Economies after Colonialism

Despite Ghana's strong democratic track record in recent decades, its economy remains underdeveloped. Industrial policies are necessary to transform the colonial trading economy that Ghana inherited at independence, but successive governments have been unwilling or unable to implement them. In this highly original interpretation, supported by new empirical material, Lindsay Whitfield exposes the reasons that the Ghanaian economy remains underdeveloped and sets her theory in the wider African context. She offers a new way of thinking about the political economy of Africa that charts a clear path away from defining Africa in terms of neopatrimonial politics and that provides new conceptual tools for addressing what kind of business-state relations are necessary to drive economic development. As a study of Ghana that addresses both the economy and politics from early colonialism to the present day, this is a must-read for any student or scholar interested in the political economy of development in Africa.

LINDSAY WHITFIELD is Associate Professor in the Department of Social Sciences and Business at Roskilde University, Denmark. She is the author of *The Politics of African Industrial Policy: A Comparative Perspective* (Cambridge University Press, 2015), *The Politics of Aid: African Strategies for Dealing with Donors* (2008), and *Turning Points in African Democracy* (2008).

Economies after Colonialism

Ghana and the Struggle for Power

LINDSAY WHITFIELD
Roskilde University

CAMBRIDGE
UNIVERSITY PRESS

CAMBRIDGE
UNIVERSITY PRESS

University Printing House, Cambridge CB2 8BS, United Kingdom

One Liberty Plaza, 20th Floor, New York, NY 10006, USA

477 Williamstown Road, Port Melbourne, VIC 3207, Australia

314–321, 3rd Floor, Plot 3, Splendor Forum, Jasola District Centre, New Delhi – 110025, India

79 Anson Road, #06–04/06, Singapore 079906

Cambridge University Press is part of the University of Cambridge.

It furthers the University's mission by disseminating knowledge in the pursuit of education, learning, and research at the highest international levels of excellence.

www.cambridge.org
Information on this title: www.cambridge.org/9781108426145
DOI: 10.1017/9781108545877

First published 2018

Printed in the United Kingdom by Clays, St Ives plc

A catalogue record for this publication is available from the British Library.

Library of Congress Cataloging-in-Publication Data
Names: Whitfield, Lindsay, 1978– author.
Title: Economies after colonialism : Ghana and the struggle for power / Lindsay Whitfield.
Description: New York : Cambridge University Press, 2018.
Identifiers: LCCN 2018012353 | ISBN 9781108426145 (hardback)
Subjects: LCSH: Ghana – Economic policy – 21st century. | Ghana – Economic conditions – 21st century. | Ghana – Commerce. | Economic development – Ghana.
Classification: LCC HC1060 .W45 2018 | DDC 330.9667–dc23
LC record available at https://lccn.loc.gov/2018012353

ISBN 978-1-108-42614-5 Hardback

In memory of Raufu

Contents

Figures

Tables

Acknowledgments

This book is about economic development in Ghana. As the great economist Alice Amsden put it, development entails moving the economy away from being a set of assets based on primary products exploited by unskilled labor toward an economy built on knowledge-based assets exploited by skilled labor. Most African countries have struggled to achieve a greater degree of economic development. In fact, few developing countries since the breakup of colonial empires and the emergence of new countries in the twentieth century have achieved significant economic development, and most of them are in Asia. This is because economic development is no easy feat to achieve. In some ways, the question should not be why have African countries not achieved more transformation of what are still substantially agrarian economies, but rather why have some countries been so successful? I have attempted to answer this question in *The Politics of African Industrial Policy*, with my colleagues Ole Therkildsen, Lars Buur and Anne Mette Kjær. This book, on the other hand, is decisively a book about Ghana. While comparative scholarship is important for generating theories and the broad understandings of social, political and economic processes that theories provide, it is still important and insightful to focus on one particular country and to examine the economic and political challenges that one country faces. This is not because Ghana's challenges are unique, or because they represent particularly African problems, but because a detailed understanding of a particular place expands our knowledge.

This book is in the tradition of, and inspired by, two earlier monographs on Ghana: Dennis Austin's classic account of politics during decolonization and the early postindependence period in *Politics in Ghana, 1946–1960*, and Eboe Hutchful's seminal discussion of the paradox of structural adjustment in *Ghana's Adjustment Experience*. With this book, I aim to provide a rich and detailed account of the politics of economic development that picks up where Hutchful left off. The goal of this book is also to combine an understanding of the politics of development in Ghana with an understanding of the economics of development – not just of economic theory, but of actually existing economies and the everyday constraints that firms and farms operating in agriculture and manufacturing face.

The literature on the political economy of development in Ghana is vast, but also fragmented. A student or scholar new to the country would have to read a large number of books and articles in order to obtain knowledge of the colonial, immediate postindependence and contemporary periods. In writing this book, I wanted to provide a single study of Ghana that covered the early colonial period up to the present day, and one that has a coherent narrative running from the emergence of agrarian and merchant capitalism in the 1880s to the advent of oil production in the 2010s. To make this coherent narrative possible, the book synthesizes the large body of literature on Ghana and combines it with original empirical research.

The book draws on fieldwork in Ghana over many years that was funded by several research projects. It draws on material collected during the Negotiating Aid project that I coordinated while a junior research fellow from 2005 to 2008 at the Global Economic Governance Programme based at University College and the Department of Politics and International Relations at the University of Oxford. I thank Ngaire Woods and the funders of the Global Economic Governance Programme for making that research possible. The majority of the empirical material for this book comes from research and fieldwork in Ghana carried out for the Elites, Production and Poverty (EPP) collaborative research program while I was a senior project researcher at the Danish Institute for International Studies in Copenhagen from 2008 to 2011. The Danish Consultative Research Committee financed this research and partially financed my position at the Danish Institute. I thank Roskilde University for financing the final round of fieldwork in 2015 that allowed me to complete the empirical research for this book.

As part of the EPP program, I worked with a Ghana research team that included Emmanuel Akwetey and Abdul-Gafaru Abdulai from the Institute for Democratic Governance and Elizabeth Asante from the University of Ghana. This was how I first met Gafaru, and although he left the team not long into the project in order to pursue a PhD at the University of Manchester, we have remained friends and colleagues ever since. We worked together to collect some of the material on the Millennium Challenge Account case included in this book. But more importantly, Gafaru has been a constant sounding board for my arguments and observations about Ghana, and I have also had the pleasure of watching him grow into an excellent scholar. I might not have finished this book if he had not been a source of constant support and encouragement. As part of the EPP Ghana team, I worked together with Elizabeth Asante to research the President's Special Initiative in Oil Palm, and material that she collected and shared with me from the PSI Secretariat was crucial to the insights garnered about the political and technical processes behind that industrial policy. I also want to thank Chris Foli and Anthony Botchwey, without whose insights and support the sector case studies would not be as rich and detailed as they are. Chris served as both a research assistant on the palm oil industry case, and a key informant based on his extensive experience gained while employed within one of the large-scale palm oil estates and then as a private consultant for the industry. Anthony Botchwey, the owner of Bomart Farms, became not only a key informant on developments in the pineapple export industry but also a friend.

The first analyses of the empirical findings from the Ghana research for the EPP program were published as working papers at the Danish Institute for International Studies in 2012. After that, the analysis was reworked, debated and reworked again through many sparring sessions with my colleagues, Ole, Lars and Mette, as we were writing *The Politics of African Industrial Policy*. The Ghana chapters of that book contain an abbreviated version of the core argument of this book, but the argument has been further developed and refined over the years as I worked on this manuscript and as I conducted further research. But my debt to Ole, Lars and Mette is even larger. This book draws upon the conceptual approach to understanding the politics of industrial policy that the four of us developed together and was first presented in *The Politics of African Industrial Policy*. While I have ventured out alone to write this manuscript, it is very much a product of our collaborative intellectual project, and I am grateful for their support and friendship over the years.

The actual writing of this book, or the very first version of what later – after many, many revisions – became this book, was started at the

African Studies Centre (ASC) at the University of Oxford. I was a visiting scholar at the ASC in the autumn of 2015 while on sabbatical from Roskilde University. I thank Jonny Steinberg for kindly accepting me into the academic life at the ASC, and David Pratten and Nic Cheeseman for allowing me to use their offices while they were away. I also thank the MSc in African Studies graduate students who provided a willing audience for me to try out the arguments from Chapter 2 of this book in a lecture called "Development, Modernization and the State."

During what turned into the many years of writing this book, numerous people have helped in small and big ways to make this book a reality. I thank George Bob-Milliar for helping me think through the arguments in Chapter 4 at a very early stage, when I was still at the Danish Institute for International Studies and he was a visiting fellow there. I am indebted to Gafaru, Festus Boamah and Pritish Behuria for reading earlier versions of the entire book and offering meticulous comments. The book is no doubt much improved as a result of the generous giving of their time. I thank Alexandra Zeitz for our discussions on macroeconomics, and Niels Fold for the comparative study that we did on the palm oil industries in Ghana and Malaysia, which proved very useful in thinking through the ideas presented in Chapter 6. Thanks also go to Jon Phillips, Kumi Yasmin and Hilary Wong for sharing their excellent doctoral and master's thesis research on Ghana, which has allowed this book to cover more industries and industrial policies than would have been otherwise possible and thus strengthen the evidence and persuasiveness of the argument. Thank you to the two anonymous reviewers, whose constructive criticisms also helped to improve the quality and presentation of the argument. Lastly, I want to thank Gavin Williams, Emily Jones, Alhassan Adam and Stefan Ouma, with whom I have discussed and debated Ghanaian politics and economic development over the years, and whose intellectual companionship and friendship are very important to me. Writing a book is a long process, and I thank my husband, Sune, for supporting me in this endeavor, and my children, Sofia and Viggo, for enduring my time away from them to work on the manuscript.

This book is dedicated to Raufu Mustapha, in memoriam, who passed away on August 8, 2017. He was the supervisor of my thesis for the MPhil in development studies at the University of Oxford, and he was the reason that I even started researching Ghana those many years ago. He sent me off to Accra in the summer of 2000 with nothing more than the name of one research contact and a place to stay with a Ghanaian family in the New Achimota suburb of Accra. As a supervisor, he was tough but fair; he was generous with his time but subscribed to the pedagogical approach of criticize first and praise later. The persistence, endurance and meticulousness that I have as a scholar, I owe to him. As I moved from being a student to a colleague, I never ceased to learn from him. He was an inspirational teacher, a great researcher and a remarkable intellectual.

Map of Ghana

BURKINA FASO
UPPER EAST
Bolgatanga
UPPER WEST
Wa
NORTHERN
BENIN
Tamale
TOGO
CÔTE D'IVOIRE
BRONG-AHAFO
Sunyani
ASHANTI
Lake Volta
Kumasi
Ho
EASTERN
VOLTA
Koforidua
GREATER ACCRA
Bight of Benin
WESTERN
CENTRAL
Accra
Cape Coast
Sekondi
Gulf of Guinea

Introduction: The Ghanaian Economy, Fragile Still

"I'll like to repeat without exaggeration that the Ghanaian economy is in a crisis," said Kwesi Botchwey, pointing to the high inflation, double-digit budget deficit and depreciation of the Ghanaian cedi.[1] Botchwey was the finance minister under the Provisional National Defence Council (PNDC) military government led by Jerry John Rawlings in the 1980s and under the first term of the National Democratic Congress (NDC) elected government in the 1990s. He is well known for being the lead negotiator with the International Monetary Fund (IMF) and World Bank on the first structural adjustment program, and he takes the title of Ghana's longest-serving finance minister. When the NDC returned to government in January 2009 after defeating the incumbent New Patriotic Party (NPP) in the December 2008 elections, Botchwey assumed a new role as a public intellectual. Laying out the country's options, Botchwey continued, "The country can decide that we will not go to the IMF for funds; we can decide instead of medium term drawing at lower cost from the IMF, we will borrow from international markets at greater cost and short tenure and with pretty much the same conditions."

On August 9, 2014, when the Mahama-led NDC government announced its decision to request an IMF bailout, the cedi had plummeted 36 percent since the beginning of the year, the fiscal deficit was set to reach 9.5 percent of GDP and public debt to GDP had exceeded 60 percent. The massive depreciation of the Ghanaian currency led international financial commentators to call the cedi one of the worst-performing currencies in Africa that year.[2] Inflation was into the

1 "Economic Crisis: 2014 Could Become Worse – Prof. Botchwey," June 4, 2014, peacefmonline, http://ghanaweb.com/GhanaHomePage/NewsArchive, accessed on September 1, 2015.

2 "Ghana's Cedi Zambia's Kwacha Worst African Currencies in 2014," December 31, 2014, Reuters, http://af.reuters.com/article/investingNews/idAFKBN0K90MS20141231, last accessed on September 10, 2015.

double digits, and growth had declined dramatically. In the context of high inflation and currency depreciation, the purchasing power for much of the population fell precipitously. In April 2015, the government signed the IMF loan after implementing a series of "prior actions" to show its commitment to rectifying its problem of twin fiscal and trade deficits.

None of this is new. Ghana's economy experienced macroeconomic crises (of varying degrees) in 1992, 1996, 2000 and 2009. In fact, since the first structural adjustment loan in 1983, there have been only short periods when Ghanaian governments were not drawing on loans from the Bretton Woods institutions for balance of payments support. A country's balance of payments summarizes its economic transactions with the rest of the world. Ghana has a chronic problem of importing more than it exports and not having enough capital inflows (through foreign direct investment or portfolio investments) to make up the deficit, and of spending more than what can be covered by government revenues, leading to a build-up of domestic and external debt.

The latest macroeconomic crisis that began after the December 2012 elections led to a severe economic downturn. The rate of growth fell sharply, partly as a result of the exceptional growth spike after 2010 when the country began exporting oil, and it fell continuously, with growth in 2016 estimated at 3.6 percent, the lowest in over two decades. Growth was projected to rebound in 2017 due to the revival of the oil and gas industry, but the Ghanaian economy continued to be plagued by high fiscal deficits, especially after the December 2016 elections.

Recurrent macroeconomic crises in Ghana result from the "fragile" nature of the economy. The term "fragile" was first used in the opening line of the Seers-Ross report on the Gold Coast colony (now Ghana) in 1952 carried out by an economic mission from the British Colonial Office: "If we were forced to sum up the Gold Coast economy in one word, the word we would choose would be 'Fragile'."[3] By fragile, the authors of the report were referring to the general tendency of the economy towards instability caused by several factors. Almost all of the territory's exports (cocoa beans, gold, diamonds, manganese and timber) depended on the world market because they were not

[3] "Report on Financial and Physical Problems of Development in the Gold Coast," Dudley Seers and C.R. Ross, Government Printer, Accra, July 1952.

consumed domestically. This made exports vulnerable to fluctuating global demand and volatile world market prices, which in turn led to instability in the amount of foreign exchange available in the country. The colonial territory was dependent on imports because little of what was imported could be produced domestically, people preferred imported brands, and there was great instability in domestic food production due to widespread rain-fed agriculture and an inefficient distribution system. The colonial government's budget was dependent on revenue derived from exports and imports. Together, these factors made the British colony susceptible to balance of payments problems, budget deficits and inflation. The Seers-Ross report concluded that the structure of the economy had to be changed by bringing domestic demand and domestic production more in line, by diversifying exports and by increasing agricultural production and productivity.

By the 2010s, these economic goals still had not been achieved. The structure of the Ghanaian economy was very similar to the one inherited at independence in 1957, which is referred to in this book as the colonial trading economy. This kind of economy is *shallow* in terms of what is produced domestically and the production capabilities of local firms; *narrow* in terms of the basket of exports and their complexity; and *thin* in terms of linkages within the economy among domestic producers of intermediate goods and services. In other words, there had been limited economic transformation. Economic transformation involves several separate but interconnected processes, including export diversification, increasing agricultural productivity, industrial deepening through creating backward and forward linkages between industries in the economy, industrial upgrading by moving into the production of more complex technological activities within national industries and global production networks, and building the technological capabilities of local firms and farms.[4]

International and domestic observers are often puzzled about why Ghana's economy has not performed better, especially given the country's strong democratic record in recent decades compared to most African countries. This book aims to unpack that puzzle. It is a story of the economic and political challenges to economic transformation in

[4] The literature on economic development uses the terms structural change, structural transformation and economic transformation interchangeably to refer to the same set of processes.

Ghana. These challenges have their origins in the economy inherited at independence and the political struggles for power that emerged during decolonization, which created path dependencies that have proven very difficult to break.

Moving through the decades of the postindependence period up to the present, the book explains why successive governments have not been able to transform the colonial trading economy. The argument emphasizes the necessity of industrial policy to catalyze economic transformation and concludes that Ghanaian governments have not been very successful in implementing industrial policies. Industrial policy is a broad term that refers to any government initiative targeted to support the development of specific industries and even firms. Industrial policy has to be targeted because industries face different institutional challenges and have specific needs related to the type of production and export markets.[5]

There is renewed interest within academic circles as well as international organizations and African governments regarding the need for industrial policy. In the early 2010s, arguments that African countries required economic transformation in order to generate self-sustaining growth and rising incomes gained attention in international and national fora.[6] The renewed discussion on economic transformation reopened the debate on the need for state intervention and industrial policy, what kinds of politics were necessary to support industrial policy and whether this kind of politics could be found or nurtured in African countries.[7]

This book contributes to that debate by looking at the particular case of Ghana, which differs significantly from countries such as Ethiopia and Rwanda that have so far dominated the discussion on industrial

5 This book does not provide a review of the literature on economic transformation and industrial policy, nor of the debates regarding industrial policy, as these topics are covered elsewhere. See for example chapter 2 in Whitfield et al. (2015), and chapter 1 in Oqubay (2015).

6 See for example, ECA (2011); Dinh et al. (2013) at the World Bank; and Amoako (2011), President of the African Center for Economic Transformation in Accra, Ghana.

7 See for example, the collective volume *Good Growth and Governance in Africa* edited by Noman and colleagues (2012); *The Industrial Policy Revolution II: Africa in the Twenty-First Century* edited by Stiglitz and colleagues (2013); *Business, Politics and the State in Africa* by Kelsall and colleagues (2013); and *The Politics of African Industrial Policy* by Whitfield and colleagues (2015).

policy in Africa.[8] All industrial policies are difficult to implement because they are inherently political, but some country contexts are more difficult than others due to the distribution of power in society. Ghana's context of competitive clientelism with weak domestic capitalists is one of the most difficult.

Competitive clientelism emerges in developing countries where the distribution of power in society is highly dispersed, and as a result there is a large group of fragmented political elites who enter shifting alliances to form a coalition strong enough to govern the country and the state apparatus. The highly fragmented nature of political elites means that a ruling coalition faces strong political opposition and also that the ruling political elites are fragmented and in constant competition with each other for political positions and state resources to gain and maintain those positions.[9] In addition, the political leaders of competitive clientelist coalitions enjoy strong political support among highly mobilized and organized groups, but these groups in turn constrain the resource allocation decisions of the leadership through their distributional demands or resistance to changes in the existing allocation of resources.

Competitive clientelism is actually the most common form of clientelism in developing countries because informal power in society is highly dispersed in most developing countries.[10] It is called *competitive* clientelism, because political leaders compete for lower-level supporters in a relatively open system of bargaining and coalition formation. Ruling political leaders can attempt to "buy in" groups and supporters of the opposition, and discontented leaders of highly mobilized groups and political factions within the ruling coalition can leave and join the opposition. But the specific nature of competitive clientelism can, and does, vary across developing countries as a result of differences in the intensity and the exact nature in which informal power is dispersed across groups in a particular society. This book

[8] See Oqubay (2015) on Ethiopia, and Booth and Golooba-Mutebi (2012) and Behuria (2016) on Rwanda.

[9] The term ruling political elites refers to the group of people who wield power as a result of their position in government, where they occupy offices in which authoritative decisions are made. Ruling coalition refers to the ruling elites, as well as the groups and individuals behind the rise of the ruling elites and/or those groups or individuals that keep the ruling elites in government by organizing political support for them.

[10] For a discussion on why this is the case, see Migdal (1988) and Khan (2010).

describes the particular form of competitive clientelism in Ghana as a result of historical developments and their legacies.

Through multiparty elections, the political configuration of competitive clientelism can result in political stability because voting is a test of the relative organizational strength of different parties, which are political coalitions. A successful change in government through elections, however, requires that the different political coalitions accept that the election outcomes are an accurate representation of their factional strength and thus that there was not significant electoral fraud. Ghana's political stability and successful changes in the ruling party through elections under the Fourth Republic are due to relatively free and fair elections, an Electoral Commission that is seen by political elites as a neutral referee, and an Inter-Party Advisory Committee that brings together political elites from the main parties to negotiate changes deemed required to maintain free and fair elections and thus an accurate representation of their relative strengths.[11]

While competitive clientelism can lead to political stability, as shown in the case of Ghana, it is not good for industrial policy. It makes it difficult for ruling political elites to pursue and implement industrial policies because there is a high degree of contestation among political elites and their elite factions combined with large distributional demands from lower-level groups and supporters within the ruling coalition. The more competitive elections are, the higher the contestation and distributional demands. Countries that have had some success with industrial policy despite having competitive clientelism, such as Thailand, are ones in which a relatively large group of domestic capitalists with investments in productive sectors already existed and were able to wield some political influence.[12]

In contrast, competitive clientelism in Ghana has occurred alongside weak domestic capitalists. The term weak domestic capitalists is used as shorthand to denote that individual domestic capitalists in productive sectors – that is, agrarian and industrial capitalists (and not merchant capitalists involved only in trading) – are weak. They

[11] For commentary on the democratic nature of the December 2016 elections and the role of the Electoral Commission and Inter-Party Advisory Committee, see Cheeseman, Lynch and Willis (2017). Elections are discussed in Chapter 3 of this book.

[12] For a discussion of competitive clientelism in Thailand, see Doner and Ramsay (1998).

are weak in the sense that they have low productive and organizational capabilities and thus cannot produce much at international levels of efficiency and meet international quality standards. They are also weak in the sense of having limited political influence over policy content and implementation.

This book argues that the combination of competitive clientelism with weak domestic capitalists produced a structure of incentives that shaped the political survival strategies of ruling political elites and in turn their policy choices. In order to keep their ruling coalition together, political leaders needed to meet the distributional demands of elite factions and lower-level supporters within the coalition. At the same time, domestic capitalists had only limited political influence on how state resources were allocated and invested, and their low level of capabilities provided them with little motivation to make risky investments in productive sectors with the small resources they were able to capture without broader state support to make sure those investments became profitable. This distribution of power resulted in two key features that have characterized the policy choices of nearly every government since the country's independence.

The first key feature is that ruling political elites, calculating the short-term need for political survival against rival political elites, chose government expenditures that consisted mainly of distributive spending that could reward patron-client support networks and provide individual and collective benefits for voters. As a result, resources were consumed but were not reproduced in the sense of productive investments that would lead to growth and thus generate more resources through taxes, jobs and incomes. The short time horizon of ruling elites in pursuit of political survival also led them to avoid policies or programs that involved significant changes in the allocation of existing resources, especially if they involved short-term negative effects on a large portion of the population. Since most industrial policies involve some change in the immediate distribution of benefits, political elites did not pursue and implement many of the institutional changes required to increase production and productivity in agriculture and manufacturing.

Second, when ruling political elites in Ghana did pursue productivity-enhancing expenditures, they chose state-led investments in agriculture and manufacturing rather than industrial policies that incentivized private investments and supported the development of productive capabilities among private domestic firms. This is because state-led investments allowed the ruling party to take credit for the investments at election time, in an attempt to sway voters, and to control the generation and distribution of rents, which they channeled through patron-client networks to reward supporters and keep them in the coalition. The motivation of ruling elites was to try to keep control over economic opportunities and wealth accumulation due to the competitive nature of rival coalitions, but *paradoxically* the rival sources of power and elite fragmentation within ruling coalitions made it difficult for political leaders to implement state-led industrial policies. As a result, state-led industrial policies were poorly implemented. Both kinds of government expenditures that were popular with Ghanaian governments – distributive spending and state-led industrial policies – had limited impacts on developing the productive sectors of the economy and thus economic transformation.

Ghana is not unique in having weak domestic capitalists. On the African continent, domestic capitalists have been small and relatively weak in terms of their productive capabilities and political influence for historical reasons, except most notably in Mauritius and South Africa.[13] However, due to differing historical developments and legacies that affected political elite formation and the mobilization and organization of social groups, not all African countries are characterized by competitive clientelism. In African countries where the distribution of power at independence was not highly dispersed, or in countries where internal or external shocks such as civil wars changed the distribution of power, we see different political configurations.[14] This variation in political configurations largely accounts for the differences in the extent to which African governments actively pursue and successfully implement industrial policies. In countries where the distribution of power in society is less dispersed and where political elites are less fragmented, governments have more success in

[13] For a summary, see Whitfield et al. (2015: 90–96). For a seminal work on this topic in the case of Senegal, see Boone (1992). On South Africa, see Handley (2008), and on Mauritius, see Brautigam (2009).

[14] The other broad types of political configurations in developing countries, based on the distribution of power in society, are strong dominant party, weak dominant party, and vulnerable authoritarian. For a discussion of these types and their implications for industrial policymaking and implementation, see Khan (2010), Whitfield et al. (2015), and Kelsall et al. (2013).

implementing industrial policies and even state-led investment projects, as in Ethiopia.

Nevertheless, there are a significant number of African countries that are characterized by competitive clientelism, and a number of countries that are increasingly heading towards competitive clientelism as elite factions break away from dominant parties, such as in Uganda. Therefore, Ghana's story is one that resonates with the experiences of many African countries and can illuminate broader issues and challenges to economic transformation on the subcontinent. Furthermore, the diversity across African countries in term of variations in the political configurations and the strength of domestic capitalists highlights the importance of taking into account the political dimension of industrial policy. "What works" cannot be generalized, but rather industrial policy advice has to be tailored for each country, taking into account the distribution of power and its implications.

Elaborating the Challenges to Economic Transformation

The Gold Coast and then independent Ghana experienced an average annual growth rate of 4.1 percent between 1950 and 1960, which dropped to 2.2 percent between 1960 and 1970 as the country hit its first macroeconomic crisis and its first coup d'état in 1966. Between 1970 and 1981, the years of political turmoil, the economy actually contracted, with a negative average annual growth rate of –0.3 percent as government after government failed to implement economic reforms to reverse the trajectory.[15] The economic decline was not reversed until 1983, when the government began economic reforms with financing from the World Bank and IMF. On the back of the structural adjustment lending and policy prescriptions, Ghana experienced sustained but modest growth in the 1990s and 2000s, achieving lower-middle-income status in 2010.[16] However, the growth turnaround was not accompanied by significant changes in the structure of the economy.

[15] These growth statistics are from Rimmer (1992: 208).

[16] When the Ghana Statistical Service changed the way that it calculated GDP in 2010 through a revision of the base year from 1993 to 2006, per capita income was revised upward to $1,289, qualifying it as a lower-middle-income country. The base year influences estimates of the size of the economy as it indicates which economic activities are captured and their relative importance. The revision in the national accounts estimates was based on incorporating a considerable amount of data from new surveys that allowed for wider coverage of economic activities

The structural adjustment reforms halted the country's economic decline, but they also had the effect of reviving the colonial trading economy structure, after the failed attempts in the 1960s and 1970s to catalyze economic transformation through state-led industrial policies. This is because the reforms liberalized imports while only directly supporting the revival of the traditional export industries: cocoa and gold. The structural adjustment loans helped to rebuild infrastructure, social services and pay for imports, but they had little impact on developing other export sectors, increasing agricultural productivity in food crops or helping locally owned manufacturing firms to compete in the domestic market in the context of rapid trade liberalization. As a result, agriculture and manufacturing growth rates tailed off in the 1990s, and the service sector became the largest sector of the economy from the mid-2000s. Economic growth became increasingly consumption-driven and led by the service sector, which includes public services, services in the informal sector and services linked to oil, gas and mining. By the end of the 1990s, the urban population surpassed the rural population and continued to grow. This urbanization led to "consumption cities," where services and other nontradable activities were the main employment creators and sources of nonagricultural income (Kolavalli et al. 2012). Thus, Ghana achieved urbanization without industrialization.

Ghanaian governments still depended on gold and cocoa exports, and then oil, for generating foreign exchange and for a significant amount of government revenue. Production capabilities were limited due to generally low productivity in agriculture and stagnating manufacturing, so little of what citizens consumed was produced in the country. The absence of a takeoff in other productive sectors, especially ones oriented to exporting, left the economy in a vulnerable position: a limited base for generating export revenue, dependence on imports for most consumer goods in addition to intermediate and capital goods, and little formal employment generation in the private sector, which meant heavy reliance on the public sector to create jobs.

In explaining the puzzle of limited economic transformation in Ghana, this book has two objectives. The first is to demonstrate that

(Jerven and Duncan 2012). The previous way of estimating the national accounts reflected the structure of the Ghanaian economy in 1993 and thus overemphasized the decline in previous sources of growth such as state-owned enterprises.

economic transformation involves overcoming specific challenges to increasing production and productivity in agriculture, which is also a requirement to create viable agro-processing industries, and to building competitive firms that can compete in liberalized domestic markets and enter nontraditional export sectors. The second objective is to examine the *policies* that Ghanaian governments pursued in agriculture and light manufacturing, and whether those policies responded to these specific economic challenges, as well as the *politics* that explain those policy choices and their outcomes.

In African countries, locally owned firms in industries new to the country are initially unprofitable due to their low productivity. Low productivity stems from two types of constraints.[17] First-order constraints on productivity concern factors external to firms and farms that lead to high production costs, but which are costly or impossible for individual firms or farms to address on their own. They include the lack of or poor state of infrastructure, the high cost and poor terms of finance, the absence of skilled labor and the cost of acquiring or training labor, problems in accessing land and insecurity of land rights, and the lack of coordination and collective action among producers. These features of the economic context drive up the cost of production for firms to a level that makes them uncompetitive in export markets as well as in domestic markets where trade liberalization means that firms must compete with imported goods from more advanced economies. Industrial policy is required to address these constraints, either directly with public institutions, policies and expenditures, or indirectly by subsidizing the costs for firms, industry associations or third-party actors to find solutions.

Second-order constraints concern factors internal to firms and farms, and have to do with what are called technological capabilities. Technological capabilities are knowledge-based assets. They are the technical, managerial and organizational skills – the soft technology – that allow firms to utilize equipment and scientific knowledge – the hard technology – efficiently and profitably. Technological capabilities are inherently composed of tacit knowledge, and thus can only be acquired through learning by doing. But learning by doing is costly and risky. Firms have to undergo a period of learning in which they

[17] I borrow the terminology of first- and second-order constraints from Vrolijk (2016).

may operate at a loss, and it is uncertain if and when a firm may become competitive. The risk is highest for the first investors when the knowledge and infrastructure required to become competitive in new economic activities do not yet exist and have to be acquired and adapted to local conditions. Industrial policy is necessary to encourage investments in economic activities that are new to firms and farms by underwriting risk and financing losses incurred while firms and farms are becoming competitive in domestic and international markets.

These problems are very real in Ghana. Yet there is little written about Ghana's economy from this perspective. Despite a rich literature probing these issues in the first decades after independence, contemporary studies of the Ghanaian economy focus mostly on macroeconomic and general sectoral dynamics.[18] There are few industry case studies, most of which focus on cocoa exports, and even fewer studies on the first- and second-order constraints facing specific industries and domestic firms operating in those industries. This book is motivated by the need to start filling that gap. Industry studies are not only academic exercises but also critical to formulating good industrial policy initiatives.

The point of industrial policy is to find solutions to first-order constraints in land, labor and capital markets, and second-order constraints by incentivizing and supporting firms to invest in building their technological capabilities; industrial policy can also help solve coordination and collective action problems among firms within specific industries. All developing countries struggle with implementing industrial policies, because it is not a technical process but rather a political one. Addressing industry-specific constraints entails decisions about the prioritization and allocation of scarce government revenue, about property rights, and about providing subsidies to groups of firms or farmers in return for investments in learning to produce more efficiently and with new technology and organizational practices. It almost always involves changing the distribution of economic benefits, and thus creates conflicts and tensions between immediate winners and losers – even though in the longer term, production and productivity increase, and more wealth and jobs are created. Thus, industrial policy is difficult to implement because it entails basic political

[18] For example, see Aryeetey, Harrigan and Toye (2000), Hutchful (2002), Aryeetey and Kanbur (2008), and Aryeetey and Kanbur (2017).

struggles over the allocation of resources, institutional changes and the enforcement of new rules in the context of a given distribution of power in society. Consequently, explaining how and why Ghanaian governments have or have not responded to the first- and second-order constraints on productivity, and with what outcomes, requires a broader understanding of Ghanaian political economy.

Summary of the Argument

This book draws on political settlements theory to explain Ghana's particular form of competitive clientelism and its implications for the politics of industrial policy. The book builds on the existing Ghanaian literature, but also advances it through the use of a comparative theoretical framework that allows us to understand the different distributions of power in African countries and explains their origins as well as their implications for economic performance. A major contribution of this book is to explain the origins of competitive clientelism and weak domestic capitalists in Ghana, as well as why this context persists, and thus also explain why ruling elites continue to use distributive expenditures to hold the ruling coalition together and choose state-led industrial policies in order to control the accumulation process.

The origins of competitive clientelism are found in the particular precolonial and colonial experiences in the territories that became Ghana, which resulted in a situation where power was highly dispersed. The decolonization struggle was not so much a struggle between Africans and the British as one among societal groups in the colonial territories. The distribution of power in the colonial society created a high degree of elite fragmentation as the result of several strong and relatively autonomous societal groups that produced their own (aspiring) political elites who had strong organizational capabilities and who entered into shifting alliances with each other in order to form political coalitions. The political elites were not just fragmented; they became polarized along particular social cleavages that existed before independence but were politicized during the decolonization process and solidified over time.

This combination of political elite fragmentation and polarization meant that all political factions could not be incorporated into one coalition, and thus the group of political elites in government always faced a group of powerful excluded political factions. This situation made ruling elites highly vulnerable to being ousted from governing the new state in Ghana, and thus made them dependent on the societal groups whose support kept them in power. High vulnerability led to short time horizons of ruling elites, while dependence on an array of local groups and alliances meant a large number of distributional demands being placed on ruling elites in return for that support. Ruling elites distributed state resources and economic opportunities linked to the state as patronage to keep the ruling political coalition together and as a strategy to win elections. However, the high degree of elite fragmentation within political coalitions meant that no one group of ruling elites could centralize control over the distribution of resources and opportunities, which led to spending outside of budgeted priorities and beyond budget ceilings.

The stymied development of domestic merchant and agrarian capitalists during the colonial period, and even earlier, resulted in weak domestic capitalists at independence who could not influence the ruling political elites to pursue political survival strategies that incorporated synergies in productive sector investments between state and private capital. The political elites of the Convention People's Party (CPP) that entered a power-sharing government with the British in the early 1950s began to undermine the accumulation strategies of the weak domestic capitalists based in the cocoa and import-export trading sectors, and then later shifted to state-controlled industries in an attempt to both direct and control accumulation processes. However, the implementation of state-led industrial policies was undermined by competitive clientelism, which led to poor management of state-owned enterprises and farms.

The two features characterizing the CPP ruling elites' economic policy choices had important legacies that were hard for subsequent governments to escape, even when the economic consequences were devastating. This path dependence was not broken until the early 1980s with the second coup led by J.J. Rawlings, but it was only a partial break. The political configuration of the PNDC ruling coalition, with Rawlings at the head, differed from the previous decades because the distribution of power in society had (temporarily) changed due to internal shocks. The depths of the economic decline in the late 1970s and early 1980s left the old political factions with little legitimacy. In this context, the PNDC did not need to have a strong lower-level support base, and the higher levels consisted of a small group of relatively cohesive elites. However, during the process of rebuilding the economy, the PNDC ruling elites did not make an alliance with domestic entrepreneurs, largely because the surviving businessmen were seen to be aligned with rival political groups. Instead, the PNDC made an alliance with the IMF and World Bank, albeit one fraught with tensions. In return for financing trade and budget deficits, the Bretton Woods institutions and other donors were able to exert extensive influence on policy content and the direction of reforms, even if not the full extent of policy influence that these donors desired.

The interests of the PNDC elites and the Bretton Woods institutions converged in important ways. In particular, they both emphasized rebuilding the traditional export sectors of the economy, cocoa and gold, which rejuvenated government revenues and foreign exchange earnings. For the PNDC elites, this economic revival strategy was also a political one, as it did not involve the risk of supporting domestic entrepreneurs whose political loyalties could not be controlled. The cocoa sector involved relations between the state-owned cocoa marketing board and smallholder farmers; whereas the gold sector involved rehabilitating state-owned mining companies with the intention to attract foreign direct investment. PNDC elites were less concerned with other productive sector policies, and thus did not temper the World Bank's proposals for rapid liberalization, privatization and deregulation to the same extent that they did in the cocoa sector. As a result, the structural adjustment reforms failed to address the supply side constraints on private sector investment and to actively support domestic farms and firms to become internationally competitive in the face of trade liberalization. The consequence was a return to the structure of the colonial trading economy.

The PNDC ruling elites could not keep rival political elites from competing for power for long, especially after excluded political groups joined together to lobby for the return to multiparty elections. The PNDC elites agreed to elections in late 1992 and converted the PNDC into a political party, the NDC, by including a larger group of political elites and creating a political machine with patronage networks at the constituency level. In government, NDC ruling elites needed to deliver public services, jobs and incomes widely in order to win elections. The same proved true under the NPP government in the 2000s.

Many international and domestic observers, as well as academic scholars, expected that the NPP government led by President John Kufuor that came to power in 2001 would mark a break with past political strategies, business-state relations and economic policy choices. They contrasted the hostile PNDC and NDC governments led by J.J. Rawlings to the business-friendly NPP government and pointed to particular policies as potentially signaling a new way of the state working with the private sector.[19] Yet the NPP government (2001–2008) exhibited the same preference for distributive expenditures and state-led industrial policies that characterized the NDC governments that preceded it (1993–2000) and followed it (2009–2016). Furthermore, there are indications that the economic policy choices of the second NPP government led by President Nana Akufo-Addo, which took office in January 2017, are following in the same direction.

This book explains the continuity in policies and practices between two political parties whose ideological tags indicate that they should act quite differently, with the NPP the liberal, pro-market party and the NDC the social democratic, pro-state intervention party. The configuration of power within both political parties was characterized by elite fragmentation and strong lower-level groups within the party, leading to a high degree of contestation among ruling elites as well as a high level of distributional demands placed on ruling elites. In addition, the increasingly competitive nature of elections led to a high degree of vulnerability of ruling elites and created large political financing needs.

The high degree of vulnerability of ruling elites led to short time horizons, and in the context of short time horizons, ruling elites chose a two-pronged political survival strategy. They must deliver enough visible "development" projects, goods and services to a broad section of the population in order to win over floating voters: those who are not loyal to a specific party and who increasingly decided the outcome of elections. They must also placate constituency-level party organizations and the party activists and financiers in their patron-client networks. This led to policies that emphasized distributive, consumption-driven expenditures.

[19] For example, see Handley (2008: 202–205), Arthur (2006) and Taylor (2007: 211–214).

The scope and scale of distributive expenditures was amplified by the high degree of intraparty competition that resulted from elite factionalism and strong lower-level factions within the ruling party. Elite fragmentation led to increased contestation over resource allocation as well as rent creation and distribution, and made it difficult for any one group of ruling elites to exert control over budgeting and actual budget outlays, or to centralize the process of rent distribution. As a result, politicians were constantly seeking resources that they could use to deliver to their constituency in general and their clients in particular, as well as to line their own pockets to pay for future campaigns and to generally benefit from political office. The distributional demands were high, both within the higher and lower levels of the ruling coalition, and the increasingly competitive nature of elections made ruling elites more attuned to these demands. They also led them to see state-controlled industrial policies as better political strategies for winning elections, and to avoid policies that were economically necessary but would have immediate negative economic effects and thus high political costs in the short term. These political drivers directly contributed to budget overruns and fiscal laxity.

As a group, domestic capitalists in productive sectors had limited political influence, because they were not important to the key economic sectors of cocoa and gold, to financing the state or to financing political parties. Ruling political elites were more concerned about supporting businessmen and -women within their ranks or who were closely linked to their party as a means to ensure political financing. The goal was often immediate accumulation, and thus the businesses that benefited were typically not in productive sectors, where accumulation was riskier and took longer. Domestic capitalists tended to be individually politically networked into a ruling party, through which they could access some loans and other resources.

A high level of vulnerability of ruling elites and a high level of fragmentation and contestation within ruling coalitions combined with weak domestic capitalists in productive sectors forms a difficult environment in which to pursue and implement industrial policies. The fragmented ruling elite continuously contests resource allocation decisions, making it difficult to pool and prioritize state resources for productive investments (as they have to be widely disbursed) or to change the distribution of economic benefits (if it entails economic or political costs for members or groups considered part of the ruling coalition). Ruling political elites within both political parties engaged in intense internal political jockeying with each other for the top positions in government and contested the distribution of resources to different ministerial portfolios as well as to different regions and constituencies.

As a result, many of the productive sector policies since the 1990s were donor-driven, and donors and consultants influenced their content more than domestic firms did. Their implementation lacked the political imperatives that would come from stronger relations between ruling elites and domestic capitalists. Domestic capitalists tended to be networked into a ruling coalition through individual political connections, but did not have enough influence to shape productive sector policies in the face of other influences driven by the political survival imperatives of ruling elites or the requirements of donor-funded projects.

When ruling elites were the ones driving industrial policy, the same political factors that made state-led industrial policies attractive undermined their implementation: the dispersion of power within the ruling coalition made it difficult for the particular political elites pushing the industrial policy to secure its funding and for bureaucrats implementing it to resist distributional demands from other ruling elites or important lower-level groups to benefit from the policies. Furthermore, state-owned enterprises were poorly managed and could not respond quickly to challenges and address constraints on productivity. Thus, when Ghanaian governments pursued industrial policies, they generally failed to have a significant impact.

Sector and Industrial Policy Case Studies

The evidence supporting these arguments comes from a multilevel analysis, including national level economic policies and outcomes, selected productive sectors and their development over time, and key industrial policies targeting those sectors and their implementation and outcomes. At the level of the national economy, the book analyzes a broad range of productive sector policies implemented by Ghanaian governments in the 1990s, 2000s and 2010s. It covers the traditional cocoa and gold sectors rehabilitated under structural adjustment, as well as government policies focusing on agriculture and manufacturing more generally, including donor-driven projects. The analysis focuses on the content and impact of these policies, contextualized within broader economic trends and the general constraints on economic transformation. This level of analysis is based on a combination of government reports, donor project evaluations, reports from local and international research institutes and NGOs, published and unpublished academic papers, and interviews with civil servants in the Ministry of Food and Agriculture and the Ministry of Trade and Industry.

The analysis moves to the sector level in order to highlight the specific constraints on productivity in two selected productive sectors, horticulture and palm oil processing, and to examine the politics surrounding the formulation, implementation and outcomes of specific industrial policies targeting these sectors. The sector case studies trace the development of the sector over time, explain government policies affecting the sector in the 1980s, 1990s and 2000s, and examine their economic impacts. At the sector level, we can get a better understanding of the constraints that firms and farms face in agricultural production and light manufacturing (agro-processing) and why these constraints cannot necessarily be overcome without industrial policy. The sector level analyses also provide greater evidence on the causal linkages between competitive clientelism, the two features characterizing ruling political elites' policy choices, and poor economic outcomes.

In particular, the horticulture sector study sheds light on the economic and political challenges to achieving export diversification. Horticulture products collectively were one of the largest categories of nontraditional exports in the 2000s, even though they comprised a small percentage of total nontraditional exports. Horticulture production and export began in the 1980s as a result of private initiatives from a handful of Ghanaian entrepreneurs looking for a way to make money in a context of limited economic opportunities. The PNDC government did not have a concerted response to the constraints faced by the nascent pineapple export industry, as the Ministry of Finance was focused on macroeconomic reforms and revival of the traditional export sectors. However, the industry did receive crucial support from the Secretary (Minister) of Trade and Industry. This industrial policy was the personal initiative of the minister, which involved a degree of mutual interests and collusion, and definitely did not fit any textbook model of what industrial policy should look like.

But it solved the immediate constraints on productivity facing the small group of pineapple producer-exporters and allowed the industry to expand in the late 1980s and catalyzed further private investments.

The private investors in commercial pineapple production for export did well, but these pineapple producer-exporters were new to agribusiness and exporting, so they started with low technological capabilities and did not perceive the importance of investing in building their capabilities. In the late 1990s, the industry faced a series of constraints that required collective action among the firms and with the state in order to solve them. The NDC and NPP ruling elites were not interested in the horticulture export sector and thus left it to donor-driven projects. The types of public-private coordination of actions and investments needed were not forthcoming, occurred on a very limited scale or did not come at the right time. When a crisis caused by changes in international competition hit the industry in the mid-2000s, the pineapple producer-exporters were not able to respond quickly and sufficiently, and thus pineapple exports contracted in 2006 and generally failed to recover.

The palm oil sector study illuminates the economic and political challenges involved in modernizing traditional agro-processing industries. Manual and small-scale palm oil processing has a long history in Ghana, given the origin of the palm oil tree in West Africa. The first postindependence government created industrial palm oil processing through state-owned oil palm plantations and mills. As a result, Ghana has a dualistic industry structure in palm oil characterized by two distinct but overlapping subsectors: small-scale production for home consumption and large-scale production for industrial use in downstream manufacturing industries. In the context of a customary land tenure system, palm oil estates had challenges to acquire large tracts of contiguous land with which to expand their own oil palm plantations, and thus were dependent on buying from smallholders. But the dualistic industry structure created several first-order constraints on improving productivity in oil palm cultivation and in palm oil processing, including organizing the supply base among scattered smallholders, improving production techniques among smallholders and introducing higher yielding varieties, and enforcing contracts with smallholders. These constraints caused stagnation in the sector and limited opportunities for developing secondary industrial refining of crude palm oil. These first-order constraints are not unique to the palm oil sector, but rather characterize most agro-processing industries in Ghana.

When the PNDC government began reforms to halt the economic decline in the early 1980s, it sought to revive industrial palm oil processing, which was barely operating. Crude palm oil had to be imported, and reviving domestic production would reduce import bills and save foreign exchange. It was also the case that the palm oil sector, like the cocoa and gold sectors, was dominated by state-owned companies and thus its rehabilitation could be controlled by the state. The PNDC government successfully implemented industrial policies to revive the industrial palm oil processing sub-sector, with most of the state-owned estates becoming profitably just before the return to multiparty politics in 1992. The NDC government's policy toward the palm oil sector in the 1990s demonstrates the pressures of competitive clientelism. Facing large fiscal deficits, NDC ruling elites used privatization of the palm oil estates to plug deficits without a strategy to use foreign direct investment to achieve objectives related to developing the sector. As a result, constraints on the expansion of the supply of raw materials in the traditional palm belt remained after privatization, limiting growth in the sector. Under the NPP government, a group of NPP elites tried to address the shortage of raw material, but ultimately failed to achieve much.

The analysis moves to the policy level in order to examine in detail the politics of industrial policy formulation, implementation, and outcomes. It focuses on the politics of industrial policy under the Kufuor-led NPP government from 2001 to 2008. Specifically, it examines the Millennium Challenge Account project targeting the horticulture export sector, and the President's Special Initiatives, which included an initiative targeting the palm oil sector. The Millennium Challenge Account project is an instructive example of how the group of NPP politicians in charge of formulating and negotiating the project shifted the initial focus on supporting the horticulture export sector, which came about through engagement with industry actors, into a massive distributional initiative that had little to do with promoting horticulture exports. The case of the President's Special Initiatives demonstrates how another group of NPP politicians linked to President Kufuor tried to promote selected productive sectors, but they did so through state-led industrial policies. An analysis of the Oil Palm President's Special Initiative shows that this group of NPP politicians chose a state-led approach to address constraints in the sector despite alternatives put forth by existing palm oil estates, and how contestation among NPP ruling elites undermined the implementation of the state-led initiative. Thus, the Millennium Challenge Account case illustrates the first feature where ruling elites choose distributive expenditures over productivity-enhancing ones. The President's Special Initiatives case illustrates the second feature where ruling elites, when they do pursue productivity enhancing expenditures, choose to do so through state-led initiatives that fail to achieve their objectives due to competitive clientelism.

The two sector studies and the examination of specific productive sector initiatives under the NPP government draw on new empirical material collected and generated during fieldwork in Ghana between 2008 and 2011, and again in 2015. Detailed descriptions of the sources for the sector case studies and industrial policies case studies are provided at the beginning of the relevant chapters. Appendix B at the end of the book contains a complete list of interviews on which the book draws.

Structure of the Book

Chapter 1 demonstrates how the literature assessing Ghana's economic performance since independence largely converges on the argument that political elites prioritized distributive, consumption-driven expenditures as a political survival strategy, and that when political elites did pursue productive sector investments in order to increase wealth in the country and tackle trade deficits, they chose state-led industrial policies over support for private domestic capitalists. However, this literature is less clear and systematic in providing explanations of the origin of these two features of Ghanaian political economy and why they continue to persist. The chapter shows how a political settlements theoretical approach provides the conceptual tools to understand the origins of the two trends in the nature of competitive clientelism and weak domestic capitalists in Ghana, and also provides a better framework for understanding the kind of business-state relations needed to drive successful industrial policy.

Chapter 2 explains the origins of competitive clientelism by looking at the distribution of power in society on the eve of independence and why it was that way. It also explains why domestic capitalists were weak at the time of independence by tracing the processes of agrarian capitalism and merchant capitalism that began in the 1800s in response to changes in the global economy and how they slowed or were actively stymied during the period of formal colonial rule. The chapter then shows how the distribution of power that emerged in the 1950s shaped how ruling coalitions were constituted and political support mobilized in the context of independence, which in turn forged the two defining features regarding the political survival strategies of ruling political elites. Finally, the chapter details how Nkrumah's independence government left legacies that shaped the economic and political context in which later ruling coalitions had to function, and how their choices of political survival strategies and economic policies within this context led to economic decline, which was only reversed under extreme political and economic circumstances.

Chapter 3 explains the politics that made economic reforms possible under the PNDC government in the 1980s, but also why the change in the distribution of power was only temporary and competitive clientelism reemerged. It then describes the nature of competitive clientelism under the Fourth Republic. In particular, the chapter demonstrates how the NDC and NPP political parties were organized and financed within the specific distribution of power in Ghana, and it draws out the implications for political elites' choices of political survival strategies: strategies concerning how to win primaries and general elections. In turn, these political survival strategies shaped ruling elites' choices in terms of government expenditures and economic policies, and ultimately led to recurrent macroeconomic crises. Chapter 4 presents data on the country's economic performance showing the return to the colonial trading economy structure and how it was reinforced by the kinds of economic policies pursued by the NDC and NPP governments in the 1990s and 2000s.

Chapters 5 and 6 present the sector case studies. The analytical narratives regarding the development of the horticulture export and palm oil processing sectors are told chronologically, identifying policy choices and outcomes under the PNDC government in the 1980s, the NDC government in the 1990s and the NPP government in the 2000s. Chapter 7 then looks at particular industrial policies of the NPP government targeting these sectors and demonstrates the causal mechanisms at work between ruling elites' political survival strategies, policy choices and economic outcomes.

Chapter 8 describes the development of the oil and gas sector under the Mills- and Mahama-led NDC government. It shows how competitive clientelism shaped the development of the oil and gas sector, as well as how oil revenues were allocated and spent. The NDC government's strategy for using the oil revenues was to invest much of it back into the oil and gas sector, which it described as industrialization based on natural resources. Part of the explanation of this strategy lies in the political influence of NDC elites governing the state-owned oil company, Ghana National Petroleum Corporation, which had the ambition to become commercially independent. The ambitions of this group led to factional fighting within the NDC, which negatively affected the development of the gas sector and cost the government a large amount of resources. A significant part of the oil wealth went back to the oil and gas sector, leaving a relatively small portion for the government to use in the annual budget. The ways in which the NDC II government spent them mirror the two features characterizing political elites' economic policy choices: distributive consumption-driven initiatives and state-led industrial policies.

Despite the advent of oil exports, the economy remained fragile, still. This was made clear by the macroeconomic crisis sparked by overspending around the 2012 elections combined with the simultaneous decline in international market prices for cocoa and gold. The concluding chapter considers what kind of industrial policies Ghana needs in order to spur economic transformation, but also what would be politically feasible.

1 *Ghanaian Political Economy and the Politics of Industrial Policy*

Two features have characterized the policy choices of Ghanaian governments since independence. Ruling elites have prioritized the requirements of their political survival over economic growth, and because they had short time horizons, their political survival strategy included distributive, consumption-driven expenditures that ended up depleting the wealth of the country without reproducing it, much less expanding it. When governments attempted to expand production, they typically did so through industrial policies in which the state played a central role as manager or owner of the productive investments and which neglected or even marginalized private domestic capitalists. This argument is based on a reading of the extensive literature on Ghanaian political economy in the 1960s and 1970s. No one scholar put forth the argument in this way, but most scholars emphasize one or both of these features to explain the poor economic performance of Ghana in the immediate postindependence decades. The first part of this chapter demonstrates how the literature assessing Ghana's economic performance in the 1960s and 1970s converges on these two features, and how the literature on Ghana's economic performance under the Fourth Republic makes similar points, reinforcing the idea that the two features reemerged with the return to multiparty rule in 1992.

In explaining the dominance of these two features, scholars typically point to the pervasive clientelism in the country's political system, indicating that it led to the short time horizons of political elites, and to the small class of domestic capitalists who had limited political influence. However, scholars are less clear and systematic in their explanations of the origin of the two features. The theoretical approaches used in the Ghanaian literature cannot explain why clientelism in Ghana has resulted in economic policy choices and outcomes that differ from other African countries, because these theoretical approaches have been applied to explain economic outcomes in Africa generally. For example, the neopatrimonial approach, which has dominated studies on the political economy of development in African studies, cannot explain why clientelism in Ghana was more economically detrimental than the form of clientelism in neighboring Côte d'Ivoire.[1]

More generally, there have been limited attempts to move beyond the neopatrimonialism approach in African studies. An exception is the work of Tim Kelsall and colleagues, which argues that not all forms of clientelism are detrimental and explains the conditions under which clientelism does not undermine, and can even facilitate, economic development, focusing on the degree of centralized rent management and the time horizon of political leaders (Kelsall et al. 2013). They use the term developmental patrimonialism for political regimes that are characterized by a high degree of rent centralization and a long time horizon, and use the term competitive clientelism for political regimes characterized by a low degree of rent centralization and a short time horizon of leaders. The work of Kelsall and colleagues has been very important in advancing the discussion in African studies by arguing that not all clientelist political systems are the same, and that neopatrimonialism cannot be used writ large to explain the poor economic performance of African countries because many governments with neopatrimonial features in Africa (and other parts of the world) have implemented industrial policies successfully. However, the developmental neopatrimonialism model does not go far enough in teasing out the causal pathways between different forms of clientelism and implementing industrial policy, nor does it adequately explain the origins of different forms of clientelism. Kelsall et al. (2013) point to several factors that affect whether long-horizon rent centralization emerges: presence of a visionary leader, creation of a dominant party system with a top-down patron–client network, and a competent but politically disciplined bureaucracy. But the emergence (or not) of these factors still has to be explained.

The second part of the chapter presents political settlements theory and uses its conceptual tools to explain how the two features that characterize the policy choices of Ghanaian governments result from the incentive structure which emerges in the context of competitive clientelism combined with weak domestic capitalists. The political

[1] For an extended discussion of the limits of the neopatrimonial theoretical approach, see Gray and Whitfield (2014).

settlements theory emphasizes the structural features of countries, in particular the distribution of power in society, which shape how coalitions are constructed and the consequences for how bureaucracies work and whether political leaders are able to exercise longer time horizons. It also provides a better comparative theoretical framework in which to examine and explain the origins of competitive clientelism in Ghana as opposed to the developmental patrimonialism approach. This chapter draws on the elaborated political settlements theory first presented and discussed in Whitfield et al. (2015).

Political settlements theory also differs in important ways from the theoretical perspectives used in the existing literature on Ghanaian political economy in terms of assumptions about what is required for economic transformation. There is an implicit argument in much of the literature, including more recent work on the Fourth Republic, that reducing the role of the state in the economy and separating the interests between political elites and economic entrepreneurs is necessary to move from politicized businesses to independent production-driven capitalism, or full-blooded capitalism as Tony Killick (2008: 22) calls it. However, it is argued here that state interventions in the market through industrial policies are necessary to spur private sector investment in productive sectors and that such state interventions usually only come about as a result of close, even collusive, business–state relations. The political settlements theoretical approach emphasizes the necessity of politically driven processes of accumulation for the emergence of a production-driven domestic capitalist class and how these processes shape the politics of industrial policy. The political settlements approach also shares with developmental patrimonialism an emphasis on the importance of rents to economic development and on focusing on how governments are able to manage rent creation and distribution.

In other words, economic transformation does not require the elimination of collusive business–state relations and state interventions in the market but rather a particular kind of business–state relation and particular ways in which the state needs to intervene in the market. In this sense, the political and economic challenges to economic transformation may be even greater than is typically thought, as "getting the politics right" is much harder than the "rolling back the state" and "getting the prices right" prescriptions of previous decades. These arguments are taken up in the third part of the chapter.

Explaining Ghana's Poor Economic Performance

The first postindependence government of the Convention People's Party, led by Kwame Nkrumah, tried to transform the colonial trading economy. However, the government's strategy of rapid industrialization through state interventions in the economy used up the country's foreign exchange reserves, which had been accumulated from cocoa exports during the colonial period. It created many state-owned factories and farms, but most of them did not become profitable and had few if any linkages with other sectors in the economy. The Cocoa Marketing Board, with its export monopoly, made these state interventions possible by setting the producer price lower than the world market price and using the difference to finance investments in social services, infrastructure and state-owned enterprises as well as prestige projects. The state slowly came to dominate the formal economy, making the public sector the main source of formal employment.

When government expenditure began to exceed revenue and the available supply of foreign exchange declined as the global price of cocoa fell, the government maintained high investments by borrowing from the central bank and foreign creditors. Deficit financing led to inflation and an overvalued, inconvertible currency, as the government refused to devalue the currency. These policies led to the smuggling of cocoa out of the country and to falling incentives for farmers to engage in cocoa production, both of which reduced the export base and led to further government regulations and administrative controls. Import tariffs were used to protect state-owned enterprises, import controls were used to regulate the use of scarce foreign exchange but not in a way that prioritized production, and price controls were used to combat inflation but only led to the emergence of a black market in goods. Even when global commodity prices picked up in the mid-1970s, the producer price paid for cocoa did not, which, combined with the overvalued currency, led to a further decline in cocoa production.

There were several attempts to devalue the currency, privatize parastatals and liberalize markets in order to reduce inflation, parallel markets, and budget and trade deficits as well as to incentivize cocoa production. However, they were always short-lived and often resulted in the overthrow of the government through a military coup. In the second half of the 1970s, government fiscal deficits skyrocketed and were covered by borrowing from the central bank (printing money), and revenues

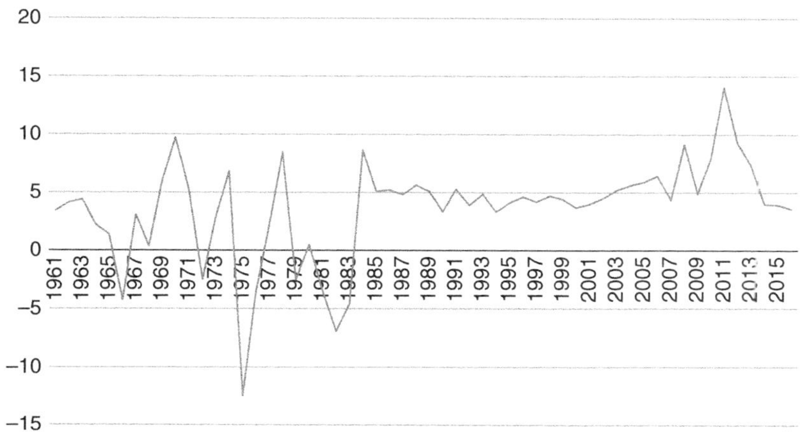

Figure 1.1 Ghana GDP Growth, 1961–2016
Source: World Development Indicators 2017.

increased only marginally. There was a sharp decline in production for the domestic market as well as exports. These factors led to hyperinflation and the most overvalued currency in Africa by a large margin, which in turn led to administrative corruption in the context of price and import controls, smuggling and parallel markets.[2] The economic decline was not reversed until the start of the Economic Recovery Programme in 1983, as shown in Figure 1.1, which was supported by structural adjustment loans from the IMF and World Bank.

There is a large body of literature concerned with the specific question of why Ghanaian governments were unable to adjust the country's economic policies that were so clearly having a detrimental effect on the economy and population as a whole. Within this literature seeking to explain the "failure to adjust," I identify four broad types of arguments: (1) the rational choice argument about the urban coalition; (2) the qualified trade-off argument about short time horizons; (3) the lack of state autonomy argument that draws on the developmental state theory; and (4) the lack of an independent capitalist class argument. In some ways these arguments are linked to particular scholars, but a close reading of the works on this period shows that scholars often

[2] This summary of the economic conditions comes from Hutchful (2002: 6–7).

adopted or fused several of these arguments, and that they largely agree on the basics despite different theoretical starting points.

The first type of argument is the rational choice/urban coalition argument found in the works of Douglas Rimmer (1992) and Jonathan Frimpong-Ansah (1991). These authors were theoretically inspired by the New Political Economy approach, which argued that a revenue-starved state captured by a coalition of price-conscious consumers, profit-seeking industries, and dependent farmers preys on the bulk of rural producers, who are producing the country's exports and thus wealth.[3] This behavior is in the individual, short-run best interests of these groups, but harmful to farmers and collectively deleterious. The arguments of Rimmer and Frimpong-Ansah were inspired by this approach but did not always follow it strictly. Rather, they emphasized that governments are typically more interested in how to make use of resources (distribution) than how to increase them (growth). The short-term interests of social groups that had captured the state were in conflict with the national or public interest in economic growth, and thus a trade-off existed between economic growth and the government's own interest. In particular, Rimmer (1992: 10) argued that Ghana "lacked any social group that was both powerful enough to shape policy and possessed an interest better served by economic growth than by public protection and patronage." This explains, according to Rimmer, why governments were unable to change economic policies.

The second argument, which partly stems from a constructive critique of the rational choice approach, is what I call the qualified trade-off argument about short time horizons. In his review of the work by Rimmer and Frimpong-Ansah, Gareth Austin (1996) notes that there is some merit in the trade-off argument but makes several qualifications to it. The first is to recognize the importance of statist ideology at the time in shaping policy choices, and thus that they were not driven purely by self-interest. The second is that politicians can gain politically from economic growth in such a way that there does not necessarily have to be a trade-off. In the case of Ghana, the time horizons of politicians and policymakers were "too short for the pursuit of growth-

[3] Some of the most influential writers within the New Political Economy approach included Robert Bates, Deepak Lal and Anne Kreuger. See the concise review of this literature in Frimpong-Ansah (1991: 45–47).

oriented economic policies to have become politically rational or, more generally, to have become optimal from the perspective of the personal interests of the policy-makers" (Austin 1996: 565).

Tony Killick (1978) comes to a similar conclusion on short time horizons in his thorough review of economic policies under the first three postindependence governments. However, Killick sees the short time horizon in terms of prioritizing consumption in the present rather than sacrificing current consumption for investment in production that would increase wealth and expand consumption in the future. This is epitomized in the use of the public sector to generate employment. He argues that short time horizons occur in postcolonial countries generally, and not just Ghana, because the drive for development comes from consumers rather than producers. Killick argues that development for Ghanaians means the goods and services associated with the welfare state in industrialized countries, and not economic growth per se. Thus, it is a demand for modernization without growth, without the economic innovation and adaptation that created wealth and made modernization possible. Popular pressure to deliver development is the source of politicians' short time horizons, because the pressures and uncertainties of political life tend to induce decisions based upon immediate rather than longer-term advantage. Defeated or deposed politicians often had few employment alternatives, increasing the incentive to do the popular thing even if unwise from a longer-run viewpoint (Killick 1978: 339).

Killick's explanation for why the "failed policies" were not changed in 1966 after the overthrow of Nkrumah's government emphasizes nationalism and the diffusion of economic costs. Nkrumah's government changed tack to a state-led industrialization strategy partly to deliver economic independence in the context of an economy that was largely dominated by foreign companies at the time of political independence – or at least that was the official discourse. But this discourse resonated within society, especially among urban populations. To change strategies would be to return the economy to foreign economic dominance, something that ruffled nationalist sensitivities. Furthermore, the economic costs of the policies tended to be diffused over the consuming public, whereas the benefits were enjoyed by highly specific groups of public sector workers and parastatal managers as well as businesspeople enjoying access to import licenses or import protections. Private businessmen and -women were neither strong enough nor well-regarded by the civil service. Thus, Killick argues, there were no social forces supporting a radical liberal approach to the country's economic problems, and thus it was not advantageous for politicians to support the approach (Killick 1978: 347).

This point resonates with Gareth Austin's argument that while urban bias is partially accurate as a description of the outcome of economic policies, the concept of urban coalition does not have much explanatory power. Austin notes that authors using the concept do not discuss the causal mechanisms through which the urban coalition mobilizes and translates its interests into action. Instead, he argues that the answer is in why there were no rural social forces with political influence. To understand why, claims Austin, more attention needs to be paid to how Nkrumah's power-sharing government during the decolonization process successfully demobilized cocoa farmers in the 1950s and to the continued demobilization of cocoa farmers under subsequent governments, which was a necessary condition for the economic policies adopted in the 1960s and 1970s.

Austin also finds that the urban coalition argument breaks down from the mid-1970s, when the previously existing balance between government support to the cocoa sector and government extraction of income from cocoa producers collapsed as extraction outweighed support. This shift to unrestrained rent-seeking requires an explanation, and Austin finds the personal rule argument, advanced by authors such as Richard Jeffries (1989) and Richard Sandbrook (1985), more convincing. This is because personal rulers, as the theory explains, build political support through patronage networks rather than through a coalition of interest groups, and the clients who receive rewards from patrons in return for political loyalty are not able to exert influence on the government. Therefore, patronage networks allow for a greater distance between the interests of groups in society and the ruling elites, which seemed to explain what occurred under the Acheampong government in the 1970s.

In contrast, Robert Price (1984) provides a different explanation for the economic chaos during the second half of the 1970s, one that draws inspiration from the developmental state literature. His argument is not that ruling elites were too detached from the rest of society, but rather that they were not insulated enough from distributional demands within society. The original developmental goals of state economic interventions were turned into tools for securing political incumbency and distributing state resources as patronage, rather than the state acting as an economic entrepreneur to pool and direct resources towards productive investments. This happened, according to Price, because the postcolonial state in Ghana was permeated by society. Society was characterized by ethnic and regional divisions that existed before independence, as well as by the social and economic demands of the relatively large, well-organized and mobilized urban strata. These centrifugal forces (that challenged central authority) and high expectations for immediate improvements in material living standards put extreme political pressures on new Ghanaian officials, who had few resources with which to consolidate state power and political survival. Due to "political malintegration," he argues, political support was purchased from the socially mobilized strata of society, which developed into a utilitarian relationship in which groups in society came to expect the state to serve their material needs and the survival of ruling elites depended on doing so (Price 1984: 187–190). This strategy was successful for political integration, but not for the economy, because material resources were consumed without being replenished given that they were not aimed primarily at increasing production and productivity. As the resources were eroded, the pool from which political support could be purchased shrank. The failure of statist economic policies, argues Price, was not so much because they were ill-conceived, but because the state lacked the requisite autonomy to implement them.

Eboe Hutchful's analysis is quite similar to that of Robert Price in terms of the intensity of society's demands of the state and the structural constraints that it created. Hutchful (2002) refers to a postcolonial social compact that resulted from the particular trajectory of decolonization experienced in the colonial territories that became Ghana. The decolonization struggle pitted an aspiring political elite coalition against an older political elite class that partially overlapped and was allied with rural capitalist cocoa farmers and chiefs (who were often cocoa farmer-traders) as well as urban businessmen. The "upstart" political group won the founding elections through the political coalition it built, which was primarily urban, southern and semi-educated and whose members looked to the state and political processes rather than the market and economic processes as the basis for accumulating wealth and social status. The ruling coalition thus favored a strong central state with an active role in the economy, especially in creating state-owned enterprises. In this sense, it also resonates with Tony

Killick's argument about short time horizons stemming from consumers' demand for development. Hutchful acknowledges, as Killick did, that Nkrumah's big push was as much about modernization and social welfare as it was about industrialization. It was about free or subsidized healthcare, education, housing, water and so on. The choice of industrialization through state and foreign capital investment was a means of delivering modern industrialization quickly.

Hutchful also argues that rational choice theorists underestimated the magnitude of the structural challenges posed by balance of payments constraints, and thus the policy options available in responding to them, and as a result overplayed the role of political will. While late colonialism had a more developmental approach and created the marketing boards, which provided the means to tap into cocoa wealth to fund government expenditure, the economy was still a colonial trading economy characterized by "fragility." Nkrumah's big push was driven by a need to overcome this fragility. However, the dilemma is that any attempt to transform the economy through industrialization also results in an expansion of imports (at least initially), leads to greater inflation, and puts pressure on the balance of payments. This is a classic problem that all developing countries have faced in achieving economic transformation from largely agrarian economies, including now advanced capitalist countries.[4] There are limits to the extent to which export earnings can be expanded rapidly enough to earn the foreign exchange required for imports of capital and intermediate goods, especially when what is exported are the same kinds of commodities that other developing countries are exporting and oversupply leads to falling prices. Therefore, countries attempting industrialization tend to experience chronic balance of payments crises. The only solutions are external finance or foreign direct investment. In Ghana, foreign direct investment was not forthcoming during the Nkrumah period, as discussed in the next chapter, and depending solely on external financing led to a debt crisis.

Hutchful's explanation for why subsequent governments continued with Nkrumah's policies even when they were unsustainable hinges on the social compact constructed under the first

[4] For a good summary of this dilemma in the contemporary period, see Fischer (2009). For a historical overview of this dilemma of all countries trying to "catch up" with the first industrializing country, Great Britain, see Schwartz (2010).

postindependence government that served to legitimize the state and the political coalition governing it. Under this compact, the state was to generate the economic and social welfare structure of a modern society, which was to be managed and implemented by a technocracy. Political legitimation of the leaders governing the state was produced through delivering this welfare, as well as patronage. Hutchful agrees with Price that a large part of this social compact was a unifying exercise – to bind constituencies to the state and establish its centrality – and that as a result, state–society relations became defined in utilitarian terms in which distributive spending and patronage increasingly constituted the glue.

Hutchful refers to a fiscal coalition to capture the broad consensus in society regarding the fiscal and economic responsibilities of the state. It is not an actual coalition of interest groups, but rather a coalition based on common ideas. He uses the term fiscal paradigm to describe the substantive fiscal assumptions represented in this consensus. The fiscal paradigm did not work equally in the interests of everyone, but nonetheless, there was substantive support for it diffused through society. Hutchful argues that the fiscal coalition had an urban core, seeming to agree with Rimmer and Frimpong-Ansah, but also emphasizes that it transcended the rural–urban divide because some rural middle-class groups with strong connections to the state were also beneficiaries. Hutchful agrees with Price that as state resources shrank, ruling elites were less able to respond to popular expectations and thus to maintain the broad political mobilization structures that necessitated and legitimated redistribution.

There were tensions within the fiscal paradigm, according to Hutchful. The first was over the requirements of political reproduction and economic growth, with technocrats emphasizing directly productive investments and political leaders emphasizing social expenditures that could also be used as political patronage. Another tension concerned whether state power should be used to support the market and domestic private entrepreneurs, or to substitute them. It was not just Nkrumah's government that suppressed the emergence of an independent capitalist class free from bureaucratic controls, but also the next two governments. Therefore, it seems that the consequence of the fiscal paradigm was for the state to usurp the leadership of economic development and to suppress the small autonomous capitalist class.

What Hutchful, Rimmer and Austin all imply but do not directly discuss is that this was possible due to the absence of a strong domestic capitalist class not dependent on the state for wealth creation. This point is explicitly made by Antoinette Handley (2008), who argues that, at independence, the state was stronger than the nascent entrepreneurial class, which allowed the state to overexploit the main economic sector – cocoa – and to take over the economy. State-led economic development in turn led to the emergence of a business class dependent on the state, which she calls a neopatrimonial business class. Thus, we can see a fourth line of argument that emphasizes the lack of a strong domestic capitalist class at the time of independence, or a growth constituency, as Rimmer (1992) phrased it, which shaped the incentives and decisions of ruling political elites and created path-dependent effects.

This review of the literature attempting to explain the economy's downward spiral in the second half of the 1970s shows that there is more of a consensus among scholars of Ghanaian political economy than disagreement. This consensus centers on *two features* that characterized Ghanaian political economy and their outcomes. First, Ghanaian governments prioritized the short-term requirements of their political survival, which involved distributive, consumption-driven expenditures across a broad spectrum of society as well as targeted distribution (or patronage) to specific groups linked to the ruling political elites. Second, when governments did promote productive investments, they privileged the public sector over domestic capitalists, partly because it was the fastest way to create the jobs and modern amenities that Ghanaians expected and partly because independent domestic capitalists posed a potential political threat. Both of these features had the effect of undermining the productive sectors of the economy, by creating disincentives for private investment in their reproduction and expansion.

However, there is not much discussion of why these two features emerged and why they were so much more destabilizing in Ghana than in neighboring Côte d'Ivoire, for example. There are similarities in the trajectories of African countries in that most of them experienced economic crisis in the 1980s, but Ghana's was one of the more extreme. Other African countries, and indeed other developing countries, faced similar challenges of political integration and centralizing state authority, with different results, and other African countries also lacked a strong domestic capitalist class at independence.

An exception is the work of Richard Crook (1989, 1990) comparing the political and economic development trajectories of Ghana and Côte d'Ivoire. Crook emphasized the strongly mobilized, competing social groups incorporated into Ghanaian political competition in contrast to the central control exercised by a united ruling elite and weaker social groups within the ruling coalition in Côte d'Ivoire. He coined the term developmental patrimonialism, in arguing that the form of clientelism in Côte d'Ivoire under Houphouet-Boigny was more conducive to economic growth than the form of clientelism in Ghana and other African countries because Houphouet-Boigny was able to centralize the management of economic rents within the ruling party, and, because he had no strong political rivals, he had a longer time horizon and devolved authority to a competent economic bureaucracy. Crook's work provides an excellent starting point for explaining Ghana's experience in comparative perspective, but we still need more conceptual tools to understand the drivers of political clientelism and why clientelism was more pervasive and economically detrimental in some countries than in others. These tools are introduced in the next section.

As noted above, the early political economy literature was concerned with explaining why political elites failed to stop the economic decline. But it did finally stop, under the Provisional National Defence Council (PNDC) military government set up by J.J. Rawlings after yet another coup on December 31, 1981. How and why did it happen? Hutchful (2002) offers the only systematic explanation. The lower levels of the military revolted, which resulted in a temporary revolution of the lower classes in urban and rural areas. These classes had not been benefiting from the existing distribution of economic benefits. Rawlings rode this wave of popular mobilization and encouraged it in order to destabilize the existing political elite groups and prevent them from reorganizing. The economic crisis, which had reached proportions where basic economic activities were not reproducible, had led to a legitimacy crisis for the political elite and to a large extent for the state. The twin economic and political crises provided an opening for a new group to take control of the government, a group with few connections to the existing political organizations (and factions within them) and whose political legitimacy was not linked to clientelist exchange.

The result was to break with the first feature that had characterized all previous governments. The PNDC government implemented radical economic reforms despite the short-term costs to sections of the urban population and prioritized productive investments over consumption-driven ones. This pattern of government spending was broken because the trade-off changed. It was actually in the political interests of the PNDC elites to rebuild the fiscal basis of the state by rehabilitating the traditional export sectors and to provide infrastructure to rural sections of the population and geographically neglected parts of the country (such as the northern regions) as a political survival strategy. This period proved Gareth Austin's point that economic growth could be in the interests of political elites (Austin 1996).

Economic adjustment under the PNDC government included reforming the Cocoa Marketing Board but not dismantling it, despite the board being singled out by many writers as one of the main causes of poor economic performance.[5] In fact, the Cocoa Marketing Board became crucial to the revival and relative success of the cocoa sector since the 1990s. But while the PNDC government used the marketing board to tax cocoa for rebuilding government revenues, it no longer needed to use revenue extracted from the cocoa sector to finance social expectations and political reproduction. This was because official foreign aid came to fulfill this role, which remained the case under subsequent governments, with sovereign bonds and oil receipts substituting, to some extent, for foreign aid in the 2010s. Furthermore, the new floating exchange rate and capital account liberalization removed the possibility of overvalued exchange rates, although it introduced new problems of currency instability and capital flight.

Thus, the worst excesses of the past were gone, but things did not change as much as was hoped. This is because the PNDC government did not break with the second feature of pursuing state-led investments over support for domestic capitalists. The PNDC ruling elite feared that a viable private sector might create a new center of power, underwrite the emergence of an alternative political force, or finance another coup. Therefore, PNDC elites tried to neutralize existing domestic capitalists (or what was left of them after decades of economic crisis), particularly those they perceived to be linked to the opposition Danquah-Busia

[5] See for example, Frimpong-Ansah (1991), Killick (1978) and Herbst (1993).

political tradition, and at the same time, sought their own socioeconomic mobility through control of the state and thus the creation of businesses tied to them.[6] Their efforts were buttressed by the ideological positions of the World Bank and IMF staff, whose organizations were financing a significant proportion of the economic reforms and who viewed direct government support to domestic capitalists as market-distorting interventions.

Soon the country was once again caught between a rock and a hard place as the return to multiparty rule at the end of 1992 led to the reemergence of the first feature of prioritizing consumption-driven expenditures over (or even at the expense of) productive sector investments. This time around the trade-off was not between economic growth and political survival, because the country did experience modest economic growth, albeit marked by recurrent macroeconomic crises that led growth rates to dip and then recover. The government did not overexploit the cocoa sector, and it pursued the "right" policies according to the World Bank, the IMF and other donors who were financing the state. As a result, cocoa exports increased and policies remained relatively liberal, and the government continuously turned to international financial institutions and donors to plug its trade and budget deficits. Growth continued, but the public sector remained large, and limited growth in the productive sectors meant that the economy failed to generate formal private sector jobs to keep pace with growth of the labor force.[7] This time around the trade-off was between political survival and economic transformation.

The literature on Ghanaian political economy since the Fourth Republic highlights the reemergence of the two features characterizing government policy choices and spending.[8] In seeking to explain the moderate economic success in the 1990s and early 2000s, Killick (2008: 27) argues that governments continued to emphasize short-

[6] For authors supporting parts of this argument, see Hutchful (2002), Arthur (2002), Tangri (1992), Handley (2008), Ninsin (1996), Opoku (2010), Kraus (2002) and Hart and Gyimah-Boadi (2000).

[7] The public sector accounted for half of formal (recorded) employment in 2003, and total public sector expenditure was equivalent to more than half of GDP between 1999 and 2001 (Killick 2008).

[8] The key works include Hutchful (2002), Handley (2008), Booth et al. (2004) and Killick (2008). Notably, they cover the 1990s and early 2000s. There are no extensive analyses of the NPP government (2001–2008) and the second NDC government (2009–2016).

term appropriation and distribution of resources by the state, rather than economic growth and wealth creation. Many scholars thought change was on the way in the 2000s under the New Patriotic Party (NPP) government, but it became clear that the NPP political elites did not behave significantly differently in government, nor did they pursue initiatives to support domestic capitalists to invest in productive sectors. Emmanuel Gyimah-Boadi (2009) observed that NPP politicians forced technocrats to take a back seat to the stark realities of electoral politics as politicians attempted to take into account the social costs of their economic policies. Ernest Aryeetey and Andrew McKay (2007) agree that spending by the NPP government was driven by political expediency and a lack of prioritization, resulting in fiscal deficits and no clear commitment to implementing structural change through increased agricultural productivity and private sector development.

The main theoretical perspective used to explain these two features in the contemporary literature on Ghana under the Fourth Republic has been neopatrimonialism. The neopatrimonial state refers to a situation where the state and its resources are more or less completely captured by patronage networks, which results in a state with limited policy autonomy (Booth et al. 2004: 6). This situation is explained as originating partly from the precolonial social orders on which the colonial state was imposed, which were characterized by obligations and entitlements governing kinship and community at local levels. Under colonial rule, these personal bonds of loyalty and obligation were expanded to different arenas and then to the state in the post-independence period. Powerful individuals were obliged to support their kin and followers. The outcome of neopatrimonialism, as explained by Booth and colleagues (2004), is the lack of state autonomy in policymaking. Handley (2008) also refers to neopatrimonial collusion, in which formal institutions are subverted by a patrimonial logic in which officeholders almost systematically appropriate public resources for their own uses and political authority is based on clientelism.

However, the neopatrimonial framework is inadequate as an explanation because everything gets subsumed under the logic of patrimonialism rather than really explaining why things are the way they are, and it offers no explanation for why neopatrimonialism plays out differently in Ghana and Tanzania, for example, because there is only one logic. Booth and colleagues (2004) recognize these limitations and try to overcome them by highlighting the ways in which Ghana's particular form of neopatrimonialism differs. They emphasize the complexity of Ghanaian society's organizational groups and associations; the varied forms of social loyalty and identity that are available to be mobilized politically; and the ways in which political parties sought support by engaging with local factions in order to win elections. These observations are a better starting point than traditional ties of loyalty and obligation. We must return to the origins of pervasive political clientelism in the context of weak domestic capitalists if we are to understand why ruling political elites continue to pursue distributive expenditures and state-led industrial policies.

Taking a Political Settlements Approach

Ghanaian governments since independence have engaged in distributive, consumption-driven expenditures resulting in large fiscal deficits, which in turn negatively affected economic growth and transformation. This tendency is driven by pervasive clientelism in the political system, the history of which could be summarized as follows. Since independence, political elites purchased political support from the socially mobilized strata of society in order to construct political parties and win elections. This also occurred under military regimes as a means to create political support, albeit the width of the clientelist exchange narrowed, particularly as the economic crisis persisted and the financial resources of the state dwindled. A utilitarian relationship developed in which groups in society came to expect the state to serve their material needs, and the survival of ruling elites depended on doing so. This utilitarian view of the state created popular pressures to deliver social welfare and modernization, which, combined with the uncertainty of remaining in power, led political leaders to have very short time horizons and thus to make decisions that prioritized their immediate political advantage. The latter resulted in distributing material benefits and economic opportunities to key political groups and loyal supporters that ruling elites saw as essential to staying in power.

There is nothing about this story that is unique to Ghana. This utilitarian relationship driving clientelism is generally true for all developing countries. So why has clientelism in Ghana been more economically detrimental than in other countries? Referring to the patrimonial origins of clientelism in African countries is not convincing, nor does it help to explain variations across African countries in the forms and effects of clientelism. Mushtaq Khan's political settlements theory provides a framework for conceptualizing how and why clientelism takes different forms, and the implications of the different forms of clientelism for economic transformation.

The starting point is that political clientelism is the dominant feature of all developing countries, and we need to understand why that is before we can understand variations in clientelism. Developing countries are called "developing countries" because they experienced the partial collapse of precapitalist economies and the political systems attached to them as a result of interactions with areas of the world that were already capitalist, which had more advanced technologies and greater wealth and which challenged the status quo in precapitalist territories in the world.[9] In many places, this process began even before formal colonial rule through interactions of merchants and producers within the global economy, including in the southern territories that became part of Ghana. This interaction started processes of capitalist transformation, with varying degrees of success. The emerging capitalists and market-based formal institutions in the typical developing country were not productive enough, however, to make the beneficiaries of these formal rights the dominant group in these societies. At the same time, the dominant property owners in the precapitalist system were no longer able to politically dominate these societies.[10]

Therefore, what Mushtaq Khan calls intermediate class organizations (borrowing the term from Michael Kalecki) came to dominate the societies of developing countries. Intermediate classes were not asset-rich (with incomes derived from profits, land or finance) but also were not so asset-poor that their incomes stemmed primarily from their labor (Khan 2005a: 718). Their main tool was their organizational capabilities and social legitimacy: their ability to organize and mobilize supporters based on ideology, identity and symbols of legitimacy as well as the use of economic resources. These intermediate classes emerged during the colonial period and trajectories of decolonization. For example, colonial powers selectively recognized

[9] For two good books, among many, on this process, see Wood (2002) and Schwartz (2010).

[10] The summary presented here is based on Mushtaq Khan's explanation of the origins of clientelist political settlements and why they differ from capitalist political settlements (Khan 2010).

the "rights" of organizationally powerful groups as a method of political stabilization, and these groups usually played a dominant role in forming political coalitions during decolonization to take over the postcolonial state.

In postcolonial polities, political competition involved political entrepreneurs from the intermediate classes competing to achieve a distribution of income and assets that favored them. They were unlikely to share common interests or to be constrained by the fate of the small capitalist sector. Political competition was organized primarily through patron-client networks. Making a similar point with reference to African countries, Chris Allen (1995) argued that in the absence of strong class cleavages, (aspiring) political elites, in the context of rapid decolonization from British and French rule, built political parties using patronage to bind local powerbrokers to the party and local voters to the candidates.

Thus, (aspiring) political elites use clientelist practices to mobilize and organize coalitions that allow them to obtain and maintain power and political order. Capitalist firms and farms do not provide the means of income and employment for the majority of the population, who live in low productivity agriculture or survive through informal activities like petty production and trade. The small capitalist sector also does not provide the major source of government revenue, and the low productivity of the majority of the economic activities means that the tax basis of the state is small. Political organizations compete to achieve a distribution of income and assets that favor them. Ruling elites distribute resources to accommodate groups in society who are part of the coalition supporting the ruling elites and groups who can threaten political stability. They use resources that are part of budgeted funds, as well as off-budget resources raised through legal and illegal practices. Ruling elites also appoint critical clients to government positions or positions on parastatals, where clients have the opportunity for personal accumulation.[11]

Colonial rulers installed political and economic institutions in their colonial territories, before recognizing their independence, which mirrored the ones in their own countries, but which had emerged as a product of capitalist transformation in their societies. These formal

[11] For a greater elaboration of these points, see Gray and Khan (2010) and Khan (2010).

institutions – of an impersonal rule of law that benefits capitalist property rights upheld by impersonal bureaucracy governed by a democracy where political parties are organized generally along class lines – did not function in newly independent postcolonial territories as they had in Western countries, because they were not backed up by the (informal) power of a large productive capitalist sector and the diffusion of capitalist property rights throughout society. Therefore, the distribution of power embodied in the formal institutions did not match the distribution of power in society, which resulted in the subversion of formal institutions to the claims of powerful groups in society.

Informal institutions such as patron-client networks also became central to capital accumulation, because it is not possible to transfer assets and resources in a transparent and formally regulated way. Such non-market transfers are referred to as primitive accumulation. All capitalists have emerged through close relationships with political groups controlling state power, which allowed them to benefit from non-market-based means of accumulation. However, primitive accumulation only drives capitalist transformation if captured resources are channeled into productive investments. Otherwise, primitive accumulation results in conspicuous consumption and, at worst, predatory behavior that can lead to economic collapse.

The set of economic and political logics described above are present in all developing countries and account for why political clientelism is a common feature among them. But despite the presence of personalized politics and rent-seeking, developing countries have experienced different economic outcomes: the growth of capitalist sectors has been greater and faster in some countries than others. This is because the pace of economic transformation depends on how the political logics of maintaining power through clientelism and the economic logic of groups who seek to reallocate or capture resources through primitive accumulation shape the final pattern of resource and asset allocation and capture in a particular country (Khan 2010). More specifically, it depends on how the competition between political factions affects the emergence of capitalist sectors, the acquisition of technologies by local firms and farms, and the ability of local firms/farms to compete in global markets (Khan 2005a). These patterns in turn depend on the preexisting distribution of power among groups in a given society.

Thus, the country-specific differences in the distribution of power in society are the source of variation.

Which groups have power in different countries cannot be generalized, but it is possible to generalize the variables relating to the distribution of power in a particular society that are significant in shaping the final pattern of resource allocation and capture. The first is the distribution of power between political groups included within the ruling coalition and those excluded. The second variable is the distribution of power within the ruling coalition, among elites as well as between elite factions and lower level supporting factions. The third is the relative power of domestic capitalists vis-à-vis ruling elites.[12]

The reason why political clientelism can be more pervasive in some countries than in others is related to the first two variables. The more diffused the distribution of power in society, the more vulnerable political leaders in government are to being replaced and the harder it is to manage demands for patronage as patronage becomes central in holding the ruling coalition together. For example, if there are powerful political factions that are not included in the ruling coalition, then political leaders are vulnerable and likely to have a short time horizon, which leads to prioritizing immediate political gains over political strategies that can deliver only over a longer time period. Distributional political strategies deliver more quickly than those based on productive investments and economic growth. If power is highly fragmented among ruling elites, then it is difficult for any particular group of elites to centralize and manage the clientelist system; instead, it becomes a free-for-all as elites, in a common strategy of building political support, try to capture and distribute resources in ways that most enhance their own political survival, which is based on their individual political support base and is only loosely linked to the survival of other elites. If the lower-level support groups of the ruling coalition have significant power vis-à-vis the political leaders, because the latter are dependent on the former to keep them in power, then lower-level groups in the ruling coalition will demand and be able to extract more patronage resources in return for that support.

Pervasive clientelism exists in Ghana for these reasons. As illustrated in the next chapter, on the eve of independence, power was highly

[12] For a more intensive discussion of these variables, see Khan (2010) and Whitfield et al. (2015).

dispersed as a result of precolonial and colonial processes that bequeathed a configuration of several strong political organizations and a high degree of political mobilization and organization in urban and rural areas. Political elites were fragmented as a result of the existence of several strong and relatively autonomous societal groups. These groups produced their own (aspiring) political elites who had strong organizational capabilities and who entered into shifting alliances with each other to form political coalitions. Local political elites exchanged their loyalty to national political elites in return for patronage. The political elites were not just fragmented, they were also polarized along particular social cleavages that existed before independence, became politicized during the decolonization process, and solidified over time. Thus, despite their fragmentation, political elites tended to coalesce into two broad political coalitions based on a mixture of political ideology, family history, social status and ethnicity. This is the origin of Ghana's de facto two-party system, one in which political parties are coalitions holding together a highly fragmented elite.

Therefore, Ghana has been characterized by what Mushtaq Khan calls competitive clientelism. Competitive in this context refers to the distribution of power in society. It means that the number and strength of political factions resulted in many power centers that could not be accommodated within a single ruling coalition. On the other hand, attempts to keep strong political factions out of power by legal means or military force would not work either and would only lead to political instability. Within the ruling coalition, the president and top elites are not able to centralize and control the creation and distribution of patronage due to factional competition. Increasing clientelist competition, within and outside the ruling coalition, can become so intense that the military typically intervenes. However, rather than reducing clientelist competition, military involvement often intensifies it, leading to endemic instability with continual attempts to overthrow governments, as witnessed in Ghana. Thus, competitive clientelism is typically associated with electoral democracy, because elections allow powerful elite factions to rotate in and out of government in an orderly way and provide a mechanism (the ballot box) for testing the organizational strength of competing coalitions. However, elections are only successful if competing coalitions perceive that election results actually reflect the balance of organizational power on the ground.

A situation of competitive clientelism has characterized Ghana since independence. The existence of powerful factions outside of ruling coalitions explains why political leaders have had such short time horizons under military governments and elected governments. During periods of democratic rule, political parties mobilized coalitions that could win elections by picking up the support of local elites, who in turn mobilized their supporters and already existing local organizations, and by building their own direct patronage networks. This political mobilization strategy was continued under the Fourth Republic by both the National Democratic Congress (NDC) party and the NPP, as shown in Chapter 3. Once in government, both the NDC and NPP built strong and wider patronage networks in which different types of actors were essential to financing campaigns and mobilizing votes on election day. These groups within the party have significant leverage due to their importance in winning elections and thus are able to make demands of political leaders regarding the distribution of resources and economic opportunities.

Even military governments had to build a support base by cultivating loyalty in return for patronage. The early period of the PNDC government was the only time that political leaders did not rely on strong lower-level factions to constitute their political support base. This was a unique situation: PNDC political leaders did not need a strong support base given that excluded political factions were (temporarily) weakened because of the severe economic crisis over which they had presided. The presence of strong political organizations outside government means that these excluded political elites can lure away the supporters of the ruling coalition with promises of better patronage, whether individual, collective or quasi-public goods. When excluded political elites and their organizations are weak, ruling elites face less vulnerability, and as a result, the political costs of policy reforms are lower and they can fend off the distributional demands of lower level supporters without worrying about their political survival. Eventually the PNDC ruling elites had to build a support base through patronage, but the flow of resources to the lower levels of the coalition were much smaller than what was expended after the return to multiparty rule and the need to mobilize a coalition that could win elections.

The point that African countries had different clientelist systems at independence due to the distribution of power in society that set countries on particular path-dependent trajectories is best illustrated by comparing Ghana with its neighbor Côte d'Ivoire. The PDCI (*Parti democratique de la Côte d'Ivoire*) was able to construct a one-party system in Côte d'Ivoire because there were fewer autonomous power centers and the few groups challenging the PDCI could be brought into the ruling coalition. The one-party system was maintained through a clientelist system in which patronage was centralized and controlled by leaders at the top of the system.[13]

But competitive clientelism on its own is not enough to explain why Ghana's form of clientelism is so detrimental to economic transformation. Other developing countries with competitive clientelism, such as Thailand, have experienced economic growth and significant transformation.[14] To be sure, Thailand has benefited from greater foreign direct investments in the manufacturing sector than Ghana, but another key aspect concerns the presence of domestic capitalists at independence who had greater financial assets and technological capabilities than those in Ghana and who had greater political influence with factions of political elites.

The relative power of domestic capitalists depends on their wealth, the extent to which they dominate key economic sectors, and their ability to organize and engage to protect or further their interests through a political process. But it also depends on the organization of the ruling coalition, which determines if and how political influence of domestic capitalists can be wielded (Khan 2010). The greatest source of power for domestic capitalists is their direct contribution to government revenue and foreign exchange, and their ability to offer political financing that ruling elites need to build and maintain ruling coalitions. If ruling elites perceive that they do not need existing domestic capitalists to do either of these things, and if ruling elites can create or rely on their "own" business class based on access to state resources, then domestic capitalists in productive sectors will be politically weak and have little influence over policy direction and choices (Whitfield et al. 2015).

Earlier scholarship has noted that the economically detrimental form of clientelism in Ghana was due to the absence of strong domestic capitalists who could check the excesses of the government and form

[13] For a comparison of Ghana and Côte d'Ivoire, see Boone (2003). For an excellent overview of the clientelist system in Côte d'Ivoire, see Crook (1989).

[14] On the case of Thailand, see Khan (2010) and Doner (2009), for example.

a politically influential group in favor of economic reforms. The weakness of the domestic capitalists also led Nkrumah's government, as well as successive governments, to pursue state-controlled industrial policies over supporting domestic capitalists. As the next chapter shows, the Nkrumah government's decisions in the early 1960s had important legacies: ruling elites' predilection for state-controlled industrial policies reduced the scope of and support for the development of private domestic capitalists in productive sectors, further weakening domestic capitalists and thus reinforcing the tendency of ruling elites to adopt a statist approach.

But we still need to explain why domestic capitalists were such a small group at independence and why this group lacked political influence. To do so, we need to start from Gareth Austin's point about the cocoa farmers that Nkrumah's power-sharing government demobilized in the 1950s, but we need to take it further (Austin 1996). It was not just a demobilization; it also involved an expropriation of wealth and closing of opportunities for accumulation by the cocoa capitalist farmers through the internal cocoa trade, as shown in the next chapter. Nkrumah's government was able to do this because the cocoa farmers were a diverse group, some more capitalist in orientation than others, that also cut across social hierarchies and ethnoregional politics, and embodied tensions between migrants and indigenes in communities governed as traditional areas under local chiefs. In turn, this situation has its origins in the 1920s with colonial policies that aimed to slow, if not stop, capitalist transformation in cocoa growing areas. The absence of a domestic industrial capitalist group can also be linked to stymied development of the indigenous merchant class as a result of their inability to compete with European merchants in the precolonial period and then colonial policies that privileged European merchants. This is important, as there are strong links in early capitalist development between accumulation through commerce and the move into industrial production.

My approach is in line with that taken by Antoinette Handley (2008), who emphasizes the importance of taking a historical focus on how political processes and class formations unfold, and that relationships and institutional paths that inform the productive capabilities and political influence of the business class were laid down historically. However, I differ from Handley in my interpretation of what the critical junctures in Ghana's history are. Handley argues that the immediate postindependence period was the most important because it shaped the emergence of a neopatrimonial business class: businesses that emerged simultaneously with the postcolonial state and formed a dependency relationship with it. This occurs, she argues, because when independent domestic capitalists do not already exist, states are not constrained in their quest to centralize and consolidate their power. Thus, it matters whether it is business or the state that emerges first. I agree that weak domestic capitalists at independence allowed the political elite to dominate economic sectors and suppress the emergence of an independent capitalist class, instead supporting a managerial and business class connected to the state through parastatals. But I argue that the critical juncture is to be found in the precolonial and colonial periods, in which nascent agrarian and merchant capitalists emerged but were subsequently weakened. It was this weakened cocoa capitalist class that tried but failed to defend its interests during the decolonization struggle of the 1950s. Cocoa capitalists were not so much too "young" but rather too "weak," as capitalist development had been stymied in previous periods, undermining the formation of a strong agrarian capitalist class. This is why Chapter 2 begins with the precolonial and colonial periods when tracing the historical origins of weak domestic capitalists.

Lastly, there is a consensus among scholars of Ghanaian political economy that Nkrumah's Convention People's Party (CPP) suppressed any independent business, including cocoa farmers, because the political elite saw private independent capitalists as a political threat. The outstanding question is why did they see private business as a political threat, when this was not the case in Nigeria or in Côte d'Ivoire. Some scholars point to Nkrumah's socialist ideology as an answer, but it could also be that Nkrumah adopted the socialist rhetoric because it fit preexisting objectives. While many lower-level members of Nkrumah's political coalition believed in socialism, I argue that ideology was not the key motivation of the CPP political elites, especially not of Nkrumah. It was the heightened level of political competition, a strong opposition and thus extreme vulnerability that led Nkrumah and many CPP political elites to squash independent centers of accumulation and to connect all accumulation to the state, and thus political loyalty, as a means to ensure political survival. As Chapter 2 shows, political leaders supported the creation of businesses loyal to them, which could be used to finance their ruling coalition, and they also engaged in business opportunities through their contacts and access to state resources – a form of primitive accumulation that was politically aligned and thus non-threatening. This imperative still drives ruling political elites to a significant extent today. Ruling political elites under both NDC and the NPP governments pursued state-led industrial policies in the 1990s, 2000s and 2010s, and domestic capitalists in productive sectors that were not politically aligned were ignored, neglected and sometimes expropriated.

The Politics of Industrial Policy

While there is considerable agreement in the existing literature about the two features characterizing Ghanaian governments' policy choices and how they negatively affected economic transformation and even economic growth, there is less discussion about the political and economic conditions necessary to drive economic transformation and seemingly little agreement. This is important because one cannot offer a full explanation of Ghana's poor economic performance without a theory of what drives economic transformation. It is here that this book diverges significantly from the existing literature on Ghana. Douglas Rimmer, Tony Killick and Antoinette Handley implicitly or explicitly indicate that the problem is too much state intervention, an overbearing public sector that soaks up all resources and a politicized business class that results in a "parasitic business class" (Handley 2008) or "crony capitalism" (Killick 2008). These scholars argue that state and business interests need to be separate, and that domestic capitalists need to be organized enough to solve conflicts among themselves and engage with the government about a set of policies collectively agreed and pursued by domestic capitalists. The business-state relations strand of the comparative political economy literature supports this line of argument, emphasizing the importance of the formal, institutionalized and transparent influence of organized business.[15] However, this literature draws on developing country experiences where a relatively strong group of domestic capitalists already existed. This conceptualization does not account for how private domestic capitalists in productive sectors emerge in the first place. While business

[15] For a review of the business-state relations literature, see Whitfield et al. (2015: 10–11).

will develop interests distinct from the state eventually, in the early phases of capitalist transformation, economic and political elites can be fused because a private domestic capitalist class is still emerging.

I argue that an "enabling business environment" would not be enough to drive economic transformation in Ghana, nor would a complete break between business and political elites. My approach is closer to that of Eboe Hutchful. In his seminal book, Hutchful (2002: 2–3) assesses the impact of structural adjustment reforms and concludes that while many macroeconomic policies initiated were overdue and produced major gains, they failed to address embedded problems of the Ghanaian economy: "the notion that 'freeing markets' and rolling back the state would free and revolutionize productive forces turned out to be an illusion." Revolutionizing productive forces, he argued, would require a synergy between state and market, and a closer relation between the state and capital than had been the case under the PNDC and then NDC governments.

Not only are industrial policies necessary to drive economic transformation, a certain degree of collusion between business and political elites is necessary if governments are to pursue industrial policies in the first place. The central challenge to economic transformation in Ghana is not the existence of collusion and a politicized business class per se, but rather its specific configuration.

Industrial policy is essentially about creating, allocating and managing rents.[16] Government policies and investments supporting the emergence and development of specific industries involve providing incentives for entrepreneurs to invest in productive sectors, providing access to capital below market rates, subsidizing the cost of training or acquiring skilled managers, and using import tariffs or other forms of protection to subsidize the costs of learning because while firms are operating below the level of efficiency of international competitors, they would operate at a loss. Rents are necessarily created as government initiatives help firms to overcome the first- and second-order constraints on productivity discussed in the previous chapter.

[16] Rents are often defined in (neoclassical) economics as excess incomes, meaning all those income flows that are additional to prevailing market-based profits and wages. Even though rents are excess incomes in terms of what recipients would have received in the market, they are not excess payments because they are necessary in order for recipients to produce the good, provide the service or carry out the economic activity in question (Khan 2000).

However, the processes of creating and managing rents as part of industrial policy easily becomes entangled with the processes of rent creation and distribution linked to political stability and political survival of the ruling coalition. Rent-seeking can lead to the productive use of such rents, or it can result in unproductive uses, depending on how these political processes play out. The successful use of rents in implementing industrial policy requires several conditions to be met: mutual interests, pockets of efficiency, and learning for productivity (Whitfield et al. 2015).

The political incentives for ruling elites to create rents for productive uses by capitalists have to be substantial. The strongest motivation is the existence of what we call mutual interests between a group of ruling elites and a group of domestic (or foreign) capitalists. Mutual interests are created in various ways. Capitalists may be able to influence policy formulation and the creation of rents to help them in existing activities or move into new activities in exchange for providing political financing, for example for political parties. Capitalists may also have political influence because of their importance as a source of government revenue or foreign exchange, which ruling elites need to pursue other important programs essential to their survival in government. In the absence of mutual interests, ruling elites may pursue industrial policies for other reasons, such as ideas of economic nationalism or as a political survival strategy that emphasizes delivering jobs and raising incomes. However, when industrial policy is not backed by a group of firms or farms with a strong interest in it, the emergence of resistance within and outside the ruling coalition can undermine implementation of that policy, and rents created as part of an industrial policy may be diverted for unproductive uses.

But even when there are mutual interests, successful implementation of industrial policy is not ensured, as the state bureaucracy needs to be able to formulate and implement policies. This does not require a complete Weberian bureaucracy in which civil servants work only according to the formal rules and are appointed on meritocratic grounds, but rather only pockets of efficiency. It requires pockets within the state bureaucracy in which civil servants have political backing from ruling elites and a significant degree of autonomy from political pressures and distributional demands generated within the ruling coalition. In other words, the group of ruling elites pushing the particular industrial policy must be able to exert enough control over factions within the ruling coalition in order to shift resources, change institutions (which often involves changing the distribution of economic benefits) and overcome any resistance to the policy. This pocket gives state bureaucrats just enough relative autonomy from particularistic demands to be able to design and implement industrial policies. However, on their part, bureaucrats must be knowledgeable about the targeted industry: not just technical knowledge but also practical knowledge about the actual industry in the country, regular contact and working relations with industry actors, and an understanding of the constraints on productivity that capitalists face in order to design initiatives that will help them to overcome these constraints. This is the "efficiency" part, in the pocket of efficiency.

The hardest part of industrial policy is making sure that the targeted firms and farms use the rents, which were created to help them overcome constraints on productivity, for that purpose and actively invest in learning. Thus, policy enforcement is important. This is easier if the government demands that in return for access to rents, firms/farms must show specific results in terms of increasing production and achieving international levels of efficiency. In order for state bureaucrats to enforce the rules and conditions attached to rents provided for firms, the owners of those firms cannot have so much political influence that they are able to leverage their political connections to undermine enforcement. In other words, benefiting capitalists need to have enough political influence to shape the content of industrial policy but not so much political influence that they could use it to block enforcement of the reciprocal requirements attached to rents. This condition is what we call learning for productivity.

There are many ways in which industrial policies can fail to meet their stated objectives, because these three conditions do not all emerge. This is why we are not seeing more successes across African countries. But the distribution of power in a given society determines just how difficult it will be to implement industrial policy. Where domestic capitalists are weak and small farmers are fragmented (in other words, they do not have strong organizations for collective action and coordination), mutual interests are rare, except with foreign capitalists or state-, party-, or military-owned firms. Where the distribution of power in society is highly dispersed, the resulting implications for the configuration of power within and outside the ruling coalition means that changes in resource allocation, institutions governing economic benefits and the creation and allocation of rents are constantly contested, and rent management is difficult to centralize. As a result, pockets of efficiency rarely emerge. Without mutual interests and pockets of efficiency, there is little chance that rents will make it to the targeted firms and little chance that those firms will be sufficiently incentivized to use the rents to build their technological capabilities and thus enhance their productivity and international competitiveness – which, after all, is the end goal of industrial policy.

The difficulties of developing new sectors or upgrading existing ones are often underestimated in analyses that stay at the level of the national economy. Firms/farms also have different interests across sectors as well as within a single sector, especially in agro-processing where the interests of producers and processors can be opposed in the short term. Therefore, it is important to break down the category of "business" and to move to the industry level in order to understand the constraints on productivity in specific industries and the array of firms and farms and their interests, as well as the potential political costs/gains of policies to address industry-specific challenges and the political calculations that drive the actual policies selected and how they are implemented. That is what this book aims to do, using the industry case studies of horticulture exports and palm oil processing. The difficulties of implementing industrial policy can also be underestimated, as they involve not only incentivizing learning among locally owned firms and first-generation capitalists, but also solving complex problems involved in increasing the raw material supply base for agro-processing industries – which typically involve conflicts over access to land and the distribution of the benefits of agricultural production, as well as organizing a large number of scattered small farmers. The specific cases of industrial policy examined in this book illustrate just how hard industrial policy is to implement among the myriad of social, economic and political interests within a given society.

Conclusion

This book builds on existing arguments within the Ghanaian political economy literature, but it also diverges from it in important ways in order to explain the limited extent of economic transformation achieved in Ghana since independence, and especially since the 1980s after the structural adjustment reforms. It argues that Ghanaian governments in the past and the present tended to pursue distributive, consumption-driven expenditures rather than targeted industrial policies. This occurred as a result of the high vulnerability of ruling elites due to powerful political factions outside the ruling coalition that were capable of winning elections (or, in earlier periods, capable of mounting a coup), combined with a high level of fragmentation within the ruling coalition that resulted in large distributional demands that had to be met in order to keep the coalition together and intense contestation among ruling elites over resource allocation and changing the distribution of economic benefits.

When ruling elites pursued industrial policies, they tended to be state-led and even state-controlled. In other words, governments used the creation of state-owned firms, or joint-venture firms that partnered the state with foreign capital or management, to pioneer new productive sectors. When sectors already existed, state-led industrial policies tended to ignore existing firms and implement initiatives to expand production in collaboration with entirely new investors or through arrangements where the state played a key role in organizing smallholder farmers to increase production and even created firms owned by farmer cooperatives. Industrial policies in Ghana have rarely involved the state supporting existing domestic firms to expand production and increase productivity, where the state takes a backseat in implementation and only incentivizes firms to invest in building their capabilities. One case where this occurred, the pharmaceutical industry, is considered in the Conclusion of this book. In general, Ghanaian political elites' affinity for state-led industrial policies led to a paradox in that the same political imperatives generated by competitive clientelism that made state-led industrial policies attractive as a political survival strategy also undermined their implementation.

The next chapter examines the origins of competitive clientelism by looking at the distribution of power in society on the eve of Ghanaian independence, why it was that way and how it created a set of path dependencies. It also explains why domestic capitalists were weak at the time of independence by tracing the processes of agrarian capitalism and merchant capitalism that began in the 1800s in response to changes in the global economy and how they slowed or were actively stymied during the period of formal colonial rule.

2 *Origins of Competitive Clientelism and Weak Domestic Capitalists*

The origins of competitive clientelism in Ghana can be found in the transformations of societies in the territories that became the British colony called the Gold Coast during the precolonial and colonial periods. The Gold Coast was an amalgamation of the Colony (the coastal part), where societies had a long history of interaction with European traders; the Ashanti territory, which encompassed the core of the large Asante precolonial centralized kingdom (including the present-day Brong Ahafo region); Togoland (covering the present-day Volta region), which had been part of the German empire but after World War I came under the British mandate[1]; and the Northern Territories (the present-day Northern, Upper East and Upper West regions), which were administered separately until quite late in colonial rule.[2] These territories had different experiences of social and economic change as result of their varying interaction with the colonial government and with export agricultural production. The large and fragmented group of political elites was concentrated in the Colony and Ashanti territories, where all of the agricultural and mining production for export took place and where blue- and white-collar workers resided.

1 People in British-controlled Togoland voted on whether to become part of the Gold Coast, or to rejoin the French-controlled part of Togo in 1956, the year before independence.

2 There were several centralized and hierarchical kingdoms (precapitalist states) in the southern part of Ghana. The most powerful was the Asante, but there were other smaller ones as well (see Austin 1964). The British signed a treaty with several Fanti chiefs in 1844 and then extended their jurisdiction inwards over the southern part of contemporary Ghana, declaring it the Gold Coast Colony in 1874. British expansion provoked a war with the Asante kingdom, whose military fought the British imperial army several times before finally losing in 1901. British rule was extended over the Asante kingdom and its hinterland to the north, which became the Northern Territories.

Africans living on the coast had a long history of contact with Europeans, which provided opportunities of social and economic advancement and led to the emergence of an educated elite. These elites came from aristocratic families in indigenous kingdoms (chief lineages) who had acquired Western-style education; they also came from wealthy coastal merchant families, some of whom were the descendants of European merchants and officials and had been educated in Europe.[3] The coastal elite were organized and active in colonial politics from the beginning of colonial rule, and their representatives participated in the colonial administrative organs and were vocal on issues regarding rights for Africans. Their first political organization founded in 1897 was called the Aborigines' Rights Protection Society.

This chapter explains how the educational and economic opportunities in the Colony and Ashanti territories during the precolonial and colonial periods resulted in multiple distinct but overlapping social groups with varying economic interests, which often conflicted with each other as well as the colonial government and foreign firms. These conflicts of interests led to a high degree of political mobilization and organization, which led to a high dispersion of power and thus a fractured nationalist movement and a prolonged period of decolonization from 1951 to 1957. The political struggle during decolonization saw different groups of political elites and politically engaged social groups forming and reforming alliances, but in the end, the Convention People's Party (CPP) had the biggest political coalition, which had been tested through elections, and formed the first postindependence government in 1957.

The British system of indirect rule brought the chiefly families into the ruling coalition that governed the Colony and Ashanti territories, effectively as lower level factions that could keep political support for British ruling elites. As the chapter illustrates, British rule created a neotraditional elite that consisted of chiefs who had acquired a Western education, new administrative functions, and new economic interests. The relationship between paramount chiefs and colonial officials that emerged during the colonial period had important implications for the evolution of property rights, accumulation based on

[3] The best source on this educated elite is Kimble (1963). The first European school in the Gold Coast was established in Cape Coast in 1751. Missionary activity exploded in the mid-1800s. By 1881, there were 139 schools, concentrated along the coast, with only three of them operated by the colonial government and the rest by missionaries (Busia 1956: 425).

land wealth, and agricultural production. British commercial interests did not enter agricultural production and processing, but rather focused on export marketing and import retailing.

The origins of weak domestic capitalists can also be found in this time period. The chapter shows that forms of agrarian and merchant capitalism emerged in the Colony and Ashanti territories in the late 1800s and early 1900s as a result of the production and export trade in palm oil and then cocoa. However, capitalist development was slowed, stymied and then reversed: first due to policies pursued by the colonial government and then by those of the power-sharing government during the 1950s that was composed of the Gold Coast colonial authorities and the CPP political elites.

The second part of the chapter demonstrates how the two features characterizing Ghanaian political economy emerged in this context of competitive clientelism and weak domestic capitalists, during the fifteen years from 1951, when the first power-sharing CPP government began, to 1966, when the government was overthrown through a military coup. It shows why the CPP ruling elites prioritized the short-term requirements of their political survival in the context of high vulnerability and extreme contestation within the changing composition of the ruling coalition. This short time horizon strategy involved distributive, consumption-driven expenditures across a broad spectrum of society as well as more targeted distribution (or patronage) to specific groups linked to the ruling political elites. The chapter also explains how and why the power-sharing CPP government reversed the past patterns of capitalist development and accumulation. Central to this reversal was the policy creating monopoly rights over cocoa purchasing, which were then given to a farmers' organization aligned with the ruling CPP party, eliminating both the foreign and private domestic actors in the internal cocoa trade. This policy served to organize some farmers in support of the CPP and to eradicate cocoa trading as a platform of the political opposition. It also shifted incomes away from cocoa farmers into the hands of a small section of farmer-traders aligned with the CPP. But this was arguably only possible because the cocoa capitalist farmer-trader class was not strong enough in the face of the organizational capabilities of the CPP. In general, CPP ruling elites slowly undermined independent patterns of accumulation by monopolizing economic opportunities and linking them to whoever controlled the state. The expansion of state-led and state-controlled industrial policies in the early 1960s, and the marginalization of private domestic businesses not directly linked to the CPP, was part of that process.

The final part of the chapter summarizes how the Nkrumah era left important legacies concerning the economy, which created path dependencies after the overthrow of the CPP government. Overspending and a large external debt in the context of declining cocoa prices led to twin trade and fiscal deficits, and to the country's first macroeconomic and debt crises in 1966. The cocoa sector, through the Cocoa Board, became the largest source of government revenue, which led governments to overexploit this sector, and state-owned enterprises became a significant source of employment and political patronage. All subsequent ruling elites were faced with the predicament of how to resolve the debt, balance of payments and fiscal crises without getting thrown out of government. In general, they oscillated between economic reforms and the status quo because the reforms delivered benefits to the larger population in the medium to longer term, but had high short-term costs. Accumulation strategies became linked to who controlled the state but not in a way that benefited the emergence of a stronger domestic capitalist class, nor effective state-owned enterprises, as the politics of competitive clientelism led to political instability and undermined stable accumulation and business-state relations.

The Development of Agrarian Capitalism

The rise of a peasant-based agricultural export economy predated cocoa and the colonial period. Farmers and traders in the Akwapim Hills produced and exported palm oil to Europe starting in the 1820s to meet demand generated by the industrial revolution. When international palm oil prices fell in the late 1880s, the peasant palm oil producer-exporters looked for new opportunities and entered the more remunerative and less labor-intensive cocoa cultivation. They migrated in the 1890s to southern Akyem Abuakwa (in what is now called the Eastern Region), because cocoa grew better in the forest of the Akyem area and in recently cleared mature forest than in fallow land.[4] They purchased

[4] On the early period of cocoa production and export, see Hill (1963), Hopkins (1966) and Austin (1987, 2003, 2005); on the early importance of cocoa to the colonial economy, see Kay (1972).

land from Akyem chiefs in low populated areas.[5] There was a second wave of cocoa expansion in the areas of southern Ashanti between 1900 and 1916.

The rapidly increasing demand for chocolate in industrializing Europe stimulated cultivation of cocoa to such an extent that the crop eventually took over as the territory's major agricultural export commodity. Investment in cocoa became more profitable than palm oil, and most peasants engaged in the cultivation of oil palm trees switched to cocoa trees from 1910 onwards. Cocoa produced in the eastern part of the Colony and in the Ashanti territories became the most important export by 1910, and by 1920 it accounted for 83 percent of total exports.

An incipient agrarian capitalism in cocoa production emerged in the Akyem area, as land and labor relations were transformed with the selling of land and the selling of labor through wage contracts.[6] The increased output was due to the more intensive application of labor than to radical changes in agricultural techniques. Land under cultivation expanded by devoting more land and farmers' time into cocoa production and away from food production.

High world cocoa prices were sustained from around the turn of the twentieth century through World War I (despite fluctuations) and culminated in the boom of 1919–1920, but were then followed by a period of depressed world prices during the interwar period. Rising prices after 1945 led to the third wave of cocoa expansion in the late 1940s and early 1950s, as cocoa farmers migrated to underdeveloped areas in the Ashanti and Brong Ahafo regions. Farmers migrated to these areas because it was more profitable to plant cocoa on freshly cleared forest land than to replant trees on old cocoa farms, giving rise to what is called the "forest

[5] Local men of the Akyem area were already engaged in goldmining, rubber production, and the kola nut trade, and thus it was largely the in-migrants who cultivated cocoa (Austin 2003).

[6] Farmers in the Ashanti region who adopted cocoa production initially used the labor of people who were brought into the household via lending or purchase, such as pawns or slaves or descendants of slaves. Slavery was abolished in 1908, but within the Ashanti area it took almost a decade for the British colonial government to enforce it (Austin 2005). As profits from cocoa increased, farmers could afford regular wages high enough to attract voluntary recruits, and there was a shift to wage labor.

rent."[7] Thus, the cocoa industry was sustained by a continued expansion westward through the forest belt.

The emerging agrarian capitalism in cocoa production presented major problems for the colonial government. The commercial organization of cocoa production acted as a dissolvent on the "traditional" chieftaincy structures through which the British sought to exercise their authority. But on the other hand, it provided the fiscal basis of the colonial state. The British-controlled mining industry did not achieve a size where it could yield profits to investors and still cover the capital costs of the railway transport system, which was vital to its operations, as well as the administrative costs of the colonial state. Cocoa exports, through taxation, paid for colonial administration and covered the loans from London that financed the construction of transport systems.

This tension between the need for economic resources and for political stability was solved through thwarting the advance of agrarian capitalism.[8] Around the 1930s, a new version of the *abusa* sharecropping system that became increasingly prevalent in the Colony and Ashanti territories marked a shift away from market transactions in land and labor. Under the *abusa* system, migrant farmers did not purchase land, but rather asked local chiefs for permission to cultivate lands controlled by chiefs (stool lands). This shift occurred due to a combination of factors from above and below. From above, the colonial government observed how Akyem chiefs sold large areas of land to migrant farmers and feared the concentration of land in the hands of a few African rural capitalists and the freeing of farmers from the political control of chiefs. Therefore, the colonial government persuaded chiefs in the Colony and Ashanti territories to prohibit the sale of land, and enacted policies that gave chiefs extensive powers to collect land tribute from migrant farmers. From below, in the Ashanti territory sharecropping was requested by laborers, mostly migrants from the Northern Territories or neighboring colonies, as a way of getting more of the cocoa profit margin.

[7] It is more costly to maintain high yields in an old cocoa farm and to replant trees, because production and replanting costs increase in relation to the costs of planting after forest clearing. Forest rent is defined as the difference between the production cost of a ton of cocoa from a plantation after forest clearing and that of a ton of cocoa resulting from replanting an old farm or fallow land (Ruf 1995).

[8] This paragraph is based on Boone (2003: 149–151), Berry (1993), Konings (1986) and Austin (1987, 2005).

Lower world prices in the 1920s meant that farmers were unable to attract long-term wage labor, so they agreed to sharecropping, where the laborer operated the farm for a season and received one-third of the crop.

This shift away from capitalist relations in cocoa production coincided with the advent of British indirect rule, in which the principle of "native" land ownership was a central pillar.[9] The British Colonial Office adopted the stance in West Africa of supporting customary land ownership and created the Native Administration system as a way to indirectly control land, as paramount chiefs were dependent on the colonial government for their new powers over land, which brought with it new opportunities for accumulation. The British position was a change in strategy after decades of trying, unsuccessfully, to take control over the administration and allocation of land rights in the Gold Coast, through the Land and Forestry Bills of 1894, 1897 and 1912. The British colonial government was prompted to establish public/state ownership and control of the forest reserves due to fear of foreign companies acquiring control of the land through speculation and purchasing concessions from local chiefs during the mining boom. However, the African lawyers and merchants of the Aborigines' Rights Protection Society joined an alliance with chiefs in opposing the legislation, leading the colonial government to abandon it. The coastal educated elites and neotraditional elites in the Aborigines' Rights Protection Society combined with British anthropological work in the 1920s to produce a powerful argument regarding community ownership of land, which laid the basis for indirect rule. The Native Administration Ordinance of 1927 strengthened the position of paramount and divisional chiefs at the local level by recognizing traditional state councils, defining procedural rules in destoolment cases and giving chiefs the power to suppress "subversive" political activities within their traditional areas. It also strengthened the judicial powers of the traditional state councils and rationalized the hierarchy of the chiefs.[10]

9 This paragraph and the next one are based on Amanor (2008), Boone (2003), Crook (1986), Kimble (1963), Mikell (1989) and Simensen (1974).

10 However, in the Northern Territories, land remained under the control of the state, a situation that persisted until 1979 (Berry 2013: 37). The application of indirect rule in the Northern Territories was relatively easy due to the lack of an educated social stratum and of an extensive cash economy, and chiefs were

The expansion of the cocoa economy, the *abusa* system, and the buttressed powers of chiefs under indirect rule enriched the chiefs and the stools. Chiefs used their new control over the land, and the wealth generated from that control, to go into cocoa farming. More generally, the neotraditional elite (chiefs, other traditional political officeholders and elders) were able to develop their landholdings into much larger farms than the average peasant farm of a few acres, as well as to invest in transport and trade. This created even further problems for the colonial government, because a class of capitalist farmers emerged from within the neotraditional elite, and because the expansion of the cocoa economy was at the core of chieftaincy politics: rivalries for control over land and over people (or their labor), and the division of surpluses appropriated in the name of the stool (Boone 2003: 153). The colonial government enacted various laws and reforms aimed at preventing the chiefs who were also capitalist farmers from consolidating into a landed gentry.

Regardless, chiefs in the cocoa belt of southern Ghana had both the political authority conferred by the institutions of indirect rule and the economic resources that stemmed from using their control over land to accumulate through the cocoa economy. This combination gave chiefs great authority over peasant households and the capacity to mobilize community collective action. But it also gave rise to class-like tensions between chiefs and "commoners," who saw chiefs as privatizing stool resources, exploiting tenants and abusing debtors. As a result, commoners led an increasing number of campaigns to "de-stool" chiefs.[11]

In sum, agrarian capitalism started with indigenous commercial farmers producing export commodities but was hampered by the colonial government's fear of political instability caused by social change and its need to govern through a system of indirect rule using chiefs. While the development of capitalist markets in land and labor were slowed and somewhat overturned through chiefs' control over land use and allocation as well as sharecropping arrangements, chiefs

already very dependent on the colonial administration to legitimize their authority (Ladouceur 1979: 40–44). The British even created chiefs where none existed before their occupation, particularly in the northwest.

11 For examples of such campaigns to de-stool chiefs, see Simensen (1974, 1975) and Allman (1990).

used their control over land to participate in commercial cocoa production for export. This gave rise to a chiefly cocoa capitalist farmer class, which also developed commercial interests in the cocoa trade, and thus a weakened form of agrarian capitalism continued to develop.

The Development of Merchant Capitalism

Linked to the educated elite in the coastal towns and palm oil production in the precolonial period was the rise of an African merchant capitalist class from the 1850s, based in Cape Coast and smaller towns nearby.[12] The economic opportunity to enter into oversees trade was made possible by the high demand (and high prices) of palm oil in Britain and Germany, and by the advent of new steamships that docked more frequently at small towns along the Gold Coast. Competition between shipping lines and British and German trading houses resulted in reduced freight rates as well as the easing of credit and commission terms for shipment of manufactured goods. These conditions allowed small-scale African businessmen with limited capital to enter the import-export trade, which they then developed based on experience working in the European merchant houses in the Gold Coast and using social connections leveraged from royal lineages and kinship networks.[13] Raymond Dumett (1983:672) estimates that there were twenty-five African merchants that could be classified as large-scale, most of which controlled their overseas import-export trade and sizeable inland trading operations.

However, these African merchants struggled after the drop in palm oil prices around 1885, which also led palm oil producers to stop selling. The limited liquidity of the independent African merchants meant that they could not absorb periods of slow or interrupted trade for that long. Although the commercial development of wild rubber in the 1880s allowed the merchants to diversify slightly, the Cape Coast merchants declined by the turn of the twentieth century due to dependence on a two- or three-product crop economy, which made them

[12] This paragraph and the next paragraph are based on Dumett (1983).

[13] Dumett (1983: 671) notes that a significant number of leading African merchants of the 1870s and 1880s were members of their local royal lineage: that is, they were the sons, nephews, grandsons or grandnephews of kings and chiefs.

vulnerable to swings in world trade cycles, and to the absence of local banks providing commercial credit to Africans. In addition, economic opportunities changed as the colonial government's railways shifted the main port stops to Accra/Tema and Sekondi/Takoradi, and as the European shipping companies engaged in price-fixing cartels with discounts denied to African companies. Thus, these African merchants could no longer compete with their European counterparts.

As the Cape Coast overseas merchants declined, the rise of the cocoa industry in the eastern part of the Gold Coast gave rise to a new group of African import-export firms linked to the cocoa economy. In 1918 there were 292 registered African companies competing against 98 European firms (Dumett 1983: 692). However, the size of these firms is not known. Some African merchants were exporting cocoa directly. But the African merchants were falling behind the European firms, which had formed limited liability companies, mobilized additional finances and established branches in the interior of the Gold Coast (Hopkins 1966). The economic depression of 1920 and the mergers among European firms (mainly British firms) reduced the market shares and economic opportunities of African merchants. For example, the United African Company was created in 1929 by the merger of three of the largest trading companies, which gave it half the market in cocoa-buying and allowed it to organize price-fixing pools during the 1930s (Bauer 1954; Stockwell 2000). African participation in the import-export trade was reduced to being brokers for the European trading houses.

These developments caused significant economic grievances among the African merchant class. As early as the 1880s, these merchants had seen themselves as a native capitalist class that could take the lead in commercial agriculture, mineral development, and even industrialization, but knew that they needed external assistance (Dumett 1983: 686–687). They petitioned the colonial government for financial support in agricultural and industrial ventures, with minimal effect. Several Cape Coast merchants attempted diversification into commercial agriculture, mining, banking and agro-processing ventures, but their efforts were inhibited by insufficient working capital. There was no local bank until 1897, and even then the British colonial banks put restrictions on loans to Africans.

The African merchants linked to cocoa continued this vision and also understood that the colony needed more local economic institutions (banks, agricultural cooperatives, marketing cooperatives, shipping facilities) and the deepening of the local economy away from the dependence on cocoa exports. They made several attempts at setting up banks, cooperatives in commerce and collective marketing of cocoa, none of which succeeded (Hopkins 1966). What did succeed, partially, were the cocoa hold-ups, especially the one in 1937–1938, which tried to force cocoa prices up in the context of falling world prices and the cartel among European firms that controlled most of the international market in cocoa (Howard 1976). The extensive role of chiefs as cocoa farmers and traders, and the political authority they had amassed, was an important factor in the success of the cocoa holdup, which also included a boycott on buying imports from expatriate firms, from October 1937 to April 1938. However, it neither succeeded in breaking up the cartel of major European firms nor in raising the price of cocoa.

Therefore, the 1930s saw the emergence of more radical ideas. Where previously the African capitalist class had sought to carve out a greater space for itself within the colonial economy, the younger group among the African merchants concluded that the colonial economy needed to be changed. It was no longer enough to seek a place within an economy exporting raw materials and importing manufactured goods, but rather the resources within the colony should be developed to meet domestic demand. It was J.B. Danquah, and not Kwame Nkrumah, who first said, "It is not enough to live in the old agricultural economy. We must manufacture and buy our own goods. We must industrialize our country."[14] And it was J.B. Danquah who commented that the colonial government would not assent to industrialization, as it would be detrimental to its interests as an exporter of manufactured goods. Therefore, the balance of political power would have to be altered before the economic structure could be changed. Danquah became the general secretary of a new political organization that included the elite groups, but also drew on the educated commoners and their various clubs, societies and unions emerging in the towns during the 1920s and 1930s.[15] This organization was the precursor to the United Gold Coast Convention.

[14] J.B. Danquah, *Self Help and Expansion* (Accra, 1943), p. 15, cited in Hopkins (1966: 151).

[15] On the various political organizations in the 1920s and 1930s, see Boahen (1975), Kilson (1970) and Wight (1947).

The situation during World War II further aggravated these economic grievances, as official trade controls sanctioned and extended the European firms' monopoly on trade. The key area of contention was the cocoa marketing arrangement put in place by the Colonial Office during the war, in which the British government would buy the entire cocoa crop in the Gold Coast at a fixed price, but established trading firms would act as licensed buying agents to actually buy from farmers and market the cocoa (Alence 2001). This arrangement was largely in response to the requests of the European firms that dominated West African trade. The British government agreed, as it did not want a repeat of what happened during World War I, when local cocoa prices dropped by half due to shipping disruptions. The colonial economy had become completely dependent on cocoa exports, and the recent cocoa holdups demonstrated the political tensions around cocoa prices. This marketing arrangement not only fixed the price, but also institutionalized the prewar market-sharing agreement among the European firms (which had prompted the 1937 cocoa holdup in the first place), because quotas were distributed to firms based on their market shares over the previous seasons. As a result, only a small number of quotas were set aside for African merchants.

The cocoa marketing arrangement did insulate farmers from shipping disruptions, but in 1943 that threat disappeared and yet the arrangement continued. The new rationale for keeping the arrangement was the need to depress farmers' incomes. Colonial officials feared that increasing cocoa farmers' incomes while imported goods were still very scarce (due to the British colonial policy to reduce exports to the colonies) would cause severe inflation, which in turn would lead to political instability as inflation eroded the purchasing power of everyone. The extreme dependence of the Gold Coast on imported manufactured goods made it vulnerable to inflation.[16] Rod Alence (2001) notes that the colonial government was caught between the need to keep export volumes high with high producer prices, and to keep inflation low with low producer prices.

[16] Supply disruptions and shortages created opportunities for profiteering by those with access to scarce goods. While prices could be fixed at the main retail shops, goods were sold and resold through trading networks into the interior part of the country. Thus, shortages in the supply of goods always led to inflation, and increases in incomes in a context of shortage only served to fuel inflation.

The Colonial Office decided to make controlled marketing a permanent feature of the West African cocoa trade in order to stabilize global market fluctuations and to stabilize producer prices (Alence 2001). The Gold Coast colonial government also supported the scheme, but it saw the scheme as a way to take control from the European firms and the UK treasury, and proposed revoking guaranteed quotas and gradually increasing the share of African shippers. The government's Cocoa Marketing Board appointed licensed buying agents, including farmer cooperatives, to buy cocoa from farmers at a set producer price, advancing them capital and remunerating them with official buying allowances. The Cocoa Marketing Board accumulated the surplus between the producer price paid to farmers and the export price paid by the shipping firms, which would be used to promote agricultural research and price stabilization.

In sum, merchant capitalism also emerged in the late 1800s driven by the coastal educated elite based on the export of palm oil and then cocoa. But African import-export businesses failed to compete with European merchants, partly because European companies formed cartels to capture more of the international trade and partly because African businesses did not have access to the kinds of economic institutions necessary to compete in international trade. Colonial policies also disproportionately benefited European merchants, but rather inadvertently, as colonial governments sought to deal with the challenges of international trade during World War II.

Decolonization Political Struggles and the Suppression of Domestic Capitalists

Despite macroeconomic indicators that looked good in the late 1940s with relatively high GDP and substantial external reserves due to the Cocoa Marketing Board, the economy was very "fragile" (Krassowski 1974: 10–11). The income earned from cocoa and mineral exports, and activities catering for these industries, accounted for about 40 percent of GDP, and thus the fortunes of the whole economy were sensitive to changes in the global economy. Furthermore, low savings and a high demand for imported goods, with a lag time between increased demand and arrival of supplies of imports, meant that increased export proceeds tended to force up the general price level. Agriculture was underdeveloped and very dependent on climatic conditions. Other than the introduction of cocoa, there were no innovations or changes in the first half of the century in agricultural methods. Cocoa accounted for over one-third of all income from agriculture, and growing cocoa provided the most important source of cash income in the economy. Although there were many large cocoa farms, the typical farm holding was small, about five acres, and cultivation was labor-intensive with few purchased inputs. Furthermore, the "swollen shoot" cocoa disease killed one-eighth of the tree stock in 1948. In an attempt to control the spread of the disease, the Gold Coast government required farmers to cut out not only trees already affected but also the surrounding healthy ones. The cocoa disease, compounded with problems of soil fertility on old farms, adversely affected cocoa production.

The manufacturing sector remained basically artisanal, dominated by small firms using craft techniques and most having no paid employees, and supplied basic needs such as furniture and clothing. People were used to, and preferred, imported consumer goods. Thus, food production was unable to respond to increased demand, and manufacturing was unable to respond in areas where demand was growing fast. Infrastructure was poor, and electricity and water supplies were inadequate to meet household/residential and commercial demand. The education system was well developed by African standards, but the country lacked the economic structure to absorb the educated people, except for the public sector.

It was in this economic context that political mobilization among the local population occurred, which precipitated decolonization.[17] These factors included the concern of urban populations with unemployment and inflation, as the prices of imported goods rose continuously but wages lagged behind. This point, combined with the conditional sales used by European trading houses, which meant people had to buy goods they did not want along with those they needed, led to a volatile situation in the towns as people perceived the colonial government to act in concert with the European firms. This led to a campaign to boycott the imported goods of expatriate companies in October 1947 that lasted until the early months of 1948. In the rural areas, cocoa farmers' opposition to compulsory

[17] This paragraph is based on Austin (1961, 1964), Bauer (1954) and Stockwell (2000).

cutting-out led farmers' organizations to support the anti-colonial sentiment.

During that time, the United Gold Coast Convention (UGCC), represented by J.B. Danquah and the newly hired general secretary Kwame Nkrumah, traveled through the Colony and Ashanti territories, spreading the idea of self-government and soliciting the support of the youth associations.[18] The boycott committee (composed primarily of neotraditional elite) and the UGCC (the more radical of the educated elite/merchant class) were not working together, as the boycott committee refused to be part of the UGCC, but the local leaders of the youth associations saw both as part of the same mounting demand for self-government. During the boycott, a march by the ex-servicemen's organization to demonstrate their economic grievances ended in a gun shooting incident with the police, which in turn led to rioting and looting of the stores owned by the expatriate companies in Accra and other towns. The colonial government blamed the six leaders of the UGCC for the disturbances and jailed them. The real instigators of the "disturbances" included the Ghana Farmers' Congress; the chiefs and local youth associations; the trade unions in Accra and Takoradi; and the urban mobs. Nevertheless, the leaders of the UGCC rocketed in popularity with these discontented social groups.

This is when the political movement fractured. The colonial government asked the UGCC leaders and several chiefs to constitute a committee on constitutional reform for greater local autonomy, but excluded Nkrumah. The politically conscious youth organizations also felt stifled by chiefly power and generational hierarchy (Austin 1964; Allman 1990). Nkrumah's exclusion led him and the youth organizations that he had helped organize in the Colony and Ashanti to break away from the UGCC and then form the Convention People's Party (CPP) in June 1949. This division, which saw Nkrumah break away from the educated elites and merchant class and create a separate political organization, was a division that shaped not only the decolonization period but also the postindependence period, as it laid the foundation of the Danquah and Nkrumahist political traditions.

18 "Youth" in this context is a social category. It was used in the 1920s, 1930s and 1940s to refer to educated commoners who held no stool or traditional office (Boahen 1975: 136). This definition included lawyers as well as shopkeepers, clerks, teachers, artisans and so on.

Based on proposals from the constitutional committee, the 1951 constitution created a Legislative Assembly of predominantly African representative seats, with elections held that year. The constitution provided for one directly elected seat for each of the five municipalities, with the rural seats indirectly elected through electoral colleges and seats reserved for representatives from the Provincial Councils of Chiefs. The CPP won all of the direct elections and 29 out of 33 seats from the electoral colleges of the Colony, Southern Togoland and Ashanti.[19] Its strong showing was based on the youth associations, but also on gaining the support of existing social and economic organizations by aligning with their economic grievances. Thus, the CPP garnered the support of the railway and harbor workers, as well as cocoa farmer-trader organizations by echoing their critique of the Cocoa Marketing Board and promising to give farmers control over the vast funds accumulated by the board. The party also promised to make local gin manufacturing legal, and thus linked into broader arguments about supporting local production and African self-sufficiency.

The colonial government invited Nkrumah to become Leader of Government Business and appoint six ministerial posts in the Executive Council. Certain key ministries remained under the control of the British, and the governor maintained the right of veto over policy. The opposition to the CPP came from the UGCC and the State Council of Chiefs, who either stood as candidates or used their machinery of subchiefs to support prominent local people.[20] The majority of representatives of the chiefs were not sympathetic to the CPP government, but with the support of the northern representatives, the CPP had a working majority. After joining the power-sharing government, Nkrumah and CPP politicians sought to undermine their political opposition by reducing the political authority and economic base of chiefs. Its two key strategies in achieving this objective were in the cocoa sector and in local government reforms.

Regarding the cocoa sector, Nkrumah sought to undercut the chiefly cocoa farmer-trader group, which had been instrumental in organizing cocoa farmers in the cocoa holdups and in the 1948 boycott. The CPP

[19] This paragraph is based on Austin (1964: 140–149), Jeffries (1978), Beckman (1976) and Akyeampong (1996).

[20] As the only party in the Assembly, the UGCC became the opposition. It changed its name to the Ghana Congress Party.

attacked their control over farmers and their economic base in cocoa trading profits (Beckman 1976). Initially, the CPP leaders sought to gain influence with the existing Farmers' Congress, asking leaders of the congress to support the CPP in return for influence in the Cocoa Board. When the leaders of the Farmers' Congress refused, the CPP turned to a new strategy of establishing its own licensed buying agent, the Cocoa Purchasing Company, as a subsidiary of the Cocoa Board and directly entering the internal cocoa trade. The company had privileged access to capital from the Cocoa Board and government, which it used to advance loans to farmers in order to get control of a significant part of the internal cocoa buying market. The CPP then created its own farmers' organization, the United Ghana Farmers' Council, to organize trading and credit activities at the local level.

The CPP also used local government reforms to shift political authority away from the chiefs.[21] The British colonial government had been in the process of reforming local government institutions, but still envisioned chiefs playing the lead role. Nkrumah's CPP insisted that the local councils that were to replace the Native Authorities consist of two-thirds elected members, and only one-third appointed by chiefs. The CPP then created local party organizations to contest for these seats across southern Ghana, taking a majority of the elected seats. It did so through using patronage resources and building new patron-client networks. Some chiefs resisted, refusing to turn over revenues to the new local governments. But the CPP used chiefly politics to divide and rule, freeing subchiefs from their superiors.

In 1954, elections were held for a National Assembly in which all the seats were directly elected based on single-member constituencies throughout all the territories. The CPP won, but it was a very different election, and its support base began shifting. The first time around the CPP capitalized on anti-colonial sentiments, but now the CPP was part of the colonial government and the anti-colonial movement began to fracture. New groups were drawn to the CPP because of the clout it wielded as the ruling party and as the keeper of state resources. An important group was what Richard Rathbone calls the aspirant businessmen, who for a variety of reasons were prevented in the late 1940s from expanding or even starting their own enterprises

[21] This paragraph is based on Apter (1972), Austin (1964), Boone (2003: 165), Owusu (1970) and Rathbone (2000).

(Rathbone 1968, 1973). This is because they did not have access to the patron-client networks that favored the neotraditional elite, old merchant families and expatriate commerce. Once the CPP was in government, it had control over contract allocation, licenses and credit giving. Aspiring businessmen aligned themselves with the CPP in the hopes of benefiting from that control, and as they did, others joined the CPP also in hopes of benefiting from the alliance. In return, these businessmen contributed money to the party and played a mobilizing role as employers and patrons.

Conversely, some groups defected because they felt they could no longer pursue their social and economic interests through the CPP. The CPP's central party committee tried to control candidate nominations, but lower level factions of the party resisted it. As a result, 160 candidates were considered CPP "rebels" who failed to get the party's nomination and stood for election anyway, capturing over a fifth of the vote (Austin 1964: 210–211). The large salaries, perks and increased social status that accompanied a seat in the Assembly were too tempting to pass up and candidates believed they had a chance given their personal ties. Not only did a place in the Assembly provide personal gain, but it also carried the hope of material benefit for the community from which the representative came. Nkrumah expelled these "rebels" from the party. Furthermore, new regional and ethnic-based political parties emerged in the Northern Territories and Togoland.

The 1954 election was supposed to be the final contest legitimizing in whose hands the British would transfer political authority. However, the emergence of a new political organization in the Ashanti territory, the National Liberation Movement (NLM), which made alliances with the other smaller parties, compelled the British to hold yet another election in 1956. The NLM was driven by small Ashanti businessmen who found their economic opportunities blocked by CPP patronage networks (Rathbone 1973). These businessmen often included farmers who had diversified investments into property and services, and also included chiefs who were both farmers and businessmen. Members of this aspirant group belonged to the Ashanti youth organization, which had been concerned about more legislative seats for Ashanti, the direction of public investments and scholarship allocations. They sought new allies with cocoa farmers and chiefs in the territory (categories which themselves overlapped). They were aided in doing so by the Nkrumah government's decision to freeze the producer price of cocoa at a time of a rising world market price, which had an economic rationale (as explained further below) but unsurprisingly angered cocoa farmers and compounded existing grievances with the state-controlled marketing board. It is important to note that by the 1950s, Ashanti was the major cocoa-growing area, given the decrease in cocoa production in the Colony due to the swollen-shoot disease that affected cocoa trees. The Ashanti cocoa farmers left the umbrella cocoa farmers organization, which the CPP controlled, and set up a new one, and the NLM took up the farmers' demands for a higher cocoa price. The neotraditional and educated elites in Ashanti backed the NLM (Allman 1990; Austin 1964).

The CPP won the 1956 elections and formed the first fully independent government, but by the 1956 election several political trends were clear. A reciprocal relationship often characterized the interface between political parties and local communities in which electoral support was exchanged for outside assistance in local disputes, particularly the influence and resources of the ruling party.[22] Young men seeking social and economic mobility stood on the platform of the party most likely to bring them success, and the benefits of being on the "winning side" had become more attractive. The CPP sought to bring the chiefs within the CPP's fold, and the advantages of supporting the ruling party, which could provide or deny local development projects, were not lost on many southern chiefs. State patronage became the dominant tool in building a political coalition. The CPP's cohesiveness stemmed from its ability to provide social status, jobs and power. An early lesson learned by aspiring politicians was that remuneration for services rendered in the political sphere was favorable to other occupations, and the party became a vehicle for social mobility for its members; ideologies and nationalistic principles waned. The CPP did not so much mobilize social groups as much as social groups used the CPP to further their interests. The pursuit of local agendas, or regional ones, tended to erode the possibility of a cohesive political organization with a cohesive national agenda.

The fully independent CPP government took several steps after 1957 to consolidate its political base by taking its previous strategies to their

[22] There is strong agreement on this point in the Ghanaian literature. See Apter (1972), Austin (1964, 1976), Peasah (1975), Lentz (2002) and Rathbone (2000).

logical conclusion.[23] Through further local government reforms, all seats in the local councils were directly elected. It declared the United Ghana Farmers' Council as the only officially recognized farmers' organization, and then gave it monopoly-buying powers. This full state monopoly on cocoa buying and credit undermined the economic base of the political opposition, combined with the seizure by state agencies of assets of private farmers' organizations. The CPP government passed laws regulating land rents, which were supposed to protect tenant (migrant) farmers, and state agencies asserted control over the use and allocation of stool lands and revenues. Chiefs were formally stripped of their authority over communal land; however, this situation was temporary and the powers of chiefs were restored after the CPP was overthrown in 1966. In the end, the CPP did not succeed in removing chiefly authority in relations of agricultural production and access to land.

The Emergence of the Two Features of Ghanaian Political Economy

The problems with the Gold Coast colonial economy espoused by J.B. Danquah in the 1930s was the economy's mercantilist nature: exports depended on world prices that producers had no control over and the economy depended on imported goods that it also had no control over, which made it incredibly vulnerable to shifts in the global economy, in which European companies colluded, set prices and dominated wholesale trade. While Nkrumah and the youth upstarts of the CPP usurped the nationalist platform from Danquah and the older generation of merchant and professional elites, they argued for the same goals: restructuring the economy through export diversification and the development of local manufacturing production.

However, these stated economic objectives were undermined by political imperatives. The CPP faced the challenge of maintaining its ruling coalition in the context of powerful excluded political factions and the need to keep the support of a sufficient number of politically organized and mobilized lower-level groups in a context of shifting alliances. As a result, policies and institutions with sound economic objectives were made to serve the political objectives of consolidating

[23] This paragraph draws on the argument of Catherine Boone (2003: 169–177).

the support base of the CPP through political patronage (and thus also taking away economic opportunities of the political opposition) as well as attempting to deliver on the nationalist expectations of the population through massive public investments as quickly as possible. Here we can see the first feature emerge. The result was to undermine the CPP government's own goals, as patronage undermined the efficacy of efforts at economic restructuring, and the massive public investments absorbed the large reserves from budget surpluses accumulated during World War II and during the postwar years when revenue from cocoa exceeded government expenditure.

The consequences of these policies led to a balance of payments crisis. Nkrumah's government responded with greater state controls on imports and exports combined with foreign borrowing to solve the balance of payments problem, rather than currency devaluation and reducing the public investment program. The CPP ruling elites also responded with state-owned firms and farms in agricultural and industrial production as a way to achieve economic restructuring more quickly, rather than trying to provide incentives for private domestic and foreign investments. Here we can see the second feature emerge. These strategies ended in macroeconomic crisis and mounting debt. The state-controlled industrial policies led to building the infrastructure of modern factories and farms, but not the capabilities and the national supply chains that would make them profitable, because building capabilities is much harder and because state-owned enterprises became tools of political patronage.

Feature One: Politically Expedient Government Spending

The Colonial Office in London sent an economic mission in 1950 to assess the colony's economic problems and its capacity to implement a development plan. The Seers-Ross report produced in 1952 concluded that the immediate cause of inflationary pressure and economic instability was the rapid growth of cocoa incomes in the context of the low supply elasticity of domestic consumer goods and limitations on the supply of imports.[24] The economic mission found that cocoa farmers spent a large part of their income on consumer

[24] Report on Financial and Physical Problems of Development in the Gold Coast, Dudley Seers and C.R. Ross, Government Printer, Accra, July 1952.

imports or housing, with the latter putting strain on the building industry and the available supply of materials. It advised the government to stabilize cocoa farmer incomes, because rising incomes would fuel inflation and thus erode the purchasing power of the additional income. The report suggested that stabilizing cocoa farmer incomes would make space for greater public investments to spur economic restructuring through diversification of exports away from cocoa and through achieving a better balance between the structure of domestic output and of domestic demand. This was the view, widely shared among colonial officials, that led to the freeze on the producer price of cocoa in 1954 in the context of a rising world price.

The colonial government decided to use accumulated reserves from cocoa earnings to finance investment in other sectors, but had not decided which sectors.[25] The CPP government wanted to pursue industrialization, so it invited the eminent development economist W.A. Lewis to report on the potential for industrialization and its contribution to future development. CPP leaders were surprised when the Lewis report suggested that the priority should be increasing the productivity of food crop production and investing in public services. Lewis recommended that the development of manufactures should wait:

> In unenlightened circles agriculture and industry are often considered as alternatives to each other. The truth is that industrialization for a home market can make little progress unless agriculture is progressing vigorously at the same time, to provide both the market for industry, and industry's labor supply. If agriculture is stagnant, industry cannot grow ... The most certain way to promote industrialization in the Gold Coast is to lay the foundation it requires by taking vigorous measures to raise food production per person engaged in agriculture ... A high standard of living cannot be built upon an economy in which half the population are scratching the ground for food with a hoe.[26]

Lewis only suggested strengthening the Industrial Development Corporation (IDC), which had been created by the colonial government in 1948 to support African industrialists, to make it more effective. The Lewis report noted that the IDC lent money without

[25] This paragraph is based on Tignor (2006: 118–134) and Krassowski (1974: 19–20).

[26] Report on Industrialisation and the Gold Coast, by Professor W.A. Lewis of Manchester University, 1953, printed by the Government Printing Department, Accra, Gold Coast, p. 2.

exercising any supervision, and thus much of the money was not used for the purposes for which it was lent and would not be recovered. Around the time that Lewis was conducting his review of the Gold Coast economy, some government officials, which at this time included CPP members, suggested that the IDC stop making loans to small African industrialists and rather use public funds to finance large factories wholly or partly owned by the government, which could later be sold or leased to African entrepreneurs after the "teething" problems were over. Lewis did not disagree with the idea that the government should pioneer new industries, but he clearly stated that it was not an alternative to helping African entrepreneurs. He also suggested shifting the emphasis away from lending people money to start new businesses in industries in which they had no past experience, towards lending to businesses that were already in existence and showed good prospects.[27] In fact, he argued that African enterprises could not be built up simply by lending money: "What potential African industrialists lack is not primarily money; it is rather technical knowledge, and experience of factory organization. If the government lends money it should do this only as a supplement to rendering technical and managerial assistance."[28]

Lewis was making the argument that local entrepreneurs acquiring technological capabilities is at the heart of economic transformation, and he argued that industrial policy that promotes African entrepreneurs is necessary, but difficult, because technical and managerial knowledge can only be acquired through experience. This aspect of industrial policy is more difficult to implement than capital expenditure on constructing things, its returns are not visible, and its benefits may not be immediate and are initially confined to a small group. It also requires cooperation with entrepreneurs, with public and private investment working together. (This is, by the way, the same argument that I am making in this book.) The CPP government tended to associate industrialization with building things, instead of building capabilities, for political and practical reasons.

After the 1951 election, the CPP government felt it needed to keep strong political support of the population, in light of the growing

[27] The Lewis report also highlighted the relative insignificance of handicraft industries in the Gold Coast, which in so many other countries had provided a starting point for industry.

[28] Report on Industrialisation and the Gold Coast, p. 12.

political opposition and shifting alliances, by delivering jobs, better urban conditions, a steady supply of food and other basic consumer goods, and imports at "fair" prices. The CPP was also anxious to start building a modern Ghana: railways, harbors, roads, schools, hospitals, power stations, mechanized farms and factories (Krassowski 1974: 18–21). Additionally, Nkrumah and CPP politicians thought that the public investment push in education, infrastructure and public services would on its own attract new industries. Therefore, Nkrumah wanted a bigger and faster public investment push than the colonial government had envisioned, and he got it.

Between 1950 and the end of 1954, government spending increased by 250 percent on capital expenditures and over 300 percent on recurrent expenditures. Given the large amount of public revenue at the time, this did not cause a budget deficit, the government continued to accumulate reserves, and the balance of payments was still positive due to high world cocoa prices. Therefore, further big additions were made in planned public investment. However, revenue fell sharply from 1955, but budget spending continued to rise. From the end of 1955, the government began to experience budget and balance of payment deficits, and had to draw on its reserves. This growth in government spending was not predominantly related to productive sectors, and most money was spent on projects that would not generate further revenue (Krassowski 1974: 25–38).

Remember that the political environment changed dramatically between 1951 and 1954, with the shifting political alliances and the rise of the NLM and thus growing opposition to the CPP. Therefore, the CPP ruling elites faced greater vulnerability. These political factors led Nkrumah and many CPP politicians to use government programs and spending to create and dispense patronage in order to build and maintain the CPP coalition. This led to the inclusion of many projects for political reasons and undermined attempts at planning, as budgets were routinely ignored and projects added that were not in the five-year plans of the Ministry of Finance and did not meet the priority criteria set out in the plans. Government spending also included prestige projects, such as regional airports, international conference centers, a yacht for VIPs and so on, which were more for the benefit of ruling elites than those at the lower levels of the political coalition. W.A. Lewis expected the

Industrial and Agricultural Development Corporations to spearhead economic development by linking the interests of private capital with those of the state and demonstrating the state's commitment, but these key industrial policy initiatives were also undermined by their use as vehicles of political patronage (Tignor 2006: 130–161).

Lewis was aware of the substantial pressures on Nkrumah and the CPP elites to use government funds to solidify their political support and to build patron-client relationships (Tignor 2006: 178). However, he did not agree with this practice, or the drive of the CPP elites to enrich themselves, and he expressed this to Nkrumah several times. In his last written confrontation with Nkrumah on this issue, Nkrumah replied,

> [Ghana] cannot expect you to risk [your international reputation] by political decisions which I consider that I must take. The advice you have given me, sound though it may be, is essentially from the economic point of view, and I have told you, on many occasions, that I cannot always follow this advice as I am a politician and must gamble on the future.[29]

Ultimately, Lewis resigned his advisory position over the politically expedient spending.

There was a further surge in government spending between 1959 and 1961, increasing expenditure by £44 million each year. In the 1950s, government plans were unencumbered by a hard budget constraint, given the large government budget surpluses and the reserves, which were drawn upon in the second half of the 1950s to balance budgets. Things changed in the 1960s. Budget deficits increased, eating further into the country's foreign currency reserves. The current account turned to deficit in 1959, due to the high propensity to import out of additional income generated by public spending, but exports rose by much less, with increasing deficits the following years. The world cocoa price began to fall in 1960, and it fell consistently for the next five years.

By the end of 1961, the country's reserves were declining rapidly, and by 1962 they were exhausted. However, the spending spree of the 1950s trapped the CPP government into maintaining a high level of public spending for political reasons when the country could no longer

[29] Nkrumah to Lewis, 18 December 1958, Lewis Papers, Box 9, cited in Tignor (2006: 173).

afford it; it increased the recurrent expenditure needed to maintain completed projects to a level that absorbed almost all tax revenues; it strained the supply of skilled personnel, which reduced the efficiency of public services; it competed with the private sector for scarce resources and skilled labor; and it increased the country's dependence on imported goods. Instead of curbing government expenditure, the CPP government decided to curb imports by imposing additional duties and levies on imports, and when that did not work, it introduced rigid controls on imports and on foreign exchange transactions. Import controls, while introduced for economic reasons, increased the opportunities for corruption and political patronage, and stifled the growth of smaller domestic enterprises (Krassowski 1974: 45–60).

Feature Two: State-Led Industrial Policies

The balance of payments crisis in 1962 prompted Nkrumah to shift to a statist import-substitution strategy as a way to restructure the economy.[30] At this point, Nkrumah turned fully to the state as the means to promote economic restructuring.[31] The more conservative and business-oriented high-ranking CPP members in the government voiced their opposition and were forced out. The most notable of these included Minister of Finance Komla Gbedemah, who went into exile. In their place, more radical CPP members entered, who looked to the example of the USSR experience and proposed bypassing the private sector, both domestic and foreign, and expanding the state-run industrial and agricultural firms to produce for domestic and export markets.

But the statist turn was not only due to the leftist ideology of the CPP. State-driven investments in the productive sectors could also deliver results more quickly, because the ruling party could control and direct public investments; whereas, the state trying to direct private investments was much more difficult, and the existing technological capabilities of domestic entrepreneurs were very low in manufacturing. As early as 1953, the CPP government had already pursued statist

[30] Notably, an import-substitution strategy would not show results in the short run but rather do the opposite: add to the already high import bill. Therefore, it did not offer an immediately effective solution to the foreign exchange problem.

[31] This paragraph and the next few are based on Tignor (2006: 181–184), Esseks (1975), Killick (1966b: 289) and Krassowski (1974: 45–88).

industrial policies through the Industrial Development Corporation, which deviated significantly from the strategy suggested by W.A. Lewis. The IDC concentrated resources on creating companies controlled entirely by the IDC as well as joint-venture arrangements with firms of proven business capacity. Similarly, trying to improve the agricultural productivity of smallholder farmers was seen as a difficult task that would take a long time and required extensive manpower. There were also political reasons for the state to take over the economy, as the line between state and party was blurred, and the party controlled many of these enterprises and organizations and thus the economic opportunities for accumulation.

The CPP government sought to use foreign credit as a way to avoid cutting back in the total volume of investment already planned, as well as embark on major new spending programs while maintaining the rate of spending on old programs. The government relied significantly on external supplier credits, which was made possible by the willingness of Western European companies, and later Eastern European governments, to supply on credit the factories, equipment, technical knowledge and sometimes managerial expertise. Their main interest was to sell, and their incentive was to offer credit. Over twenty countries were involved in supplier credits, but the most important creditor country was Britain, with a majority of the credits guaranteed by the suppliers' governments. The CPP government also relied on domestic deficit financing by issuing Bank of Ghana treasury bills.

Credit agreements financed twelve new state-owned factories between 1962 and 1965. The foreign credits only covered about 40 percent of the total capital costs. Some of the factories had an economic rationale, and were on the list that Lewis had made in his report on industrialization of areas that had prospects. But they also included areas Lewis had dismissed as not economically viable, as well as projects that had been "sold" by interested suppliers and not initially demanded by Nkrumah or his ministers. Planning behind the factories was often poor, and there was a great deal of corruption. On the supplier side, the foreign companies overcharged, provided defective or secondhand equipment, and failed to carry out tasks according to payments made. On the government side, a contribution to CPP funds became a normal feature of private supplier credit contracts.

Notably, it was at this time that three state-owned canneries were established with supplier credits from Yugoslavia. The canneries included one for pineapple in Nsawam, one for mango and tomato at Wenchi, and one for tomato at Pwalugu. These factories never functioned, as the available supply of raw fruits was only enough for a fraction of what was planned. The case of these factories is a classic example of the path dependency that has occurred in Ghana as a result of the investments made by Nkrumah's administration. Again and again, Ghanaian governments sought to revive these state-owned factories as a means to both promote industry in the country and achieve political gains. Even the Kufuor-led New Patriotic Party government in the 2000s played this game, attempting to revive the Pwalugu and Wenchi tomato factories. The Nsawam pineapple factory was no longer owned by the state at that time but was equally used as a political pawn. It had been bought during the privatization period in the 1990s by a company owned by Nana Konadu-Agyemang Rawlings, the wife of ex-president J.J. Rawlings, who tried to use it as a campaign tool in her unsuccessful bid for the NDC presidential nomination in 2011, proclaiming to have rehabilitated it.

The state farms established by the CPP government to drive the modernization of agriculture became controlled by the CPP as party tools. The State Farms Corporation, United Ghana Farmers Council, and the Workers Brigade controlled sixty-nine farms and all of the public agricultural extension services. A significant amount of public funds were poured into these organizations, yet they controlled only 5 percent of cultivated land (Krassowski 1974: 69). These initiatives included the promotion of large-scale oil palm plantations and modern processing of palm oil, as discussed in Chapter 6. Oil palm plantations were established on land that was acquired compulsorily, and the State Farms Corporation established new palm oil mills. The Workers Brigade employed youth in the oil palm growing areas to cultivate oil palm trees and sell their fresh fruit bunches to the mills.

The state farm approach pursued by Nkrumah's government after 1961 is in sharp contrast to the approach pursued by Houphouet-Boigny's government in neighboring Côte d'Ivoire, which encouraged the expansion of agriculture through a combination of foreign and state investment in large-scale plantations linked to smallholder farmers through contract farming. Cyril Daddieh (1994) argues that Nkrumah's agricultural policy was predicated on creating a "public sector peasantry" rather than creating conditions for the emergence of agrarian capitalism, whether foreign-dominated or domestic. But

Nkrumah's policy was also part of a political strategy. The CPP government, through various legislations, had repressed the urban political elites of the opposition party, and used political patronage and destoolments to either gain the support of chiefs or replace them with more loyal chiefs.[32] Although the CPP had been committed to extinguishing the power of chiefs, political expediency led it to reinstate the colonial situation in which chiefs depended on the national government for their maintenance and survival, who in turn supported the government, but this reciprocal arrangement meant leaving in place the rural institutions through which chiefs governed people and access to land.

In Côte d'Ivoire, Houphouet-Boigny's government did not face the same political landscape of a strong, chiefly cocoa farmer-trader class, nor one that had links to a political opposition, as the CPP government had to face, and Côte d'Ivoire did not have strong chieftaincy institutions (from precolonial kingdoms) in the southern part of the country as Ghana did (Boone 2003: 177–199). Thus, part of the explanation of Nkrumah's different approach stems from the different political configuration – a higher dispersion of power – in which the CPP had to maneuver, and which shaped ruling elites' political survival strategy and economic policy choices made in large part to serve that strategy.

Poor Economic Outcomes

By the time his government was overthrown in February 1966, the structure of the economy had changed to some extent, but as Andrzej Krassowski (1974: 97–101) notes, it is not clear that the changes were due to policy nor that they made the economy less "fragile." In food production, patterns and techniques of cultivation were largely unchanged, and the country remained dependent on food imports, due to shortages rather than preferences for imported food as was the case in 1950. Industry had expanded due to large-scale private, public and joint-venture enterprises as well as private small-scale manufacturing establishments using artisanal methods. Private and joint-venture firms, which accounted for the majority of the firms, operated at a commercial return; whereas, the state-owned enterprises in operation

[32] See for example, Rathbone (2000), Staniland (1975: 140–147) and Simensen (1974).

were commercially unsuccessful as a group and many had not come into operation yet. The choice of industries for state-owned firms had not been strategic, and they made only a small net contribution to value added, new employment and foreign exchange savings.

The limited local manufacturing industry at independence meant that it was not attractive to newcomers who would have to be the risk-takers. The Lewis report had underscored the challenges in production and marketing: few local industries that could supply intermediate inputs; lack of skilled staff; uncertain supply of raw materials; a small and unprotected domestic market with strong brand-loyalty for existing products and a high-status value attached to buying imports; and competition from expatriate companies engaged in the local distribution of imports. The CPP government offered some incentives to defray these costs, but the IDC poorly administered these incentives. Domestic private investment and activity was stimulated, but mainly by new demand created from government spending and government contracts and to only a small extent by improvements that directly affected private sector productivity or production costs.

The state-owned companies set up by the IDC did no better. Out of the twenty-two state-owned and nine joint-venture companies established by the IDC, only eight of the state-owned companies were profitable by 1962 when the IDC was shut down. The problems were not only political, but also economic. Many factories were built without considering the supply side: securing a consistent supply of quality raw materials at an affordable price for the factory. In addition, the state-owned firms suffered from inadequate working capital, and a shortage of technical and managerial personnel.[33] These problems equally affected the success of the state-owned enterprises established in the 1960s under the import-substitution program. They continued to plague state-owned agro-processing companies in the contemporary period, as discussed in Chapter 7 regarding the Ayensu Starch Company set up by the Kufuor-led NPP government in the 2000s.

Much of the public investment had gone into the provision of education and public buildings and into long maturing projects. Public spending in the 1950s resulted in more railway lines, new harbors

[33] There is agreement on this point between Killick (1966b: 289–293) and Krassowski (1974: 26–31, 64).

and fishing ports, public transport, telephone and postal services, water supplies and other public services. But it also resulted in the implementation of prestige projects with few economic benefits. Furthermore, funds were spent on new projects without adequately planning for the recurrent costs of already completed ones, particularly in terms of maintenance, so that the overall effect was to skyrocket the claims on recurrent expenditure.

Lastly, the Volta River Project to build a hydroelectric dam at Akosombo across the Volta River and include an aluminum smelter to process Ghana's bauxite into aluminum had a negligible effect on the economy. Nkrumah pursued this project vigorously as part of his vision of turning Ghana into a modern state. He also thought that the provision of electricity would promote industrialization and the smelter would diversify exports.[34] In his eagerness to see the project become a reality, Nkrumah accepted a deal that was sub-optimal, to say the least. The US-based multinational company Kaiser Aluminum and Chemical Corporation was the only firm interested, apparently after persuasion from the US government which was keen not to see Nkrumah turn to the Russians for financing. The resulting deal with Kaiser was a very one-sided deal. The multinational company got electricity well below the rate that would make the dam profitable (secured over a fifty-year period) and it did not have to use Ghanaian bauxite but rather imported alumina from its subsidiary companies in other countries to Ghana for processing into aluminum and then exportation.[35] Furthermore, the government paid for most of the financing through loans from the World Bank, the US and the UK. In the end, aluminum exports constituted a very small proportion of total exports, and the foreign exchange earnings from it were almost entirely offset by the payments made for imported alumina and the machinery for the VALCO smelter.

By the time of the 1966 coup, the country was bankrupt and massively in debt.[36] The total debt obligation at the beginning of 1966 was

[34] This paragraph is based on Tignor (2006: 193–204), Krassowski (1974: 49–53), Faber (1990), and Killick (1978: 45).

[35] The original idea was that a large company was necessary to act as the major buyer of electricity in order to make the dam investment profitable, but the terms of the deal with Kaiser defeated this purpose, as other consumers of electricity would be paying a higher price and thus subsidizing the cost of electricity for the VALCO aluminum plant.

[36] On this point, see Esseks (1975) and Krassowski (1974: 92).

at least £255 million, of which 64 percent was due within five years, and the average debt burden was £33 million a year, giving an average debt burden of 20–30 percent of exports from 1966 to 1970. Furthermore, the average Ghanaian experienced rising prices, growing shortages of goods, declining real incomes, reduced job opportunities and heavier taxation.

The Nkrumah Legacies and Path Dependence

The Nkrumah era left important legacies concerning the economy. Growth was dependent on public spending and employment dependent on the public sector, which led to chronic budget deficits. The importance and value of public sector employment cannot be overestimated.[37] The relatively large educated class, compared to the structure of the economy, sought employment comparable to its perceived qualifications, which created stiff competition for high salaried positions in the civil service and pressure to expand the bureaucracy. The economy's dependence on imports had increased, which led to chronic trade deficits that grew when the terms of trade fell for the country's limited export basket. Agricultural productivity had not increased, which led to a dependence on food imports. The expansion of state-owned enterprises continued to absorb government expenditure under subsequent governments in order to try to make them work and as a means to provide employment and political patronage. Lastly, the huge foreign debt further contributed to chronic balance of payments problems and thus macroeconomic instability.

All of these legacies shaped the economic and political landscape in which later ruling coalitions had to function, and thus shaped their choice of political survival strategies and economic policies. The country faced an extremely difficult task of economic adjustment given the structure of the economy and debt obligations, but such adjustments had to be made in the context of existing popular discontent with harsh economic conditions and a high degree of political

[37] Genoud (1969:28) notes that by 1960, the public sector employed the bulk of the professionally qualified working population. Colonial salary scales were maintained, which were way out of proportion to the standard of living and income of the rest of the population. Public office also had major financial significance for northerners, as most of them were either teachers or local council officials prior to entering politics (Ladoucer 1979: 213).

Table 2.1 *Governments of Ghana, 1966–1992*

Time period	Name of Government	Type of Political Regime
1966–1969	National Liberation Council (NLC), led by E. Kotoka and A.A. Afrifa	Military-bureaucratic
September 1969–1972	Progress Party (PP) government, led by K.A. Busia	Multiparty democratic *Second Republic*
1972–	National Redemption Council (NRM), led by I.K. Acheampong	Military-bureaucratic
1975–	Supreme Military Council (SMC I), led by I.K. Acheampong	Military
1978–1979	Supreme Military Council II (SMC II), led by F.W.K. Akuffo	Internal military coup
June 4, 1979	Armed Forces Revolutionary Council, led by J.J. Rawlings	Military
September 1979	People's National Party (PNP) government, led by H. Limann	Multiparty democratic *Third Republic*
December 31, 1981–1992	Provisional National Defence Council (PNDC), led by J.J. Rawlings	Military-bureaucratic

mobilization and organization that increased the vulnerability of ruling elites. No political coalition was able to stay in government for more than six or seven years, as shown in Table 2.1. Coup d'états by sections of the military were prompted by macroeconomic crises, but the military ruling coalitions could not maintain power for long in the face of mounting pressures from excluded political elites.

Military coups and repeated regime changes resulted from a rigorous competition between different factions of an enlarged elite for control over the state. The disunity and fragmentation within the elite resulted from the various cleavages dissecting it. Eboe Hutchful (1979) shows that this elite group included a commercial stratum composed of merchants, petty-traders, owners of small enterprises in the service and extractive sectors, small-scale manufacturers and professionals, as well as a rural sector of commercial cocoa farmers and rentier chiefs; and it included the state bureaucracy composed of high civil servants, judges, military and police officers, managers of state-owned enterprises, as well as politicians responsible for political decisionmaking. Only one cross-section of this elite directly controlled the state at any given time, but their control was contested by those excluded.

Postindependence governments retained the customary land ownership and tenure system constructed during the colonial period, which gave chiefs and their traditional councils control over access to land and enhanced their authority. The institution of chieftaincy not only survived in this period, but gained strength after the 1966 coup.[38] Chiefly authority over land was reaffirmed in the 1969 and 1972 constitutions. The 1969 constitution of the Second Republic restored chiefs' authority to allocate land rights and receive land tribute. The 1979 constitution of the Third Republic equally did so and went further to emphasize that the central government had no right to recognize or refuse to recognize chiefs, as it was the sole right of the community. In land under the jurisdiction of paramount chiefs, property rights were not secure but rather governed by "customary law," which could be ambiguous, contradictory and open to manipulation by chiefs. Chiefs translated their constitutionally mandated authority over land into wealth and influence at the local and national levels.

Following the example of the British colonial government, postindependence governments created enclaves in which land was owned by the state and could be bought and sold, and where the government sought to enforce property rights. Ato Onoma (2010) argues that this dual strategy of neglecting property rights institutions in the majority of the country while attempting to enforce them in enclaves of state-owned land was an intentional political strategy in which political elites allowed chiefs the right to control land in exchange for political support, or nonopposition. Thus, postindependence political elites retained the compromise struck by British colonial officials in which arbitrary power over land rights was central to the government's control over chiefs and the chiefs' control over people living in their

38 This paragraph is based on the work of Sara Berry (2001, 2013) and Richard Rathbone (2000).

traditional area.[39] Ghanaian political elites did so as a result of the high dispersion of power within Ghanaian society that resulted in a high degree of political vulnerability of ruling elites and fragmentation within the ruling political coalition. Ruling political elites used political accommodation with chiefs as a means to buttress their political legitimacy and to ensure that chiefs did not support excluded political factions.

Dealing with the Structural and Fiscal Crises

By the time of the February 1966 coup that overthrew Nkrumah's government, the country was locked in a cycle of insolvency (Esseks 1975: 37). The country could not pay its arrears and debt service payments due in 1966, most of which was owed to Western companies whose supplier credits were backed by guarantees from their governments. Ghana also depended on these Western countries for its exports, and thus the new National Liberation Council (NLC) government had to negotiate debt rescheduling and access to imports, otherwise the economy would collapse. It did so by signing a stabilization agreement with the IMF, which provided foreign exchange to pay for imports and secured the IMF's help in negotiating with the country's creditors. Thus, Ghana has a long history of seeking help from the IMF that started before the structural adjustment programs in the 1980s.

Furthermore, the package of measures aimed at achieving macroeconomic stabilization in 1966 included the same measures at the heart of all IMF programs in Ghana. The two-year IMF stabilization program (1966–1967) entailed reducing central bank financing of the budget deficit, reducing the current account (trade) deficit to a level that could be supported by foreign exchange from capital inflows; and reducing the budget deficit. The key measures to cut the budget deficit included reduced public spending and public sector employment. Key measures to cut the trade deficit included devaluation of the currency by 30 percent, and partial import liberalization through reform of the import licenses, tariffs and duties. But the devaluation was not enough to reduce import demand to a level that could be supported by the

[39] This argument is made, explicitly or implicitly, by many scholars of Ghanaian politics, but is put forth most clearly by Ato Onoma (2010).

capital inflows, so foreign exchange and price controls were maintained (Killick 1978: 302).

In return, the IMF helped the NLC government to negotiate four different agreements with its creditors, which meant that it paid about one-ninth of the debt service that was due in 1966 and also a reduced amount in 1967 (Krassowski 1974: 122–133). The debt rescheduling and IMF credits gave the NLC government the breathing space to continue importing and to achieve the stabilization measures without the economy contracting more than it did in the previous years. But the debt was just pushed back a few years, and further debt negotiations were held in 1968, which pushed the debt back a few more years, but that was as far as the Western governments, who held most of the debt, were willing to go, and in the process they added a large interest rate on debts being rolled over. This provided some space, but meant that the debt would come due under the elected Busia government.

Despite implementing measures to curb budget expenditure, the NLC government only succeeded in reducing the budget deficit slightly during the stabilization period, and even then, it did not change the allocation of public spending, as it confronted the same difficulties and pressures that Nkrumah's CPP government had faced (Krassowski 1974: 112–114). Thus, government spending remained skewed towards educational, social and general government expenditure, with no clear priorities in favor of productive sectors, and imports privileged consumer goods over imports essential for maintenance and productive investments.

The stabilization measures caused a recession as government spending generally fell, unemployment rose sharply and private investment stagnated. As a result, the NLC government relaxed the austerity measures in 1968–1969, in fear of the social and political costs. Recurrent spending increased under the NLC government as a result of increased public service remuneration; demands on education and social service programs agreed before 1966, which the NLC did not overturn; and the knock on effects of devaluation (Krassowski 1974: 117).

The Busia government continued with expansionary budgets, increasing capital and recurrent expenditure, on the back of higher cocoa prices in 1969 and 1970 (Killick 1978: 306–308). The government also liberalized imports, but without any measures to tax incomes, which led to a massive import boom in 1970 and 1971.

The largest increases were in consumer goods, which were not essential, and thus the imports were not used strategically. The 1971 budget was based on deficit financing, and thus led to inflation. In 1971, the world price of cocoa fell dramatically, and the balance of payments and budget situation deteriorated rapidly. In early January 1972, the Busia government enacted austerity measures, including a large devaluation of the currency in an attempt to reduce import demand. The devaluation provided the backdrop for Acheampong's military coup, just as it had done in 1965 for the military group that overthrew Nkrumah's government (see Killick 1978: 154).

In dealing with the chronic problem of foreign exchange shortages and excess import demand, the governments in the 1960s and 1970s alternated between a monetarist approach (currency devaluation) and state-administered controls, but both approaches failed to deal with the structural issues and constraints on production in the domestic economy that led to balance of payments instability (Hutchful 1989). All governments retained the focus on state-owned enterprises as a means to increase production, and most of them continued to neglect agricultural production.

Industrial Policy and Dependence on State Corporations

Despite pressures from the IMF under the stabilization agreement to privatize the state-owned enterprises created during Nkrumah's era, the NLC government, and later the Busia government, did not radically change the approach to industrial development. The pace was slowed down, and contracts for enterprises not yet constructed were terminated. But the main approach of the NLC government was to make the industrial state corporations profitable by increasing capacity utilization and improving their management.[40] The privatization path was tried, but of the forty-six state-owned enterprises at the time of the coup, only a few were sold and a few made into joint ventures. The problem with privatization was that few locals had the capital to buy the state enterprises, and there was public opposition to selling the enterprises predominantly to foreigners, partly due to ideas of economic nationalism coming out of independence but equally due to

[40] There is consensus on this point by the best works covering this time period; see Krassowski (1974: 116–117) and Killick (1978: 310–313, 218–219).

the fact that local businessmen did not want foreign ownership in the economy to increase and would choose state capitalism over foreign direct investment. Tony Killick (1978) notes that what was missing in the industrial policy of the NLC and Busia governments was a rationalization of the system of industrial protection and the willingness to shut down the least profitable state-owned companies. They kept the high import tariffs based on the infant industry argument, that domestic firms needed support to survive and gain market share away from imported brands. Thus, the NLC and Busia governments continued to put money into the state-owned enterprises, which in turn claimed the majority of local bank credit and a large portion of industrial imports.

After the 1972 coup, Acheampong's National Redemption Council (NRC) government unilaterally rescheduled the debt and reinstituted import controls. The NRC government's industrial policy emphasized import-substitution in selected goods that constituted a large portion of the import bill, such as crude palm oil. It did so through a two-pronged strategy: using the state-owned enterprises, and encouraging foreign investment in agro-processing in joint ventures with state capital. The latter strategy included incentives as well as compulsions, such as blocking the repatriation of dividends by foreign firms already operating in the country unless they invested in productive sectors, especially in the agricultural sector. This was important in developing the palm oil industry, as shown in Chapter 6.

The only significant difference in productive sector policies of the NLC and Busia governments compared to the Nkrumah period was in the cocoa sector. Cocoa production was revived through increases in the producer price and currency devaluation, and the government provided support for pesticides, disease control, replanting old trees with high yielding trees, and extension services (Krassowski 1974: 120). The United Ghana Farmers Council's monopoly on cocoa buying was eliminated, and the multiple buying systems were reestablished. However, private traders and farmers' cooperatives were not able to reestablish themselves in the trade (Boone 2003: 171). Their assets that had been seized by the CPP government were not returned. This liberalization of internal cocoa marketing was short-lived, however, as Acheampong's government reinstated the single state-controlled cocoa marketing system.

In agriculture more broadly there was less change. The NLC and Busia governments did not abandon the State Farms Corporation and

Workers Brigade, but rather only reduced their scale. A major feature of agricultural policy in the early 1970s was the formation of single product development boards for commodities to offer advice and incentives to peasant farmers and to oversee the production of agricultural raw materials for the newly established factories. The government also instituted minimum guaranteed prices. Agricultural policies were supported by a rural development scheme designed to provide basic infrastructure of roads, water and electricity. However, reality fell short of intentions (Killick 1978: 311, 316). The Busia government also had to deal with high food-import dependence and rising prices, and did so by blaming inflation on exploitive middlemen and establishing a government agency to deal with food distribution issues.

The Acheampong government's response was to create the Operation Feed Yourself program and agricultural development programs for all regions. The former resulted in self-sufficiency in rice production between 1974 and 1975, mostly produced by state farms and large-scale commercial farms with connections to the military government, but this success was short-lived, due to the declining macroeconomic environment and contradictory government policies.[41] Agricultural production then declined from 1976 to 1982 in the context of a deteriorating macroeconomic environment, which meant that the agriculture sector suffered from a shortage of the required imported inputs and reduced government spending in rural areas.

Economic Decline

Fixed exchange rates in the 1970s and early 1980s led to the overvaluation of the cedi and appreciation of the real exchange rate.[42] Budget deficits rose between 1971 and 1977, with the total money supply rising by 500 percent, leading to inflation and a steep fall in the black market rate of the cedi, which governments then tried to contain through price controls. The prices for over 700 goods were fixed in the formal sector, resulting in long queues, empty shelves and black market activities. This led to a period of hoarding, smuggling and

[41] For more details on the rice case, see Nyanteng and Seini (2000: 269), Konings (1986) and Shepherd (1981).

[42] This paragraph and the next are based on Hutchful (2002: 11–14) and Gymiah-Boadi and Jeffries (2000).

profiteering by businesses, bureaucrats and ruling elites, which Ghanaians called *kalabule*. People with access to import licenses and foreign exchange at official rates of exchange could, and did, make huge profits out of selling goods on the black market. Government officials in charge of allocating import licenses and foreign exchange demanded a share of such profits through kickbacks, and later the ruling elites of the Supreme Military Council government tried to monopolize the allocation of import licenses and foreign exchange for their personal benefit. By the mid-1970s, black market transactions accounted for between 25 and 42 percent of the Ghanaian economy.

J.J. Rawlings led a coup d'état on June 4, 1979 and established the Armed Forces Revolutionary Council, which carried out a brutal campaign against *kalabule*. The AFRC government executed eight senior military officers, including Acheampong, and burned markets, including the Makola market in Accra – blaming *kalabule* and women market traders for the economic crisis. The AFRC organized elections, and the Third Republic was inaugurated with President Hilla Limann and the People's National Party, which held a majority in Parliament. The People's National Party was founded by former CPP politicians and claimed Nkrumah's legacy. Unfortunately, the Limann government presided over a significant decline in the world price of cocoa, exacerbating the already bad fiscal situation. But the newly elected government did not enact austerity measures and budget deficits continued. The government was at a policy impasse; economic reforms were needed to stem the economic crisis, but the new group of ruling political elites would not reduce spending or devalue the currency. Eboe Hutchful (2002: 14) argues that the PNP ruling elites, especially the party financiers, were opposed to devaluation and liberalization measures with the support of an IMF lending arrangement, because they wanted to exploit the import licensing and administrative controls in order to recoup the money they had spent on the elections. The youth wing and party leftists also opposed economic reforms for ideological reasons. President Limann had little control over the politicians and party financiers, so the government did nothing and the crisis worsened.

Declining real producer prices of cocoa due to inflation and overvalued exchange rates (which acted as an additional tax on cocoa farmers) created disincentives for cocoa farmers, and cocoa exports declined by 60 percent between the mid-1960s and mid-1980s.[43] The decline in cocoa exports exacerbated the balance of payments crisis, deprived the industrial sector of foreign exchange, and devastated the revenue base of the government – sending the economy from stagnation into decline.

Conclusion

On the eve of the 1981 coup, the economic crisis had reached proportions where basic economic activities were not reproducible. J.J. Rawlings led another coup to overthrow the Limann government, but this time he called it a "revolution," a campaign against *kalabule* and against an economic system that benefited only a few. Rawlings' so-called revolution acted as an internal shock that temporarily altered the distribution of power and made it possible for the Provisional National Defence Council (PNDC) government to implement economic reforms, as shown in the next chapter.

Faced with a bankrupt economy, external debts and few alternatives of external financing, the new ruling elites turned to liberalizing the economy as the only way to squeeze out *kalabule* operators, and to rehabilitating the cocoa and gold export sectors as a political survival strategy. Rebuilding the cocoa and gold export sectors made sense because it meant rebuilding the fiscal basis of the state and supporting sectors where the state was a dominant actor and thus could control the economic reform process. This survival strategy involved the PNDC elites entering an alliance with World Bank and IMF staff, and later a wide group of donor agencies, who provided foreign exchange to pay for imports, paid for the reforms in the cocoa and gold sectors, and financed "development" projects (i.e. distributive spending) in lieu of the bankrupt government.

The process of designing and implementing the economic reforms was one of the PNDC elites negotiating with World Bank and IMF staff based on their perceived interests. The economic reforms did not involve an alliance or negotiations with what was left of private domestic capitalists, but rather continued the trend of their marginalization and limited political influence within policymaking processes. In contrast, the new group of elites in the PNDC coalition sought to

43 On the decline of cocoa exports, see Aryeetey and Harrigan (2000) and IMF (1998).

create their own businesses, through their privileged access to state information and resources and by capitalizing on the economic liberalization process. This gave the new group of PNDC elites an economic base that they would then use to fund their new political party as the country transitioned to multiparty elections and democratic rule. With the anticipation of the founding elections of the Fourth Republic in late 1992, competitive clientelism reemerged in the 1990s.

It took extreme political and economic circumstances before the economic decline of the 1970s and early 1980s was reversed. However, the distribution of power that emerged in the 1950s shaped how ruling coalitions were constituted and political support mobilized in the context of independence, which in turn forged the two defining features regarding the political survival strategies of ruling political elites that continued into the twenty-first century. The next chapter examines the nature of competitive clientelism under the Fourth Republic. In particular, it explains how the political parties were organized and financed within the specific distribution of power in Ghana, and draws out the implications for political elites' choices of political survival strategies: strategies concerning how to win primaries and general elections. In turn, these political survival strategies shaped the incentives facing political elites when in government and thus the kind of policies they pursued and their implementation arrangements, as demonstrated in later chapters by examining general policies in the productive sectors, selected industry cases, and specific industrial policy case studies.

3 *Return to Competitive Clientelism in the Fourth Republic*

The Provisional National Defence Council (PNDC), led by J.J. Rawlings, was able to overcome the economic impasse and restart economic growth. It implemented economic reforms that previous governments were unwilling to undertake, backed by structural adjustment lending agreements with the IMF and World Bank. The government's Economic Recovery Programme involved exchange rate liberalization and currency devaluation, ending price controls and liberalizing marketing systems, reducing budget deficits and increasing government revenue, rehabilitating infrastructure, and eliminating smuggling and black market activities. Tight controls on the economy were gradually reduced as the massive structural imbalances in imports and exports, and between production and consumption were rectified.[1]

The first part of this chapter explains the politics that made these economic reforms possible. It argues that economic recovery was possible because competitive clientelism was temporarily suppressed due to changes in the distribution of power in society resulting from internal shocks. Within this context, Rawlings was able to put together a ruling coalition with a very different configuration of power than previous ruling coalitions, and thus was willing and able to absorb the short-term political costs of economic reform. However, the PNDC elites pursued a political survival strategy that ostracized domestic capitalists and instead chose an alliance with World Bank and IMF staff.

The PNDC ruling elites could not keep rival political elites excluded from competing for power for long, especially after rival political groups joined together to lobby for the return to multiparty elections. The PNDC elites agreed to hold elections in 1992 and converted the

[1] This chapter does not go through the structural adjustment reforms or the reforms process in detail, which is covered in Aryeetey, Harrigan and Nissanke (2000) and Hutchful (2002).

PNDC into a political party, the National Democratic Congress (NDC), by including a larger group of political elites and creating a political machine with patronage networks at the constituency level. The NDC won the 1992 and 1996 elections by capitalizing on Rawlings' popularity in the rural areas and northern parts of the country.

The return to multiparty rule led to the reemergence of competitive clientelism, which looked similar to previous periods. The group of political elites was large and fragmented, but they coalesced into two broad political coalitions organized around the poles of the Danquah-Busia and Nkrumahist political traditions that emerged during decolonization. The NDC party effectively usurped the Nkrumahist political tradition, branding itself as the new alternative to the Danquah-Busia tradition. Political elites within the Danquah-Busia tradition created the New Patriotic Party (NPP) and were able to mobilize a significant amount of support due to the founding mythology and institutional networks binding chiefly families, professionals, and ethnic identity.

Initially, the New Patriotic Party's support base was largely urban and the professional strata of society, with strongholds in the Ashanti and Eastern regions – the traditional strongholds of the Danquah-Busia political tradition. The NPP barely garnered enough votes to win the 2000 presidential election by a small margin in a run-off election, but once in government, the NPP was able to build up its political support base at the lower level using state patronage and benefited from its new credibility as a political coalition that could win elections.

Between the 1992 and 2016 elections, the NDC and NPP alternated in government after two terms, as shown in Table 3.1. The NDC and NPP accounted for over 90 percent of the total votes in every election. There were several smaller parties, historically linked to the Nkrumahist tradition but unable to unseat the dominance of the NDC. The electoral percentages of these smaller parties, and their representation in parliament, gradually declined after 1996, to the extent that they won only one parliamentary seat in the December 2012 elections and none in the December 2016 elections. The few independent candidates were actually NPP or NDC party members who failed to win their party primary but felt they had the local political support base to win the election and thus ran as "independent" candidates. Independents moved back into the party's fold once they were in parliament. Individuals could be successful in such temporary breakaway moves, but not at the party

Table 3.1 ***Governments and Parliamentary Composition, 1993–2020***

Elected term	Political party in power; president	Parliamentary composition
1993–1996	NDC; President Rawlings	200 seats. NDC: 189; NPP: 0, because it boycotted the parliamentary elections. Smaller parties: 9; Independents: 2
1997–2000	NDC; President Rawlings	200 seats. NDC: 133; NPP: 61 Smaller parties: 6
2001–2004	NPP; President Kufuor	200 seats. NDC: 92; NPP: 100 Smaller parties: 4; Independents: 4
2005–2008	NPP; President Kufuor	230 seats. NDC: 94; NPP: 128 Smaller parties: 7; Independents: 1
2009–2012	NDC; President Mills*	230 seats. NDC: 116; NPP: 107 Smaller parties: 3; Independents: 4
2013–2016	NDC; President Mahama	275 seats (138 required for a majority) NDC: 148; NPP: 123 Smaller parties: 1; Independents: 3
2017–2020	NPP; President Akufo-Addo	275 seats. NDC: 106; NPP: 169

Source: Created by the author with data from the Electoral Commission of Ghana, except the 2016 parliamentary election results, which are from Peace FM online, http://ghanaelections.peacefmonline.com (last accessed August 14, 2017).
* Vice President Mahama became president after Mills died in office in July 2012.

level. The several breakaway factions from the NDC that established new parties failed dramatically in presidential and parliamentary elections.

Rather than fragmenting, the NDC and NPP grew in strength as umbrella parties encompassing several elite factions. The factions were organized around key leaders, embodying personality conflicts but also reflecting historical struggles among political elites.

Table 3.2 *Margin of Victory between the NDC and NPP Presidential Candidates, 1992–2016*

Election year	Total votes of NPP candidate (%)	Total votes of NDC candidate (%)	Margin of votes between NDC and NPP (%)
1992	30.30	58.40	28.10
1996	39.70	57.30	17.60
2000 (run-off)	56.90	43.10	13.80
2004	52.48	44.64	7.81
2008 (run-off)	49.77	50.23	0.46
2012	47.74	50.70	2.96
2016	53.72	44.53	9.19

Source: Created by the author with data from the Electoral Commission of Ghana.

Factional dividing lines could shift over time as political elites aligned and realigned, especially around choosing presidential candidates. The formal party organization rules regarding party primaries meant that (aspiring) politicians needed their own patron-client network in order to win party primaries against fellow party members, and the first-past-the-post electoral system in single member constituencies reinforced the importance of politicians having a personalized support base. As a result of party factionalism, there was a high degree of intraparty competition. This competition played out in contests for executive positions in the political party organizations as well as parliamentary primaries, where elite factions vied to get "their people" elected. This competition could and did lead to situations in which the top party executives belonged to one faction and the presidential candidate to another.

The NDC and NPP became increasingly competitive with each electoral cycle. As Table 3.2 illustrates, the margin of votes by which candidates won the presidency declined between the 1992 and the 2012 elections. Notably, the 2008 and the 2012 elections were extremely close and the most competitive under the Fourth Republic, with the margin of victory increasing in the 2016 elections.

The highly competitive nature of presidential and parliamentary elections meant that in order to win elections, NDC and the NPP presidential and parliamentary candidates became increasingly dependent on party organizations at the constituency level and on local-level party activists. In return, these lower-level factions placed greater demands on national political elites, in terms of greater influence in selecting party candidates as well as material benefits and economic opportunities. Increasingly competitive elections and intraparty competition to win party positions and nominations increased the amount of financing required to win primaries and general elections, as well as the general financing needs of the political parties to hold party-wide events. Ruling parties in general, and individual incumbent politicians in particular, raised political financing through a myriad of legal and illegal methods linked to the state, which could be used to finance the next election and as a safety net in case they lost the election.

The second part of this chapter elaborates these structural features of competitive clientelism under the Fourth Republic, and the political incentives regarding policy choices that result from them, using evidence from the NDC government in the 1990s and the NPP government in the 2000s. It explains how the NDC and NPP were organized, focusing on the elite factionalism and relations between the higher and lower levels of the party organizations, and how expensive electoral campaigns became as well as the sources of political financing and their implications. Moving beyond the composition and financing of the party organizations, the chapter then assesses the importance of floating voters in winning elections and the incentives this generated in terms of electoral strategies and policy choices. Bringing together the distributional demands of core (loyal) and swing (floating) voters, and the difficulties of financing and winning elections, we can see how competitive clientelism led to overspending and macroeconomic crises – a topic taken up in the next chapter. Lastly, this chapter examines the political influence of domestic capitalists, or rather the lack of it, which explains why they could not provide a counteracting influence on government policymaking.

Composition of the PNDC Ruling Coalition

The PNDC ruling coalition was characterized by lower vulnerability in government because excluded political factions were temporarily weakened, and by a political support base that had less leverage over ruling elites. The severe economic decline of the late 1970s and early 1980s led to the loss of legitimacy of the political elite class as a whole among large sections of the population. Flight Lieutenant J.J. Rawlings mobilized junior ranks in the military to overthrow the elected Limann government and called for a people's revolution, which resulted in popular mobilization against the wealthy elite. Rawlings rode this wave of popular mobilization and encouraged it, in order to destabilize the existing political factions, but then demobilized these lower-level supporters and reduced their influence within the ruling coalition by seeking out alternative sources of political support. As a result, Eboe Hutchful (2002) notes that Rawlings and the PNDC government had several different bases of political support but no individual political group had significant influence over Rawlings and the PNDC elite. This allowed the PNDC ruling elites to implement politically difficult economic reforms without worrying about their political support base.

The first two years of the PNDC government were characterized by coup attempts from members of the PNDC as well as policy battles between radical Marxists and pragmatists. By 1985, all of the original PNDC members were gone, except for Rawlings, around whom power was concentrated and centralized.[2] The new set of PNDC elites was less ideological and more pragmatic, and represented a wide spectrum of society: trade unions, traditional authorities, Nkrumahist politicians, established elites and a parastatal manager. It included military personnel, but an equal number of civilians. The key point was that none of the individual PNDC ruling elites, besides Rawlings, had a power base of their own. There was also a large degree of cohesion among the ruling elites, albeit this cohesion was achieved through a measure of force: members of the ruling elite who fell out with Rawlings were forced out of the ruling elite. The PNDC elite included four types of people: (1) technopols who were in charge of economic policy, and who came from the universities or had served in previous governments; (2) a conservative wing composed of traditional authorities and established elites, who were largely in charge of the political strategy after 1984; (3) leaders of the

[2] This paragraph and the next few are my interpretation of the empirical details provided in Ray (1986), Nugent (1995), Ninsin (1996) and Hutchful (2002: 43–50).

revolutionary organs, who after 1984 had little political or policy influence; and (4) securocrats, who were responsible for security of the ruling coalition.[3]

After 1984, the revolutionary organs were marginalized, and Rawlings sought new political constituencies and shifted his support base, which limited his dependence on specific lower-level factions. Rawlings' rhetoric shifted from idealizing urban workers to romanticizing rural workers (peasants), who were benefiting more from the economic reforms; however, these rural beneficiaries were not mobilized. The PNDC's organizational power came mainly from the armed forces, from which Rawlings had emerged, and the revolutionary organs, which were kept in existence and acted more as clients who encouraged support for the regime in return for material benefits. The PNDC elites decided to create new local government bodies, district assemblies, as a strategy for securing nonurban support. Similar to the local government reforms introduced by Nkrumah's CPP government, only two-thirds of the members of the district assemblies were elected, but this time, instead of the chiefs having control, it was the central government that appointed the remaining one-third, as well as the head of the assembly, thus creating new patronage structures in the rural areas. The PNDC ruling coalition did not require much financing initially, because these patron-client relations with certain organizations did not require large resources and because the lower-level factions were weak.

Rawlings not only overthrew an elected government in 1981, but also the entire Ghanaian political establishment, in the sense that those who came to power were not from the existing political coalitions organized around the Nkrumah and Danquah political traditions.

[3] I borrowed the term securocrats from Eboe Hutchful. While Hutchful refers to the first group as technocrats, I have called them technopols, to emphasize that these people were both technocrats and politicians. John Williamson (1993) used the term technopol in his argument about the political economy of reform in developing countries. Williamson's use of the term referred narrowly to economists who accepted political appointments and thus political responsibilities, and who had the potential to become successful applied economists and successful politicians. I use the term more widely to refer to politicians who also had technical training, even if not in economics, but who also combined within their person the political imperatives of remaining in power with the economic imperatives of managing state resources to achieve economic development.

These outsiders took control of the state through the PNDC and came to constitute new political elites, many of whom had no previous experience in political office or a family tradition of political office.[4] The established political elites were seen as the major cause of the country's economic decline, and thus temporarily had little legitimacy with which to challenge the PNDC and were limited to their urban-based organizations and networks.

The relative autonomy of the PNDC ruling elite from organized societal interests combined with insulation from demands among the lower-level factions of the ruling coalition were not the only reasons that the PNDC government was able to implement economic reforms that previous governments had been unwilling to undertake. The PNDC government also had unprecedented financial support from the Bretton Woods institutions. Large aid inflows from the World Bank and IMF helped to buffer the impacts of the economic reforms, such as import liberalization, and reduced the temptation of the government to revert to administrative controls when faced with balance of payments problems, such as occurred after the sharp fall in cocoa prices in 1988 (Harrigan and Younger 2000).

Increased aid flows also softened the blow to the population from massive cuts in government expenditure and public sector employment, price increases and currency devaluation. Foreign aid allowed the PNDC government to increase "development" spending. Particularly important was the construction of new roads and electrification in the rural areas, especially in the northern regions of the country that had never had electricity.[5] The shift in government spending away from parastatals and urban sectors to focus on rural areas and previously marginalized parts of the country, such as the northern regions, formed the basis of Rawlings' popularity in these parts of the country, which he transformed into votes in the 1992 elections.

The PNDC government had an antagonistic relationship with the small group of domestic capitalists that had survived the economic

[4] This point is based on an examination of the backgrounds of the key PNDC members in E. Aggrey-Darkoh, 2009, "Mapping Political Elite in Ghana, 1982–2008," a paper that I commissioned as leader of the Ghana country team, within the Elites, Production and Poverty research program (2008–2012), based at the Danish Institute for International Studies, Denmark.

[5] There is consensus among scholars on this point; see Jeffries (1998), Nugent (1995: 206), and Bob-Milliar (2011).

downturn. During the "revolutionary" years after the first coup led by Rawlings in 1979 and again in the 1980s, Rawlings attacked domestic capitalists as the source of the country's economic problems through public statements. Just after the 1981 coup, the PNDC ruling elites created new justice institutions through which it put domestic capitalists on trial, and subsequently jailed them and confiscated their assets.[6] Many were forced or ran into exile. Even after the launch of structural adjustment reforms in 1983, many of the PNDC elite distrusted businessmen, especially leading businessmen linked to the excluded political factions. Thus, the PNDC elites were not in favor of private capitalism, but rather state-led capitalism, and pursued a strategy of persecuting what had survived of the domestic capitalist class.[7] They feared that a viable private sector could create a new center of power, underwrite the emergence of an alternative political force, or finance another coup. Top PNDC officials publicly criticized prominent businessmen, and the PNDC government preferred alliances with foreign capitalists through joint ventures.

Kwame Ninsin (1996) argues that the PNDC ruling elite, and later those in the National Democratic Congress party, were not only threatened politically by existing capitalists, but also economically, as they sought socioeconomic mobility through control of the state.[8] In the early 1990s, the PNDC elites sought to produce their own businessmen through two strategies. The first strategy was accumulation among the PNDC elite, which began in the late 1980s as the moral fervor of the revolution died and wealth accumulation was sanctioned in the PNDC public discourse. Strategies of accumulation for the new elite included skimming off state resources and setting up businesses to benefit from new economic opportunities linked to the structural adjustment reforms. The second strategy was rewarding entrepreneurs who supported the PNDC. Aspirant businessmen linked themselves to the PNDC to benefit from new economic opportunities, such as contracts for public works in road construction and electrification. They became a social base of support for the PNDC, repeating the strategy that Nkrumah and the CPP had used in the 1950s.

6 For more details, see Hansen (1991).
7 On this point, see Tangri (1992), Hutchful (2002) and Arthur (2002).
8 Paul Nugent (1995: 203–204) makes a similar point.

Not surprisingly, relations between the PNDC government and the established business associations were characterized by a lack of collaboration.[9] The main business associations, the Ghana National Chamber of Commerce and the Ghana Manufacturers' Association (later renamed Association of Ghana Industries) were politically marginalized, and business association leaders had very limited access to the PNDC economic policymakers. Leaders of the business associations were perceived to be part of the Danquah-Busia political faction. The most obvious example was the President of the Ghana Manufacturers' Association in the 1980s who was a high-ranking member of the Danquah-Busia tradition political elite and had been a deputy minister of trade and industry under the Busia government.

In sum, the PNDC ruling coalition had limited linkages to existing domestic capitalists, who were seen to be linked to the excluded political elites, especially in the Danquah-Busia political tradition. Instead, the PNDC elites made an alliance with the Bretton Woods institutions, albeit one full of tensions, which unlocked foreign exchange and budget financing. The PNDC political elite could ignore domestic capitalists because the latter were not central to the key economic sectors and thus not important for generating foreign exchange and government revenue. In fact, the PNDC elites sought to undermine the financial base of the political opposition by marginalizing businesses associated with excluded political factions and by creating their own businesses.

Creating the NDC out of the PNDC

Forming a political party to compete in the 1992 elections required different organizational structures and more financing than the PNDC ruling elites previously had. Therefore, they created the National Democratic Congress party as a broad-based political machine that could win elections. In doing so, they made use of the revolutionary organizations from the PNDC period to mobilize political support and turn out votes at election time. They also created new organizations that received state resources in return for delivering the political support of their members and co-opted existing organizations through the

[9] This paragraph is based on Hart and Gyimah-Boadi (2000), Opoku (2010) and Kraus (1991, 2002).

same kind of patron-client exchange that had characterized earlier periods of competitive clientelism.[10]

Central among the revolutionary organizations that became key parts of the new NDC political machine was the 31st December Women's Movement. The movement was led by Nana Konadu-Agyemang, the wife of J.J. Rawlings, who turned it into a nongovernmental organization in the 1990s. It was a women's network stretching across the country that carried out projects to assist mainly rural women through the grants and assistance it received from donors and international NGOs. Since Nana Konadu-Agyemang led the movement, its activities were seen as largesse from the NDC. Other revolutionary organizations that were important for mobilizing votes included the Committees for the Defence of the Revolution, which continued to play a mobilizing role and whose members had become part of the District Assemblies and thus also had some influence over the allocation of resources at the local level.

Among the new auxiliary organizations, the Council of Indigenous Business Associations and the Ghana Private Road Transport Union were the most important. The Council was created by the PNDC as one of its last acts in early 1993. It was composed of twenty associations of petty commodity producers. The NDC government gave it a starting grant when it was established. Council officials acquired political leverage over members through the responsibility given to them by the NDC government regarding the allocation of credit, subsidized equipment and work sites to small entrepreneurs. Council officials also were granted the right to collect taxes from members on behalf of the Internal Revenue Service in exchange for a commission. The Transport Union was granted the right to collect daily tolls in lorry parks around the country and received government loans, which were unlikely to have been repaid.

Another result of the shift from the PNDC to the NDC was a shift in the balance of power from the technopols of the PNDC era to the party brokers in charge of running and financing the NDC party machinery (Hutchful 2002: 219–222). Initially there were large continuities between the PNDC and NDC ruling elites, with key PNDC officials retained in Cabinet and the President's Office. As power drifted from the technopols to the party brokers, Rawlings was detached from the

10 See, for example, Nugent (1995) and Sandbrook and Olebaum (1997).

party and depended on the party brokers. Two of the top party brokers were Obed Asamoah, the chairman of the party finance committee who also served in ministerial positions, and Nana Konadu-Agyemang, who had a formidable support base and independent source of financing through her leadership of the 31st December Women's Movement.

Eboe Hutchful (2002) documents the conflicts that emerged between the party brokers on the one hand, and the technopols who led on policy issues and the securocrats who were in charge of security issues on the other. During the PNDC period, the technopols and securocrats had worked closely together. Now, they were losing political power, and as they did, many resigned. Policymaking increasingly lacked focus, and the government's commitment to economic reforms wavered. The Minister of Finance who had led the economic reform process under the PNDC resigned in 1995, in protest against his inability to restrain excessive budgetary demands of the public sector. After he left, the Ministry of Finance was purged of much of the technical team behind the Economic Recovery Programme. The Chief of Staff, who was also a technopol, was demoted in 1996, prompting him to resign, and shortly after the chief securocrat retired. Other key technopols left, so that by 1997, the macroeconomic team that had negotiated the structural adjustment program was gone.[11] As a result, negotiations with the World Bank and IMF weakened, coordination was lost, and the new economic policymakers lacked a strong vision for what policies were to achieve. Vice President John Atta Mills was put in charge of economic policy in 1998, but he lacked the political clout to make Cabinet ministers stick to spending targets or account for the running of their affairs.[12] John Atta Mills had a background in tax law, taught at the University of Ghana, and had been Director of the Internal Revenue Service before becoming the vice presidential candidate in the 1996 elections. He had no history of PNDC activism and no political support base of his own (at that time).

Factional divides within the NDC elite formed around the party brokers, and later around other prominent NDC members, as NDC political elites jockeyed for support in different electoral contests for party leadership and for the presidential nomination. For example,

[11] This point made by Eboe Hutchful (2002: 222) was also confirmed in an interview with Kwesi Botchwey, April 12, 2008, Oxford, UK.

[12] *Africa Confidential* 2000 Vol. 41, No. 23, p. 2.

there was increasing factionalization within the higher ranks of the NDC in the lead-up to selecting the party's presidential candidate for the December 2000 elections, which Rawlings could not contest due to constitutional term limits.[13] Each faction within the NDC supported a different presidential candidate.[14]

Furthermore, the NDC party executives decided not to hold primaries in the run-up to the 2000 parliamentary elections, with most sitting MPs confirmed but some new candidates were given to constituencies: a process reflecting factional struggles at the center of the party. Constituency-level party members did not like this decision, and some NDC members sought to defy the party leadership and run in their constituencies as independent candidates. This put some NDC parliamentary seats that were considered "safe" at risk, where locally popular candidates who did not win the NDC nomination stood as independents and split votes.

The NPP was able to capitalize on a deteriorating economy and NDC factionalism in the run up to the 2000 elections. It also extended the party's reach beyond its traditional urban- and elite-based support and its concentration of rural support in a few southern regions.[15] Even then, the NPP only won the December 2000 national elections by a slim margin, relying on the support of the small parties to win the presidency in a run-off election. Once in government, however, the party built up its lower-level factions using its access to state resources and positions in the subnational state apparatus. Not surprisingly, the NPP won the 2004 elections with a greater percentage of the vote.

Intra-Elite Struggles within the NPP

The organization of the NPP came to be very similar to the NDC in terms of the high degree of elite factionalism and strong lower-level groups, as the formal and informal party structures of the NPP evolved

[13] *Africa Confidential* 1998 Vol. 39, No. 3, pp. 1–2.

[14] *Africa Confidential* 1999 Vol. 42, No. 23, p. 2. For more evidence of elite factions, see Bob-Milliar (2012b) on the NDC under the Mills-led NDC government.

[15] The NPP Vice Presidential candidate in the 2000 elections, Alieu Mahama, was a major financier of the NPP in opposition; he was a successful building contractor in the capital of the Northern Region. He is credited with creating party alliances in the three northern regions that delivered crucial votes for Kufuor in the 2000 elections. *Africa Confidential* 2002 Vol. 43, No. 8, p. 6.

to give considerable power to constituency-level party organizations. One of the key divides in the party was between the Kufuor and Akufo-Addo factions. It started when J.A. Kufuor won the presidential nomination in 1998 over Nana Akufo-Addo, but it actually has a longer history. There was a broad split within the Danquah-Busia political tradition between the Danquah and Busia factions, which dated back to the early independence period. The division became public during the 1979 elections, when one of the factions broke away and supported its own presidential candidate. This split was considered by many political elites to have caused the Danquah-Busia tradition to lose the 1979 general election, and it became a source of factionalism within the NPP political organization.

This division emerged again around the 1998 leadership contest to select the NPP's presidential candidate for the 2000 elections.[16] Akufo-Addo had a long history within the Danquah-Busia tradition and was seen by some parts of the party as the rightful heir to the party's top position, after Adu Boahen, who was the party's flagbearer in the founding 1992 election.[17] However, J.A. Kufuor was the more astute politician and mobilized grassroots support within the party. Akufo-Addo fell into the same elitist trap that his predecessor J.B. Danquah had done in the 1950s, but felt betrayed nonetheless. Kufuor won the party's presidential nomination for the 1996 general election (though he lost the election to J.J. Rawlings), and again for the 2000 general election. When Kufuor won the presidency in the 2000 election, it fueled resentment among parts of the NPP that it should have been Nana Akufo-Addo. But Akufo-Addo and his supporters did not give up and were still waiting for their turn, when Kufuor's two terms would be up.

Kufuor's control over the party and over the government was challenged by this factional split quite early in his presidency. To get a firmer grip on the party, he monopolized control over party finances, which only further undermined his support within the party and increased support for the Akufo-Addo faction.[18] The Akufo-Addo

[16] This paragraph draws on internal NPP politics as recounted by Agyeman-Duah (2006) in his biography of J.A. Kufuor.

[17] His father, Edward Akufo-Addo was a one of the six UGCC members jailed, along with Kwame Nkrumah, after the 1948 boycott and riots, and he was the titular president of Ghana during the Busia administration.

[18] Personal communication with Kwesi Jonah, political scientist at the University of Ghana, Legon; *Africa Confidential* 2005 Vol. 46, No. 25, p. 3.

faction also capitalized on dissent from party activists who felt that they were not being rewarded for their effort to get the party into government. As a result, the Kufuor faction lost control of the top party positions to the Akufo-Addo faction in elections at the 2005 party congress (Kennedy 2009: 6).

Within the government, President Kufuor used his constitutional powers of appointment and control over parliamentarians to reward loyal supporters and punish his detractors. The president is able to co-opt parliamentarians through his powers to appoint ministers (of which the constitution requires that 50 percent come from members of Parliament) and to appoint persons to seats on boards of parastatals and boards related to government departments and agencies. Ministerial portfolios provide a 50 percent increase in salary and perks, and put parliamentarians in a better position to meet constituents' distributional demands. In 2003, President Kufuor appointed a total of eighty-three ministers, deputy ministers, ministers of state and regional ministers, as well as twenty-seven highly paid special assistants.[19] According to Staffan Lindberg (2009), in Kufuor's second term in office, 43 percent of NPP parliamentarians held a ministerial portfolio. There were also frequent reshuffles of ministerial portfolios during Kufuor's two terms in office.

The split between the Kufuor faction and the Akufo-Addo faction persisted throughout Kufuor's presidency and afterwards.[20] Kufuor's preferred candidate to win the NPP presidential nomination for the 2008 general election was Alan Kyerematen, a close friend and ally. Kyerematen founded the Young Executives Forum in 1992, along with other businessmen within the NPP.[21] The forum made financial contributions to the party for the 1992 and 1996 elections, and Kyerematen had been directly involved in Kufuor's campaigns to win the NPP presidential nomination in 1996 and 2000. Kufuor's preference for Kyerematen was perceived among NPP political elites as early as 2003 when Kufuor moved Kyerematen from US Ambassador to Minister of Trade and Industry, and charged him

19 *Africa Confidential* 2003 Vol. 44, No. 10, p. 2.

20 On these two factions, see Agyeman-Duah (2006) and Bob-Milliar and Bob-Milliar (2010).

21 Alan Kyerematen had been a senior corporate executive with Unilever Ghana, and also worked for a number of years as a consultant for a management consultancy firm.

with leading the President's Special Initiatives.[22] Kufuor supported Kyerematen's bid in 2007 for the presidential nomination in the 2008 general elections, which Kyerematen only barely lost to Akufo-Addo. This rivalry between Kufuor and Akufo-Addo over the future of the party is central to understanding Kyerematen's efforts at industrial policy while he was the Minister of Trade and Industry, especially with the President's Special Initiatives, and their poor implementation, as shown in Chapter 7.

The contest for the presidential nomination in 2007 included such a large number of candidates that no candidate received the required amount, and a run-off was required between the top two: Kyerematen and Akufo-Addo. Akufo-Addo was well in the lead, so Kyerematen withdrew in order to avoid a run-off, but then resigned from the party shortly afterwards, claiming harassment of his supporters contesting as candidates in the party's parliamentary primaries. He only rejoined the party after mediation from top NPP political elites. Thus, the party emerged from these primaries highly fractured.

In addition to the deep-seated split among the NPP political elite, there was a general fragmentation and lack of discipline within the higher levels of the party. For example, seventeen NPP politicians competed to be the party's 2008 presidential candidate. Eight of the candidates were senior ministers who had ministerial portfolios that they had to resign from in order to enter the contest. Not only does such a number of ministers relinquishing their post at the same time create a problem of governance. It also signals an absence of cohesiveness among leading members of the ruling coalition and an absence of internal party discipline.

Party Organization and Intraparty Competition in the NDC and NPP

By the 2000s, both the NDC and NPP held primaries in which parliamentary candidates were selected at the constituency level by party delegates. The primaries became contests based on money, where party members "bought" delegates and sometimes paid for

22 This point is based on informal conversations with several politically appointed technocrats in the Ministry of Trade and Industry, who were NPP members and close to Kyerematen.

the primaries themselves.[23] Party delegates were active in this process, demanding that primaries be held and increasing the payout in constituencies where its party was sure to win.[24] Furthermore, intra-elite factionalism also influenced the primaries. Party primaries included a formal process of vetting candidates by party executives, but the outcome was determined by informal power where elite factions jockeyed to get their favored candidates selected by disqualifying the other candidates. In cases where party candidates felt they lost the primary due to unfair intervention, they would stand as independent candidates and take their supporters along with them. This happened frequently, especially in seats considered "safe" for a particular party. Once in power, the independent candidates went back within the party fold.

Intraparty competition for the party's nomination also played out between incumbent MPs and district chief executives, who were the government-appointed political heads of the district assemblies. The office of the district chief executive provided fertile grounds for launching a bid to unseat incumbent MPs, because it controlled the local government and the District Assembly Common Fund, a transfer from the central government budget (Daddieh and Bob-Milliar 2012). In contrast, MPs had access to a much smaller common fund to be used to initiate development projects in their constituencies. In instances of rivalry between the district chief executive and MP from the same party, the two politicians undermined each other and used their funds on politically expedient projects.

In addition, lower-level factions wielded significant power within both parties. Members of Parliament could lose their seats if constituency party members felt that the incumbent MP did not deliver enough constituency-level "development" or enough for the lower-level party members. For example, in the NPP parliamentary primaries before the

23 This paragraph is based on the work of Daddieh and Bob-Milliar (2012) and Ichino and Nathan (2012).

24 For this reason, ahead of the NDC's party congress to select presidential and parliamentary candidates for the 2016 elections, the party decided to open the primary elections to all card bearing members, and not just delegates as in the past. This change was intended to reduce the role of vote-buying in the primary elections and to ensure the selection of candidates who are going to poll well in the national elections because they have the support of loyal NDC voters.

2004 elections, twenty incumbent members of Parliament, including ministers, lost renomination in the primaries.[25]

In addition to selecting party candidates, lower levels of the party machinery were strong because the higher levels depended on party activists, the so-called foot soldiers, to mobilize votes at election time.[26] Based on survey work, George Bob-Milliar (2012a) notes that foot soldiers are people who devote exceptional amounts of their time and energy to canvassing support and votes for a party and its candidates and to undermining the activities of the rival party. Foot soldiers had been crucial building blocks of political parties since decolonization, and they reemerged with the return to multiparty politics. They were mostly poorly educated and engaged in the informal sector, and they invested in party activism as a way to secure their livelihood: finding work through political patronage. They viewed political parties largely as vehicles for ambitious people to seek power and take control of resources located within the state, so if their party won, they expected to get "their share."

Given such a high level of competition among political elites, both within and across parties, what accounts for the relatively high degree of political stability of the Fourth Republic? The answer is that political elites across the NDC and NPP share social networks that straddle party affiliation as well as ethnic identity and have a high measure of trust in one another. Thus, while political elites are fragmented, leading to a high level of contestation within the political parties, they nonetheless constitute a socially united political class. Based on an analysis of political elites elected to Parliament in 2012, Anja Osei (2015) shows that a high level of interaction takes place among MPs across party lines both informally and formally through institutions such as the Inter-Party Advisory Committee. While the NPP has a larger percentage of MPs of Akan origin, ethnic cleavages are muted by the fact that MPs from the Akan ethnic group have a dense social network that straddles party lines. While Ga and Ewe networks dominate the NDC and are more excluded from NPP MP networks, Northerners are also fairly well integrated across party lines.

25 *Democracy Watch* 2004 Vol. 5, No. 2&3, pp. 10–11. *Democracy Watch* is a quarterly newsletter of the Ghana Center for Democratic Development.

26 *Democracy Watch* 2007 Vol. 7, No. 3, pp. 4–6.

Financing of the NDC and NPP

Securing the party's nomination for parliamentary or presidential candidate and then winning national elections became an increasingly expensive affair. Aspiring parliamentarian and presidential candidates spent large amounts of money in campaigning for primaries and national elections from their own pockets and from their financiers. There was neither a legal limit on the amount of donations that could be made to political parties (or politicians) nor on the amount of money that could be spent on elections.

For example, the NPP spent at least US$30 million on the 2004 elections and $100 million in the 2008 elections on advertising and entertaining supporters (Daddieh and Bob-Milliar 2012). Incumbent and aspiring presidential and parliamentary candidates spent a lot of money on campaigning (and allegedly vote-buying) within the NPP to get the party's nomination. To illustrate this point let us return to the example of the seventeen NPP members that ran for the party's presidential nomination in 2007. Each candidate paid a US$25,000 nomination fee. Accounts of campaigning ahead of this presidential primary indicate that "big" money was spent on campaigning around the country and giving "inducements" to constituency-level party members.[27] Rampant use of money by aspirant presidential and parliamentary candidates to buy off party functionaries increased divisions within the party organization and increased patron-client relations between "party big men" and lower-level party functionaries (Kennedy 2009: 7). After securing the party's nomination, candidates then ran expensive campaigns starting about a year before the national elections.

Constituency-level party organizations and parliamentary candidates depended on money received from the central party office to undertake campaign activities. Being a wealthy aspiring parliamentary or presidential candidate who could contribute to funding one's own campaign was a bonus for the individual and for the party. For this reason, the NDC party brokers opened the party to moneyed individuals in the 1990s in order to finance its political campaigns, and they

[27] At that time, NPP party rules were such that the identities of party delegates to the national congress were only revealed a few days before the congress. On campaign spending, see Bob-Milliar and Bob-Milliar (2010) and *Africa Confidential* 2007 Vol. 48, No. 24, p. 1.

favored parliamentary candidates aspiring to run on the NDC ticket who were wealthy and could contribute their own financing (Nugent 1999). Eboe Hutchful (2002: 225) refers to these party financiers as carpetbaggers. Some of the carpetbaggers were politicians in previous civilian governments who were opportunists or political entrepreneurs, "investing in politics" in order to benefit materially from political positions.

Party financiers became important in both the NDC and the NPP. George Bob-Milliar (2012a) describes these financiers as patron activists: party members who are not highly visible in the party but who contribute substantial funding and other logistics for the sustenance of the party. Patron activists see their activism as an investment, sponsoring candidates for party positions or national office and funding national and constituency campaigns in return for mostly private goods, such as a position as cabinet minister, regional minister or district chief executive, or by getting business contracts.

Individual politicians and party financiers expect to recoup their "investments" in political campaigns, if the candidate or party is successful. Recouping investments and refilling party coffers was typically done through kickbacks on state contracts and awarding state contracts to party members. For example, Richard Sandbrook (2000: 106, 114) notes that kickbacks on state contracts and awarding state contracts to party loyalists were an important source of financing the NDC in the 1990s. Illegal financial transactions were especially prominent in road building contracts, where false claims, overstated claims, and overpayment were said to have totaled US$ 30 million during the second term of the NDC government.[28] The NPP ruling elites followed a similar strategy of raising political financing, for the party and themselves, through kickbacks on state contracts and awarding state contracts to NPP-aligned businesses.[29] Politicians also found other ways to siphon state resources and direct them to party coffers, such as holding ministry workshops in hotels owned by party loyalists.

[28] This figure comes from the audit carried out by the NPP government, upon taking office in 2001, on payment claims presented by contractors to the Ministry of Finance between December 1996 and April 2001. *Africa Confidential* 2003 Vol. 44, No. 10, p. 2.

[29] *Democracy Watch* 2005 Vol. 6, No. 3&4, pp. 10–12. *Africa Confidential* 2005 Vol. 46, No. 25, p. 3.

A mainstay of NDC party funding in the 1990s was party members who exploited the provision of loans, grants, lucrative contracts, implicit exemptions from taxes and other incentives to enter business (Opoku 2010). Political interests of the party and the personal and business interests of key political elites were increasingly factored into policy decisions.[30] For example, Kwabena, Kwesi and Ato Ahwoi (the Ahwoi brothers) were part of a key faction within the P/NDC coalition.[31] Prior to entering politics through the PNDC, they were all civil servants with no business background. They started private businesses in the early 1990s through exploiting their close ties to the government. The most successful business was Cashpro. In 1992 when the internal marketing of cocoa was liberalized, Cashpro was one of the six firms granted a license to buy cocoa beans (licensed buying agent). These agents still had to sell to the Cocoa Board, but they received concessionary loans from the Cocoa Board for their operations. There is very little written about Cashpro. One of the few sources speculates that Cashpro may have operated as an affiliate of the NDC's rural political machine created at the end of the 1980s and relied on in the 1990s to win elections (Oelbaum 2002). *Africa Confidential* notes that Cashpro was the major financier of the NDC party and that, in the early 2000s, Cashpro owed millions of dollars in unpaid loan advances.[32]

Divestiture of medium and small state-owned enterprises in the 1990s was not only used by the NDC ruling elites to reward party loyalists, but also exploited by the top political elite for personal accumulation. It was a major avenue by which the party sought to create an independent economic base for itself. Darko Opoku's research into the Divestiture Implementation Council reveals that leading members of the 31st December Women's Movement and NDC political elite served on the board of the Divestiture Implementation

30 See Hutchful (2002) and Interview with Kwesi Botchwey.

31 Kwabena Ahwoi was minister of local government and rural development for much of the PNDC/NDC period. Kwesi Ahwoi was head of the Ghana Export Promotion Council from 1985 into the early 1990s. Ato Ahwoi was minister of trade and industry around 1985–1986, and also headed the National Investigation Committee and the Internal Revenue Service under the PNDC. This data comes from Aggrey-Darkoh, "Mapping Political Elite in Ghana"; see also Opoku (2010: 147–148).

32 *Africa Confidential* 2002 Vol. 43, No. 22, p. 5; *Africa Confidential* 2004 Vol. 45, No. 14, p. 7.

Council and ensured that state-owned enterprises that were sold to Ghanaians went to regime allies (Opoku 2010: 153–155). Opoku also finds that members of the council acquired public assets, made nominal deposits, and then had their debt defrayed by end-of-service benefits when they left the council (presumably with the change of government in 2001). Notably, Nana Konadu-Agyemang Rawlings used the 31st December Women's Movement as a personal vehicle for wealth accumulation, creating a subsidiary corporation of the movement called Caridem Corporation, through which she acquired several public enterprises. Financial reports of the Divestiture Implementation Committee indicate that Caridem Corporation acquired four public enterprises between 1994 and 1995.[33] However, none of these businesses functioned after being sold to Caridem. Some of them were bought for the real estate and infrastructure on the site. For the others, it seems that Caridem lacked the entrepreneurial and technological capabilities to turn them around, despite access to government-guaranteed loans.[34]

Caridem Corporation also benefited from a line of concessional credit (US$18 million) from China secured by the NDC government in 1995 (Tsikata et al. 2008). The credit was to promote joint ventures between Ghanaian and Chinese companies, and it was disbursed to three companies in gold mining, cocoa processing and fishing rope manufacture. An amount of US$8.75 million went to Calf International Cocoa, a cocoa-processing company that was a joint venture between Caridem Corporation and China International Cooperation Company for Agriculture, Livestock and Fisheries. By 2002, the cocoa-processing factory (costing US$6.9 million) was completed and equipment installed, but the then minister of finance (of the NPP government) refused to authorize the Eximbank to release the last tranche of money (US$1.8 million) on the grounds that it did not think Caridem could repay the loan. The project was also widely viewed as a vehicle to help finance election expenses for the NDC.

The NPP ruling elites equally were looking to benefit personally from their control of the state in terms of business opportunities. For example, the NPP government decided to create Ghana International

33 Divestiture Implementation Committee, financial reports, available at www.dic.com.gh.

34 Interview with the former Executive Secretary of the Divestiture Implementation Committee, July 8, 2011, Accra.

Airlines, a joint venture between the government and a US-based consortium, following the bankruptcy of the old national carrier Ghana Airways. Transactions establishing the company are unclear and involved negotiations with the Minister for Roads, but what is clear was that an NPP regional party chairman held a stake in the airline company through his US-based consultancy firm.[35]

Another example is the scandal over the stake in the Jubilee oil field held by the EO Group, a Ghanaian company headed by two NPP members close to President Kufuor that had no track record in the oil business.[36] EO group was credited with getting the US-based Kosmos Energy a stake in the Jubilee oil field, and in return Kosmos gave the EO Group a 3.5 percent equity stake in its operations (see Chapter 8). When Kosmos wanted to sell its stake in Jubilee oil block to ExxonMobil in 2009, the EO group stood to make US$300 million from the sale of their stake alongside the Kosmos-Exxon deal. Thus, the Mills-led NDC government at the time tried to prohibit the sale (Phillips et al. 2015). The investigations triggered a US Department of Justice investigation of Kosmos Energy, which cleared Kosmos and the EO Group but forced the EO Group to sell its shares to Tullow Oil. However, the NDC government made sure that the EO Group could only receive the proceeds of the sale after the 2012 elections, for fear that the company's profits would find their way into NPP election financing (Mohan and Asante 2015: 19). The EO Group sold its 3.5 percent stake in the Jubilee field to Tullow Oil for an estimated US$305 million: US$100 million in cash and US$205 million in Tullow shares.

Electoral Strategies of the Political Parties

Both the NDC and the NPP have core voters, including foot soldiers and financiers, but as constituency elections in most regions became increasingly close contests, parliamentary candidates needed to garner more and more support from floating voters, also called swing voters (Lindberg and Morrison 2005, 2008). Swing voters are citizens who

35 *Africa Confidential* 2006 Vol. 47, No. 9, p. 8; *Democracy Watch* 2006 Vol. 7, No. 1, pp. 1–2.

36 *Africa Confidential* 2009 Vol. 50, No. 21, p. 3; "Ghana: First Act, Long Drama," Patrick Smith, *The Africa Report* No. 25, October–November 2010, pp. 22 & 24; *Financial Times*, January 8, 2010.

are not solidly committed to one party and whose vote can be influenced by the electoral strategies of individual politicians or the incumbent party's performance in government. Swing voters switch from one party to another and effectively decide the outcome of elections. The percentage of swing voters in Ghana in the early 2000s was estimated at 18 percent by Lindberg and Morrison (2005), but between 20 to 40 percent by the Ghanaian pollster Ben Ephson.[37] At the end of the 2000s, the percentage of swing voters was estimated to be even higher, between 44 and 53 percent of citizens, according to the survey carried out by Keith Weghorst and Staffan Lindberg (2013).

As a result of the core/swing voter dynamic, some regions have been strongholds for the NDC or NPP, while others are swing regions. Strongholds contain a large number of core voters for one of the two parties and thus there is not much competition between parties. However, there is a high degree of intraparty competition at the party primaries, as these are effectively safe seats (Ichino and Nathan 2012). The strongholds for the NPP have been the Ashanti and Eastern regions – home to the Ashanti and Akyem (subgroups of the Akan ethnic group) who are linked to cocoa production and to the tradition of Danquah-Busia. The NDC strongholds have been the Volta Region as well as the three northern regions: Northern, Upper West, and Upper East. However, the NPP increased its competitiveness in these regions during the 2000s, especially in the Northern Region (Whitfield 2009).

Weghorst and Lindberg (2013) developed a measure of the swing voter, showing that voters vary in the degree to which they can be persuaded as well as in what persuades them, and applied this to survey data from Ghana taken before the 2008 elections. Their analysis shows that some swing voters can be persuaded by individual personal benefits, whereas others are less persuaded by that kind of political clientelism but rather are concerned with the provision of "development" in their community, the performance of parliamentarians in lawmaking, and/or the economic performance of the party in power as judged by the effects on the everyday livelihoods of the voter. Lindberg's further analysis of the same survey data showed that citizens interviewed expected parliamentary candidates to provide personal gifts and favors as well as community development goods such as schools, health clinics, and boreholes, but that that the provision of

[37] Ben Ephson, Countdown to 2008 Elections, Allied News Ltd, Accra, 2008.

such clientelism did not necessarily influence their vote. (Lindberg 2013). Rather, voting patterns were better explained by citizens' evaluations of how the economy and government policies affected their livelihoods.

The multiple expectations placed on parliamentarian candidates to deliver individual, community and national goods and services that improve livelihoods within a four-year time period shaped the political survival strategies of individual MPs and the party as a whole. The work of Staffan Lindberg (2010) among parliamentarians shows that incumbent MPs from both parties pursued a mixed strategy of providing private goods and building patron-client relationships with loyal voters as well as providing community or constituency-level goods and some national public goods. Getting a high position in government offered better opportunities for MPs to deliver to their constituencies. MPs without a ministerial position resorted to lobbying ministries, departments and agencies for development projects in their constituencies, but they also provided such projects through the MP's share of the local government budget or their personal funds. In competitive constituencies, MPs faced greater pressure to provide private and club goods (Lindberg 2010). The result was an intense politicization among ruling elites over the allocation of resources and political interference in the implementation of government programs.

In addition, core voters, especially party foot soldiers, put pressure on the ruling party to use state resources and official positions to meet their distributional demands. For example, NPP foot soldiers voiced persistent complaints that the Kufuor administration "neglected to look after them" in terms of providing employment opportunities, and in his second term, President Kufuor promised to do more for them.[38] The NPP government introduced the National Youth Employment Scheme in 2005 officially as a means to address chronic unemployment, but in practice it was used to reward party foot soldiers. The scheme was highly politicized, with the recruitment of personnel, operations and management along party lines. The same situation occurred with the Microfinance and Small Loans Centre (MASLOC), established by the NPP government in 2006. Some

[38] See the evidence presented in Bob-Milliar (2012a); *Democracy Watch* 2006 Vol. 7, No. 2, p. 1; *Africa Confidential* 2006 Vol. 47, No. 25, p. 3 and Vol. 48, No. 15, p. 2.

evidence points to positive effects on the livelihoods of loan beneficiaries, but also a loan default rate of over 90 percent. Such a default rate undermines the very purpose of the credit and loan scheme, as Aryeetey and Owoo (2015: 12) point out. It also indicates the political purpose of the Centre: loans were a reward for NPP activists and thus not to be repaid. Notably, the NDC government that came to power in January 2009 maintained the National Youth Employment Scheme, apparently replacing NPP activists with NDC activists.

Combined, swing voters and core voters place large distributional demands on incumbent politicians, and high interparty competition puts heavy pressure on ruling elites to deliver. The combination of these factors produced incentives for ruling elites across both parties to pursue politically expedient public spending. For individual political survival, this spending included providing private and collective goods to members of their personal political networks as well as securing the allocation of state amenities for their electoral constituencies to influence floating voters. For the survival of the party, ruling elites pursued initiatives that could deliver immediate visible benefits to a large section of the population. These political survival strategies resulted in ruling elites prioritizing policies and expenditures with large distributional effects, while productivity-enhancing measures were pushed to the bottom of the agenda or warped in their implementation in order to meet distributional needs. In addition, high interparty competition means that ruling elites avoided implementing policies that had immediate negative effects on large sections of the population, although they had longer term benefits for them and the economy as a whole, because of the high short-term political costs.

Political Influence of Domestic Capitalists, or the Lack of It

The PNDC elite, including the economic reform team leaders, did not involve the business associations in the formulation and implementation of the structural adjustment reforms. As noted above, this was largely because they perceived domestic capitalists to be aligned with the excluded political elites, especially in the Danquah-Busia political tradition. However, internal problems within the two main business associations contributed to their political marginalization.[39]

[39] This paragraph is based on Hart and Gyimah-Boadi (2000), Opoku (2010) and Kraus (1991, 2002).

Before the economic reforms, these associations were oriented towards operating in a regulated economic environment, and their main function had become negotiating with the government for individual permits and import licenses for its members. With the economic reforms, this function was no longer required. Import liberalization not only led to many manufacturing firms going into debt or collapsing, and thus reducing the resource base of the associations, but equally important, it led to the irrelevance of the associations because they no longer provided direct benefits for members. These associations found it difficult to shift to a new role in the changed economic environment. The associations lacked the organizational capacity to marshal information, formulate proposals on the speed and direction of reform, and argue economics with government officials whose key relationship was with the World Bank and IMF. Lastly, the industrialists and the commercial importers disagreed over some policy issues, notably the optimal degree of trade liberalization. The Ghana Chamber of Mines was the only business association that had good access to government to resolve sector problems, which reflected the resurgence of gold as a key export. The Chamber of Mines, led by Ashanti Goldfields, played an influential role in designing the 1986 Minerals and Mining Act, which gave mining companies major benefits.

Under the Fourth Republic, domestic capitalists continued to lack a collective influence on economic policymaking. Firms in productive sectors who suffered the most from macroeconomic instability did not act as a brake to deter macroeconomic crises, nor did they exert a counteracting influence on the incentives facing ruling elites. They were too small in number, had a relatively low level of technological capabilities, and typically struggled to form strong industry associations that would speak with one voice and lobby the government, as shown in Chapters 5 and 6. Domestic capitalists also continued to have a limited role in the key economic sectors – gold and cocoa – and the sectors in which their businesses resided were not yet big enough to leverage political influence, because they did not provide a significant amount of foreign exchange, government revenues, or employment. Furthermore, the high level of elite fragmentation within the political parties made it even more difficult for domestic capitalists to exert political influence over policymaking, when this was difficult for ruling political elites to do themselves.

In the 1990s, the NDC government remained antagonistic to the large domestic capitalists, as the PNDC government had been. Jon Kraus (2002) argues that the NDC government showed a clear preference for multinational corporations over Ghanaian capital. The transition to constitutional rule made it harder for Rawlings and the NDC political elites to get away with harassing businessmen aligned with the political opposition. Democratic institutions and new private media gradually led to changes in business-state relations in terms of restricting the arbitrary actions of the government. However, only one member of the NDC political elite had a background in business prior to taking government office, which unsurprisingly was in a parastatal. He had also been a key technopol during the PNDC period, and tried to forge links with business and promote business interests, but he lost influence during the shift in power within the P/NDC from the technopols to the party brokers and was politically marginalized by the end of the first NDC administration.[40]

President Rawlings continued to run the government in personal ways when he could. Connections to Rawlings mattered, and falling out with him was (potentially) dangerous. Businessmen who were close to Rawlings and rejected his political advances to be part of the NDC and finance the party were also persecuted. In one case, Rawlings even put his political agenda before the health of one of the pillars of Ghana's economy, gold mining, as evidenced in the relationship between Rawlings and Sam Jonah, the top manager of Ashanti Goldfields, the biggest gold mining company. Rawlings appointed Jonah, a Ghanaian national, to the position in 1982, when the government had a controlling 55 percent ownership of the company. Ayowa Afrifa Taylor (2006) attributes the revival of Ashanti Goldfields in the 1980s and early 1990s to the support that Rawlings gave to assist the company with accessing credit through the International Finance Corporation (the commercial wing of the World Bank), industrial relations, flotation of company shares on the Ghana and London stock exchanges, and multinational expansion. However, the relationship soured when Rawlings wanted Jonah to be his vice presidential candidate in the 1996 elections and Jonah declined, and when Jonah

[40] This point draws on Eboe Hutchful's analysis of the P/NDC elite (Hutchful 2002: 144, 223).

declined to provide financial backing for the NDC because he wanted to "stay out of politics." When the company hit a financial crisis in 1999, Rawlings tried to use the opportunity to remove Jonah, which prolonged the crisis and reduced the fortunes of the company.[41] According to Antoinette Handley (2008: 193), as Jonah's national and international status grew, Rawlings and some of the P/NDC political elites saw him as a political threat. Jonah did not have political influence because he was the Managing Director of Ashanti Goldfields, a major mining company, but rather because of his relations with J.J. Rawlings and Nana Konadu-Agyemang Rawlings. When he fell out with both of them, his political influence was reduced.

Given the lack of close relations between the NDC political elites and domestic capitalists, business associations had some influence on economic policies such as customs operations, the privatization process, and investment codes, but had little influence on government fiscal and monetary policies (Kraus 2002). The World Bank and the United States Agency for International Development pushed the NDC government into dialogue with business associations as a condition for aid, so the government set up several business-state consultative forums, but they were more for show to the donors. The NDC ruling elite focused on keeping the political opposition out of business, rather than building connections with productive entrepreneurs. As Elizabeth Hart and Emmanuel Gyimah-Boadi (2000: 22) observed at the end of the 1990s:

> The logic of competitive politics in the nineties has had the short-term effect of exacerbating the poor relations between the Rawlings government and key elements of the domestic private sector. In the politically expedient quest to disadvantage or at least not advantage its opponents, the government appears to have little or no incentive to be consultative with a domestic private sector that is also widely perceived to be the home of many opposition stalwarts. CIBA [Council of Indigenous Business Associations] and other associations that could be organized into a neo-corporatist network provide a more politically acceptable mode of engagement between the Rawlings government and the domestic private sector.

Business participation and input into policymaking were not institutionalized, but rather depended on personal relationships between business representatives and particular government officials, which

[41] See also *Africa Confidential* Vol. 40, No. 24, p. 3.

ended when the individual left office or was moved from that official position.

Furthermore, NDC government officials viewed the policy positions taken by business with contempt, especially calls for certain forms of assistance to indigenous business. On their part, business association leaders could not advance a coherent argument for such assistance beyond simple references to the success story of East Asian countries (Opoku 2010: 131–34). At the same time, the World Bank pushed the government to pursue policies that were detrimental to the interests of businesses and that were often in opposition to what the business associations advocated, especially in manufacturing for the domestic market, as discussed in Chapter 4. Ironically, the World Bank and the US aid agency did not seem to consult businesses substantially on the content and design of their aid projects.

The NDC political elite did court the support of small local businessmen who could contribute to party financing at the regional and district levels. Darko Opoku (2010) finds in his research on prominent businessmen in the Brong Ahafo Region that the relationship between the NDC and business was one of reciprocal needs and provision of favors. For the ruling party, business offered donations that funded its activities, especially election campaigns, and in return these businessmen were given offers and inducements. Those who refused to "play the game" could be harassed and their businesses declined. Well-placed local NDC functionaries used their positions to enter business themselves or assisted their friends and family to do so. District chief executives were key players in the NDC ruling coalition, since they owed their position to presidential appointments. These executives controlled the allocation of district funds, especially construction and procurement contracts to local businessmen. The loyalty of local businessmen to the NDC party (usually through donations) resulted in contracts, acquisition of state-owned enterprises, and not being harassed. However, many businessmen were tactical: publicly supporting the NDC and covertly cultivating ties with the NPP or seeking other strategies, so that in case the NDC lost the next elections their business would not suffer under the NPP (i.e. because they were seen as too closely aligned with the NDC). The exceptions to this tactic were a minority of entrepreneurs whose antagonistic relationship with the NDC was irreparable, and a small group whose closeness to the NDC precluded a relationship with the NPP.

In the 2000s under the first NPP government, many Ghanaians in the diaspora returned to Ghana, private sector investment increased, and property rights were more secure relative to the previous period (Killick 2010: 455–463). The exit of Rawlings from the presidency increased the confidence of entrepreneurs to invest in the economy, and the NPP government declared it would usher in a Golden Age of Business. However, in many ways, relations between NPP ruling elites and domestic entrepreneurs were quite similar to what occurred during the NDC government. This point can be made by looking at several aspects of business-state relations that were key features of the NDC period.

The NPP government favored businesses aligned with its party and discriminated against businesses clearly aligned with the NDC or owned by the NDC political elite (Killick 2008). The NPP created new companies to bid for government contracts, and also canceled existing procurement arrangements in order to give contracts to NPP-aligned businesses. Consultancy contracts became a new highly profitable economic opportunity in the 2000s, as donor agencies and the government increasingly contracted out policy work to local consultants or required that foreign consultancy firms find local partners. The use of local consultancy firms by government ministries, departments and agencies became a new source of patronage for government ministers.[42]

Furthermore, domestic capitalists continued to have little influence on economic and sector-specific policies and implementation during the NPP government, despite the creation of a Ministry for Private Sector Development. President Kufuor created the Ministry for Private Sector Development as a means to ensure that the various institutions of government supported the development and growth of the private sector. The flagship initiative of the ministry was the private sector development strategy, launched in 2004. The strategy and the new ministry became a focal point for donors, but was soon subsumed in intradonor conflicts, while the NPP politician in charge of the ministry sought to benefit personally from his ministerial position.[43]

42 Based on the author's observations in the Ministry of Trade and Industry and the Ministry for Private Sector Development.

43 On the donor conflicts, see the detailed discussion in Whitfield and Jones (2009: 201–202). The Minister for Private Sector Development, Kwamena Bartels, was accused of corruption in the Ghanaian media. See "Kwamena Bartels Exposed

By 2006, the Ministry for Private Sector Development was integrated into the Ministry of Trade and Industry during a ministerial reshuffle, indicating its loss of importance, and the private sector development strategy failed to achieve much for domestic capitalists. President Kufuor also created the Ghana Investor Advisory Council composed of prominent businessmen to advise him and to hold government ministers to account and to serve as a tripartite institution for dialogue between the government, donors and the private sector in relation to the private sector development strategy. However, the council ceased to function in 2006.[44]

Sector-specific industry associations involved in the horticulture and palm oil industry case studies did not have more political influence with the NPP government than they had had with the previous NDC government. This was true despite the fact that the chairman of the Ghana Oil Palm Development Association, who owned Juaben Oil Mills, was a high level NPP member. The case study on the President's Special Initiative (PSI) in Oil Palm in Chapter 7 shows that not even the owner of Juaben Oil Mills could wield significant influence over the PSI in Oil Palm, as a result of elite fragmentation within the ruling coalition and political imperative to use the initiative to meet political survival objectives through state-controlled industrial policy. In short, individual capitalists that were networked into the NPP ruling coalition could access benefits, but more organized business-state collaboration to benefit particular industries as a whole was not evident during the Kufuor administration.

Conclusion

The incentives stemming from high *interparty* competition led ruling elites to prioritize projects that benefited a large number of citizens and to dampen the negative effects of economic conditions through subsidies, as well as to target the distribution of goods, services, jobs and public appointments to their electoral constituencies and to their core

Again," www.ghanaweb.com, October 11, 2007; "How Bartels Sprinkled 4 Billion Cedis," www.ghanaweb.com, October 8, 2007.

44 External Evaluation of the Private Sector Development Strategy, final draft, 2008, prepared by a team of international and Ghanaian consultants, for the Ministry of Trade and Industry and donors in the Private Sector Development Working Group.

political supporters and financiers. High *intraparty* competition led to politicization within the party over the allocation of resources to ministries, projects and geographical places in the country, as elites vied for a distribution that not only benefited the party as a whole but more importantly their electoral prospects individually. Within both the NDC and NPP, there was not one group of political elites at the apex with control over the party organization. Politicians – MPs and most ministers – owed their positions not to political elites at the top of the party organization but rather to constituency level party delegates and their own political financiers. There was little glue uniting political elites within each political party, and competition among them for top offices was rife. This meant that when a party won an election and became the ruling coalition, many people had to be accommodated and "rewarded" through political appointments and rent-seeking. As a result, rent creation and management was decentralized within the government, as no particular group of ruling political elites was able to exert control over these processes.

The composition of political coalitions, the strategies political elites pursued to gain and maintain their positions in government and the incentives for policy choices and expenditures generated by these political survival strategies produced a tough landscape within which domestic capitalists had to try to influence economic policies and their implementation. Elite fragmentation made it difficult for ruling elites to exert control over policy processes, which meant that it would be even more difficult for domestic capitalists to do so. The situation was further exacerbated by the low technological capabilities of domestic capitalists. Most businesses were concentrated in sectors that were either non-productive such as importing, real estate, hotels and consultancy, or dependent on state contracts such as construction. Domestic capitalists with investments in productive sectors were small in number, had relatively low technological capabilities, and faced collective action problems in organizing strong industry associations.

The next chapter details the economic policies pursued by the PNDC government and then the NDC and NPP governments in the 1990s and 2000s, and shows how they were linked to the incentive structures generated under the exceptional moment of the PNDC government as well as the return to competitive clientelism under the Fourth Republic. As shown in this chapter, the PNDC government faced reduced pressures to pursue distributive expenditures as a political survival strategy, which allowed the PNDC elites to pursue economic reforms. However, their antagonistic relations with domestic capitalists and their dependence on the World Bank and IMF to finance the economic reforms shaped the exact nature of the kind of economic reforms pursued by the PNDC government, as well as the impacts of those reforms in terms of economic transformation. In short, the reforms revived the colonial trading economy, with all its weaknesses. These weaknesses were not resolved under the subsequent NDC and NPP governments, as the pressures to focus on distributive expenditures reemerged, as well as the tendency to pursue statist approaches to developing productive sectors. The next chapter presents trends in economic performance, supporting the argument that the Ghanaian economy remains a colonial trading economy. It also provides an overview of the economic policies pursued by the NDC and NPP governments and their limited impacts on catalyzing economic transformation.

4 *Economic Growth, But Return to the Colonial Trading Economy*

The PNDC elites' strategic alliance with World Bank and IMF staff as part of its political survival strategy helped to implement the economic reforms desperately needed, but this alliance partly explains why the economic reforms resulted in the return of the colonial trading economic structure. This chapter shows that the strict pro-market stance of IMF and World Bank staff at that time meant that economic liberalization reforms did not take into account specific measures to help domestic capitalists survive liberalization. The World Bank and IMF were driven by neoclassical economic ideas and by quick wins for stabilizing the balance of payments and ensuring that their loans were paid back. For their part, the PNDC elites were not particularly interested in supporting domestic capitalists, but rather they were focused on reviving the fiscal basis of the state by rehabilitating the gold and cocoa export sectors. Furthermore, the state could guide and control the revival of these sectors due to its extensive role in them. The state-owned cocoa marketing board organized the internal and external marketing of cocoa beans, which were produced predominantly by smallholder farmers, while state-owned enterprises dominated the gold sector.

Subsequent NDC and NPP governments in the 1990s and 2000s continued to prioritize the cocoa and gold export sectors. For cocoa, the focus was on increasing exports through higher producer prices and direct support to cocoa producers. For gold, the strategy was to sell the majority of government shares in mining companies to foreign investors but to keep a minority stake. Together these sectors continued to provide the majority of foreign exchange, and cocoa was a major source of rural incomes in the southern part of the country while mining companies became the largest formal sector employers and taxpayers. In contrast, the agricultural and manufacturing sectors were subject to more ideologically brazen liberalization policies pursued by donors, especially the World Bank. This chapter describes the major policies and their economic outcomes in the gold and cocoa sectors, as well as for agriculture and manufacturing generally. While the cocoa and gold sector policies succeeded in rehabilitating and expanding those sectors, government policies aimed at increasing agricultural productivity and spurring manufacturing had limited effects. Agriculture and manufacturing growth rates tailed off in the 1990s, and the service sector became the largest sector in Ghana's economy from the mid-2000s.

As a result, the country's economy remained narrow, shallow and thin. The NDC and NPP governments continued to depend on a small basket of primary commodity exports that were not consumed domestically and were vulnerable to fluctuating global demand and volatile world market prices, and it depended on imports because little of what was imported could be produced domestically, people preferred imported brands and there was great instability in domestic food production. Governments had a very narrow fiscal space for capital expenditures. The final part of the chapter connects the structure of the colonial trading economy to the recurrent macroeconomic instability after the return to multiparty elections and the reemergence of competitive clientelism.

The PNDC Government and Structural Adjustment Reforms

The PNDC elites received what Eboe Hutchful (2002) calls policy rents from the IMF and World Bank, in which the latter provided foreign exchange and effectively financed the state in return for influence on policy content. The PNDC elites prioritized policy measures that resulted in fiscal gains for the state through reviving the cocoa and gold industries, and through divestiture of state-owned enterprises. The World Bank and IMF staff focused on static efficiency.[1] Their prescribed policies assumed that the way to support production was simply to get the state out of the economy and production would happen: get the prices and incentives right, and the supply side would respond positively. The World Bank and IMF promoted the country's traditional export sectors as a way to increase foreign exchange and address the balance of payments problem immediately. Thus, the

[1] Static efficiency is concerned with the most efficient combination of resources at a given point in time.

interests of the Bretton Woods institutions and the PNDC elites dovetailed on the cocoa and gold industries, and neither side advocated supporting domestic capitalists to become more competitive in the new liberalized environment.

Sector-specific programs in cocoa and gold mining were implemented vigorously, and state institutions in charge of these sectors were revived and improved. The mining sector reforms between 1986 and 1991 focused on rehabilitating the mines in order to increase their worth and thus attract foreign investment and reduce state ownership (Twerefou et al. 2007). The PNDC government facilitated and guaranteed loans from bilateral and multilateral donors for some mines, such as Ashanti Goldfields. For other mines, the government gave management contracts to foreign companies to improve their efficiency. The Mineral Commission was established, and the capacities of other government institutions dealing with the sector were increased. Lastly, the government promulgated new laws that provided generous tax cuts and allowed the retention of a significant portion of foreign exchange earnings in offshore accounts.

Reforms aimed at revitalizing the cocoa industry included increasing the price paid to cocoa producers by reducing the operating costs of the state-run Cocoa Marketing Board (Williams 2009). The staff and operating costs of the Cocoa Board were drastically reduced partly through the divestment of nonessential activities, such as running plantations and building roads, but also through retrenchments and eliminating "ghost" workers. A collaborative price-setting process was established whereby the Producer Price Review Committee became responsible for determining the division of cocoa revenues between the farmers and the Cocoa Board. As part of the reforms, farmers were compensated for replanting trees infected with disease and encouraged to replant with high-yielding cocoa tree varieties developed by the Cocoa Research Institute (Kolavalli and Vigneri 2011). By the mid-1990s, cocoa production had rebounded, productivity had increased, and the Cocoa Board had become a profitable state-owned enterprise.

The PNDC government was willing and able to implement these reforms in the cocoa industry because the cocoa export sector was key to revitalizing the economy and to rebuilding the finances of the state, and because the cocoa sector was largely organized by the state. There was also little opposition from the main losers within the Cocoa

Board because retrenched workers were given severance packages that were financed by foreign aid (Williams 2009: 29). Severance packages were expensive and became a major reason why divestiture of state-owned enterprises was slow to start in the late 1980s and early 1990s. It cost the government more to pay retrenched workers than it might receive from the divestiture, but without generous severance packages, there would be labor unrest (Tangri 1999: 52).

The World Bank and IMF pressured the PNDC government to liberalize the internal and external marketing of cocoa. The PNDC technopols held out for many years, but in the run-up to negotiating a World Bank agricultural sector credit in 1990, the technopols gave a concession and agreed to liberalize the internal marketing and allow private buyers to compete with the state-owned Produce Buying Company (Hutchful 2002: 69). Licensed buying companies were registered in 1991 and began operating in the 1992–1993 cocoa season. To "level the playing field" for private buyers, the number of buying centers of the Cocoa Board were reduced by one-third and extension centers were reduced by two-thirds. All remaining subsidies on cocoa inputs were eliminated, beginning with the 1991 season. Nevertheless, the Produce Buying Company continued to dominate internal purchasing of cocoa beans, due to its size, expertise, ability to access credit, and presence throughout the country. Notably, the PNDC technopols held out on privatizing the Produce Buying Company and liberalizing export marketing. The technopols negotiated hard on the cocoa industry because they wanted to retain state control, and technocrats in the Cocoa Board believed that centralized authority and coordination were necessary to achieve a high quality and high volume of cocoa bean exports (Williams 2009).

The PNDC government's role in the cocoa industry reforms stands in contrast to its actions regarding agricultural policy more generally. The general agricultural framework in the 1980s and the early 1990s focused on eliminating direct state support, such as farm input subsidies and guaranteed minimum prices for foodstuff and industrial crops, liberalizing input supply and domestic marketing, and phasing out state-owned enterprises (Nyanteng and Seini 2000). From around 1986, the PNDC government's agricultural policies were determined through negotiations on projects with the World Bank and a few other donors, because agricultural financing was heavily dependent on the World Bank.

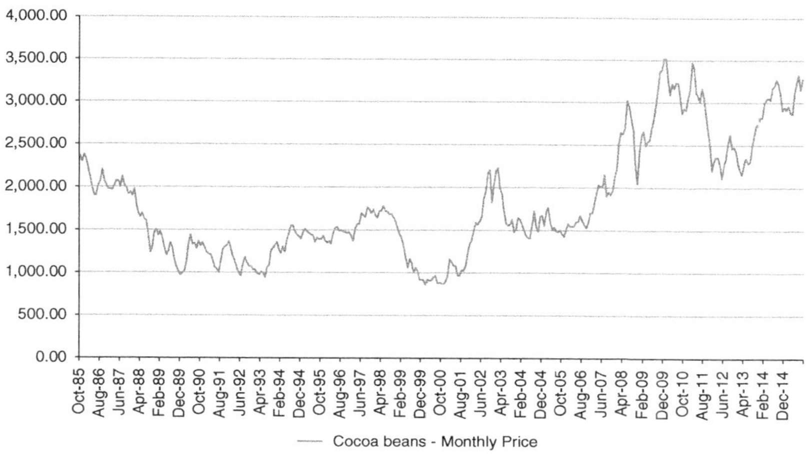

Figure 4.1 World Cocoa Price (US$ per metric ton), 1985–2015
Source: ICCO for Cocoa, quoted by way of Index Mundi: www.indexmundi.com/commodities/?commodity=cocoa-beans&months=240
Note: Cocoa beans, International Cocoa Organization cash price, CIF US and European ports, US$ per metric ton.

Declining world cocoa prices in the 1980s and their stagnation in the early 1990s, as shown in Figure 4.1, meant that reliance on cocoa was a vulnerable strategy. Nevertheless, there were no substantial targeted reforms to build up nontraditional exports or import-substituting industries to relieve the pressure on the balance of payments. There were disagreements within the PNDC economic team, and between the team and World Bank and IMF staff. Some of the PNDC technopols challenged the short-term orientation towards macroeconomic stabilization measures and the neglect of longer-term structural issues related to production that ultimately caused the balance of payments problems (Hutchful 2002: 154). It seems that the technopols who wanted to directly address some of these structural issues related to production lost out in these negotiations, but also that the PNDC team did not have any new ideas about how to promote production, and there does not seem to have been an inflow of foreign ideas or models to pit against the World Bank and IMF technocrats (Herbst 1993).

Some academic observers shared the view of the PNDC elites and World Bank staff that economic policy should focus on cocoa exports as a means to revive the economy, due to the obvious potential and existing expertise in the country. The following comment by Cord Jacobeit is instructive in this respect:

> While in the long run there appears to be a need to diversify into other nontraditional exports, a short run alternative to cocoa is not available. Every attempt to start anything else in the immediate future would be met by almost equal uncertainties and would also require substantial initial funding to get started. Flowers, tropical fruits, and fresh vegetables for the markets in the European Community, for example, require an infrastructure – reliable communication networks, cold storage depots, constant airlinks, etc. (Jacobeit 1991: 229).

One can find little support or advice within the PNDC ruling coalition or among its coterie of foreign advisors for focusing resources and efforts on developing nontraditional exports, or import-substituting agro-processing for that matter. The World Bank Agricultural Diversification project loan, which began in 1991, was the only government-implemented initiative in agricultural diversification in the 1990s. It targeted four agro-industries – coffee, rubber, oil palm and horticulture export – but the activities it supported were small and piecemeal. Horticulture as a nontraditional crop was only included in light of success in the horticultural sector spurred by a one-off initiative from the Ministry of Trade and Industry, as discussed in Chapter 5.

Maintaining the Colonial Trading Economy

The structural adjustment reforms succeeded in reviving the cocoa and gold industries, but they also had the effect of returning to the colonial trading economic structure. Gold and cocoa remained the leading exports, moving from half of the value of total exports to accounting for two-thirds of the value of total exports by the end of the 2000s, as shown in Figure 4.2. The dramatic rise in export value from 2011 in the figure marks the start of oil exports.

After subtracting cocoa, gold and timber (the three traditional export sectors) from total exports in the 1990s and 2000s, the remainder was composed of a large number of different goods, primarily agriculture-based. New products entered and exited the list of top ten exports with varying export shares. Products showing strong performance included fish, veneers and plywood, fruits and nuts, ores and concentrates of base metals, and aluminum. For example, horticulture

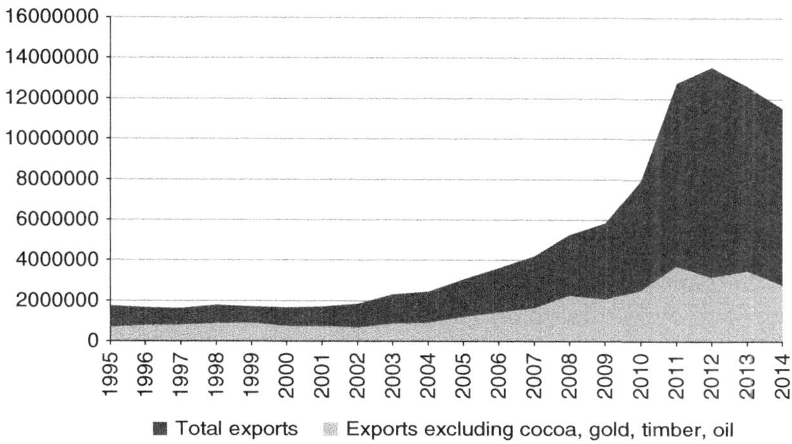

Figure 4.2 Total Exports and Total Non-Traditional Exports (thousand US$), 1995–2014

Source: Created using data on exports from the UNCTAD database, which provides disaggregated data by type of export. Nontraditional export figures were calculated by omitting cocoa (072), gold (971), wood (247, 248 and 246), and crude petroleum oil (333 and 334) from the total exports data.

grew significantly as a nontraditional export, but even then total horticulture exports, including all kinds of fruits and vegetables, were a small percentage of overall nontraditional exports. Furthermore, John Sutton and Bennet Kpentey (2012: 3) note that twenty-seven firms accounted for 62 percent of Ghana's exports by 2010, indicating the concentration of economic activity among a small number of firms.

The structure of Ghana's economy had changed by the close of 2010, due to the growth of the service sector and the advent of oil production and export. However, it had not made much progress in terms of economic transformation: increasing agricultural productivity; diversifying exports and increasing higher value exports; increasing manufacturing and knowledge-based services that rely more on knowledge-based assets to generate wealth than natural resources; and increasing the percentage of domestic firms and farms that have higher technological capabilities. The economic sectors that grew the fastest in the 2000s were construction; transport, storage and communications; and wholesale, retail, hotels and restaurants. Mining and utilities also grew relatively fast, while agricultural growth was much lower and manufacturing was the slowest growing sector.

The growth acceleration from the mid-2000s, shown in Figure 1.1, was driven by increased prices and production of cocoa and gold, and later oil exports. These drivers of growth are reflected in the spatial trends of poverty reduction and rising incomes, which occurred mostly in urban areas and largely linked to employment in services as well as in the rural forest area linked to the cocoa export sector. The percentage of the population below the poverty line (calculated by the Ghana Statistical Service based on a consumption basket) declined from 51.7 percent in 1990 to 24.2 percent in 2013, with about a quarter of Ghanaians considered "poor" in 2012/2013 and just under a tenth of the population in extreme poverty. While Ghana has met the Millennium Development Goal of halving poverty, the poverty reduction gains are highly vulnerable, as they depend on public services and the volatile international prices of agricultural and natural resource commodities.

Attracting Foreign Direct Investment in the Gold Mining Sector

The NDC and NPP governments continued to emphasize the mining sector as a key source of foreign exchange and government revenue. Foreign direct investment was key to the expansion of the gold sector from the 1990s onwards, as the NDC government sought to reduce state ownership in the sector through selling government shares in companies or awarding management contracts to foreign companies with the option to buy the company at the end of the contract (Twerefou et al. 2007). An estimated 70 percent of total foreign direct investment inflows between 1990 and 2006 went into mining, predominantly gold (Barthel, Busse and Osei 2008). In 2013, over 50 percent of foreign direct investment was still related to the mining sector.[2]

By 2013, the large-scale gold mining industry was mostly foreign-owned and accounted for 65 percent of gold production, while the

[2] "Mining in Ghana – What Future Can We Expect?," July 2015, Report of the Mining: Partnerships for Development, Ghana Chamber of Mines and the International Council on Mining and Metals, p. 5.

small-scale mining sector was reserved for Ghanaians and accounted for 35 percent of total gold production. The state maintained a minority 10 percent stake (free carried interest) in most of the active large-scale mining operations, with some exceptions, as shown in Table 4.1. Strong growth in the mining sector in the 1990s was largely due to the doubling of gold production associated with Ashanti Goldfields and heavy investments in that company after the government sold most of its shares in 1994–1995 (Leite et al. 2000: 16).

The mining sector contributed 37 percent of export revenues and 19 percent of all direct tax payments, making it the largest taxpaying sector in the economy. Exports grew by more than 400 percent between 2005 and 2012, partly due to the rising world market price for gold during this period, as shown in Figure 4.3. Royalties constituted 4 to 6 percent of total direct tax revenue, and corporate income tax constituted between 5 and 16 percent during the period 2005 to 2013.[3]

However, the gold mining sector had few forward and backward linkages with the rest of the economy. The main linkages occurred through wages, social investments and supplier expenditures. A study of seven out of the eleven main mining companies published in 2015 found that 25 percent of mining companies' total expenditures remained in the country, of which half was spent on local procurement and the other half on wages and payments to government.[4] However, the linkage through local procurement was diminished by the fact that 20 percent of expenditures on local procurement was lost to the Ghanaian economy due to subsequent imports by direct and indirect suppliers. Large-scale mining is highly capital-intensive and thus created little direct employment. The same study found that the seven mining companies together employed about 7,000 people. Projections from 2014 onwards showed gold production among the large-scale mines declining as a result of lower gold prices, but also due to the lifecycle stage of the mines.

The PNDC government legalized small-scale mining in 1989, allowing individuals to have licenses to mine small concessions for two to

[3] Of the total royalties, according to the law, 80 percent goes to the general government budget, 10 percent goes to the administration of mining oversight and 10 percent goes to district administration in mining districts.

[4] "Mining in Ghana – What Future Can We Expect?," July 2015, Report of the Mining: Partnerships for Development, Ghana Chamber of Mines and the International Council on Mining and Metals, p. 6.

Table 4.1 ***Major Gold Mining Companies in Ghana, 2013***

Mining Company Name	Government Share	Location in Ghana	Country of Origin*
Adamus Resources	10%	Teleku-Bokazo and Nkroful (Western region)	Australia
AngloGold Ashanti§	1.7%**	Obuasi (Ashanti region) and Iduapriem (Western region)	South Africa
Chirano Gold Mines	10%	Chirano (Western region)	Canada
Gold Fields Ghana	10%	Tarkwa and Damang (Western region)	South Africa
Golden Star Resources	10%	Prestea and Wassa (Western region)	Canada
Newmont Ghana	0%***	Kenyasi (Brong Ahafo region) and New Abirem (Eastern region)	USA
Perseus Mining Ghana	10%	Ayanfuri (Central region)	Australia
Prestea Sankofa Gold	10%	Prestea (Western region)	Ghana

Source: "Mining in Ghana – What Future Can We Expect?," July 2015, Report of the Mining: Partnerships for Development, Ghana Chamber of Mines and the International Council on Mining and Metals, p. 18.

* Country of origin is ascribed to the country of the largest shareholder.

** The Government of Ghana holds shares in the global company rather than the Ghana mines.

*** With respect to Newmont, the government has a 10 percent interest after the initial cost of investment is recouped.

§ In April 2004, AngloGold Ashanti was formed through a merger of Ashanti Goldfields with AngloGold, a gold mining firm based in South Africa and majority-owned by the Anglo American group.

three years. However, Gavin Hilson (2009) argues that the NDC and NPP governments generally neglected to regulate the artisanal miners. Most miners operated without a license due to the cost and time involved in obtaining one, and could survive because the state mineral marketing service bought gold from both legal and illegal miners. By the end of the 2000s, artisanal mining activity involved over one

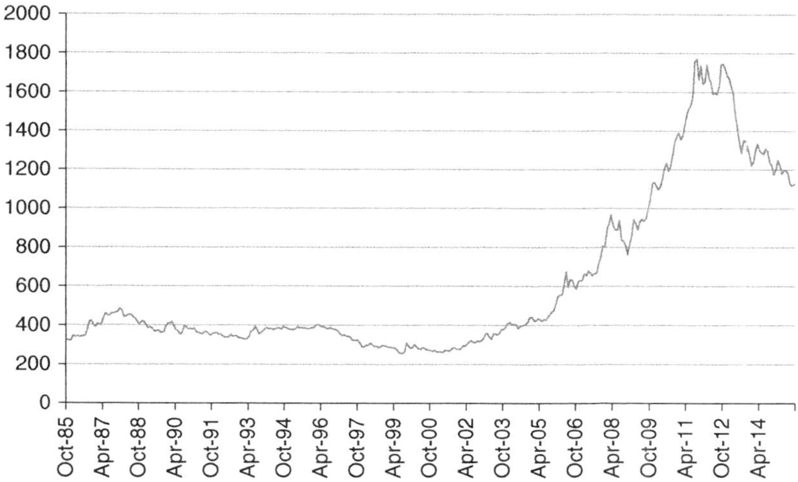

Figure 4.3 World Gold Price (US$ per ounce), 1985–2015
Source: World Bank, accessed on Index Mundi,
www.indexmundi.com/commodities/?commodity=gold&months=360.
Note: Gold (UK), 99.5% fine, London afternoon fixing, average of daily rates.

million Ghanaians. It had also become an important way for rural families to finance farm inputs for cocoa production and to sustain themselves in the context of low productivity and thus low revenues generated from cocoa farming.[5]

Continuing to Bet on the Cocoa Export Sector

The recovery of cocoa production after its all-time low output in the 1980s was slow, reaching only 350,000 tons by the 2000/2001 season, but then booming to 740,000 tons in 2005/2006, and estimated to have reached 900,000 tons in the 2010/2011 season.[6] The cocoa sector accounted for almost 10 percent of GDP at the end of the 1980s, dropped to around 5 percent in the 1990s but rose again to reach 8 percent by the end of the 2000s.[7] Cocoa accounted for 60 percent of

[5] See the work of Hilson and Garforth (2013) documenting the rise of artisanal mining among cocoa farming communities.

[6] The 2010/2011 estimate comes from the *Financial Times*, "Incentives Produce a Steadily Rising Crop," Orla Ryan, p. 6, Thursday December 15, 2011, Ghana Special Report.

[7] Data obtained from the Ministry of Finance in 2012.

export earnings in 1983 and then hovered between 20 and 40 percent in the 1990s and 2000s.[8]

Under the NDC government, reforms in the cocoa sector focused on securing cocoa export taxes and negotiating with World Bank and IMF staff over reforms in the sector.[9] The government only partially liberalized the sector, and thus the Cocoa Board continued to play a significant role. One reason that the Cocoa Board was able to partially win out in negotiations with the Bank and Fund was that the fully liberalized cocoa sectors in other West African countries did not perform as well as Ghana's cocoa sector (Fold 2002). Ghana exported the finest-quality cocoa beans in the world, fetching a premium of about 10 percent over average world cocoa bean prices. Leaders of the global cocoa industry recognized Ghana as a producer of good quality cocoa in a manner that did not involve much effort on the part of international buyers as a result of reforming but maintaining the Cocoa Marketing Board.

The high quality of Ghanaian cocoa beans was due to the role played by the Cocoa Board in organizing the product from production to marketing and centralizing the management of exports. The Cocoa Board consists of five public companies: (1) Cocoa Marketing Company, with a monopoly on the export marketing of cocoa beans; (2) Produce Buying Company, which purchases, stores and distributes cocoa to designated takeover centers, in competition with other private licensed buying companies;[10] (3) Cocoa Research Institute, which carries out research and development activities; (4) Quality Control Division, which is responsible for quality assurance and undertakes checks at the farm level and before export; and (5) Cocoa Processing Company. The Cocoa Board financed its activities from the remainder of the export price left over after paying the set producer price to farmers and the set margin to licenses buying agents. Furthermore, the Cocoa Marketing Company began borrowing abroad in 1993 to finance buying the cocoa crop, and by 1998 international banks were competing to lend funds to it because of its reputation (Williams 2009).

[8] Data obtained from the Ministry of Finance in 2012.

[9] For more details on these reforms than provided here, see Williams (2009).

[10] The Produce Buying Company acts as a buyer of last resort, penetrating difficult areas of the country to make sure that all cocoa farmers are reached, despite the higher costs of doing so.

The producer price of cocoa gradually increased from a low of 40 percent of the export price in 1983, to reach 52 percent in 1998/1999 and then 70 percent in the 2000s. The producer price increase was achieved through increasing the efficiency of the board's operations and later through reducing the export tax that went to the Ministry of Finance, which reached a low of 11.1 percent by the 2007/2008 season. While the World Bank and IMF may have played an important role in pressuring the NDC government to increase producer prices, ruling elites in the NPP government pursued a higher producer price on their own.[11]

In addition to keeping the producer price of cocoa high, NPP ruling elites encouraged cocoa revenues (controlled by the Cocoa Board) to be used on initiatives to support cocoa farmers, including building roads in cocoa areas, farmer pension and housing programs, scholarships for children of cocoa farmers and farmer bonuses. It also encouraged the Cocoa Board to pursue productivity-enhancing initiatives aimed at increasing the yields of smallholder cocoa farmers, but there were problems in the implementation. These initiatives included supplying fertilizer and other inputs on credit, as well as pesticide control. This experience illuminates some of the weaknesses in the capacity of the Cocoa Board to address constraints on productivity as a result of reforms that reduced the extension services of the board (see below).[12] By the 2000s, the Cocoa Board was an efficient state agency, but it was basically a cocoa-buying and export-marketing organization.

Productivity on smallholder cocoa farms, measured in terms of yields, increased in the late 1980s (rebounding from a low base) due to the increased use of fertilizer and the adoption of improved varieties, as part of the Cocoa Rehabilitation Program implemented by the Cocoa Board. However, the majority of increased production since the 1980s was due to clearing forest and planting new cocoa, especially in the Western Region (Kolavalli and Vigneri 2011). The boom in

[11] Interestingly, in 1999 the World Bank and IMF argued that a producer price set at 70 percent of the export price, which the 1999 Cocoa Sector Strategy aimed to achieve by the mid-2000s, was too high and that instead the government should use the resources to improve infrastructure for farmers and encourage value-added processing (Shepherd and Onumah 2003: 69). The NPP government under President Kufuor pursued the 70 percent level anyway.

[12] For more details on the NPP government's initiatives in the 2000s and problems with implementation, see Laven (2010) and Barrientos et al. (2008).

production in the 2000s was also driven by an expansion in the area cultivated, moving into new forest areas. Notably, the country was running out of new forest areas to exploit. By the end of the 2000s, cocoa yields per hectare were still far below what was achievable.

There were several constraints on increasing productivity in cocoa bean production. On one level, constraints on productivity were linked to the low profits achieved by smallholder farmers, creating a vicious circle where their low yields meant that they could not afford the high costs of inputs and labor, combined with the lack of access to credit and extension services.[13] The high costs of labor and other inputs deterred many farmers from adopting improved practices, such as re-planting old trees, using hybrid trees, and maintaining farms. Stefanie Barrientos and colleagues (2008) concluded that cocoa farming alone could not sustain the farmers if yields were not improved and farm holdings increased so that earnings from cocoa would increase.

By the early 2000s, processes related to land tenure such as share-cropping and inheritance systems had weakened capitalist cocoa farming (Takane 2002). In particular, insecurity of land rights undermined capitalist cocoa farming by migrants, who were integral to cocoa production (see Chapter 2). Migrants' access to land and the security of their tenure was dependent on recognition by chiefs under customary law. During the revival of cocoa production in the mid-1980s, chiefs reneged on land contracts with migrants and demanded arbitrary extractions of tributes and rents in some areas in the Western Region (Boone and Duku 2012). As a result, the PNDC government initially intervened in these conflicts to support the claims of migrant tenants in order to secure cocoa production. It also passed laws such as the Land Title Registration Law of 1986, which recognized the rights of "customary freeholders," indigenous families who had been granted land by chiefs in previous generators, and reduced chiefs' control over land. However, as the PNDC elites sought to build greater political support ahead of the re-introduction of multiparty elections, they reduced their hostility towards chiefs. Notably, the 1992 constitution acknowledges the right of chiefs to govern land based on customary law, foreclosing any radical reform of the land tenure system.

[13] There are plenty of moneylenders for cocoa production, but they come with high interest rates.

While cocoa output tripled over the period from 2000 to 2010 (although the figures for the 2010/2011 season likely include smuggling from Côte d'Ivoire), only a small part of this increased production could be attributed to increased fertilizer use and pesticide spraying. Based on farmer survey data, Francis Teal (2013) shows that the most important factor was increased intensity of labor on farms. He argues that this was probably the result of the higher producer price, which increased significantly over that period, and not of changes in the methods farmers used to produce cocoa.

In the 2000s, local cocoa processing increased with major foreign direct investments by the leading multinational corporations producing intermediate processed cocoa inputs such as cocoa liquor, butter and cake: Cargrill, Callebaut and ADM.[14] These multinational corporations set up factories in Ghana because the NPP government offered a discount on cocoa beans from the premium international price, which these multinational corporations said was necessary for the profitability of running a factory in Ghana. Foreign direct investment in cocoa processing spurred local investment in the sector as well, and by 2012 there were eight factories, including the state-owned Cocoa Processing Company. However, as cocoa-processing capacity expanded in the country, so did a struggle over access to cocoa beans. Since the Cocoa Board had a monopoly on the marketing of cocoa beans, processing factories were dependent on the discounted beans being released from the Cocoa Board. The Cocoa Marketing Company, the most powerful agency in the Cocoa Board, began to advocate for ending the discount on beans, as exporting a large volume of beans was essential to maintaining its power position in the existing production system and keeping producer prices as high as possible was critical to spurring cocoa production. The real problem, however, was low productivity among cocoa farmers, because if productivity increased, a higher volume of beans would be available. Processed cocoa products fetch higher prices than cocoa beans in international markets, but a processing industry can only be built on a raw material supply base that is expanding through productivity increases.

In sum, the cocoa sector grew increasingly fragile as a means of income for a large part of the southern population, as a key pillar of

14 For more detail on the cocoa processing industry, see Whitfield et al. (2015: 243–247).

the economy and source of foreign exchange, and as the foundation on which to build cocoa processing and capture higher value in export markets. The macroeconomic crisis that started in 2012 affected cocoa production and exports, which combined with other exogenous shocks, caused a 22 percent contraction in cocoa exports between the 2013/2014 and 2014/2015 seasons (from 830,000 tons to about 700,000 tons) despite world prices turning upwards. The official and unofficial reasons given for the production shortfall included bad weather, ageing farmer population, disease and smuggling (due to the weak cedi), as well as the late application of fertilizers due to late supply from the Cocoa Board and a reduction of the government spraying program resulting from funding problems.[15]

Chiefs and the Struggle for Control over Land

Control over allocating land and property rights in land remained unclear and contested under the Fourth Republic. Stools, clans and lineages held the allodial title and owned about 80 percent of all lands, while the state owned about 20 percent. Families and individuals who claimed ancestry from a given traditional area, controlled by a paramount chief, were considered indigenes and they possessed allodial land titles and usufructuary (user) rights to land. Chiefs could allocate land to migrants, people who came from other traditional areas or from outside Ghana. Land could not be formally sold, but could be leased to migrants for long periods of time, up to fifty years.

State ownership of land came through the compulsory acquisition of it, starting with Nkrumah's government in the 1960s, which accessed tracts of land for the promotion of large-scale agricultural cultivation and agro-processing through the Administration of Lands Act 1962 (Act 123). This Act empowered the president to authorize the occupation of stool land for any purpose conducive to the public welfare or the interest of the state. The PNDC government amended this law in 1983 with PNDC Law 42 in a way that effectively gave the state power over land and could have extinguished communal allodial

15 Anang Tawiah, "2014-2015 Cocoa Commodity Report," June 7, 2015, *Modern Ghana News*, www.modernghana.com/news/621813/1/2014–2015-cocoa-commodity-report.html (last accessed June 9, 2015).

rights to land. However, communal allodial rights continued to be exercised in practice (Aryeetey et al. 2007).

Land rights and rules under customary ownership were ambiguous and opaque, resulting in chaos in land markets and leading to litigation and conflict. The chaos prompted a national discussion on a new land policy, but the policy eventually adopted by the NDC government in 1999 promoted land registration as the best way to guarantee security of land tenure.[16] The Land Administration Project formulated by the Kufuor administration in the early 2000s to implement the new policy involved decentralization of land management to state-supported chieftancy institutions with Customary Land Secretariats, as well as improving land titling registration and mapping. However, the land titling aspect started only in urban areas, where the "adverse consequences" could be avoided or minimized (Aryeetey et al. 2007: 61). In effect, the land policy and land administration project legitimized and strengthened customary practices and thus chiefs' control over land and generally failed to solve the problems. The chiefs, who were the most organized group around the reforms, influenced the content of the policy and the project. In fact, during the NPP government of 2001 to 2008, chiefs lobbied through official channels as well as their political linkages for the revival of the customary system, which meant reversing the legislation of the Nkrumah government and successive governments that took away their official judicial and administrative functions and gave most of their powers to collect revenue from stool land and manage the development of land to state land sector agencies (Crook et al. 2007: 35). While they were not completely successfully, they were able to secure broad control over land because the statutory laws designed to regulate customary law were poorly implemented (Aryeetey et al. 2007).

Chiefs used their control over land to accumulate wealth, directly through tributes and other kinds of land rents exacted from migrants and indigenes and indirectly through agricultural production in sharecropping and tenant arrangements.[17] They also exploited the fact that land rights and rules under customary ownership were ambiguous, opaque and contested, in order to generate revenue from leasing land

[16] This summary of the National Land Policy and the Land Administration Project is based on Aryeetey et al. (2007) and Crook et al. (2007).

[17] This paragraph is based on Amanor (2008), Berry (2013) and Boamah (2014).

to multiple buyers and by taking away the land of migrant farmers who did not pay the agricultural tribute and recognize chiefs' political authority over land. Notably, by the 2000s, it was common for paramount chiefs in southern Ghana to be well-educated city-dwellers, sometimes with party affiliations. In short, chiefs used their control over land as a means of accumulating wealth and political influence, but the institutions of customary land tenure, sharecropping and tenant farming that were good for their accumulation in turn had negative effects on agricultural production by increasing the transaction costs and financial costs of acquiring land, and creating insecurity in land property rights for small farmers and large commercial farmers. These negative effects were discussed above regarding the cocoa sector, and they are demonstrated in Chapters 5 and 6 with the industry cases of horticulture export and palm oil processing. Many of the constraints on increasing agricultural productivity can be linked back to the way that land is governed and allocated, which creates tendencies toward fragmentation of farms and insecurity in land tenure (Goldstein and Udry 2008).

Agriculture Remained Characterized by Low Productivity

Outside of cocoa, agriculture generally performed poorly, with most crops characterized by low productivity. Agriculture also generally had weak forward and backward linkages in the economy. Weak backward linkages occurred due to the low level of inputs used in agricultural production, and weak forward linkages resulted from the export of agricultural crops in their raw form or from competition from imported goods. By 2011, the country produced 51 percent of its cereal consumption, 60 percent of its fish requirements, 50 percent of its meat, and less than 30 percent of the raw materials needed for agro-based industries (ACET 2015: 2).

The NDC and NPP governments continued to rely heavily on donors, especially the World Bank, to finance agricultural expenditures. As a result, agricultural policies emphasized eliminating state involvement in agricultural production, distribution and marketing, as well as removing obligatory credit allocation to the agricultural sector by commercial banks, and input and credit subsidies. New policies pushed private sector funding of agricultural research, a unified agricultural extension system and privatization of some parts of extension and agricultural services. These policies were largely unsuccessful in making much of a positive impact on agricultural productivity.

In the 1990s, the World Bank created an agricultural sector adjustment credit that provided balance of payments support in return for policy reforms linked to individual projects. The projects included the agricultural diversification project (1990), national agricultural research project (1991), national agricultural extension project (1992), national feeder roads project (1992), national livestock services project (1993), coastal wetlands management project (1993), environmental resource management project (1993), agricultural sector investment project (1994) (which provided village-level infrastructure) and fisheries capacity building project (1995). Their impact on any particular agricultural product or agro-industry was not significant. The World Bank's performance audit report gave five of these project loans a poor rating on outcomes and noted that all the projects were unlikely to be sustainable.[18] Given that these projects involved loans, this observation supports arguments about the questionable productivity to which aid money was put to use.

The structure of Ghana's agriculture requires large numbers of extension staff and a reliable means of transport to enable them to reach smallholder farmers scattered over large areas.[19] In the early 1990s, the ratio of agricultural extension agents to farmers was about 1:2500. The World Bank's solution was to introduce a unified agricultural extension system, which involved the fusion of cocoa, crops and livestock extension and to have one agent provide advice on all of the subsectors to the same farmer. A US$40 million National Agricultural Extension Project began in 1992 to help implement the new policy. It involved retraining Ministry of Food and Agriculture staff and another 500 cocoa services staff and providing them with housing, tools and equipment to deliver the unified services. However, the 500 cocoa services staff, who were transferred from the Cocoa Board to the Ministry of Food and Agriculture, took a pay cut because the board offered better conditions of service. As a result, these 500 transferred staff resigned, and the Cocoa Board never transferred resources to the

18 World Bank, Performance Audit Reports and Sectoral Overview Ghana, June 22, 2001, Report No. 22439, p. iii.

19 "Evolution of Ghana's Economic Policies," background paper on Ghana produced for an FAO study led by Ha-Joon Chang, whose findings were published as Chang (2009); on the cocoa extension service, see Williams (2009).

ministry in support of extension. The unified system did not work well, and actually negatively affected cocoa production, and thus in the mid-2000s, cocoa extension was transferred back to the Cocoa Board.

Other donor projects in the 1990s also had modest impacts, and when the projects ended and funding ceased, the new initiatives also ended. As a result, the Ministry of Food and Agriculture attempted in the late 1990s to coordinate donor initiatives in agriculture with the ministry's new Accelerated Agricultural Growth and Development Strategy. Implementation of the government's agricultural program required World Bank support, since it was the main donor.[20] At headquarters level in Washington, DC, the World Bank designed a new program, Agricultural Services Subsector Investment Project (AgSSIP), supporting a watered-down version of the government's proposal. It took out components related to infrastructure and credit, which it said duplicated other World Bank and donor projects, existing or in the pipeline.[21] Bank staff also inserted World Bank priorities at the time, which emphasized reforming research and extension.[22] The program proposed by the World Bank said it would address the first two objectives of the government's strategy: promotion of selected commodities through improved market access, and development and improved access to technology. However, it did not include any discussion of specific commodities and how to address the specific constraints around the production and marketing of those commodities. Furthermore, its approach to technology generation and dissemination were markedly different from what the government's national task force had envisioned.[23] The sector-wide approach fell through in

[20] Interview with a retired Ministry of Food and Agriculture official, who was Coordinator of AgSSIP, July 24, 2009, Accra.

[21] Project Appraisal Document, Agricultural Services Subsector Investment Project, Report No: 20366-GH, June 8, 2000, p. 3.

[22] The World Bank's proposal focused on institutional reforms within the ministry aimed at further decentralization of agricultural services, private participation in the provision of agricultural services, development of farmer-based organizations, and competition and beneficiary participation in agricultural research.

[23] For example, the task force's approach emphasized ameliorating problems with the availability of, and farmer access to, privately provided agricultural inputs, machinery and technology, as well as enhancing public research and extension services. To take another example, the government version also proposed shifting to agricultural college education and practical experience in agribusiness, rather than training to be extension workers, so that graduates

the end because donors could not agree among each other; in particular, several bilateral donors rejected the World Bank's proposal. Thus, the Ministry of Food and Agriculture's efforts to produce an agriculture investment program over the course of three years were in vain. And the NDC Cabinet rejected the World Bank's agricultural subsector services investment program on the grounds that there was too much "capacity building" and consultancy.[24]

Upon assuming power, the NPP Cabinet was presented with the same World Bank–proposed agricultural program that the NDC Cabinet had rejected. The NPP Cabinet also disliked the program and wanted to restructure it to include more components directly related to production (Voisard and Jaeger 2008). The NPP government signed the loan after almost a year of delays on the understanding that once signed it would be easier to make modifications rather than insisting on an immediate redesign of the project.[25] The restructuring of AgSSIP was formally approved at its midterm review in 2004, but the World Bank's project was scheduled to close at the end of 2006, so what could be achieved was actually very limited both in terms of time and resources.

The restructured AgSSIP contained aspects pushed by the World Bank such as demand-driven agricultural research through research extension liaison committees, farmer-based organization development and increased private-sector participation in extension through NGOs. Notably, the latter led the NGOs, which won the tenders, to poach staff from the Ministry of Food and Agriculture in order to carry out their mandate, and this approach collapsed at the end of AgSSIP for lack of funding. The project included a horticulture initiative that was pushed by World Bank specialists in collaboration with Ghanaian horticulture exporters, which is discussed in Chapter 5.

The restructured AgSSIP also contained aspects pushed by civil servants and by the NPP politicians. Civil servants succeeded in adding

could start their own businesses. The World Bank's proposal also wanted to shift agricultural education away from producing public sector extension workers, but its focus was on producing private extension workers rather than people educated to start up agribusinesses.

24 Interviews with Ministry of Food and Agriculture staff, April 27, 2009 and July 24, 2009.

25 Implementation Completion and Results Report, Agricultural Services Subsector Investment Project, Report No. ICR0000589, November 30, 2007, World Bank, p. 20.

the rehabilitation of irrigation schemes and development of fishing landing sites. The projects pushed by the NPP politicians included the establishment of mechanization centers and support of the President's Special Initiative in Oil Palm. The World Bank never actually funded the mechanization centers and provided only limited support for the PSI by the time AgSSIP ended in 2006.

The mechanization centers were one of the NPP's flagship initiatives in agriculture, and mechanization featured prominently in NPP discourses on how to modernize agriculture.[26] Government involvement in mechanization was not a new idea, but rather one from the 1960s, during which the Ministry of Agriculture had owned and operated an estimated 5000 tractors across thirty-two district mechanization stations in the savannah zone or northern Ghana. The low charge of services made the scheme unsustainable, and it collapsed in the 1970s. In the 1980s and 1990s, the supply of mechanization was left to the private sector, which had responded somewhat, aided by the import tariff exemption on agricultural machinery imports. Private importers were mainly small businessmen, who imported mostly used machinery (as the tractors were more affordable) and provided tractor services to meet the growing demand discussed above. However, demand outstripped the supply, so the NPP government's Agricultural Mechanization Service Centers aimed to support an increase in mechanization services available. In this case, the government sought to avoid directly managing the mechanization services centers, but rather stimulate an increase in private centers through subsidizing the cost of imported tractors and by providing participating private companies, selected by government tender, with a loan and generous terms for paying back the loan. The mechanization centers were implemented beginning in 2007 through financing from concessional loans from India, Brazil and China, but also a Japanese grant.

However, the mechanization centers operated on an unfeasible model, because the businesses only provided ploughing services, which did not generate enough clients in order to meet payments on the loan schedule. As a result, many mechanization center businesses defaulted on repayment. Tractor purchase and hire turned out to be an unprofitable business if service provision alone was the only means for investors to earn money. The mechanization service providers that

[26] This paragraph and the next are based on Diao et al. (2014).

existed before the initiative had survived because they were often farmers themselves, who used tractors first for their own needs and then for hiring out to other farmers.

Other NPP government initiatives returned to old policies eradicated under structural adjustment such as fertilizer subsidies and price supports. NPP agricultural policies also returned to the state-led and -controlled industrial policies of the past, in which the state intervened directly to increase agricultural production and agro-processing, as illustrated with the President's Special Initiatives in cassava starch and oil palm discussed in Chapter 7. Notably, the Mills-led NDC government continued with many of the NPP's agricultural policies such as the Agricultural Mechanization Services Centers project, fertilizer subsidies and block farms, and expanded them using the new oil revenues. The continuity in policy approaches, discussed in more detail in Chapter 8, underlines the political attractiveness of these kinds of policies, which are directly implemented by the government. But the direct role of the government in implementing and financing also exposes them to the politics of competitive clientelism and vulnerability to insufficient government revenue to maintain the financing.

Increased urbanization in the 1990s and 2000s had important implications for the demand of agricultural goods as well as for agricultural production (Diao et al. 2014). Urban residents preferred more easy-to-cook food than rural residents, leading to increased demand for cereals (rather than root crops) and for vegetables and fruits as well as livestock products. The production of all of these food products was more labor intensive than root crops. At the same time, rising nonfarm opportunities for rural households and increased migration of rural youth to urban areas increased the cost of scarce labor for agricultural production. While domestic food production was too low to meet all of domestic demand, increased imports simply made it harder to do so, as imported agricultural goods were cheaper than domestic ones. Import quotas were abolished and tariffs for imported agricultural goods were lowered to 20 percent as part of the structural adjustment policies. The increased demand was largely met through imports rather than domestic production, resulting in a surge in imported goods such as poultry meat, rice and tomato paste.[27]

[27] FAO Briefs on Import Surges No.5 "Ghana: Rice, Poultry, Tomato Paste," 2006, Commodities and Trade Division, Food and Agriculture Organization of

The development of agro-processing in Ghana suffered not only from import competition, but also from an inadequate supply of raw materials. Most agro-processing factories attempted to rely fully on independent smallholders or contract farmers (outgrowers), but they ran into serious problems with securing enough raw materials and had to shut down. This occurred with the former state-owned tomato factories that the NPP government attempted to revive with private investment, as well as the new state-owned cassava starch factory (Ayensu Starch Factory) that the NPP government established.[28] It was not just the volume of raw materials, but rather securing a regular supply of high volumes of raw materials of an appropriate quality for processing at a competitive price. A common problem was when parallel domestic markets for the agricultural products existed, as in the case with tomato. Due to limited supply, local "market queens" would bid up the price of products in order to secure their supply, making the price too high for factories to be competitive with imported processed goods, or in export markets.

Furthermore, smallholder farmers demonstrated time and again that they would break contracts with factories and sell their products for the highest spot market price, even when (or especially when) factories or other actors provided loans in the form of inputs and technical assistance to help increase the productivity of smallholder production (and the cost of those inputs would be deducted from the buying price). Parallel markets made it difficult to enforce contracts. Therefore, by the end of the 2000s, it became a well-known fact among investors and ministry bureaucrats that for an agro-processing firm to be successful, it had to supply at least 50 percent of its raw material from its own farm. However, this approach came up against constraints on access to land to create such nucleus farms. These challenges are illustrated in the case study chapters of the book.

Stagnating Manufacturing

With the structural adjustment reforms, manufacturing output grew in the late 1980s because factories were able to import raw materials, increase production and thus raise the percent of their total capacity

the United Nations (FAO), http://webdoc.rfi.fr/dark_side_tomato/img/fao.pdf (last accessed August 14, 2017).

28 On the case of the tomato processing factories, see Robinson and Kolavalli (2010). On the Ayensu Starch Factory, see the discussion in Chapter 7 of this book.

Figure 4.4 Manufacturing Growth as a Component of Industry (% of GDP), 1967–2016
Source: World Development Indicators, 2017.

being utilized. However, after rapid trade liberalization, many firms closed due to their inability to compete with foreign imports, and manufacturing output contracted.[29] While the share of the industry sector as a percentage of GDP increased in the mid-1990s and then remained almost constant, within the industry sector, manufacturing stagnated and even declined, as shown in Figure 4.4. Growth in the industry sector was driven by the construction and mineral industries. The manufacturing sector constituted only 7.2 percent of GDP in 2009, which was reduced to 6.2 percent in 2014, after the advent of oil production.

Besides rapid trade liberalization, other aspects of structural adjustment policies had negative effects on private manufacturing firms producing for the domestic market, such as the sharp currency devaluation and tight credit, which led to high interest rates. For example, the textile and garments sector consisted of fourteen textile companies and 138 medium and large garment factories producing for the domestic and West African regional market in the 1970s, and

[29] Evidence for this trend comes from Lall et al. (1994), Lall and Stewart (1996) and Aryeetey and Tarp (2000). A World Bank evaluation of assistance to Ghana noted that the poor design and sequencing of trade liberalization and the failure to direct credit to assist manufacturing firms resulted in a decline in manufacturing (Armstrong 1996: 49–50).

accounted for 27 percent of manufacturing employment (Sutton and Kpentey 2012: 87–89). Most of them closed down in the 1980s and 1990s after trade liberalization, including large volumes of used clothing imported from the US and Europe. Only four textile firms survived into the 2000s, but they struggled. Notably these firms included a state-owned enterprise established by the Nkrumah government, a Chinese-owned firm established in the 1960s, and a privately owned firm established during the colonial period.

The manufacturing firms that survived structural adjustment tended to be in activities with "natural" protection from imports: very small-scale enterprises making low-income or localized products and larger enterprises protected by high transport costs or based on processing local raw materials (Lall et al. 1994). They consisted of a few large modern firms with the ability to produce to international standards, a larger population of small- and medium-sized firms using some modern technology but with low levels of efficiency, and numerous informal and micro-enterprises with very simple or traditional technologies serving limited local markets.

A crucial factor behind the generally low private investment in the 1990s was the inability of firms to access credit, primarily due to government borrowing to cover fiscal deficits, which drove up interest rates. The recapitalized banks focused over 70 percent of their operations on bonds issued by the government, the Bank of Ghana and the Cocoa Board. Banks were unwilling to take risks on indebted old manufacturing firms or smaller and newer firms and nontraditional exporters. Political uncertainty, lack of credit, and low technological capabilities among Ghanaian entrepreneurs led to short-term speculative behavior in sectors where turnover time of capital was short and profitability was high, such as in trading activities (Aryeetey and Tarp 2000: 358).

NDC government policies in the manufacturing sector largely focused on the privatization of state-owned enterprises, although there were not many state-owned enterprises worthy of selling, as most collapsed in the 1980s, and the most valuable asset was the land on which the factories were located. Import substitution industrialization led by state-owned factories had left a legacy of inefficiency and technological backwardness; however, it had also left some technological capabilities, but not at the level that rapid trade liberalization could stimulate to reach international competitiveness in such a short time period. The palm oil processing estates were an exception. The NDC government invested in making these estates profitable in order to privatize them, as shown in Chapter 6, and these estates provided the raw materials for several local and foreign private manufacturing companies producing soaps, detergents, edible oils and other consumer products for the domestic market.

The NDC government did not assert its own strategy for supporting industrial development, but rather signed on to various donor projects aimed at "private sector development." The World Bank's Private Enterprise and Export Development project (1994–1998) focused on expanding nontraditional exports, but it largely provided short-term credit to cover shipments and neglected medium-term credit to cover working capital.[30] It underestimated the weak production base in Ghana. The government argued for medium-term financing during project negotiations, but did not win the argument. Later, the World Bank recognized the need for it but thought it too risky due to the deteriorating macroeconomic environment in the late 1990s.

A World Bank financial sector reform program recapitalized domestic banks strapped with bad debt, but left many private firms indebted and unable to access credit (Kraus 2002). Assistance through the World Bank for restructuring these firms was slow, so the NDC government on its own initiative established a Business Assistance Fund in 1994, financed by divestiture receipts. However, it had little impact. Academic observers note that the amount of money in the fund was quite small compared to firms' needs; there were no clear criteria for selecting firms; and the repayment rate was pitiful even though the peak business associations had representatives on the board of the fund – which led some observers to suggest collusion between the business associations and state officials where "irregular" practices were tolerated.[31]

Other policies pushed by donors focused more on what public sector institutions were supposed to do (or not do). For example, the World Bank Private Sector Development Project (1995–2000) focused on shaping public institutions that were supposed to provide commercial

[30] World Bank Private Enterprise and Export Development Project (CR.2502-GH), Implementation Completion Report, Report No: 18520, October 29, 1998.

[31] On the Business Assistance Fund of the NDC government, see Aryeetey and Harrigan (2000: 28), Hutchful (2002: 82) and Handley (2008: 185).

services (e.g. research and development) to be demand-driven; providing business services to small enterprises; and improving legal services for the commercial sector. The World Bank's internal evaluation rated the project unsatisfactory and admitted that the project focused too much on the supply of services by the government without a clear link with the domestic market and industries.[32] The business service component implemented by a private firm was also ineffective given that banks were not responding, even with improved business proposals.

The NPP's 2000 election manifesto criticized the NDC government for its passive role in letting much of Ghana's nascent industrial capacity crumble under import liberalization. The NPP's development vision set out in the manifesto focused on macroeconomic stability, partnership with the private sector, and an active state role in fostering the development of the domestic private sector. Once in government, the Kufour-led NPP ruling coalition effectively adopted a two-pronged approach in which it pursued a set of initiatives of its own design for economic and political reasons while continuing to cater to donors and to accept donor-driven projects. However, neither the donor-driven projects nor the NPP's own initiatives in agro-processing and other manufacturing areas made significant impacts.

Donor support centered on the private sector development strategy, which was initially coordinated within the Ministry for Private Sector Development, but when that ministry was dismantled in 2006, the strategy was housed at the Ministry of Trade and Industry. The strategy was a program for public sector reforms to create a better business environment – the kinds of reforms that donors wanted to see. It did not include the objectives of increasing the competence and competitiveness at firm level, which were left to other donor-financed projects that focused on providing business development services to small and medium enterprises. Notably, an external evaluation of the private sector development strategy observed that these projects had little impact on increasing the competitiveness of Ghanaian firms. Furthermore, political backing for the private sector development strategy eroded as the strategy was not seen to address "bread and butter" issues of creating jobs and incomes.[33]

[32] World Bank Private Sector Development Project, Implementation Completion Report, Report No. 21547, December 21, 2000.

[33] External Evaluation of the Private Sector Development Strategy, final draft, 2008, prepared by a team of international and Ghanaian consultants, for the

Most of the NPP government's initiatives to support industrial development were driven by Alan Kyerematen, a senior member in the NPP. When Kyerematen became Minister of Trade and Industry, he set out his vision in the Industrial Reform and Accelerated Growth Programme. It was probably the first time since the 1980s that the Minister of Trade and Industry had a vision for what the ministry should do. The Programme aimed to promote an export-led industrialization strategy focused on agro-processing and other manufacturing and involving mass mobilization of rural communities, and an import competing strategy aimed at stimulating the competitive production of import substitutes, especially processed foods and agricultural products. Kyerematen had ideas for several projects to put these strategies into practice, including the President's Special Initiatives (PSIs) and the District Industrialization Program. The District Industrialization Program attempted to harness the capital of the diaspora to invest in manufacturing enterprises based in rural areas, but it had little success. When that did not work, Kyerematen shifted the focus to encouraging foreign direct investment and reviving a few state-owned enterprises in agro-processing or manufacturing that were located in rural areas. These included the Pawlugu and Wenchi tomato processing factories that had been established in the 1960s under Nkrumah's government. The PSIs were characterized by a similar state-led approach, especially the PSIs targeting the palm oil industry and the creation of a cassava starch industry. Chapter 7 discusses in more detail the PSIs as industrial policy and what went wrong during implementation with these two PSIs.

The PSI in Garments did not take a state-led approach, but also had little success in stimulating the apparel industry because the industrial policy did not provide enough support for private firms to develop the capabilities to compete in apparel exports, or in the liberalized domestic market where secondhand clothing imports dominate. The Ministry of Trade and Industry used the World Bank Gateway project for financing the PSI in Garments. The Gateway project aimed to construct an export processing zone in Tema (the port city next to the capital city, Accra), but the ministry restructured it in 2005 to create a multipurpose industrial park that would provide offsite and onsite infrastructure,

Ministry of Trade and Industry and donors in the Private Sector Development Working Group.

allow domestic firms to operate there, and allow a percentage of goods produced there to be sold on the domestic market.[34] As part of this restructuring, the Gateway project was used to finance the establishment of a Garment Village just outside Tema, composed of 110 factory units to be rented out to local entrepreneurs as well as foreign garment producing companies. The Garment PSI intended to help firms take advantage of the African Growth and Opportunity Act, which offered trade preferences for African exporters to the US market.[35] The PSI established a clothing technology and training center to train sewing operators for the factories, and the PSI facilitated renting out production space and the purchase of equipment. However, only five companies actually set up in the free zone in Tema, and including the areas in Accra, there were only a total of twenty-four garment factories established (Farole 2011: 92). The sector subsequently collapsed, leaving only four firms by 2009. Thomas Farole argues that the collapse was caused by the phasing out of the MultiFiber Agreement in 2005 (the WTO agreement on textiles and clothing that involved quantitative import restrictions), which allowed global buyers to source more from China and thus lowered the prices global buyers were willing to pay. In addition, illegal imports of cheap Chinese-made clothing, counterfeit Ghanaian fabric, and the influx of secondhand clothing undermined production for the domestic market. Another study notes that there were nine garment firms producing by the early 2010s, but two were not operating and one was on the verge of collapse, but they all suffered from low productivity compared to their global competitors, even with trade preferences to the US market, and thus their profit margins were low and workers unmotivated (Quarcoo et al. 2013).

Thus, the Garments PSI incentivized investments in garment factories but did not provide additional support to help firms increase their productivity in order to be able to compete in the international market, nor did it regulate and protect the domestic market in order to provide factories with a source of demand while they were improving their productivity. As a result, firms went out of business.

[34] World Bank Ghana Trade and Investment Gateway Project, Implementation Completion and Results Report, Report No ICR00001460, June 30, 2010; and interviews with the Coordinator of Gateway Secretariat, March 2007 and May 2009.

[35] Presentation by Alan Kyerematen, Ministry of Trade and Industry, on the PSIs. Copy of PowerPoint presentation slides. Undated, but most likely from 2003.

The pharmaceutical industry is one of the few manufacturing industries that expanded significantly in the 1990s and early 2000s, and perhaps the only case of successful industrial policy. This expansion was led by private investment, which is even more surprising given that it is a capital-intensive industry. There were thirty-four licenced pharmaceutical manufacturing firms by 2005; however, after the mid-2000s, there were fewer new firms entering the industry because the standards required for factory buildings and production processes were raised in order to be compliant with the World Health Organization's basic global standards (Wong 2017). Pharmaceutical firms mostly produced basic "over-the-counter" medicines with imported ingredients; although some foreign firms and joint ventures were producing more complex medicines such as anti-malarials and anti-retroviral drugs. The Conclusion chapter discusses the conditions under which industrial policies were pursued and successfully implemented in the pharmaceutical sector, compared to the examples of failed industrial policies presented throughout this book.

In sum, by 2010 the manufacturing sector in Ghana consisted of agro-processing; woodworking; textiles and garments; metals, engineering and assembly; chemicals; plastics and rubber; building materials; and pharmaceuticals. Of the fifty leading companies in these industries, the government or foreign investors established twenty-three of them. Within the firms started by private Ghanaian entrepreneurs, half of the investors had moved from importing goods (trading) to producing them locally, and the other half entered as start-up firms in manufacturing (Sutton and Kpentey 2012). Although many of the state-owned enterprises were privatized or divested in the 1990s, it is important to note that almost half of the large-scale manufacturing firms have their origins in government initiatives and foreign investments that date back to the 1960s and early 1970s.[36] This observation illustrates the limited role of private domestic investment in the formal economy, and the small number of domestic capitalists with capabilities to run large firms in manufacturing and agro-processing, whether for the domestic market or export. For example, the metals, engineering and assembly sector largely revolved around VALCO, established by the US company Kaiser Aluminum during Nkrumah's government

[36] This observation is based on the data of fifty leading firms profiled in the enterprise map by Sutton and Kpentey (2012).

but which became wholly owned by the government. It sold aluminum ingots to Aluworks, which manufactured them into aluminum products for sale to small and medium firms downstream that made consumer products such as roofing sheets and kitchen utensils. Aluworks was owned previously by Kaiser, then taken over by the government and then divested under an initial public offering on the Ghana Stock Exchange. Tema Steel Company, one of four companies that manufactured steel from scrap, was initially built for the government-owned Kwame Nkrumah Steel Works in the mid-1970s. Of the other three companies, the privately owned Ghana Metal Fabrication and Constructed Limited had historical links to Kaiser Aluminum.

Most of the country's manufacturing firms remained small and informal. According to one study, micro and small-scale enterprises constituted 96 percent of all manufacturing businesses, in both the formal and informal economy, while medium-scale enterprises constituted 3 percent and large-scale enterprises constituted 1 percent (Ablo and Overå 2015: 394). Indigenous Ghanaians owned the micro and small firms, while foreigners, the government or local diaspora (such as Lebanese-Ghanaians) primarily owned the large firms. This finding corresponds to the fifty firms mapped by Sutton and Kpentey (2012), in which Ghanaian nationals of Lebanese descent were the owners of many of the Ghanaian-owned firms.

Poverty Reduction and Employment in the Colonial Trading Economy

The sectoral composition of GDP after the rebasing exercise in 2010 gave the impression that the Ghanaian economy had moved from being an agricultural economy to a service-based economy, because the service sector had become the largest sector in terms of contribution to GDP. Services mainly included wholesale and retail trading, restaurants and hotels, transport, communication, real estate, finance, and public administration. In 2014, the service sector contributed 50 percent of GDP, followed by industry at 28.5 percent of GDP, and then agriculture at around 21 percent. Table 4.2 provides a more detailed breakdown of the sector composition of GDP and its change between 2009 and 2014.

While the service sector accounted for a significant amount of the jobs that were created, most of the jobs were in the public sector and the

Table 4.2 ***Composition of GDP, 2009 and 2014 (% of GDP at current prices)***

	2009	2014
Agriculture, forestry, fishing & hunting	32.9	20.7
Of which fishing	*2.5*	*1.5*
Mining and quarrying	2.1	9.5
Of which oil	*0.0*	*6.3*
Manufacturing	7.2	6.2
Electricity, water and gas	1.2	1.1
Construction	9.1	12.8
Wholesale & retail trading; repair of household goods; restaurants and hotels	12.5	10.3
Of which restaurants and hotels	*6.4*	*4.8*
Transport, storage and communication	12.8	13.9
Finance, real estate and business services	5.3	6.7
Public administration and defence	7.2	8.5
Other services	9.7	10.4

Source: Okudzeto et al. (2015: 4), based on data from the Ghanaian authorities.

informal sector (Okudzeto et al. 2015: 5). According to the most recent Ghana Living Standards Survey in 2012/2013, the informal sector engaged about two out of every five (41.9%) of the employed persons 15 years and older, as shown in Table 4.3. About three-fifths of the employed urban population is engaged in the informal sector. In the rural areas, the main source of employment is in agriculture, and in general, the agricultural sector still employed about 45 percent of the workforce. Taken together, the informal sector and agriculture accounted for 88 percent of all "jobs." Official unemployment figures in 2012/2013 were low, stating that only 4.1 percent of Ghanaians over 15 years old are without jobs and potentially available for jobs, but this statistic ignores the large informal sector in which many people are "employed" but engaged in activities with limited productivity and very low associated incomes.

The 2012/2013 Ghana Living Standards Survey indicates that about a quarter of Ghanaians were poor and under a tenth of the population was in extreme poverty. The number of people living in poverty was 6.4 million, while the number of people living in extreme poverty was 2.2

Table 4.3 *Type of Employer for Employed Population aged 15 Years and Older (%), 2012/2013*

	Urban			*Rural*			*Total*		
Type of employer	*Male*	*Female*	*All*	*Male*	*Female*	*All*	*Male*	*Female*	*All*
Public Service									
Civil Service	5.0	2.6	3.7	1.5	0.7	1.1	3.2	1.6	2.4
Other public service	6.7	4.0	5.3	1.8	1.0	1.4	4.2	2.5	3.3
Parastatal	0.4	0.1	0.2	0.1	0.1	0.1	0.2	0.1	0.2
Private Sector									
Formal	14.2	5.8	9.8	2.7	1.1	1.9	8.2	3.4	5.7
Informal	52.8	69.3	61.5	19.6	26.8	23.3	35.5	47.8	41.9
NGOs	0.5	0.1	0.3	0.1	0.0	0.1	0.3	0.1	0.2
Cooperatives	0.2	0.1	0.1	0.1	0.0	0.1	0.2	0.0	0.1
International Organization	0.3	0.0	0.2	0.1	0.0	0.1	0.2	0.0	0.1
Agri-business	19.7	17.8	18.7	74.0	70.2	72.1	48.0	44.4	46.1
Other	0.2	0.1	0.2	0.0	0.1	0.0	0.1	0.1	0.1

Source: Ghana Living Standards Survey Round 6, Main Report, Ghana Statistical Service, August 2014, p. 49.

Table 4.4 *Poverty Incidence by Locality (%), 1991–2013**

Geographic Area	1991/1992		1998/1999		2005/2006**		2012/2013	
	Poverty Incidence	Contribution to total poverty	Poverty Incidence	Contribution to total poverty	Poverty Incidence	Contribution to total poverty	Poverty Incidence	Contribution to total poverty
Greater Accra	23.1	3.7	4.4	1.3	12.0	4.4	3.5	2.2
Urban Coastal	28.3	4.7	31.0	4.6	6.4	1.3	9.9	2.1
Urban Forest	25.8	5.5	18.2	5.4	8.7	4.0	10.1	9.0
Urban Savannah	37.8	3.9	43.0	5.2	30.1	5.1	26.4	8.6
Rural Coastal	52.5	14.4	45.6	16.7	27.2	9.3	30.3	6.9
Rural Forest	61.6	35.5	38.0	30.1	33.1	29.1	27.9	30.1
Rural Savannah	73.0	32.6	70.0	36.6	64.2	46.9	55.0	40.8
Urban	27.7	17.8	19.4	16.6	12.4	14.8	10.6	22.0
Rural	63.6	82.2	49.5	83.4	43.7	85.3	37.9	78.0
All Ghana	51.7	100	39.5	100	31.9	100	24.2	100

Source: Created by the author based on data from *Pattern and Trends of Poverty in Ghana, 1991–2006*, Ghana Statistical Service, April 2007; Poverty Profile in Ghana (2005–2013), Ghana Living Standards Survey Round 6, Ghana Statistical Service, August 2014.

* Poverty incidence is calculated based on an upper poverty line that incorporates essential food and nonfood consumption. Individuals consuming at levels above this are considered able to purchase enough food to meet their requirements and to be able to meet their basic nonfood needs. An extreme poverty line is also calculated, using the cost of the consumption basket needed to meet the nutritional requirements of household members.

** The poverty line was recalculated for the sixth round (2012/2013) of the survey because of changes in the consumption basket used to construct the poverty line. Based on the poverty line for 2012/2013, the welfare levels for 2005/2006 were adjusted, putting the poverty incidence for 2005/2006 at 31.9 percent, higher than the previous calculation of 28.5 percent. The survey reports are available at www.statsghana.gov.gh.

million. There was significant variation in poverty incidence by region and in terms of urban and rural areas, which mirrors the structure of economy and the drivers of growth over the past decades.

The overall poverty incidence decreased by 7.7 percent between 2006 and 2013, as shown in Table 4.4, but this decrease was driven largely by declining poverty in the Greater Accra metropolitan area and masks the slight increase in poverty in many parts of the south. The survey results show that the decline in poverty was linked to growth in the service sector, given that the large proportion of individuals engaged in service sector activities were above the poverty line. Over the period from 2006 to 2013, public sector earners experienced a reduction in poverty as a result of increases in public sector wages as part of the public sector wage rationalization process. While poverty increased in parts of the south, it fell consistently across the northern regions, but the uneven distribution of gains between urban and rural areas remained, with urban areas seeing most of the benefits as a result of growth in the service sector. The 2012/2013 survey shows that the highest poverty incidence remained among food-crop farmers. Households engaged as private employees and self-employed in non-agricultural sectors were less likely to be poor than those engaged in the agricultural sector.

With a service sector that is highly dependent on public expenditures and public sector employment, the gains in poverty reduction are vulnerable. According to Table 4.3, the public sector employed slightly more people than the formal private sector in 2012/2013. This dependence on the state for employment, in the context of a small private sector, is an important factor behind the consistent budget deficits and thus recurrent macroeconomic crises, as discussed in the final section of this chapter.

The Colonial Trading Economy and Recurrent Macroeconomic Crises

The colonial trading economy left governments dependent on revenues generated from the extractive sector, the import trade, and the value added tax (which was introduced in the late 1990s to replace dependence on taxing cocoa exports), as well as foreign aid. In this context, the reemergence of competitive clientelism led to recurrent macroeconomic crises in 1992, 1996, 2000 and 2008 – which were all election years. The crises were caused by the same three factors, regardless of the party in power: the large public sector wage bill, utility subsidies and politically expedient expenditures, which led to government overspending.

NDC and NPP governments spent a large part of government revenue on public sector wages and salaries (recurrent expenditure), as well as public institutions and state-run utilities and other companies. Due to the small size of the formal sector, the government became the largest employer, and public salaries became a political tool used during election campaigning. However, the large portion of government revenue that went to the public sector wage bill and public institutions left very little fiscal space for capital expenditures, and made it difficult to cut government spending without cutting salaries or jobs.[37]

Fuel, electricity and water subsidies also consumed a large portion of government expenditure, as successive NDC and NPP governments chose to subsidize utilities and fuel as a political tool in their electoral strategies.[38] Water, electricity and fuel are items consumed by all of the population, and thus their prices affected everyone. Furthermore, the water and electricity utilities were inefficient, with constant shortages of supply and thus rotation systems, and increasing the price of poorly delivered services was also politically costly. Fuel and utility tariffs were supposed to be adjusted automatically by an independent agency, as a result of conditions set in the IMF and World Bank lending agreements in the second half of the 1990s, but political interference kept the adjustments from being implemented regularly.[39]

The NDC and NPP governments also spent in excess of what was budgeted, with extremely high spending during election years.

37 For more on these trends, see World Bank (2014: 5) and Poverty Profile in Ghana (2005–2013), Ghana Living Standards Survey Round 6, Ghana Statistical Service, August 2014, p. 4.

38 The Ghana National Petroleum Corporation had a monopoly on the importation of crude oil and through an arrangement with another government parastatal, the Tema Oil Refinery, it became the sole wholesale supplier of petrol products to oil marketing companies in Ghana. Therefore, domestic prices of petrol products were set by the government, and failure to adjust prices in response to increases in international market prices or depreciation of the cedi resulted in government subsidizing the cost – costs which are deducted from petroleum taxes and registered as a fall in government revenue from petrol taxes.

39 On the public water utility and water tariffs, see Whitfield (2006) and Hirvi and Whitfield (2015). On fuel pricing and the automatic adjustment mechanism, see Whitfield and Jones (2009).

Overspending occurred due to problems with prioritizing the allocation of scarce budget revenue, with actually disbursing money as budget allocations indicated, and with keeping expenditures under the budget ceilings. Annual budget allocations did not always follow the government's stated development priorities due to party political pressures to distribute resources widely. Financing too many projects with not enough resources caused delays in disbursements, leading to delays in the completion of projects and thus costly extensions. Resources were not always disbursed according to budget allocations, again due to political pressures. Individual politicians and influential political elites lobbied for disbursements that benefited their constituencies, and whether or not they were successful depended on the influence they wielded within the ruling party.[40]

How these three factors led to recurring macroeconomic instability in the 1990s and 2000s is demonstrated by looking at specific actions of the NDC and NPP governments during this period. In the election year of 1992, government expenditure increased from 13.7 percent of GDP in 1991 to 17 percent in 1992, largely due to a substantial salary increase to civil servants, at the same time that total revenue and grants fell from 15.2 percent of GDP to 12.2 percent, the lowest since 1982 (Hutchful 2002: 215). The resulting budget deficit was financed almost entirely through domestic debt, driving up inflation by 27 percent. At the same time, there was a sharp deterioration in the balance of payments due to higher imports and falling export revenues, resulting from falling international prices of cocoa and timber and lower export volumes. As the PNDC government was under IMF and World Bank lending agreements, this macroeconomic situation meant that the government missed performance targets stated in the agreements, and the World Bank and other donors suspended disbursements, leading to a further loss of external inflows. The IMF program was also suspended in 1992, and a new one was not put in place until 1995 (Leite et al. 2000: 37).

The newly elected NDC government decided to tackle the fiscal deficit after the 1992 elections through increasing revenue rather than decreasing public spending. One avenue for increasing revenue was

[40] Tony Killick (2008) provides evidence of this trend in Ghana's health sector, and Abdul-Gafaru Abdulai (2012) provides evidence of this trend within the education sector under both the Rawlings-led NDC government and the Kufuor-led NPP government (see also Abdulai and Hickey 2016).

divesting government shares in some of the most profitable state-owned enterprises (Leite et al. 2000: 49). Between 1994 and 1996, the sale of profitable enterprises amounted to US$569 million, most of which was accounted for with the sale of the government's shares in Ashanti Goldfields in 1994/1995 that brought in US$454 million. The revenues from divesting Ashanti Goldfields were not used strategically, but rather helped offset the impact of major shortfalls in long-term concessional lending in the absence of IMF support. The government ran fiscal deficits every year between 1992 and 2000 except for 1994 and 1995 as a direct result of revenue earned for divesting shares in Ashanti Goldfields.

On several occasions, the NDC government delayed important initiatives for collecting revenues or reducing subsidies in response to resistance or in the run-up to elections. In the election years of 1992 and 1996, the NDC government delayed increasing petrol prices until after the elections, and again in 1999, when urban groups such as doctors, nurses and university students threatened to strike, the government rescinded its decision to increase petrol prices (Leite et al. 2000: 30–36, 54).[41] The government also withdrew the value added tax in 1995 after a major political demonstration against the new tax in which different excluded political factions joined forces and mobilized a wave of broad popular protest, and did not reintroduce it until 1998 after reducing the rate and making changes to the design (Osei 2000).

External indebtedness increased rapidly in the 1990s from US$3.5 million in 1990 to about US$7 billion in 1999, largely due to the fact that foreign aid receipts declined in response to the government's failure to satisfy certain IMF performance targets in the second half of the 1990s. As a result, the NDC government could not rollover foreign aid receipts to pay its external debt. New foreign aid receipts were less than scheduled repayments on external debt, because interest payments exceeded expenditure on development projects, excluding those financed with external loans and grants. Interest payments even exceeded the wage bill in 1997 to become the leading expenditure item in the government recurrent budget, constituting 35.4 percent of recurrent expenditure. As a result, the government was squeezed. In response, the Bank of Ghana stopped honoring government checks in

[41] See also *Africa Confidential* Vol. 40, No. 24, p. 3.

1998. While this led to improvements in macroeconomic indicators on the surface, it resulted in government ministries, departments and agencies running large debts to private companies, and thus effectively transferring the debt burden from government to the private sector, which had the effect of stifling economic activities (Hutchful 2002: 216–217).

During 1999 and 2000, economic performance declined dramatically, and donors withheld foreign aid due to what they saw as policy slippages by the government. Lower than expected foreign aid inflows were exacerbated by drops in the international prices of cocoa and gold, the country's main exports, combined with a higher international price for oil, which the country imported. The Bank of Ghana tried to fend off currency devaluation that resulted from trade deficits by buying cedis, but this failed and further depleted the country's foreign exchange reserves. At the same time, the government borrowed from the Bank of Ghana to finance its growing budget deficits, which resulted in an upsurge of inflation and a sharp depreciation of the cedi, which lost 75 percent of its value relative to the US dollar between November 1999 and April 2000 (Hutchful 2002: 218). The upcoming December 2000 elections exacerbated these pressures, and a currency black market appeared. This severe macroeconomic instability is one factor explaining why the NDC lost the 2000 elections.

The new Kufuor-led NPP government inherited an economy in deep crisis: rising inflation, currency depreciation, a huge domestic debt, shortfalls in aid flows and massive external debt servicing. The NPP government could not balance the 2001 budget despite cuts in public expenditure and faced the proposition of either cutting public expenditure massively or asking the international community for more foreign aid. President Kufuor chose the latter. Since Ghana's major official aid donors were pushing the government to sign up to the Heavily Indebted Poor Country Initiative (HIPC) as a prerequisite for more aid, it did (Osei 2008: 125). Accessing debt relief required meeting a series of conditions specified in the HIPC agreement and World Bank and IMF lending agreements (Whitfield and Jones 2009). All increased investment expenditure came from aid flows, while government revenue went toward payments on domestic and external debt, public sector salaries, administration, statutory payments and counterpart funding for donor projects.

President Kufuor's government was successful in meeting the debt relief conditionality, and the government benefited from debt relief starting in 2002. Notably, 20 percent of the HIPC savings was used to pay off interest on domestic debt. The remainder of the HIPC savings was spread thinly across ministries, which decided how to use the funds, as well as across district assemblies, which decided the micro-projects on which the money would be spent. HIPC resources were spent largely on the provision of social services, with the health and education ministries the largest beneficiaries.[42] The micro-projects in rural areas, such as a school block or a public toilet, were given big signs with the words "HIPC Benefits" printed on them, and became an important electioneering tool for the NPP government in the December 2004 general elections.[43]

During President Kufuor's second term in office, new external sources of financing the state emerged. These sources included the international capital market, and Chinese investment and official concessionary credit. However, Chinese involvement was largely confined to infrastructure projects, such as the building of the Bui hydroelectric dam. Parts of concessional loans and grants from the Chinese and Indian governments were used to finance distinctly unproductive investments, such as building a new presidential palace, constructing a new Ministry of Defence building, and rehabilitating the Peduase Presidential Lodge.[44]

The first NPP administration achieved macroeconomic stability, but things changed under the second NPP administration, especially after its agreement with the IMF ended in 2006. Fiscal deficits grew from 2006 onwards due to government overspending. Some of the main drivers of fiscal expansion were necessary to support production such as investments in infrastructure and energy, given major electricity shortages in 2006 and 2007. Other drivers were distributive, such as higher wages and salaries, social transfers to finance progress towards the Millennium Development Goals, and continuing with the previous government's strategy of utility subsidies. Furthermore, in 2008, the government initiated several measures intended to mitigate the global

42 "Where Did Ghana's HIPC Funds Go?," unpublished report by SEND-Ghana, 2006.

43 Author's observations.

44 On the Indian loan/grant for the presidential palace, see *Democracy Watch* Vol. 6, No. 3&4, p. 4, CDD-Ghana. On Chinese aid, see Tsikata et al. (2008: 25).

food and oil price rises, including reduced taxes and levies on petrol products, abolishing import duties on staple foods, and an untargeted fertilizer subsidy program. Considerable government outlays in 2007 and 2008 were spent on unproductive prestige projects, such as Ghana@50 to celebrate fifty years of independence (US$100 million), building three new football stadiums for the African Cup of Nations (US$77 million), and building a new presidential palace (about US$80 million).[45]

To finance the growing fiscal deficit, the NPP government tried the previous NDC strategy of issuing domestic government bonds and using divestiture proceeds (for example, from the resale of Ghana Telecom). To this mix it added a new strategy: using proceeds from the first Eurobond issue.[46] Nevertheless, the budget deficit surged to 14.5 percent of GDP in 2008, and the trade deficit ballooned due to rapid growth in non-oil imports and increases in the oil bill, despite good export performance. The currency depreciated, inflation soared, and by January 2009 the country was in a macroeconomic crisis of its own making that had little to do with the global financial crisis. The NPP government had to deal with increasing international oil prices throughout its tenure in office. But this factor did not prompt a change in the NPP government's spending patterns regarding subsidizing the cost of petrol, nor did it lead to ruling political elites seriously prioritizing expenditures that would create new sources of foreign exchange through export diversification or ways to save foreign exchange through production aimed at import substitution.

In sum, the causes of macroeconomic crisis were the same, and were linked to the return of competitive clientelism. Both the NDC and NPP governments engaged in overspending, particularly in election years,

[45] The Ghana@50 committee spent five times the amount of money approved by Parliament, and an inquiry into the expenditures carried out by the Atta Mills NDC government in 2009 showed that large amounts of money had been lost in bad decisions and negligence, partly as a result of people trying to make money out of the opportunities it afforded. *Democracy Watch* 2010 Vol. 8, No. 4, pp. 8–9; Report of the Commission. On the football stadiums, built by the Chinese, see *Africa Confidential* 2005 Vol. 46, No. 25, p. 3. The presidential palace was to be funded using a US$60 million loan/grant from the Export and Import Bank of India. It was supposed to cost US$36.9 million, but the final cost was much higher. *Democracy Watch* 2005 Vol. 6, No. 3&4, p. 4; www.ghanaweb.com, "Presidential Palace Is Ready," November 7, 2008, and "Mills works from Jubilee House for first time," November 10, 2009.

[46] *Africa Confidential* 2008 Vol. 49, No. 17, p. 9 and 2009 Vol. 50, No. 2, p. 2.

but not only then, and they tended to prioritize distributive, consumption-driven policies. Governments actually had a narrow fiscal space for discretionary expenditures, which was part of the problem. The small size of the formal sector reduced government revenue and led it to depend on revenues from the extractive sectors, the import trade, and the value added tax, as well as foreign aid.

Government revenue went almost entirely to pay for state administration, the public wage bill and state institutions and companies. Governments depended on donors to finance capital investments and social sector expenditures, as well as the IMF to supplement the country's foreign exchange earnings, as exports increased but not enough to keep pace with imports. Thus, when governments wanted to increase spending in order to meet electorate expectations and patronage needs, they had to subvert it from existing programs, borrow it from domestic banks, sell some state assets (of which there is a limited pool) or borrow from the central bank. While the NPP government had a greater range of financing avenues to choose from, such as financing from nontraditional donors and from issuing Eurobonds on the international capital market, NPP political elites used the increased revenue on consumption-related expenditures, on long-term infrastructure projects, and to write down domestic debt.

Conclusion

The Ghanaian economy recovered in the 1980s, but the structural adjustment pathway pursued by the PNDC elites resulted in recovery of the colonial trading economy, which the country had at independence. This pathway was the result of the PNDC elites not only having limited links to domestic capitalists, but also actively seeking to marginalize the surviving domestic capitalists. As a result, the PNDC elites formed a stronger alliance with the IMF and World Bank, which they relied on to finance the reforms and soften the immediate economic hardships involved with economic liberalization. Maintaining but reforming the Cocoa Board resulted in the continued role of the state in the sector, which produced benefits for the government in terms of revenue, control over foreign exchange and capturing economic gains through the external marketing company that could be invested back into the cocoa sector. It also produced benefits for the sector in terms of high-quality cocoa that fetched a premium price with international buyers. The gold sector was more important in terms of generating government revenue, through retained government shares in privatized large-scale mining companies, through royalties, and through corporate taxes.

Outside these two sectors, governments had little to show. The PNDC and NDC governments did not pursue many initiatives targeting other productive sectors or supporting domestic firms and farms to adjust and become competitive in the rapidly liberalized environment. The PNDC ruling elites mostly negotiated on the margins of the projects put forward by donors, especially the World Bank. As shown in this chapter, most of the World Bank projects had limited positive impacts, and sometimes had negative ones, such as with the cocoa extension service. Bank projects were driven more by ideas than by the actual needs of farmers and industrialists. The idea was to reduce the scope of the state in order to make the government's budget manageable and the development path sustainable, but they underestimated what was required to boost production and productivity (the supply side) and to catalyze new industries and exports. In the end, donor projects proved no more sustainable than the previous state interventions. The constraints on the supply side had to do with access to credit, technology and infrastructure as well as finding institutional solutions to insecure land tenure, contract enforcement, and financing learning within firms. The NPP government pursued more government expenditures on production and productivity-enhancing initiatives in agriculture and manufacturing, but most of them were poorly designed, did not go far enough in supporting domestic firms, or bypassed domestic firms in favor of state-led and state-controlled investments. Chapter 7 looks in more detail at some of these initiatives and why they had limited economic outcomes.

The lack of significant progress in developing export-oriented or import-substituting industries and in increasing the productivity of agriculture meant that the formal private sector in Ghana remained quite small. Most of the population remained "employed" in the informal sector and in agriculture, with food crop farmers the poorest members of society. The public sector employed as many people as the formal private sector, making a significant part of the population directly dependent on public sector wages. The low incomes of much of the population meant they were sensitive to price changes in utilities and fuel. These factors, combined with pressures from competitive clientelism to increase government expenditures and spread them widely, led to government overspending, especially in election years. The NDC and NPP governments financed budget deficits through domestic debt, external debt and borrowing from the central bank, which led to inflation, currency depreciation and increasing expenditures on debt servicing – further squeezing the fiscal space for government spending and reinforcing the vicious cycle of macroeconomic crises. Governments consistently sought to increase revenue rather than decrease spending, in the context of increasingly competitive elections.

The next two chapters turn to the industry case studies, which allow for more detailed exploration into the causal mechanisms between the pressures of competitive clientelism combined with weak domestic capitalists, the political survival strategies adopted by ruling political elites to win elections and stay in office, the specific policy choices of ruling elites and to what extent they address the constraints on productivity in these industries, and the implementation and economic impacts of those policies. The industry case study chapters show that the PNDC government was the most responsive to the needs of the horticulture export and palm oil processing industries and more successful with implementing industrial policies than the NDC and NPP governments. This difference is due partly to the dire state of the economy in the 1980s and thus a greater political motivation to pursue productivity-enhancing initiatives, but also to the different political configuration of power inside the ruling PNDC coalition and outside of it. Individuals within the PNDC governing elite supported specific firms in these two industries to increase their production and productivity, which involved state-owned firms in the case of palm oil processing but privately owned firms in the case of horticulture exports. However, support for these firms declined under the NDC and NPP governments, as the state-owned palm oil estates were privatized and as Ghanaian-owned horticulture firms had little political leverage after the return to competitive clientelism. Both of these industries subsequently encountered problems and stagnated. Firms in the horticulture export sector failed to overcome constraints on productivity and respond to increased global competition, while firms in palm oil processing faced constraints on expanding oil palm cultivation through direct land acquisition and in organizing the raw material supply from smallholder farmers.

5 Challenges to Diversifying Exports

Accessing Global Markets and Learning to Learn

To train up African enterprise must naturally be one of the major objectives of economic policy ... the crucial test of an industrialization policy is not how rapidly it increases employment or output, but how rapidly it builds up African enterprise ... African entrepreneurship is deficient in technical knowledge, in managerial capacity, and in capital. Of these three ... lack of managerial capacity is more difficult to remedy ... much can be learnt only by experience.[1]

This quote from W.A. Lewis in his report on industrialization in the Gold Coast is as important for Ghana today as it was in 1953. Industrial policies in Ghana have continuously neglected this aspect of industrialization. In countries with domestic firms that have very low technological capabilities, firms must even "learn to learn" (Lall 1996). The story of the rise and fall of the pineapple export industry in Ghana is a story of learning to learn, but unfortunately not before most of the pineapple producer-exporters' firms collapsed.

The purpose of this chapter, and the next one, is to explain the productivity constraints on agribusiness and agro-processing in Ghana, and to show how the PNDC, NDC and then NPP governments did or did not address these constraints in specific industry cases. This chapter focuses on the constraints encountered when building international competitiveness in a new agribusiness export sector: high-value horticulture. In addition to solving first-order constraints related to commercial farming and second-order constraints related to building technological capabilities in a new economic activity, diversifying exports also entails accessing global markets and negotiating relations with buyers. The horticulture export sector is a significant case because horticulture products were one of the country's largest categories of nontraditional exports in the 2000s and because the horticulture sector

[1] Report on Industrialisation and the Gold Coast, p. 12.

has great potential to drive economic transformation given Ghana's economic structure.

The global fruit export market grew significantly from the 1980s, as importing countries were willing to pay for access to fresh fruit all year round. Ghana has a comparative advantage in the tropical fruit market through the ability to offset growing seasons of the northern hemisphere countries and given the country's physical proximity to key markets in Europe. Agribusiness firms that can produce fresh fruit for export to European markets are not simple farms. They require technological capabilities to manage complex production and organizational processes and respond to changing consumer demands, buyer specifications and international competition. Thus, horticulture exports can spur the development of technological capabilities among domestic capitalists. Horticulture production can also act as a bridge between agriculture and manufacturing. Processing fruit not only provides an outlet for non-export-grade fruit, but also leads to firms developing agro-processing capabilities that lay a foundation from which to move into other light manufacturing industries. Finally, horticultural production has great potential for import substitution by supplying supermarkets with fresh fruit and vegetables, and supplying local processing firms that produce juice and other processed products for the domestic market through formal outlets such as hotels, supermarkets and restaurants.

Pineapple was the major horticulture export product in Ghana from the 1980s through the mid-2000s. Pineapple exports grew slowly from 650 tons exported by air in 1984 to 10,000 tons by 1991, but then took off around 1995, reaching a peak of 70,000 tons in 2004. Pineapple commercial production for export started as the result of private initiatives from a handful of Ghanaian entrepreneurs looking for a way to make money in a context of limited economic opportunities. By the mid-2000s, pineapple production for export was split between approximately twelve large farms (300–700 ha), forty medium farms (20–150 ha) and 10,000 smallholders (0.2–10 hectares). The pineapple producer-exporters constituted a rare group in a country where large-scale capitalist farming was not a widespread form of agricultural production. They also constituted a new form of agrarian capitalism, one characterized by urban investors and links to export markets that required higher technological capabilities. Foreign and domestic private investments in fruit processing companies occurred in the late

1990s and early 2000s on the back of the boom in horticulture production in general, and pineapple production in particular.

Taking advantage of the economic opportunities in horticulture exports and fruit processing required addressing first- and second-order constraints such as building new capabilities among local agribusiness firms, coordinated investments in infrastructure, and solving institutional problems related to land and finance as well as training labor and creating a wage labor force in agribusiness. Specific to the fresh fruit export industry, it required creating supply chain logistics and meeting safety and quality standards for export to European markets. Creating a profitable fruit-processing sector required integrating farmers with processors to provide high volumes of low-cost raw material, access to finance, high-quality logistics and skilled management.[2]

The PNDC government did not have a concerted response to the constraints faced by the nascent pineapple export industry, as the Ministry of Finance was focused on macroeconomic reforms and increasing foreign exchange and government revenue through revival of the traditional export sectors. However, the industry did receive support from the Ministry of Trade and Industry, through an ad hoc industrial policy led by the secretary (minister), which involved a degree of mutual interests. This initiative gave the small group of pineapple producer-exporters access to inputs and finance, solved collective action problems within the group and reduced the financial risks of these pioneers – addressing the immediate constraints that they faced in the mid-1980s. This initiative was short-lived as the Secretary of the Ministry of Trade and Industry fell out of favor with Rawlings and left the PNDC ruling coalition.

During the NDC and NPP government, most of the support to the horticulture sector in general, and the pineapple export industry in particular, came from donor-funded projects – which were piecemeal, uncoordinated, and left key constraints unaddressed. The lack of interest among NDC and NPP ruling elites in the horticulture export sector is the typical orientation of ruling elites towards productive sectors under the Fourth Republic. In the context of

[2] The processing segment of the horticulture sector will not be discussed in this chapter. For a good study of one of the largest firms exporting fresh-cut fruit, see Ouma (2015).

competitive clientelism, NDC and NPP ruling elites were busy with meeting the distributional needs of their individual and party support network as well as people in their electoral constituency. They could also point to donor projects in the horticulture sector, many of which required government counterpart funding, but which were negotiated between donor staff and ministry of agriculture bureaucrats, with politicians only interested to see that money was flowing. This point is clearly illustrated in the case of the Millennium Challenge Account project under the NPP government. The politics behind the formulation and implementation of this project is discussed in Chapter 7, but its negligible and even negative impact on the horticulture sector is explained at the end of this chapter.

The pineapple producer-exporters were first-generation capitalists who were also new to both commercial farming and exporting, and thus had low technological capabilities. These domestic capitalists in general did not wield much political influence individually or as a group. Individually, there was only one pineapple producer-exporter who had political connections, during the NDC government, but political relations with Rawlings could backfire, as they did in this case. The horticulture industry associations were never strong, as a result of factionalism and competition among the producer-exporters, which weakened their ability to develop a collective strategy for the industry and lobby the government to support that strategy.

The Ghanaian entrepreneurs who pioneered the pineapple export industry also largely failed to continue investing in building their capabilities. Firm-level investments in capabilities did not happen on a significant level until the external shock in 2005 caused by changing European market demands compelled such investments. However, only a small number of firms survived, and those that did continued to face many constraints that required collective solutions at the industry level. By 2009, production was concentrated in the hands of about fourteen large-scale farms, mostly Ghanaian-owned, but by 2015, only a few of them were regularly exporting. The contraction of fresh pineapple exports, as well as the inability of other fresh horticulture export products to take off on a significant scale, indicated that the horticulture export sector was foundering. Problems in the production of fresh fruit also affected the profitability of the emerging fruit processing industry as the supply of pineapples among smallholders disappeared and the overall supply contracted.

This chapter tells the story of the pineapple industry's birth in the 1980s, rise in the 1990s, crisis in 2006, and its failed revival and uncertain future by 2015. It is based almost entirely on new empirical material produced from different types of sources. The first type includes reports by international and domestic consultants who had been working in and observing the sector for several decades, which were followed up with interviews by phone and in person. The second type was firm histories, which I produced using informal, in-depth, repetitive conversations with the firm owners, as well as being on the farms, talking to other key staff at the farm, and observing the production and postharvest processes. Fourteen firms were strategically selected for the firm histories, including eleven out of the fourteen firms still exporting regularly in 2009. These eleven firms included nine firms that had complete or majority Ghanaian ownership, and two firms with foreign ownership. The remaining three firms in the firm histories include those that were important pioneer investors but no longer existed. The third type of source was interviews with, and documents collected from, staff of the Sea-Freighted Pineapple Exporters of Ghana Association; civil servants in the Horticulture Development Unit of the Ministry of Food and Agriculture; and staff members of donor agencies with projects affecting the horticulture sector in the 1990s and 2000s.

The Emergence of Pineapple Producer-Exporters

New economic activities do not emerge in a vacuum. There are always antecedents: experiences, even if failures, that lay the foundation and generate the initial capabilities, opportunities and incentives for risk-taking. In the case of horticulture exports, attempts at pineapple production and exports in the 1960s and 1970s laid the foundation for the renewed attempt in the 1980s.[3] The story actually begins with Swiss missionaries that established a botanical garden in the town of

[3] This section draws on an interview with a former employee of the Nsawam Cannery in 1985 who then became a pineapple producer-exporter, and two unpublished master's theses from Ghana: Peter Obeng, "Pineapple Production and Export in Ghana," Dissertation for Diploma in Agricultural Administration, Ghana Institute of Management and Public Administration, Achimtoa, 1992; Irene Obeng, "Effects of Domestic Policies on Production and Export of Nontraditional Agricultural Commodities: Case Study of Fresh Pineapple," MPhil thesis in Agricultural Economics, University of Ghana, 1994.

Aburi in the late nineteenth century and introduced a new variety of pineapple, Smooth Cayenne, which was adopted by peasant farmers in the surrounding area. However, as the cocoa industry expanded, farmers stopped growing pineapple. In the early postindependence period, Nkrumah's CPP government established a state-owned cannery near the town of Nsawam, which was to produce pineapple chunks and juice for local and export markets. A state-owned plantation was established, but the factory also used local farmers as outgrowers, so farmers started growing pineapple again. These developments gave rise to the pineapple belt between the towns of Aburi and Nsawam, but the political instability after the overthrow of Nkrumah's government in 1966 undermined this foundation.

The Acheampong military government supported pineapple production in an attempt to increase the supply of pineapples to the Nsawam Cannery through projects that offered agro-inputs, mechanization and extension services. Pineapple production levels increased to 34,000 tons of pineapple by 1974, the highest level in Ghana's history at that time. However, it is not clear whether this production went to the local market, cannery or export. Pineapple production decreased after 1974 and plummeted by 1979 to only 3,900 tons.

Ironically, it was around 1979–1980 in the midst of Ghana's most severe economic crisis that the seeds of the contemporary pineapple export industry were sown. The pineapple export industry emerged as the result of a handful of Ghanaian entrepreneurs identifying and exploiting a comparative advantage. Airfreight costs to Europe were cheaper for Ghana than for Côte d'Ivoire, which accounted for 95 percent of European imports in 1986 (Willems 2006). Ghana had similar agro-climatic conditions as Côte d'Ivoire and was a similar distance from Europe, but it did not have an experienced group of commercial pineapple producers, nor the infrastructure or the institutions for export, marketing and logistics that Côte d'Ivoire had developed during the early postindependence period.

The first investors in fresh pineapples for export were educated professionals working in the private and public sectors who were looking for a new way to make money at a time of economic crises. For example, the owner of Combined Farms had been working in the London branch of the Ghana Commercial Bank handling cocoa proceeds and returned to Ghana in the late 1970s. The person who established Koranco Farms had been running a trading company in Europe and also returned to Ghana around the same time.[4]

Ghana's first exports in 1984 were sent on passenger airlines because there were no cargo airlines then. When the space of passenger airlines was exhausted, the pioneer exporters found space at cheap rates on commercial cargo airplanes that were delivering part accessories to the oil fields in Nigeria and then flying northbound to Europe empty. Combined Farms and Koranco Farms used this opportunity to establish freight companies and scheduled commercial cargo planes to carry pineapples back to Europe. When they saw the profits to be made, they started their own pineapple farms, using capital accumulated while abroad and leasing land from chiefs just outside Accra. The owner of Koranco Farms went to the horticulture school in Abidjan to learn how to grow pineapple and brought his knowledge back to Ghana, translating a French manual on pineapple production into English. Other Ghanaians followed suit, and by the late 1980s, there were about sixteen commercial pineapple farms. Many of them were very small and also sourced pineapples from smallholder farmers.

Four conditions made capitalist pineapple production for export appear attractive enough for urban Ghanaians to invest. First, an economic crisis in the late 1970s and early 1980s compelled a search for new types of economic activity that could generate foreign exchange, followed by macroeconomic structural adjustment reforms that began in 1983 that made exports profitable. Second, the investment costs and tacit knowledge required to begin production were relatively low, and expertise initially could be brought into the farm by buying it. The low investment costs and the ability to access or bring in tacit knowledge of agricultural production reduced the barriers to entry as well as the risk of investments yielding a return. As a result, urbanites with no history in agriculture were willing to take the risk, because the potential return was high, or at least higher than alternative outlets for investment at the time. Third, the agricultural production area was located within a radius of 40 to 60 kilometers of Accra, and close to the air and seaports. Close proximity to Accra meant that investors could still live in the capital city and run their pineapple farms relatively easily, while proximity to the airport and seaport

[4] For more details on the backgrounds of the pineapple producer-exporters and why they invested in the industry, see Whitfield (2017).

meant that transport costs were lower. Fourth, while the emergence of commercial pineapple production was largely driven by private initiative, short episodes of external support and subsidies by government or donor projects helped the Ghanaians to create commercial farms and facilitated the learning process.

Except for the owner of Combined Farms, these commercial farmers did not have political connections with the PNDC government. The owner of Combined Farms was close to Rawlings, which probably accounts for his ability to access capital through loans provided under World Bank projects in the late 1980s (see Opoku 2010). Notably, Combined Farms was the largest exporter in the 1980s and early 1990s.

Ad Hoc Industrial Policy under the PNDC Government

The emerging pineapple export industry benefited from the general macroeconomic reforms under structural adjustment, including devaluation of the currency and exchange rate and foreign exchange liberalization. Other policies intended to benefit export sectors included fiscal concessions to nontraditional exporters, duty-free import of agriculture inputs for export production, rehabilitation of infrastructure, and privatization of agricultural input delivery systems (Anyemedu 1991).[5] These macroeconomic reforms made the takeoff of pineapple exports in the late 1980s possible, but structural adjustment on its own did not spur the takeoff. Targeted support to expand pineapple production spearheaded by the ministry during 1987 and 1988 was crucial.

The Pineapple Production Expansion Program was the personal initiative of the secretary of trade and industry (equivalent to minister). Given the dire situation in the country, with very little production and thus very little being exported, he decided to help the pineapple producer-exporters as a way to boost exports. The secretary could not get financing from the secretary of finance, who was under extreme fiscal constraints, so he raised it through importing bulk goods at the ministry and then exploiting the rising prices of imported goods at a time of rapid currency devaluation. The program financed and organized

[5] From April 1983 to 1986, Ghana's currency was devalued through a series of large discrete devaluations in order to bring it closer to the free-market exchange rate (Hutchful 2002: 56). Then the official and free-market exchange rates were unified in several stages between 1986 and 1990.

access to planting material from Côte d'Ivoire, because there was not enough planting material in Ghana, as well as access to import licenses[6] and a concessionary credit facility to finance the building of basic packhouses, irrigation facilities, farm equipment and agro-chemicals.

The producer-exporters who benefited from this government support referred to it as essential to the expansion of the industry in the 1980s because it came at a critical time when the industry was stagnating due to economic constraints and to unproductive competition. The nascent pineapple producer-exporters were loosely grouped under the Horticulture Association of Ghana. The association was plagued by a rivalry between the two largest producer-exporters, which undermined collective action within the industry and had the effect of limiting the growth of the smaller producer-exporters. State intervention through the pineapple production expansion program helped to mediate this conflict. The program also encouraged limited coordination as a requirement to receive the assistance. The secretary worked with the association to select eight of the biggest producers to receive soft loans in the first round, with the remaining eight to receive loans in the second round. He demanded that they produce business plans for expansion, but apparently there were no other conditions attached to the loans. It was difficult to substantiate whether the beneficiaries ever repaid the loans. The second batch of producers never benefited from the financial support because the secretary resigned.

What was the motivation of this particular secretary of trade and industry to create the pineapple production expansion program? He was part of the new generation of young, well-educated, radicalized Ghanaians who were called upon and were willing to join Rawlings' PNDC regime under the premise of change. He was first secretary of interior, before he was moved to secretary of trade and industry. The secretary concluded that the country's main problem was on the supply side and exports would only increase through interventions to support production. Most nontraditional exports at that time were horticulture crops, but the fact that the secretary circulated within the

[6] While the PNDC government embarked on major macroeconomic reforms starting in 1983, it initially maintained controls on foreign exchange and the import license system. Restrictions on the retention of foreign exchange were gradually removed starting in the late 1980s and not completed until 1992.

same social networks of at least two of the pineapple producer-exporters brought the industry to his attention.

While PNDC elites sought to produce their "own" businessmen, none of their efforts were through investments in the pineapple export industry. Notably, PNDC political elites who were aware of opportunities in the pineapple export industry, such as Kwesi Ahwoi who was the head of the Ghana Export Promotion Council and worked directly with the secretary of trade and industry to implement the pineapple production expansion program, did not use their political connections to enter the pineapple export industry. Rather the Ahwoi brothers went in for cashew and then cocoa and started a cocoa licensed buying company in 1992 called Cashpro (see Chapter 3). This choice probably has to do with differences between the two export industries. Cocoa was almost entirely linked to the state (so state connections could be used) and involved little risk or knowledge of production. Cocoa licensed buying agents benefited from state provision of loans and the existence of a guaranteed market. They bought cocoa from farmers and then sold it to the Cocoa Board. The pineapple export industry, on the other hand, was a much riskier investment, as it was new to the country.

The secretary resigned his post and the PNDC altogether in December 1988. His story is that he fell out with the top circle of the PNDC and was being persecuted on trumped-up charges. Paul Nugent (1995: 192) notes that the secretary was involved in corruption scandals and was being harassed for that reason. Thus, while the PNDC ruling elites were more cohesive than in periods defined by competitive clientelism, their cohesion centered on Rawlings and his approval. It was easy to fall out with him, and many did.

After the secretary left office, the head of the Ghana Export Promotion Council continued some support for horticulture exports with the limited resources that he could find and the support of a few key staff. Staff at the Ghana Export Promotion Council lacked knowledge about horticulture production and marketing, but they compensated for that by importing foreign expertise. Between 1987 and the early 1990s, donor projects funded by the Commonwealth Secretariat, the International Trade Centre in Geneva, and the United Nations Development Programme paid for international consultants to provide support to pineapple producers on production and marketing. The head of the council insisted that Ghanaian technocrats studied under the consultants, including two from the Ministry of Food and Agriculture and one from the council. The council also paid for pineapple producer-exporters to travel to other African countries to learn about commercial horticulture production and to European countries to understand the requirements of different export markets. Several interviewees acknowledged that these study tours were very helpful. Otherwise, it was left to the initiative of individual producer-exporters to fund their own travel for learning purposes, which several commercial farmers did.

The Takeoff of Pineapple Exports

The 1990s saw several changes in the landscape of the pineapple export industry. The success of the pioneers led to additional investments in the late 1980s and early 1990s. These new investors were also well-educated urban residents of Accra with international networks. Some of them previously worked in the public sector and used their salaries as investment or working capital when starting their commercial farms. JEI River is the exception because it had a history of corporate ownership.[7] The increase in commercial farmers spurred an increase in smallholder farmers producing pineapple to sell to exporters, which in turn led to the rise of pure exporters (exporters without their own farms) who bought fruits from smallholders and small commercial farmers. During the 1990s, there were between fifty and seventy companies exporting pineapples at any one time, and about 40 percent of exports came from smallholder production.

The pineapple producer-exporters generally relied on their profits for working capital. There was no financial support from the government during the 1990s. Land was leased from chiefs or family owners in the pineapple production belt, an area with a long history of cash-crop production, which resulted in the buying and selling of land to strangers more as the norm than the exception. However, there were problems, which were not insurmountable but consumed time and money. Land in the traditional pineapple belt was fragmented, having

[7] JEI River was established in 1993 when Ashanti Goldfields, a mining company, took over SCOA farms, an existing commercial pineapple farm. In 2006, the mining company sold its shares to the Agricultural Development Bank and a few other shareholders. Since 2010, one of the shareholders, a Ghanaian, has bought all the shares and is the sole owner of JEI River.

been divided among families for several generations. To acquire the size of land needed meant dealing with many landowners. Furthermore, there were often multiple claimants to land, especially when private investors were looking to buy it. This could result in land litigation, and sometimes producer-exporters lost money because they paid someone who was not the real owner of the land. Multiple claimants resulted from the absence of formal land titling. Another key challenge for investors was acquiring and sustaining skilled labor. Many producer-exporters went to Côte d'Ivoire to find farm managers, often from the horticulture school there, as Ghana did not have institutions training graduates to acquire skills in horticultural production and practical experience. It was not uncommon for commercial farms to poach skilled labor from each other.

By the early 1990s, Ghana's comparative advantage based on cheap airfreight charges to Europe was being eroded by rising fuel prices, exhaustion of available aircraft cargo space and the increasing cost competitiveness of sea-freighted exports from Central America as well as from Côte d'Ivoire. The increasing competition from Central America came particularly from Del Monte and Dole, transnational corporations with operations there, which we return to below.

In this context, a few pineapple producer-exporters spearheaded the move into sea freighting and established the Sea-Freighting Pineapple Exporters of Ghana association (SPEG) in 1994. This initiative was led by just a handful of producer-exporters who realized the importance of sea freighting to saving the international competitiveness of Ghana's industry and to expanding exports. Shifting to sea freighting required collaboration and organization among producer-exporters in a way that they had not done before. It would probably not have happened if actors external to the industry had not pushed the agenda and provided resources to support it. A private consultancy company hired as an implementing agency for a USAID project provided a feasibility study showing the cost advantage of shipping by sea and the volume that was needed to make it possible. This report was crucial in convincing four companies to take the risk.

SPEG was set up to arrange sea freight space on a refrigerated vessel owned by Compagnie Fruitière, which was traveling from Cameroon to Côte d'Ivoire and then to Europe. The consultancy company facilitated this contact and provided financial and logistical support for the operations of SPEG, until it could generate its own funds to support a secretariat. The vessel agreed to stop in Accra for a fixed minimum volume of pineapple per visit. SPEG negotiated this minimum volume and freight costs. Initially, the founding members of SPEG found it difficult to produce the minimum volume and had to pay for unused freight space – a cost shared among members. Eventually, the firms were able to expand their volume. With evidence of success, other producer-exporters began to join SPEG.

The move to sea freighting allowed the industry to expand its export volumes. Côte d'Ivoire supplied the majority of the European market, but in the mid-1990s it began to focus on French importing companies, giving Ghanaian exporters the opportunity to fill the demand for pineapples in Northwestern Europe. Production increased for large and medium-scale producer-exporters as well as among smallholder producers.[8]

The inconsistent quality of Ghanaian pineapples was a small problem when exporting by air, but it became a big problem with sea freighting. Pineapples were packed in the fields under the hot sun and manually handled. They were sorted inside trucks due to lack of equipment to lift pallets. The trucks went straight to the port, so pineapples were not cooled until they were in the refrigerated vessel. European importers demanded more fruit than individual producer-exporters could supply, so they often rushed fruit to ripen and picked fruit too early. All of these production and postharvest handling practices caused deterioration in the quality of the fruit.

The shift to sea freight required that producers and exporters improve their practices and equipment in order to ensure good quality and longer shelf life. According to a consultancy study carried out in the mid-1990s, considerable scope for improvement existed in production to deliver better quality and higher yields, in postharvest handling to deliver a better-presented and consistent product, and in more professional financial management and marketing.[9] The quality and yields of pineapple production in Ghana were more inconsistent than the production in Central America and Côte d'Ivoire. Standardized production practices key to achieving consistent good-quality fruits were

[8] TechnoServ, 2004, Partnerships for Agribusiness Development, Agricultural Trade and Market Access. A concept note for NEPAD.

[9] Grahame Dixie and Andrew Sergeant, The Future for the Ghanaian Horticulture Export Industry, 1998. Report prepared by Accord Associates for the World Bank's Agricultural Diversification Project.

not practiced among Ghanaian producer-exporters, much less among smallholders. Postharvest handling on the farm and transport of the fruit needed improving through investments in postharvest infrastructure, especially cold storage. The facilities at the main seaport were not organized for perishable exports and did not have a packing shed or cold stores. The industry also needed organized pre-shipment inspection and quality certification of exports, skilled labor in export fruit handling, and better packaging in order to increase the quality of produce.

The shift to sea freight was *not* accompanied by these changes, however, and the industry did not achieve international standards in production and postharvest handling.[10] European importers complained in the 1990s about browning inside Ghanaian pineapples upon arrival in Europe. As a result, Ghana's exports fetched declining prices and a declining reputation.[11] Ghanaian exporters also did not achieve the volumes of exports and standards of management needed to widen their profit margins and increase their leverage in the market. By the early 2000s, Ghana had fifty-five registered pineapple exporters consisting of many medium-sized producer-exporters and a large number of pure exporters, but only ten of them exported over 1,000 tons.[12] Such small volumes of individual Ghanaian exporters compared to their competitors meant that they had little negotiating leverage over

[10] Only one producer-exporter built a packhouse with cooling facilities in 1995, which was a huge innovation at that time. He relied extensively on a network of outgrowers whom he supported with finance and training, rather than a nucleus farm, and was trying to get uniformity in outgrower fruit by creating storage so that fruits could be harvested when ready and not against shipment consignment dates. He was one of the four producer-exporters who led the shift to sea freighting. No one else followed his lead until 2004. One reason given was that SPEG was using a refrigerated vessel with hatches, where all of Ghana's pineapples were loaded in the same hatch. Thus, his precooled pineapples were loaded next to other producer-exporters' pineapples that had come straight from the field, diminishing the effect of precooling. Creating a continuous cold chain required using refrigerated containers, which no producer-exporter attempted until September 2004, when one firm sent the first precooled shipment in a refrigerated container. At that time, the other larger producer-exporters were just building modern packhouses but without cooling facilities.

[11] Accord Associates, The European Pineapple Market – Reactions to Different Varieties and Ghana's Market Position, 2001. Prepared for TechnoServ Ghana.

[12] Jean-Michel Voisard and Peter Jaeger, Ghana Horticulture Sector Development Study, 2008, prepared for ESSD Department of the World Bank as part of Agricultural Sub-sector Investment Program restructuring process.

price. In 2001, the two biggest exporters in Côte d'Ivoire exported 130,000 tons combined, while the whole Ghana industry exported around 30,000 tons. Ghanaian exporters also generally lacked selling agents in Europe to perform quality inspection. Thus, European wholesalers could cheat Ghanaian exporters by strategically complaining of bad fruit, and thus not paying for them, without the exporters being able to prove otherwise (Fold and Gough 2008).[13]

Why was the shift not accompanied by changes in production and postharvest handling needed to achieve the required quality for sea freight? One argument is that the lack of access to adequate working capital was the source of substandard performance rather than the lack of technical know-how.[14] Most farmers relied solely on their profits for working capital, which resulted in limited investments in the farm and slow growth in export volumes. It is true that outside the cocoa sector, most agricultural producers lacked access to credit, except through small and short-lived donor-funded projects, and that long-term financing instruments were totally absent. The World Bank noted that the implementation of its agricultural projects in the 1990s was affected by the high cost of credit and the lack of long-term credit needed for major capital investments.[15]

Lack of access to finance for agribusiness was a serious constraint, but interviews with producer-exporters indicated that profit margins were high for airfreighted pineapple in the first half of the 1990s, and that a lot of money was made, which could have been invested in new production, postharvest handling and export practices. They cite other reasons why it was not. One reason was that producer-exporters saw themselves as only competing with Côte d'Ivoire, and they claimed to be using the same technology as the Ivorians ("doing things the same way"). To an extent, this was true (see Willems 2006). Thus, Côte d'Ivoire did not provide a good model to follow; its industry was in the process of changing, but it took a long time to implement these changes, with some only coming to fruition in the late 1990s and early 2000s.

[13] This point was also made in firm interviews.

[14] Obeng, "Effects of Domestic Policies on Production and Export of Nontraditional Agricultural Commodities."

[15] World Bank, Agricultural Sector Performance Review and Accountability Implementation Completion Reports. World Bank Report No. 20686-GH. June 30, 2000.

For example, quality assurance mechanisms were gradually created, and containerized shipping was not introduced until 2000.

Another explanation is that the decentralized and unorganized structure of the Ghanaian industry and the nature of relations within the supply chain did not encourage learning but rather deterred investments in new technology and innovating with new practices. The small-size operations of producer-exporters in the early 1990s led them to depend on smallholder farmers to increase their volumes. In trying to meet the volumes requested by their buyers, quality was not the top priority. Producer-exporters increasingly relied on smallholder production, but did not provide adequate support to smallholders in the production process to ensure good quality nor did they put in place formalized quality assurance mechanisms. Producer-exporters told smallholders when to harvest, and often rushed harvesting to meet deadlines.

Furthermore, arrangements between smallholders and producer-exporters became increasingly noncommittal as competition among exporters for smallholder fruits intensified. Even when a producer-exporter had a verbal commitment with a smallholder to buy his fruits and perhaps assisted him by providing inputs on credit, the smallholder might sell the fruits to another producer-exporter or pure exporter who offered a better farm gate price, sometimes because that price did not account for the deduction of the credit. Thus, the smallholder was effectively dodging the repayment of the loan. It is generally agreed that such side-selling was rife, and that producer-exporters intentionally "stole" smallholder fruit from other producer-exporters.

The lack of formal contractual relations between smallholders and exporters served the interest of both parties. Exporters saw it in their interest not to have formal relations because it gave them flexibility. Producer-exporters were seeking to create a backup supply in case they needed it, and did not want to have to buy all the smallholders' fruits.[16] Smallholders tried to sell for the highest price. This behavior exacerbated existing mistrust among producer-exporters. Such a situation further deterred producer-exporters from supporting

[16] Some of the larger producer-exporters had a small group of outgrowers with whom they worked more closely. These outgrowers included nearby peasant farmers growing pineapple in addition to other crops, but they also included aspiring commercial farmers who might also have worked as field staff or managers on the producer-exporter's farm.

smallholders financially and technically to improve their production practices.

The uncertainty and competition created by this industry structure not only led to inconsistent quality of exports, but also created disincentives for producer-exporters to invest in improved practices and equipment, when almost 50 percent of their supply was smallholder fruit. Lastly, some of the largest producer-exporters at the time did not shift to sea freighting until the late 1990s or early 2000s, because they still had buyers who paid for airfreighted pineapples, so they saw even less need to invest in new practices and technology.

The industry structure and relations as they formed in the 1990s were not the only disincentive to investing in technological capabilities. The early investors, who became the key industry actors in the 1990s, were individualistic in their approach and short-term in their outlook. This outlook was crucial to the emergence of the industry, but not conducive for its further development. Business was good for them individually, so they did not see the importance of industry-wide initiatives and collaboration, and they did not have previous business experience, which would have impressed upon them the importance of interfirm coordination. Finally, the expectations and standards of business success in Ghana were very low; pineapple exporters saw themselves as doing well by Ghanaian standards, which led to complacency.

In addition, many pineapple exporters sought mainly to make quick money in hard currency, and thus were not looking to reinvest as full-time commercial farmers and exporters. Often investors mixed businesses, using pineapple exports to support their import trading business. If the import business was more important, then the pineapple one suffered. As a result, there was a large turnover in exporters. One producer-exporter noted that the Horticulture Association of Ghana had about sixty members, but only twenty were really active and about 40–50 percent had only been operating for a few years. With the creation of SPEG, producer-exporters abandoned the Horticultural Association of Ghana to the smaller producers who did not directly export, weakening that organization further. Furthermore, the increased competition among producer-exporters exacerbated the existing distrust among them and lack of transparency in running the horticulture industry associations.

Donor-Driven Support in the 1990s

In addition to these disincentives and obstacles to firms investing in building their capabilities, and to the interfirm collaboration that would facilitate it, there were no incentives or imperatives to do so coming from the NDC government. Support for the horticulture export industry came through donor-driven projects, in which donor staff and international consultants liaised directly with the pineapple exporters. Ministry of Food and Agriculture bureaucrats and ruling political elites did not have much involvement in designing the projects.

There were two donor projects in the 1990s that contained components targeting horticulture exports. One was the USAID Trade and Investment Program (1993 to 1998) and its sequel, the Trade and Investment Reform Program (1998 to the early 2000s).[17] The second was the World Bank's Agriculture Diversification Project, discussed in Chapter 4, which targeted oil palm, coffee, rubber and horticulture, and took most of the 1990s to implement. Both of these projects were driven in their formulation and implementation by donor agencies, and the attention to horticulture was subsumed under a broad approach to export diversification.

The extended USAID project was very large in scope. It included two components: one aimed at policy reforms and one aimed at private sector enterprises in nontraditional exports. The winning bidder for the contract determined the content of the USAID project within the broad parameters set out by USAID, and the programs were implemented entirely outside the government's bureaucratic structure. AMEX International and two international NGOs won the bid and were the implementing agents for the private enterprises component. The project implementation evaluation report emphasizes that the component was unfocused: it included many different types of industries and the process of choosing firms to be supported was very ad hoc. As a result, it had only tangential effects on the pineapple export industry.

[17] Information on the Trade and Investment Program comes from interviews and secondary sources referring to it. Sources on the Trade and Investment Reform Program are "Ghana Trade and Investment Reform Program USAID/Ghana," Project Final Evaluation, March 2003, submitted by Management Systems International (external evaluation); USAID/Ghana Trade and Investment Reform Program Increased Private Enterprise Performance Component, Final Report, July 2005, submitted by AMEX International.

The main impact of the USAID projects was facilitating the creation of the Federation of Associations of Ghana Exporters (FAGE) from several small existing export associations. USAID used FAGE to engage with the Ministry of Trade and Industry in a tripartite committee on policy reform. Through the work of this tripartite committee, most of the legislation that constrained exports was removed and a shed at the Tema port was set aside for the use of exporters. The USAID projects also provided financial support for FAGE, which worked with horticulture export associations to encourage crop diversification and assist in marketing. But the most significant effect on the development of the industry, and notably not one originally intended by the project, was facilitating the shift to sea freighting through the work that AMEX International did in convincing some of the producer-exporters to take the risk.

The horticulture component of the World Bank's Agricultural Diversification Project explicitly built on the work started by the Ghana Export Promotion Council in the late 1980s. World Bank staff observed the effects of the pineapple production expansion program and the new smallholder pineapple farms that were springing up in the pineapple belt, and they pushed for the horticulture component and for the establishment of the Horticulture Development Unit within the Ministry of Agriculture.

The horticulture component of the Agricultural Diversification Project had two main aspects: technical assistance and the creation of Farmapine, a pineapple export company owned by smallholder farmers. The technical side included the development of agronomic packages for production, training for farmers and for the Horticulture Association of Ghana, participation in international trade fairs, visits to Côte d'Ivoire, and the rehabilitation of roads in pineapple growing areas. An international consultant worked in the Horticulture Development Unit to provide assistance on increasing productivity by adapting production practices to the Ghanaian context.[18] Farmapine was created towards the end of the project. The idea came from World Bank headquarters, but also had links with TechnoServ, a US-based international NGO, working with

[18] Interviews with staff in the Horticulture Development Unit, Ministry of Food and Agriculture.

USAID projects. It was intended to pilot the Farmer Ownership Model, which had been developed in other African countries.[19] The objective was to bring smallholder farmers together to reap the benefits of economies of scale available to large companies and to export directly.

Five pineapple cooperatives existed in the Nsawam-Aburi area, which had been receiving technical assistance from TechnoServ under the USAID projects mentioned above. These five cooperatives, which included 164 farmers with 1.9 acres as the average area cultivated per farmer, were brought together with two existing producer-exporter companies to form Farmapine Ghana Limited.[20] The World Bank project, through the Ministry of Finance, gave a loan of US$1.5 million to the cooperatives for start-up capital, which translated into 80 percent shares in the company for the farmers. The assets, markets and expertise of the two producer-exporters were valued, and they were given the remaining shares. A board was set up with representation from the farmers, TechnoServ, the bank administering the loan, and others. A management team was hired to run the production, packaging and marketing for the company. The company began operations in September 1999, and the World Bank project ended a few months later.

In the early 2000s, Farmapine was the second-largest exporter of pineapple in Ghana. However, Farmapine had problems from the beginning, which were compounded by changes in European market demand after 2005, causing it to shut down operations by 2007. Just as Farmapine began operating, the airfreight market shrank and it was necessary to export by sea. The strategy design for the company was done in 1997–1998 and was outdated by 1999, but it was not reviewed and revised. The two producer-exporters bought out for Farmapine had no experience in sea freighting, so they were paid salaries for expertise that they could not offer. The managing director of the company was a professor with management expertise, but no experience in pineapple export. Funds were used for unanticipated investments to meet new international standards in food quality, health and safety. Resources were wasted on administration buildings and a huge

19 Performance Audit Reports and Sectoral Overview, Ghana, June 22, 2001, Report No. 22439, World Bank.

20 Ibid, p. 45.

management structure. Farmapine fell into financial problems, delayed paying farmers, and farmers became less committed. The board changed the managing director in 2004. However, when European demand shifted to a new pineapple variety in 2005, the smallholder farmers in the cooperatives were not able to shift to cultivating the new variety, and Farmapine stopped exporting. These cooperatives became straddled with debt to the Ministry of Finance that they could not repay and the Ministry of Finance had to absorb. Farmapine failed because it did not possess the capabilities to compete in the international market, nor was it managed by people with their own money invested and who would have had the incentive to chase the investment.

Notably, Farmapine is similar to the kinds of state-controlled industrial policies that Ghanaian governments typically pursue: created with government financing, run by managers with no personal investment in the firm, and involving organizing smallholder farmers (by donors and NGOs in this case, rather than the state). The Cassava Starch PSI initiative under the NPP government created the Ayensu Starch Factory on this exact same model, emphasizing the qualities of the Farmer Ownership Model and the success of Farmapine (this occurred prior to the collapse of Farmapine in 2007, of course). Unsurprisingly, the Ayensu Starch Factory suffered a similar fate, as shown in Chapter 7.

By the end of the 1990s, despite these initiatives, the pineapple producer-exporters still faced major constraints, including lack of access to finance on good terms; lack of infrastructure resulting in increased production costs; poor business management resulting in low profit margins; lack of economies of scale; and limited research and technical support. The initiatives described had somewhat tried to address the issues of business management, technical support and research development, but in a limited and piecemeal way. The work done by USAID was not sustainable as it was located outside of government institutions such as the Horticulture Development Unit that would have to continue it.

International consultants employed under these USAID and World Bank projects, who had a close relationship with the pineapple producer-exporters, concluded that a project targeting the horticulture export industry was needed. The World Bank's report reviewing its agricultural projects in the 1990s stated that many of the production initiatives would be continued under its future agriculture sector support in order to increase their sustainability; however, they were not. The recommendations regarding future support for horticulture exports were not taken up in the World Bank's next agricultural program, or in a separate horticulture project. Neither was the consultants' proposal for an integrated project to develop the horticulture export industry picked up and pushed by members of the NDC government. These recommendations would remain relevant, reiterated in later World Bank–funded studies of the industry, and find their way into donor-funded initiatives in the second half of the 2000s.

But in the late 1990s, the World Bank was not interested in a horticulture project. The balance of interests within the World Bank as an organization had shifted. Interviews with World Bank staff involved at the time revealed that what gets included in a new World Bank project depends on what the World Bank team from headquarters has in mind. In 1998 when the World Bank Ghana office began project preparation for new agriculture funding, World Bank headquarters prioritized reforming research and extension as well as sector-wide approaches to financing needs rather than many discrete projects. AgSSIP was the next World Bank program. As mentioned in Chapter 4, AgSSIP focused on institutional reforms of the Ministry of Food and Agriculture related to research services, extension services and organizational functioning, with a special focus on developing farmer-based organizations. Given that the interests of the World Bank headquarter team were elsewhere, NDC Ministers would have had to push for horticulture export very strongly, which they did not do. What the Cabinet Ministers did was to reject the World Bank AgSSIP program in 2000 on the grounds that there was too much "capacity building and consultancy."

The NDC political elites ignored the horticulture export industry, despite the fact that pineapple exports were booming in the 1990s and that it employed a large number of smallholder producers. There seem to have been no mutual interests between the producer-exporters and any NDC ruling elites, or elite factions. Perhaps this was because the pineapple export industry was not dependent on anything provided by the state, so it did not lend itself to political extraction of rents in return for benefits provided by the state, as Darko Opoku (2010) shows occurred in the timber industry.

On their part, the pineapple producer-exporters tended to be individualistic and did not see the need to engage with government. Their industry association, SPEG, was not effective at forming a collective vision for the industry, communicating this to the government, and engaging with the government to achieve it. The seeming lack of interest of individual producer-exporters to engage with ruling elites may have been a strategy to remain neutral. Forming direct political linkages with Rawlings or other NDC ruling elites might bring economic rewards, but it could also be dangerous. This danger was illustrated with the case of Combined Farms, the one producer-exporter known to have political connections with Rawlings. The assets of Combined Farms were confiscated by the government when Rawlings found out that the owner, who donated money to the NDC, was secretly also donating money to the NPP and sought a ministerial appointment if the NPP won the 1996 elections (Opoku 2010).

Given the lack of political backing for horticulture exports, the Horticulture Development Unit did not have much leverage within the Ministry of Food and Agriculture. During the 1990s, the ministry had four different chief directors. According to one member of staff in the unit, the first chief director was supportive of horticulture, but the others were not. The unit was located within a ministry focused on smallholders, because they carried out most of the agriculture production in Ghana. The unit, created under a World Bank project, was never adequately financed by the government and thus became dependent on donor projects to continue its activities.

The Horticulture Development Unit also had weak linkages with industry actors and lacked knowledge of the industry and export markets. The unit compensated for its lack of knowledge by bringing in international consultants, and later some of the unit's staff undertook graduate level degrees specializing in horticulture at foreign universities. But the limited "embeddedness" of unit staff with the commercial exporting firms meant that they did not focus on the needs of the industry as a whole and did not share a common understanding with industry actors on how to meet those needs.

The limited embeddedness of the bureaucrats and their tendency to focus on smallholders overlapped with the emphasis of World Bank staff on smallholder production. This point is illustrated by the decision to create Farmapine. A 1998 consultancy report on the pineapple export industry commissioned by the World Bank recommended a long list of actions needed in order to support the industry. These actions included delivery of foreign exchange loans to producer-exporters, perhaps with a matching grant scheme where the business would be provided with technical advice; develop a R&D program that could devise crop production and postharvest techniques that would ultimately be wholly funded by the industry itself; create a training program for the industry so as to build up the expertise and management skills of the industry, including apprenticeship schemes; infrastructural activities such as cold storage and roads; and encourage expansion of the sea-freight sector so that Ghana can charter its own services. Instead of pursuing these recommendations, World Bank headquarter staff pushed for smallholders to be able to export directly through creating a company that they owned, and thus used unspent project funds to create Farmapine.[21]

The 2005 Crisis in the Pineapple Export Industry and the Donor Dependent Response

The same 1998 consultancy report warned that multinational companies Del Monte and Dole operating in Central American countries with low production costs and significant marketing muscle would create intense competition for Ghanaian pineapple exporters. Del Monte and Dole offered a homogenous product of high quality through their highly organized production, planning and export systems, and the use of information communication technologies (Willems 2006). Their pineapples were also traded under a well-known brand name, and they employed promotion campaigns aimed at consumers and retailers. They benefited from lower production costs due to vertically integrated production and good infrastructure, and from owning their own sea transport. As a result, these transnational corporations cut into the market share of Côte d'Ivoire, reducing it to just over 50 percent by the mid-1990s. However, they exported the Champaka variety, which was less desirable on European markets due to its greenish color and a less sweet taste. West African countries still had lower transport costs because they were closer to Europe, and their Smooth Cayenne variety was still the most demanded pineapple variety.

[21] Interview with a former World Bank Ghana Country Office staff member who worked on the Agricultural Diversification Project.

This situation changed in 1996 when Del Monte launched a new hybrid variety called MD2 that set higher quality standards and met export market needs: better appearance; sweeter and lower acidity; high resistance to parasites and internal rot; ability to survive cold storage for up to two weeks, which was crucial for sea freighting; and a longer shelf life (Vagneron et al. 2009). These characteristics addressed European importer concerns about Smooth Cayenne. The launch of MD2 occurred at the same time as issues of food safety became important for European retailers, and GlobalGAP certification became necessary.

Already by 1999, European demand for Smooth Cayenne began to decline as the demand for the perceived superior MD2 increased. Del Monte raised the standards of market service and produced pineapples with a better price/quality ratio. Ghana had low quality, low export volumes and high relative costs. More generally, the poor quality image of West African pineapple remained. When Del Monte turned its focus to the European market aggressively in the early 2000s, European importers embraced MD2. The switchover was gradual initially, but by mid-2005 importers were looking only for MD2 pineapples. Not only did Costa Rica exporters take over the international pineapple market, they also expanded it through increasing demand for the MD2 variety, as shown in Figure 5.1.

In addition to innovations led by Del Monte, the rise of Costa Rica as a major pineapple-exporting country is attributed to the general business environment produced by national trade and agricultural policies and regional trade agreements (Vagneron et al. 2009). These policies included tax credits, export promotion incentives (including export subsidies), easy access to land, trade preference programs with the United States, government investment in agricultural research and development, as well as technical and financial assistance to farmers. Compared to Costa Rica, Ghanaians faced higher production costs as a result of the high cost of credit or the inability to access credit altogether (due to high interest rates and/or high collateral demands) and poor infrastructure (roads, electricity, water), as well as problems with land acquisition and security of property rights in land, and a lack of skilled labor in agri-business and horticulture in particular.[22] For

[22] Many of the large producer-exporters got their farm managers from Côte d'Ivoire.

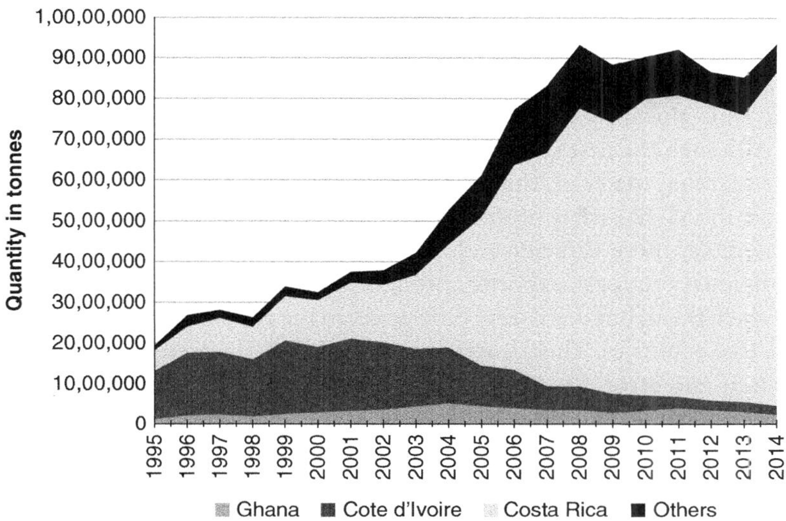

Figure 5.1 Major Pineapple Exporters to the European Market, 1995–2014 (tons)
Source: Comtrade 2015. Data from 1995 to 1998 for EU 15; data from 1999 to 2001 for EU 27; data from 2002 to 2014 for EU 28.

example, many farms were situated in rural areas that lacked electricity, so the farms operated with power generators.

Most pineapple producers did not start to cultivate the MD2 variety until after the collapse of the Smooth Cayenne market. The largest producer-exporters in the 2000s, which mostly included the early Ghanaian investors who had survived and turned into full-time commercial farmers, acquired MD2 planting material through individual efforts or sharing among informal networks. One producer-exporter started a tissue culture lab in 2002 to produce MD2 planting materials. Notably, other producer-exporters distrusted the quality of the planting materials produced in this lab and instead acquired them from MD2-producing countries like Costa Rica and Honduras. The new planting materials were initially very expensive.[23] Only a few pineapple

[23] In 2006, plantlets of MD2 were $0.36 per piece, compared to $0.01 that small farmers paid for Smooth Cayenne suckers (Ouma 2015: 202). As MD2 pineapple production in Ghana increased and MD2 suckers multiplied, the cost came down significantly; but in the first few years, replanting farms with expensive MD2 plantlets was a major barrier to entry for small farmers.

producers had significant quantities of MD2 pineapples to export. Almost all commercial farmers lost huge amounts of money when the market shifted in 2005, as they were unable to sell their Smooth Cayenne pineapples.

Although the first step to producing MD2 pineapples was accessing the planting material, this proved to be the easiest. Learning how to grow the MD2 variety profitably in Ghana's agro-ecological conditions was much more difficult and expensive than anticipated. SPEG and individual producer-exporters brought in consultants from Costa Rica to teach them, but there were differences in the climate and soil between the two countries. Thus, learning to grow MD2 involved a large degree of trial-and-error. Producer-exporters lost much of their working capital figuring out that the agronomy of MD2 is different from the traditional variety. With Smooth Cayenne, Ghanaian producers could get high yields even if agronomic practices were not the best. With MD2, production practices had to be precise to produce profitable yields. MD2 also required different land preparation techniques, more fertilizer, more irrigation, and more careful postharvest handling, which meant mechanization and a continuous cold storage chain. All of this meant massive investments in new production equipment and state-of-the-art packhouses with cold storage facilities.[24] Without doing all of these things, the yields would be low and sizes of the fruit small, and thus financial losses occurred as costs exceeded returns. MD2 is an industrial crop developed for production on large-scale plantations and most suitable for high levels of mechanization.[25]

Thus, switching to MD2 required multimillion-dollar investments. Producer-exporters who risked making the switch initially drew on company savings, but that was not enough. Accessing the necessary finance became a big problem and slowed down the learning process. In addition to the general inclination among Ghanaian banks to favor short-term loans to finance trading and to shun long-term finance for agri-business, two factors compounded the difficulty of accessing loans. First, the large number of foreclosures of pineapple farms and

[24] The estimated cost of a packhouse was between US$800,000 and US$1,000,000. Only seven SPEG members had cold storage facilities by January 2009.

[25] Natural Resources Institute, 2010, Ghana Export Horticulture Cluster Strategic Profile Study, Part II: Recommended Actions & Part III: Background Papers. Prepared for the World Bank, The Republic of Ghana Ministry of Food and Agriculture, and EU All ACP Agricultural Commodities Programme.

their huge debts increased the banks' risk averseness to lending for pineapple export. Second, the macroeconomic environment in Ghana began to deteriorate, leading to higher commercial interest rates, around 30 percent, in the latter half of the 2000s. Producer-exporters had to take loans of amounts lower than they needed, and at a high interest rate and short moratorium.

As a result, out of the fifty-four pineapple exporters registered with HAG and SPEG in 2004, only eleven were still exporting in 2008. In 2004, the capacity of SPEG and HAG pineapple producer-exporters ranged from 250 metric tons per week to 1 metric ton per week. About 60 percent of these exporters were quite small, with a capacity of less than 25 metric tons per week. Only 50 percent of pineapple exporters were GlobalGAP certified, predominantly those in SPEG and only those with capacities greater than 15 metric tons per week. With a few exceptions, only firms exporting 60 metric tons per week survived. All of the survivors had GlobalGAP certification. The small pineapple exporters in the Horticulture Association of Ghana lacked the necessary resources to cope with the change to MD2 production. As high as 90 percent of HAG members had export capacity of less than 40 metric tons per week and had no modern packing facilities and very little on farm mechanization. Thus, shifting to MD2 required even more investments for these small producer-exporters than for the larger ones. They did not have the resources to meet GlobalGAP requirements, much less those for MD2 production.

There were several initiatives in the 2000s that aimed to support horticulture export. The first two initiatives came from the World Bank and USAID – the two donor agencies that had been providing some support in the 1990s. The World Bank funded the Horticulture Export Industry Initiative, as part of the restructured AgSSIP (see Chapter 4). USAID launched a third project in its series. These initiatives spawned great interest in horticulture export among donor agencies and led to further donor projects. Table 5.1 provides an overview of the donor-driven projects targeting or affecting the horticulture industry in the 2000s.

This donor interest in horticulture exports increased the dependency of the Horticulture Development Unit on donor-funded projects, and reduced any imperative for NPP politicians to put government attention and resources into horticulture exports. There was one instance of direct government support to the industry, where the NPP government

Table 5.1 *Initiatives Affecting or Targeting the Pineapple Export Industry in the 2000s*

Donor project	Time Period	Government Institution responsible	Funding (US$)	Implementing Agency	Objectives of the project
Horticulture Export Industry Initiative (HEII) component (part of AgSSIP)	2004–2006	Ministry of Food and Agriculture (MoFA)	World Bank IDA credit ($9.5 million)	Horticulture Development Unit in MoFA	Activities: postharvest infrastructure; MD2 pineapple sourcing & development; planting material trials; research & development; food safety & quality management; and strategic support to the industry (information and studies).
Trade and Investment Reform Program, Increased Private Enterprise Performance component	1998–2004	MoFA But the implementing agents worked directly with producers.	USAID Project ($60 million)	AMEX International, TechnoServ, & CARE International	Continuation of project from the 1990s. New addition was a focus on increasing capacity of micro-enterprises and linking microenterprises/small farmers into production-marketing chain for exports.

Trade & Investment Program for a Competitive Export Economy (TIPCEE), Export Business Development component	2004–2009	MoFA Coordinated its work more with other donor projects and with MoFA.	USAID Project ($30 million total for whole project)	Chemonics, in a consortium including CARE and Technoserv	Continuation of project from the 1990s. Originally targeted high-value horticulture export crops, but later expanded to include food crops. Initiatives focus on market access and strategic partnerships and on development of information tools, for example, on production techniques, product standards, financial management.
Market-Oriented Agricultural Programme (MOAP)	2004–2013, in 3 phases	MoFA	German Technical Cooperation (GTZ) & German Development Service (DED)	GTZ, DED, Horticulture Development Unit	Components: Promotion of selected value chains in agriculture (including sugar loaf pineapple in Central region & mango in the northern region and Brong Ahafo region); support to public sector services in agriculture development; support to private sector organizations

Table 5.1 (*cont.*)

Donor project	Time Period	Government Institution responsible	Funding (US$)	Implementing Agency	Objectives of the project
Export Marketing and Quality Awareness Programme (EQMAP)	2007–2012	MoFA Initiated by the Horticulture Unit to be a successor to HEII. Project document signed in 2005.	African Development Fund ($25.85 million) and Government of Ghana ($2.8 million)	Horticulture Development Unit	Targets horticultural export crop farmers and cassava producers. Focuses on smallholders. Activities include community-owned packhouses, demonstration farms, improve feeder roads in production areas, marketing strategy, certification schemes, and regulating planting material production.

Source: Created by the author using project documents.

allocated US$2 million in the 2006 government budget to the Ghana Export Promotion Council to support the introduction of the MD2 variety, but it is not clear if this money was fully disbursed. The council used the money for producing planting material through a laboratory run collaboratively by SPEG and a government agency and for Farmapine farmers to purchase planting materials.

Donor agencies significantly influenced the priorities, design and implementation of these projects, and given the large number of initiatives dispersed over multiple donor agencies, support to the industry was fragmented and uncoordinated. As a result, the impact of donor projects on the pineapple export industry was small, mostly unsustainable and sometimes negative. Donor projects tended to address the same sorts of issues, but neglected major constraints facing the industry, partly because donor project funding was too slow, bureaucratic and rigid to meet the demands of supporting the pineapple export industry. A large focus of donor-driven projects was on GlobalGAP certification for smallholder producers due to the high cost of establishing and maintaining this certification. Other donor projects focused on research into new varieties and pest problems, certifying nurseries (which were largely used by smallholders), building roads in production areas, building public packhouses for small producers to use collectively, creating demonstration centers of best agricultural practices (aimed at smallholders) and other forms of training for smallholders in business and agricultural practices. Donor projects clearly focused on smallholder producers, often in the name of supporting "livelihoods," rather than on helping to build an internationally competitive export industry.

The NPP government's Millennium Challenge Account project financed by the United States Millennium Challenge Corporation, a new donor agency, was supposed to support the horticulture export industry. It took several years for the government proposal to become a program, with final negotiations in 2006, and in the course of negotiations with the US donor agency and in implementing the program, the focus on horticulture export was diluted. Unsurprisingly, the emphasis of the project shifted to promoting smallholder agriculture production and providing social services. Donors, politicians and bureaucrats in the Ministry of Food and Agriculture shared a common focus on the need to support smallholders, and a position that commercial farmers do not need support. For donors it was about achieving "poverty reduction" and "promoting livelihood strategies," while for NPP ruling elites in charge of the Millennium Challenge Account it was about spreading government expenditures to as large a part of the population as possible and delivering visible goods and services, as shown in Chapter 7. While the Millennium Challenge Account project did include some aspects to support the surviving pineapple producer-exporters, they were small and some turned out to have negative effects, as shown in the next section.

Decline of the Pineapple Producer-Exporters

By 2009, the industry seemed to be stabilizing. Exports stopped declining and began increasing slowly, as shown in Figure 5.2. There were only fourteen firms still exporting pineapples, but on very large-scale farms. Prior to the MD2 switch, commercial farmers were buying almost half of their pineapple exports from smallholder farmers. The surviving SPEG members expanded their farms and only exported what they produced. The total volume of sea-freighted pineapples did not fall as drastically as one might expect given the collapse of so many Ghanaian firms and the exodus of smallholders. This is because Golden Exotics, a subsidiary of the multinational company *Compagnie*

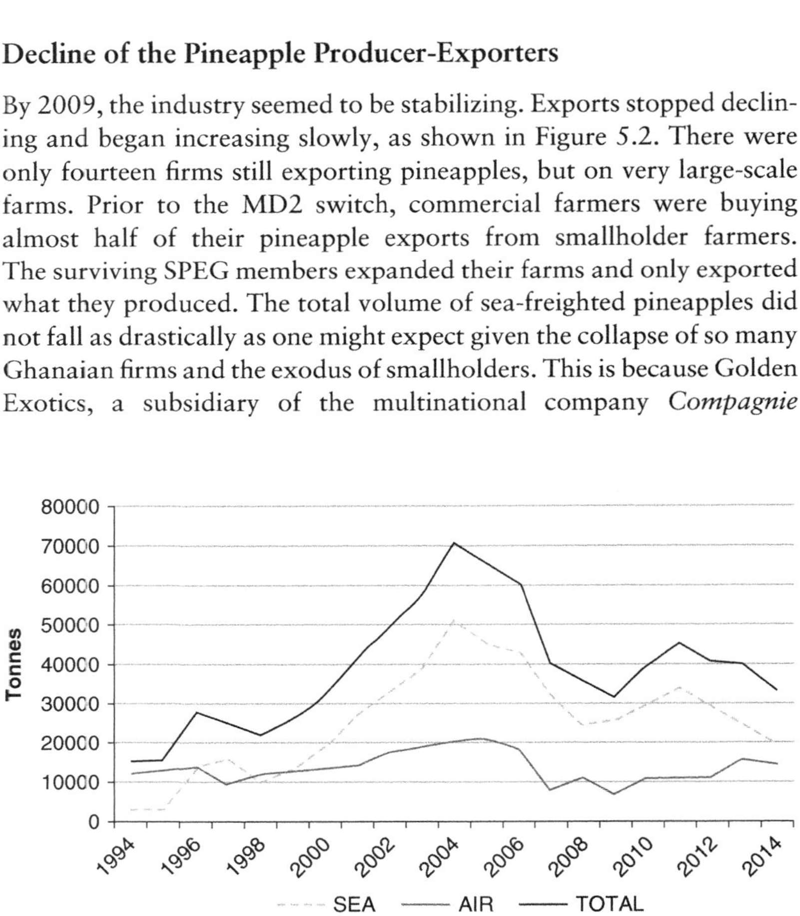

Figure 5.2 Ghana's Sea- and Air-Freight Whole Pineapple Exports, 1994–2014
Source: Data on sea and air annual exports provided by the Sea-Freight Pineapple Exporters of Ghana Association (SPEG), 2014.

Fruitière, began operations in Ghana on a large scale; by 2007 it was producing 40 percent of Ghana's fresh pineapple exports.

Those producer-exporters who made the switch to MD2 pineapple production ran down their capital reserves learning how to grow the new variety and had to take bank loans. Six producer-exporters took a package deal through the Millennium Challenge Account project that provided a custom-built packing line system for pineapple (washing, fungal treatment, sorting by grade) and cold storage facilities for the packhouse as well as generators (because electricity flow was unreliable). Most of the recipient farmers had to build new packhouses, because their existing ones were not large enough to accommodate the size of the new packing line and cold storage facilities.

By 2010, it looked like the pineapple export industry had stabilized, but the success was temporary; the firms began to have production problems. Yields became volatile and began to fall, as well as the percentage of exportable fruits that had the right external appearance. Their pineapples began having black spots, small crowns and other defects, which meant that they did not meet the exports standards set by European buyers. By 2014, Ghanaian commercial farmers were only getting yields of about 50 percent and only exporting about 50 percent of what was extracted. Sea-freight exports began declining again. By 2015, there were only a handful of pineapple producer-exporters that were still exporting, and even those remaining were producing less and operating at a loss. Some firms were no longer exporting fresh pineapple by sea, and others were selling to local processors (foreign-owned) that exported fresh-cut products and juice to European markets. There were only five firms exporting large amounts of pineapple.

The cause of the problems with yields was that the surviving pineapple producer-exporters had expanded their production significantly to achieve economies of scale and to make up for the lost volume from smallholder production, but in light of the difficulties with accessing bank loans, they did not have enough working capital to cover the costs of the planting program on what were now very large farms. Furthermore, pineapple is a labor-intensive crop, and expansion must be accompanied by continuous attention to detail, but this kind of plantation agriculture was new to Ghana. Farm laborers cut corners when not properly supervised, and there was high labor turnover, resulting in wasted resources for farms that spent time training workers who either never returned or could not be relied upon to show up when scheduled.

At the same time, the price for MD2 pineapples in the European market peaked in 2008 and began declining, as expanding global supply drove down international prices. All of the producer-exporters became squeezed between rising production costs and falling prices. They began operating at a loss and could not meet payments on the loans they had taken. Even the few foreign-owned pineapple farms were operating at a loss.

In addition to the challenges specifically related to pineapple production, the producer-exporters faced other problems in the Ghanaian environment that contributed to higher production costs. Despite paying for the connection to the electricity grid, electricity supply was increasingly unreliable, mandating the need for power generators. Some commercial farms were located close to small towns and thus had very good access roads, but others had to invest in roads around their farms, as well as making dams to access water for farming.

Ironically, their investments in water, roads and electricity, in combination with a few donor-government projects that also funded infrastructural improvements in the pineapple belt, led to the increased value of the land in these areas. At the same time, the small towns in the pineapple production belt experienced substantial growth, pushing them closer to the commercial farmland. Commercial farmers began to experience encroachment on their lands and harassment by the landowners to abrogate the lease contract early. Real estate developers from Accra were speculating that the land would be in high demand for residential area in the future and offered the landowners more money for the land than the commercial farmers originally paid. Land also was becoming increasingly scarce around the small towns and families wanted to build houses for their children. In some cases, chiefs claimed the farmland was family land, when they had not done so before. There were also disputes within landlord families over who had the right to lease the land, with one family member saying that the one who leased the land to the commercial farmer was not the one who owned it.

There was a literal fight for the land going on. The pineapple producer-exporters had leased the land from its owners (local families or chiefs), but it did not matter. People were stealing planting material, burning and stealing from the farms, and demarcating land for residences on the farmland that was lying fallow. The farms that were worst affected decided to release marginal land or land where their yields were low, in order to appease the landowners, rather than taking the issue to court, where it could take up to ten years to clear the case.[26] Given the growth of the small towns, combined with problems with soil, many commercial farms realized that eventually they would have to relocate further inland, which would require large new investments.

Key strategies for these remaining Ghanaian producer-exporters included accessing new export markets in the Middle East (which had less stringent standards for the appearance of the fruit) and selling to local processors, but many of them were still operating at a loss in 2015. Therefore, product diversification became necessary, which meant moving out of pineapple production and into other types of horticulture products. However, the pineapple producer-exporters could not access new investment capital with which to make this switch, as a result of what happened with the Millennium Challenge Account loan for the packhouse equipment. They had been unable to make the repayments within the time period specified in the contract with the US donor agency, which was by the end of the Millennium Challenge Account project in 2012. The equipment was not installed until 2010, and two years was not enough time to accumulate enough capital to pay back the loan, especially in light of the challenges outlined above.[27] The loans were supposed to be part of a revolving fund held with SPEG, in that the repaid loans would constitute a fund that could provide future loans to SPEG members. But when the initial loans were not repaid on the terms agreed, the grant for the revolving fund was withdrawn, and the US donor agency demanded that the government pay back the money owed. As a result, the producer-exporters gained a bad reputation among banks and parts of the government, and were stuck with no ability to access investment or working capital.

Conclusion

The decline of the pineapple export industry in the face of international competition was not inevitable. The pineapple producer-exporters could have acted to improve production, shipping and marketing of

[26] On the legal process for settling land disputes in Ghana, and the backlog of cases in the state courts, see Crook et al. (2007).

[27] Interview with General Manager, SPEG, May 15, 2015, Accra; and interviews for firm histories.

the Smooth Cayenne variety in the late 1990s when the threat from MD2 was detected. There was a large scope to improve pineapple production to deliver better quality and higher yields, and invest in postharvest infrastructure in order to deliver a better-presented and consistent product. If the investments that were made for MD2 had been made for Smooth Cayenne, especially washing, fungal treatment and cold storage, things could have turned out differently. Therefore, the real source of decline was the lack of learning among firms, combined with the lack of collective action and coordination among firms necessary to enforce quality control and to address challenges of marketing and research in a way that reduced the costs to individual firms and pooled tacit knowledge. At the heart of the collective action problem was one of leadership of SPEG, but it also stemmed from the fact that these producer-exporters were all first generation capitalists and pioneers in this sector, which underscores the point that "the learning process itself has to be learnt in developing countries" (Lall 1996: 32).

This problem was compounded by the fact that there was no state action to incentivize these firms to invest in learning. While the horticulture producer-exporters received some support from the NDC and NPP governments in the 1990s and 2000s, it was fragmented and driven by donor projects. Furthermore, donor-driven projects focused mostly on smallholders and supported them as part of "livelihood" and "poverty reduction" strategies, rather than attempts to support an internationally competitive horticulture export industry. Doing the latter required addressing the needs of the industry as a whole, and thus recognizing the key role of commercial farmers in the industry and the dependent links between commercial farmers and smallholders as essential to the survival and expansion of the industry. Donor agency staff, ruling political elites and ministry bureaucrats converged on their interest to support smallholders, albeit for different reasons. The convergence of interests between donor staff and political elites is discussed further in regards to the Millennium Challenge Account in Chapter 7. Neither the donors nor the NDC and the NPP politicians saw it in their interests to support the pineapple commercial farmers. This short termism of the politicians and donors in the end had negative impacts on smallholder farmers who produced pineapples, as the decline of the producer-exporters and the Smooth Cayenne variety also meant the closing of economic opportunities for them.

6 Challenges to Modernizing Agro-Processing

Struggles over Inputs, Organizing Smallholders and Enforcing Contracts

It is time for us to pay attention to the basic fact that while industrialization is the essence of fast development leading to high incomes per head, manufacturing industry is a *processing* industry. It is dependent on supplies which are the products of Nature – broadly agriculture and mining – because industrial activity consists of processing the crude products of nature. Raw materials, fuel and food are the three main products of the primary sector, and these form the "essential inputs" of the secondary and tertiary sectors.[1]

Increasing agricultural production and productivity is a prerequisite for the creation of competitive light manufacturing industries, unless all the inputs are imported. Without increased agricultural productivity, which makes raw materials cheaper for factories, the cost of value-added fabrication will not be low enough to compete on the global market or against imports on the domestic market. This is the point raised by Nicholas Kaldor in the quote above. Similar to W.A. Lewis, Kaldor emphasized the linkages between agricultural transformation and industrialization. The story of palm oil processing under the Fourth Republic is a story of stagnation due to a shortage of raw materials of an appropriate quality for industrial processing.

The purpose of this chapter is to explain the constraints on increasing the supply of raw materials for the palm oil industry, and how governments in the 1980s, 1990s and 2000s responded to these constraints. The constraints emerged from three sources: the dualistic industry structure, in which a parallel traditional market for the raw material existed; accessing land under the neocustomary land tenure system; and organizing the produce of scattered, individual smallholder farmers, and enforcing buying contracts. The palm oil industry is

[1] Nicholas Kaldor, "The Role of Increasing Returns, Technical Progress and Cumulative Causation in the Theory of International Trade and Economic Growth," 1981, reproduced in Targetti and Thirlwall (1989: 327).

a significant case because these constraints also apply to other agro-processing industries in the country.

At independence, Ghana was a net importer of crude palm oil. Postindependence governments saw the development of this sector as a way to reduce imports and thus the drain on foreign exchange reserves. They also sought to create an industrial processing segment through state-led industrial policies that created state-owned oil palm plantations and palm oil processing mills and later joint ventures with foreign direct investment in large-scale palm oil estates. Their efforts resulted in a dualistic structure of the palm oil industry shaped by the presence of two different markets – home consumption and industrial use in domestic manufacturing – leading to two subsectors. The home consumption market existed because palm oil formed the basis of cuisine and social-cultural patterns in the southern part of Ghana. The small-scale subsector included private smallholder oil palm cultivators who largely sold their fruit bunches to small-scale mills or household (largely manual) processors. The industrial use subsector consisted of medium- and large-scale oil palm plantations and mills producing crude palm oil, which they sold to domestic manufacturing companies as an intermediate input used in producing consumer products.

Political interference in running the palm oil estates through the successive changes in postindependence governments and then economic decline in the late 1970s caused the collapse of the industrial palm oil processing subsector. The PNDC government pursued and successfully implemented industrial policies aimed at reviving the large-scale state-owned palm oil estates. The palm oil sector was targeted because it could save foreign exchange and because it had attributes similar to those that had made revival of the cocoa and gold sectors appealing to the PNDC elites. It consisted of state-owned enterprises, and thus the PNDC elites could control the process of rehabilitation with the longer-term objective of making these enterprises profitable in order to attract foreign direct investment. The palm oil industry also involved a large number of smallholder farmers who had produced the raw materials required for the state-owned mills and who would benefit from their rehabilitation and government support to increase oil palm cultivation.

The NDC government's policies toward the palm oil sector in the 1990s demonstrates the overall approach of the NDC ruling elites of using privatization to plug fiscal deficits, without a broader strategy of how to utilize foreign direct investment to develop the sector. As a result, the individual large-scale estates improved production and productivity with their existing assets, but then the industry as a whole stagnated due to industry-wide problems that required coordinated actions among industry actors and between them and the government. It was these problems that industry actors hoped the NPP government would address in the early 2000s when it announced the President's Special Initiative in Oil Palm. They were sorely disappointed when the group of NPP elites heading the initiative chose to create entirely new plantations and mills, through direct implementation by the state of a farmer-owned model. The NPP's initiative had limited impacts in expanding the raw material base of the sector and addressing other constraints on the industry. The details of the NPP government's response is taken up in the next chapter.

Palm oil has significant potential to spur economic transformation given the multiple products that can be produced from palm oil and used as intermediate inputs in manufacturing processes linked to food and chemical industries. The oil palm tree bears fruit in bunches, called fresh fruit bunches (ffb). The individual fruitlets contain an outer skin, a pulp containing the palm oil, and a central nut consisting of a shell and a kernel. The nature of the crop dictates processing (milling) within 24 hours after cutting down the ffb, which necessitates strong linkages between agricultural production and industrial processing. There are two processing segments. The primary processing segment turns the fruit into two kinds of oil: crude palm oil produced from the pulp, and crude palm kernel oil produced from the nuts. Crude palm oil is used in producing soap and other nonedible products, as well as for industrial purposes. The secondary processing segment refines crude palm oil so that it can be used in various processed foods such as margarine, confectionery, chocolate, ice cream and bakery products, and nonfood manufactured goods, such as soap, candles, and cosmetics.

The refined oil can be fractionated to obtain solid (stearin) and liquid (olein) fractions, as well as oleochemical products such as fatty acids, fatty alcohols, methyl esters and glycerin, which can be used in producing agrochemicals, surfactants, biolubricants, biopolyols and glycerol derivatives. Palm oil also has health benefits, which have been increasingly promoted in recent years.[2] The limited supply of ffb and poor quality of crude palm oil in Ghana limited the expansion of the industrial palm oil processing subsector and development of secondary processing.

Similar to the horticulture sector, there were few secondary sources on the palm oil sector when I began the research, and almost none that covered the period from the 1980s onwards. This chapter is based on interviews among key actors involved in the government initiatives affecting the sector and documents collected regarding the initiatives. It also draws heavily on a study of the history of the palm oil sector commission by a key informant, who previously worked in one of the state-owned large-scale palm oil estates and in the 2000s became a consultant for the palm oil industry, and had a personal archive of reports and documents to draw upon.[3] The chapter also draws on interviews with managers of the main companies in the palm oil industry, including the four large foreign-owned palm oil estates; two (out of eight) Ghanaian-owned medium-sized mills (many of which were not fully functioning at the time); and two (out of the three) largest domestic buyers of crude palm oil for manufacturing purposes. Information on the remaining medium-sized mills was collected through written documents from the companies and grey literature.

Colonial Legacies and Historical Foundations of the Palm Oil Sector

Palm oil was the main export product of the Gold Coast from the 1830s to the 1880s. Farmers and traders in the Akwapim hills (in the Eastern Region) produced and exported palm oil to Europe starting in the

[2] It can be combined with more solid fractions, such as palm stearin, to make products of a required consistency without hydrogenation and thus has been used as a replacement for traditional hydrogenated seed oils as a strategy to circumvent *trans* fats in processed foods. The Malaysian government has sought to capitalize on these new properties in the 2010s as a way to further expand and increase the value added of its palm oil industry. See Choo Yuen May, "Malaysia: Economic Transformation Advances Oil Palm Industry," www.aocs.org/Membership/informArticleDetail.cfm?ItemNumber=18340 (last accessed November 12, 2015).

[3] The report is by Chris Foli, "History of the Oil Palm in Ghana," March 2010. It was commissioned as part of the palm oil sector study that I led in the Ghana component of the Elites, Production and Poverty research program (2008–2012) based at the Danish Institute for International Studies.

1820s to meet demand generated by the industrial revolution.[4] The British encouraged the palm oil trade, and palm oil became the principal cargo for former slave traders and ships after the abolition of the slave trade in 1807 and the abolition of slavery in 1833. Some peasant farmers cultivated oil palm trees explicitly for the export trade, migrating and buying land, but the vast majority of palm oil was produced from wild groves. In the late 1880s, palm oil accounted for 70 percent of exports from the Gold Coast, after which the international price of palm oil fell and exports declined as peasants switched to cultivating cocoa trees.

Neither the precolonial nor the colonial period generated experience with large-scale plantation cultivation in Ghana. Some oil palm plantations were established by German, British and other European interests around the end of the nineteenth century and in the early decades of the twentieth century. The British colonial government actively encouraged foreign investment in large-scale plantations and processing mills through specific production incentives in the 1910s and 1920s, hoping to revive palm oil exports. However, the plantation system failed to gain a significant hold, partly because of the internal political insecurity engendered by local warfare and by rivalry among the European powers seeking territorial hegemony, and also because of the negative attitude towards the system by the British Crown (Gyasi 1996). As discussed in Chapter 2, the Colonial Office decided in 1926 to support peasant agricultural production in West Africa over large-scale plantation agriculture as a way to maintain social stability in rural areas.

The Gold Coast colonial government then began promoting oil palm cultivation and small-scale processing among peasant farmers. But high transport costs and the low quality of the crude palm oil exports due to primitive processing techniques, combined with the drop in the international price, led to the decline of palm oil exports, which ceased altogether in the 1950s.

The international price for palm oil fell in the late 1880s due to increased production in the Dutch colonies of Southeast Asia and the emergence of temperate substitutes. Notably, the oil palm tree was taken from the Gold Coast to Malaya (Malaysia) by the British colonial rulers in the 1870s as an ornamental tree and later planted on large-

[4] On the palm oil trade, see Agbodeka (1992) and Gyasi (1992, 1994).

scale plantations with a significant industry emerging in the 1920s using mechanized processing.[5] Malaysia became one of the major suppliers of palm oil globally from the 1970s, when the global palm oil trade increased steeply, and continued to be so in the 2010s.[6] Malaysia has also developed a sophisticated oleochemical manufacturing industry on the back of its palm oil production.

Malaysia and Ghana achieved independence from British colonial rule in the same year, 1957, but they had very different experiences in terms of the development of property rights in land and plantation cultivation (Fold and Whitfield 2012). This can be seen in the fact that by the time of independence, there were about fifty-seven oil palm estates operating in Malaysia, but only one in Ghana. In Ghana, oil palm was cultivated by scattered smallholder farmers for processing into crude palm oil manually in homes and by small-scale processors and sold in local markets for use in cooking. In contrast, large numbers of British investors established large-scale plantations in Malaysia in the late nineteenth century, initially in coffee and then rubber, and these plantations were later, after World War II, linked to import-export trading houses in Great Britain that provided financial and management services to individual planters and group-owned estates in Malaysia. The development of large-scale plantations in Malaysia was made possible by the change in land rights in British Malaya. The British-controlled local Malay states (kingdoms), which owned the land, were anxious to encourage investments that developed the territory. The Malay landholders were split into two groups: those holding land under the Malay system and paying a tenth to the colonial authorities, and those without any rights to land. The latter were treated as squatters who could occupy the land, subject to conditions and decisions laid down by the landlord, in this case the colonial government. Remaining land was state land that could be allocated to prospective planters.

[5] The ecological conditions for the oil palm tree are actually more favorable in the Southeast Asian region than in Ghana.

[6] Malaysia and Indonesia together supplied over one half of total trade in vegetable oils in 2011–2012. The three major importers of palm oil at that time were China, India and the European Union. See The AOCS Lipid Library, http://lipidlibrary.aocs.org/OilsFats/content.cfm?ItemNumber=39459, last accessed on November 12, 2015.

In Ghana, the aborted legislation of the British colonial government to take control over land and the shift to indirect rule created the neocustomary system of land rights that survived into the postindependence period and was even buttressed under the Fourth Republic (see Chapter 2). But the land tenure system in southern Ghana was not static. It evolved in response to cash crop production by smallholder and small capitalist farmers, but not in ways that favored large-scale plantation agricultural production (Amanor 2010). These changes included the creation of a strategic rent system, which allowed a previous taboo of giving land to "strangers" (those not belonging to the "community") to be overcome.[7] As a result, land could be hired from landlords in return for rent, which was paid in the form of a percentage of the crop. Large tracts of land could be leased for long periods of time, such as fifty years, but not generally bought. Because land ownership was fluid, linked to the decisions of the elder of a family (for lineage land) or the chief (for stool land), land titling was not common. Furthermore, there could be multiple claimants to lands, all demanding compensation.

In short, land could not be easily bought and sold in Ghana. Acquiring large pieces of land involved a long process of negotiations with landowners, chiefs, people on the land, as well as compensation for the land, people on the land and structures on the land. And even after compensation was paid, new claims could arise, as discussed in the previous chapter in relation to the pineapple commercial farmers.

Since the colonial administration had not appropriated any large tracks of land, postindependence governments in Ghana did not have ready stocks of land available to use in large-scale agriculture, unlike in neighboring Côte d'Ivoire (Daddieh 1994). When the postindependence governments in Ghana decided to support plantation production generally, and palm oil in particular, they had to forcefully expropriate land. These forced acquisitions generated serious problems for the large-scale palm oil estates, as shown in the next section. Given the absence of oil palm plantation cultivation in the private sector, the postindependence governments pursued state-led industrial policies as the means to pool and invest capital in oil palm plantations and mills.

[7] For more on this topic, see Boone (2013).

Using State-Led Industrial Policies to Create Industrial Palm Oil Processing

The power-sharing CPP government during the period of decolonization attempted to introduce large-scale plantation cultivation in Ghana. The First Development Plan for the period 1951 to 1956 encouraged investment in oil palm plantations and processing mills through support from the state-owned Industrial Development Corporation. The Ministry of Agriculture also carried out several feasibility studies in 1954 and 1955 for plantations and mills to be located in the towns of Pretsea, Kwamuso, Assesewa, Bunso and Anyinasi. At that time, the only existing oil palm plantation and mill in operation was located at Sese.[8]

After independence, the CPP government actively sought foreign direct investment in order to modernize agro-processing, including in palm oil. Under the second Five-Year Development Plan (1959–1964), the Industrial Development Corporation was empowered to grant incentives such as tax holidays and tax waivers on imported machinery and equipment to attract private foreign investment, but the incentives succeeded in attracting only modest investment from foreign sources into the palm oil industry. As discussed in Chapter 2, at this time the Industrial Development Corporation also started setting up enterprises itself. The corporation established a few oil palm plantations, but it accumulated large financial losses and shut down in 1962 as the CPP government shifted to the state-led industrialization approach.

Under the CPP government's state-led industrialization drive, the Ghana State Farms Corporation took over management of the oil palm plantations that had been established by the Industrial Development Corporation at Prestea/Sese, Kwamuso and Asesewa. Ghana State Farms also established a palm kernel oil mill at Asesewa in the Eastern Region and planted 6,413 acres of oil palm trees at Prestea/Sese, Kwamuso and Asesewa.[9] To further increase the raw material supply for palm oil processing, sections of the Workers Brigade engaged in the cultivation of oil palm trees and sold the fresh fruit bunches to processors of palm oil and palm kernel oil for export

[8] This section is based on Chris Foli, "History of the Oil Palm in Ghana," March 2010.

[9] Proceedings of First Seminar on Food Science and Technology in Ghana, Published by Food Research Institute, Accra, May 22–23, 1967.

and domestic consumption. But an additional purpose of the Workers Brigade was to provide regular employment and incomes for the youth in areas in the Central, Western and Eastern regions.

The state-owned palm oil plantations were poorly managed, but they were also not given enough time to (literally) bear fruit by the time the CPP government was overthrown by a coup in February 1966. It takes three to four years for new oil palm trees to start bearing fruits and longer to reach optimal bearing. The impact of 1962 plantings eventually resulted in the increase in production of palm oil by 2,000 metric tons from 1966 to 1967 and by another 1,000 metric tons from 1967 to 1968. But this was a modest increase in the raw material supply, and though domestic production of crude palm oil increased from 1963 to 1969, it did not keep pace with domestic demand. The increase in demand for palm oil and palm kernel oil was due to Lever Brothers Ghana Limited, which established a soap factory in 1963 in the town of Tema.

After the overthrow of the CPP government, successor governments continued investments in the oil palm industry as a means to stimulate rural development and agricultural productivity using similar kinds of state-led policies. The continuation of state-led policies to promote palm oil processing was largely for political reasons: to control investment and accumulation in the context of weak domestic capitalists and to use it to bolster its political support base. But it was also easier. The CPP government made initial investments that subsequent governments tried to revive and build upon. For example, it was reported that the CPP government had invested £24,688,000 in oil palm plantations and palm oil mills, which is a large investment for that time. The Busia government tried to privatize the palm oil estates, but no private investors were interested in buying them because the plantations and mills were generally operating below capacity. Notably, instead of encouraging and supporting private investors to take them over by subsidizing the process of making them profitable, the Busia government sought to improve the state-owned estates directly. It granted the most viable state-owned oil palm plantation and mill at Pretsea/Sese a credit facility with which to expand its raw material base and milling capacity, as this estate was operating at capacity. The credit line assisted the Prestea/Sese estate to establish 3,240 hectares of oil palm plantation between 1970 and 1972, and increased its milling capacity from 3 metric tons to 9 metric tons in 1969. This was a rather small improvement. The other three estates were operating far below capacity due to lack of raw material (fresh fruit bunches from oil palm trees).

The Busia government was overthrown in another military coup in 1972. The new NRC government led by Acheampong pursued a more concerted effort to expand oil palm cultivation and thus palm oil processing. However, it was driven by more compelling motives. By 1972, domestic production of palm oil was meeting only about 43 percent of domestic industrial processing and human consumption needs, with the remainder being imported. The Acheampong government had to operate under hard budget and foreign exchange constraints after it unilaterally rescheduled the government's external debt obligations and tarnished its creditworthiness. Without access to external credit, it needed to reduce the import bill, and sought to do so by becoming self-sufficient in products that could be produced domestically, such as palm oil. To achieve this objective, the Acheampong government continued with the same state-led industrial policies by investing in the existing state-owned plantations and mills as well as establishing new ones. But, in contrast to previous governments, it used additional strategies that compelled foreign direct investments and sought to tap into local private capital.

The Ghana State Farms Corporation and Ghana Food Production Corporation (formerly the Workers Brigade) were used to rehabilitate and expand existing oil palm plantations and mills and to establish new oil palm plantations and mills with government funds borrowed from the state-owned Agricultural Development Bank and National Investment Bank. Seven new oil palm plantations were established at Jukwa, Okumaning, Assin Fosu, Anhwiankwanta, Akwanserem, Nkwanta and Samreboi with an estimated total size of 45,000 acres. The new plantations were managed by the Ghana State Farms Corporation, and the plantations at Jukwa and Assin Fosu were equipped with processing mills.

The Agricultural Development Bank also provided loans to private individuals to set up various types of agro-processing activities. Using these loans, local investors established a number of medium-sized palm oil mills in the 1970s (Fold 2003). Notably many of these investors were former politicians or civil servants with knowledge of the palm oil sector.

The Acheampong government also compelled foreign direct investment through controls on foreign exchange. Foreign firms operating in Ghana were not allowed to repatriate dividends, but if they invested in agri-business, they would be allowed to repatriate some. Foreign firms such as Mobil Holdings, a Petroleum Marketing Company with Mobil Ghana Limited as its subsidiary in Ghana, and Paterson Zonchonis PLC (now PZ Cussons), a pharmaceutical, soap and cosmetic manufacturing company, acquired shares in Twifo Oil Palm Plantation Limited for this reason. Twifo Oil Palm Plantations Limited was formed in 1978 from capital invested by these foreign companies combined with capital that the government borrowed from the National Investment Bank and from the European Union and Commonwealth Development Corporation. Lever Brothers Ghana Limited also jointly invested with the government in the establishment of Benso Oil Palm Plantation in 1976 at Adum Banso, in order to benefit from this incentive.

Lastly, the Acheampong government established Ghana Oil Palm Development Corporation (GOPDC) in 1977 as a wholly state-owned palm oil estate with substantial financial, technical and managerial support from several World Bank loans over almost fifteen consecutive years. The Institut Recherché d'Huile et Oligeanaux of France was engaged as management contractors of GOPDC from 1977 to 1993. The other two large estates also had foreign management teams.

In sum, three new large-scale palm oil estates were established in the 1970s through a combination of foreign and state capital. The objective of their establishment was to meet domestic industrial demand for crude palm oil, which was used to manufacture edible oils, soaps, detergent and other consumer products. These estates included Benso Oil Palm Plantation (BOPP) in the Western Region; Ghana Oil Palm Development Corporation (GOPDC) in the Eastern Region; and Twifo Oil Palm Plantation Limited (TOPP) in the Central Region. But these estates were plagued from the beginning by serious problems because the government forcefully expropriated land for setting up the estates.

The land expropriation was actively resisted by local communities, leading to land litigation, protests by peasant farmers and delays in getting the large estates operational. For example, Paul Huddleston and Matthew Tonts (2007: 271) note in relation to the Ghana Oil Palm Development Corporation:

Throughout the entire expropriation process, lawyers representing the Chiefs and families of affected villages resisted the government. Where the government did prevail, it incurred considerable costs, legal delays, violent reactions by landowners, and high compensation bills.

Smallholder schemes were established on the estates' plantations as a means to legitimize the presence of the estates by incorporating peasants who had to be resettled into the estate production. The smallholder scheme created at GOPDC provided land to local residents rent-free, which assuaged some of the anger aroused by land expropriation, but local residents never really forgave the government or the GOPDC (Huddleston and Tonts 2007). The fact that land had been expropriated also became an issue when the NDC government sought to privatize the plantations and estates in the 1990s, as discussed below.

PNDC Government Revives the State-Owned Palm Oil Estates

At the start of the 1980s, when the PNDC government took over, it was clear that most state-owned enterprises, including the oil palm estates, were not financially self-supporting and depended on government subsides. Some had even collapsed. Only eight oil palm estates and plantations were operating, according to a survey carried out by Ghana Statistical Service in 1988.[10]

The collapse of many state-owned oil palm plantations and mills is indicative of the *paradox* of state-led industrial policies in Ghana. Such policies are intended to achieve economic transformation objectives, but the *political incentives* produced by competitive clientelism and weak domestic capitalists that drive ruling political elites to choose a large role for the state in achieving these objectives, through state-owned enterprises for example, are the same political incentives that undermine the ability of state-led industrial policies to deliver good economic results. In the case of state-owned enterprises, these companies are used to generate and maintain political support, and are seen as such by those employed. Thus, they are seen more as social projects than businesses, and as a result, they are managed poorly.

[10] 1988 Ghana Directory of Industrial Establishments: Oil Palm Industry, Ghana Statistical Service Publication.

These problems were highlighted in a study of the state-owned oil palm estates, which identified the main causes for their collapse or underperformance as political interference and poor management (Gyasi 1996). The study also emphasized the negative impacts of capital constraints on the performance of the palm oil estates, and the rigidity of state economic controls put in place due to chronic macroeconomic imbalances – which were indirect effects of competitive clientelism, as discussed in Chapter 2. By the early 1980s, the palm oil estates suffered from low mill capacity utilization largely as a result of the inadequate supply of fresh fruit bunches. Inadequate raw material was due to low productivity on the oil palm plantations caused by the use of poor-quality planting materials and unsatisfactory plantation management practices.

As part of the general structural adjustment reforms, the PNDC government launched a state-owned enterprise reform program in 1988 that aimed to reduce the dependence of state-owned firms on government subventions. The government invited private participation in the palm oil estates, but it was generally not forthcoming, so instead it focused on increasing the productivity and viability of the estates. The PNDC government also wanted to achieve self–sufficiency in vegetable oil production, with palm oil being the most important, for the same reason as previous governments: to reduce the drain on foreign exchange of importing something that could be produced domestically.

The PNDC government was convinced that the four large-scale estates could become financially viable if operated by competent and independent management. These estates included BOPP, TOPP and GOPDC, as well as the National Oil Palm Plantation Limited (NORPALM) in the Western Region, which was a wholly state-owned enterprise created out of the state-owned plantations at Sese and Pretsea. The PNDC government obtained capital from various sources and channeled it to the estates. For example, it acquired funding from the European Union to undertake mill expansion and replanting of trees on the plantation at NORPALM, while GOPDC received financial support through World Bank loans. TOPP received support from the European Union and the Commonwealth Development Corporation, as well as a loan from a private Dutch financing company, and BOPP received financial support from Lever Brothers Ghana Limited, the majority shareholder.

Freed from the kinds of political inference that occurred under the pressures of competitive clientelism, managers of these palm oil estates focused on increasing productivity. The path towards productivity was led by TOPP, which by 1987 had mastered the skills and techniques required to develop and maintain the oil palm plantations at a lower cost and the oil palm trees had begun to be more productive. TOPP implemented these best practices throughout its nucleus plantation, smallholder plantations, outgrower plantations, and associated independent plantations and state farms. As a result, TOPP secured adequate raw material to increase labor productivity and maximize mill capacity utilization. Following its impressive results, TOPP managers assisted the other estates to transfer the practices from TOPP to their plantations.[11] Production increased, but the four large-scale estates still faced problems that constrained their international competitiveness, which became acute in the new context of trade liberalization.

The Ghana Oil Palm Development Association was established in 1985 to coordinate the interests of palm oil producing estates *and* the local manufacturing companies that purchased their crude palm oil. The main local buyers of crude palm oil included Lever Brothers Ghana Limited (now Unilever) and PZ Cussons, which were both subsidaries of multinational corporations based in the UK; and Appiah Menkah Complex and Ameen Sangari, which were smaller factories producing mainly soaps and detergents. Ameen Sangari was Lebanese-owned, while Appiah Menkah Complex was a private, Ghanaian-owned factory whose owner was engaged in oil palm cultivation and then set up a processing mill in 1974 and a soap manufacturing factory in 1977. Notably, the owner had been a minister in the Busia government and member of the Progress Party (the predecessor of the NPP). Lever Brothers Ghana Limited, PZ Cussons and Ameen Sangari had been importing tallow (animal fat) but switched to domestically produced crude palm oil when it became available and invested in oil palm plantations themselves.

In 1989, Lever Brothers Ghana Limited reported to the association that due to the influx of cheaper soaps and cooking oil into Ghana from Côte d'Ivoire, the Middle East and the Far East, it was very difficult to sell soaps and cooking oil manufactured goods locally. Locally

[11] Interview, a former manager of TOPP from 1979 to 1997, Accra, Ghana, 2011; and Foli, "History of Oil Palm in Ghana."

produced palm oil at the time was selling about 1.2 times higher than the world market price. To compete effectively, the local soap and cooking oil manufacturing firms required high-quality palm oil at prices lower than what BOPP, TOPP, GOPDC and NORPALM were offering. These palm oil estates refused to reduce their price for crude palm oil because the price already agreed by the association took into account their costs of production at the time.[12] Eventually, for cash-flow reasons, GOPDC was forced to sell large quantities of its palm oil at 25 percent below the agreed price to the main local buyers. But the local manufacturers buying crude palm oil from the estates continued to insist on price reductions even after this unilateral action by GOPDC. Refusing to reduce the price of their crude palm oil, TOPP, BOPP and NORPALM held large stocks of palm oil. Then TOPP started exporting palm oil to Togo, Burkina Faso and Mali in 1989, as part of its corporate plan to generate foreign exchange in order to finance loan repayments as well as spare parts, mill expansion and procurement of general inputs. This action reduced the glut on the local market and stabilized the spot market price in the country for crude palm oil.

TOPP and BOPP took advantage of this recovery of the palm oil price to push for a new pricing formula at the association in order to avoid producers such as GOPDC being forced to reduce price unilaterally. They also advocated for the regulation of imported tallow as a substitute for palm oil and of the influx of cheaper soaps and cooking oil. The overvaluation of the cedi measured against the US dollar was reflected in the high price of palm oil produced in Ghana compared to world market prices. This situation was a challenge for soap and cooking oil manufacturing industries that depended on palm oil produced in Ghana until the new palm oil price setting was adopted by the association. Under the new pricing formula, the association price was set equal to the cost of importing palm oil from Malaysia through Rotterdam into Ghana through the Tema port.

12 Between 1986 and 1989, the main local buyers of crude palm oil forced down the price of palm oil through the import of palm oil from Côte d'Ivoire or the import of tallow, which was used as a subsititute for palm oil in soap maunfacturing, whenever required. But due to further depreciation of the Ghanaian currency, tallow became more expensive than palm oil during the 1989/1990 season. Therefore, the local industrial buyers of palm oil could not import tallow, as was the case in the past, and sought a resolution with the local palm oil producers.

Following negotiations between the Ghana Oil Palm Development Association and the PNDC government, the government agreed to regulate the import of tallow, palm oil, soap and cooking oil, given the adverse effect of the 1990 palm oil glut on the palm oil estates and the Ghanaian economy.[13] The regulatory measures included the following. Permission could only be granted for the import of vegetable oil and animal fat if the local supply of crude palm oil was inadequate and after consultation with the association. When imports were allowed, the import prices of animal fat, vegetable oils, refined cooking oil and soap were to be carefully assessed to ensure that Ghanaian producers would be not crippled by subsidized imports or unrealistically low world prices.[14] Lastly, the government banned the importation of edible oil in the form of foreign aid and also asked the Ghana National Trading Company, a state-owned trading company, to suspend sales of imported edible oil from its outlets.

The Ghana Oil Palm Development Association was strong during this period, and through the association, industry actors had good relations with the PNDC ruling elites and were able to influence economic policies. These relations changed after privatization, as shown below. The palm oil estates worked with the PNDC elites to increase technical know-how and pursue productivity improvements and cost reduction measures in return for capital injections. Favorable domestic palm oil prices after the 1990 glut resulted in three of the large-scale palm oil estates becoming profitable by 1991 – the exception was NORPALM, but it started off from a less viable financial position. However, it was not long after the PNDC government's industrial policies in the palm oil sector proved successful that the configuration of political pressures changed as the PNDC elites accepted a return to multiparty elections.

Privatization under the Pressures of Competitive Clientelism

The PNDC government ran a large fiscal deficit ahead of the 1992 election through domestic financing, and at the same time experienced

13 Ato Ahwoi, Memorandum to PNDC Committee of Secretaries by a Sub-Committee of the Committee of Secretaries, April 24, 1990.

14 Letter on Dumping of Palm oil on Ghana dated September 1, 1989 and signed by W.H. Morrison Managing Director of BOPP and F.C. Quinn General Manager of TOPP.

falling export revenue due to declining international market prices for its main exports, cocoa and gold. As mentioned in Chapter 4, the deteriorating macroeconomic climate led to the suspension of the IMF program in 1992, and it was in this context that the newly elected NDC government turned to the divestiture of state-owned enterprises as a way to plug its fiscal deficits and gain foreign exchange. Thus, the NDC government initiated a process of divesting the palm oil estates that had just become profitable and could attract private investment. Table 6.1 summarizes the privatization process for the four large-scale palm oil estates as well as individual state-owned oil palm plantations.

The large estates were divested to foreign investors. In 1994, the government sold 80 percent of its shares in GOPDC to the SIAT Ghana consortium, consisting primarily of SIAT Belgium, which was given management control, and two Ghanaian investment companies. SIAT Belgium owned palm oil estates in two other West African countries. Its target market, and reason for buying GOPDC, was to sell refined palm oil products to food industries in the West African region.[15] The multinational company had accumulated knowledge and capabilities in refinery and fractionation before investing in Ghana. Regarding TOPP, the NDC government sold 50 percent of its shares to Unilever (formerly Lever Brothers), which gave Unilever 40 percent of total shares and management control of the company. BOPP was from the beginning a joint venture with Unilever, with the government having 60 percent and Unilever having 40 percent. When Unilever took over TOPP, it began jointly managing BOPP and TOPP. Unilever bought the majority of the remaining shares in TOPP in 2004 when the NPP government sold them on the Ghana Stock Exchange. The NPP government also offloaded its remaining shares in GOPDC on the Stock Exchange in 2008.

In these three estates, privatization led to significant investments in productivity, including replanting old trees, upgrading mills, and installing new technology and practices. In contrast, the National Oil Palms Limited (NORPALM) was sold in 2000 to Norpalm AS, a Norwegian company (which interestingly had the same name), but the Norwegian company did not bring additional financing for investments in productivity, such as replanting ageing trees on the nucleus plantation. This situation seems to have contravened the conditions

[15] Interviews with SIAT staff at GOPDC, Kwae, Ghana, March 2, 2010.

Table 6.1 *State-Owned Palm Oil Estates and Oil Palm Plantations Divested*

Year	Company	Transaction	Ownership	Amount Paid
1994	Juaben Oil Palm Plantation	Sale of Assets	100% by Juaben Traditional Council	¢50,000,000
1994	New Edubiase Oil Palm Plantation	Sale of Assets	100% New Edubiase Divisional Council	¢3,750,000
1994	Ghana Oil Palm Development Corporation (GOPDC)	Joint Venture	80% SIAT Ghana, 20% government	US$6,952,552
1995	Akokerri Oil Palm Plantation	Sale of Assets	100% by Thersky Oil Industries	¢75,000,000
1997	State Oil Palm Plantation, Juaso	Sale of Assets	100% by Juaso Traditional Council	¢100,000,000
1997	State Oil Palm Plantation Akwanserem	Sale of Assets	100% by Akotosu Farms Ltd/ Traditional Council	¢110,000,000
1997	Twifo Oil Palm Limited (TOPP)	Sale of Shares	40% by Unilever Ghana ltd	US$7,200,000
1999	State Farms Corporation Farm, Bunso	Sale of Assets	100% by Sun Enterprises	¢19,000,000
1999	National Oil Palms Limited	Sale of Assets	100% by Norpalm ASA, Norway	US$2,960,000
2004	Benso Oil Palm Plantation (BOPP)	Sale of Shares	100% Ownership by Unilever Ghana Limited	Not available
2008	Ghana Oil Palm Development Corporation	Sale of Shares	100% by Outgrowers/Smallholders/ Staff	¢8,000,000,000
(year unknown)	State Oil Palm Plantation, Okumaning	Direct Acquisition	100% Ownership by Ghana Oil Palm Development Company Limited	Not available
(year unknown)	Ashanti Oil Mills	Direct Acquisition	100% Direct Acquisition By Appiah Menkah Complex	Not available

Source: Created by the author with data from Chris Foli, "History of Oil Palm in Ghana," commissioned paper.

under which it won the privatization bid, but neither the NDC or the NPP government pushed the issue.[16] Thus, the management of Norpalm sold shares to PZ Cusson in order to raise capital for improvements on the estate.[17]

During the privatization process, several land litigation cases had to be settled and compensation paid to chiefs before land title could be transferred to the new private owners. Land expropriated by the government for the individual state-owned plantations generally were given (back) to the Traditional Councils of paramount chiefs in the relevant area, because the government had never paid for the lands and thus the Councils demanded that they be returned. The councils only paid for the assets of the plantations transferred with the land.[18] In at least one case, a medium-size mill owner bought a state plantation, but the surrounding community regarded it as their land and challenged the acquisition. In the end, the government "sold" the plantation instead to the Traditional Council in that community. In another case, the head of the Juaso Traditional Council, the Juaben paramount chief, was the owner of Juaben Oil Mills, and he was able to acquire the former state-owned plantation and use it for his mill company.

There were also problems with the transfer of land titles from NORPALM to the Norwegian firm that bought it. After the sale, landlords began to dispute ownership of the land. Apparently, Alexander Cecil Goff acquired the lands (on which NORPALM existed) on leasehold in the early 1900s for the cultivation of citrus, rubber and oil palm, and it was the site of the first oil palm plantation in the Gold Coast.[19] Leasehold rights to the land changed from Alexander Cecil Goff into other private hands, until it was acquired by the state in the early 1960s and incorporated as part of the State Farms Corporation. Other portions of the land, including where the processing mill is situated, were offered to the state without any financial considerations by the chiefs of Ahanta and Wassa Mpohor (in the

16 Interview, former executive secretary of the Divestiture Implementation Committee, Accra, Ghana, July 8, 2011.

17 Interviews with staff at Norpalm, Ghana, March 4, 2010.

18 Official data from the Divestiture Implementation Committee indicates that the Traditional Council paid for the plantation, but these numbers are often what was pledged, and it was not possible to access official data on what was actually paid.

19 Report of the Committee of Enquiry on lands occupied by the National Oil Palms Limited.

Western Region) for the cultivation of oil palm, in response to the call by the CPP government that land owners support the industrialization drive by releasing land for the establishment of farms and factories. The status of these parcels of land that were not properly acquired remained a source of litigation between the landlords and the state-owned NORPALM estate. When the estate was sold to the Norwegian Norpalm, landlords holding leases wanted to renegotiate leases with the new occupant, and continued to dispute the "unacquired" parcels of land by demanding constant payments for the land from the new Norwegian owners.

After the privatization process, the now foreign-owned and managed large-scale estates sold crude palm oil in the domestic market to a small number of manufacturing companies, with Unilever the main buyer until the 2000s. Unilever's factory produced a large range of consumer goods marketed in the West African region. Unilever, PZ Cussons, and Ameen Sangari invested in refinery and fractionation facilities in the 2000s, as did the new owners of GOPDC. There were a few other domestic companies that purchased crude palm oil for use in manufacturing soaps and other products. However, the volume of crude palm oil produced in Ghana was not enough to meet the needs of these manufacturing companies, which meant they had to import crude palm oil or substitutes for it. The palm oil estates exported only a small amount of crude palm oil, to other countries in the West African region or to niche markets in the US and Europe, where it was sold in ethnic retail shops to West African immigrants.

There was generally no incentive for the palm oil processing mills to export to the main importing countries India, China, Pakistan and the European Union, due to the unmet domestic demand and price setting within the Ghana Oil Palm Development Association. Since the establishment of the Association in 1985, the prices of crude palm oil and palm kernel oil were agreed between domestic producers and buyers of crude palm oil. After 1990, the price was set using the world market price quoted at Rotterdam on the last working day of the previous month plus freight charge to Ghana. Thus, producers received the same price as the price of imported crude palm oil. The buyers agreed to this formula, at the time, as a means to help the estates improve their productivity. This Rotterdam pricing formula remained in place at the end of the 2000s.

After the privatization of the large estates, the Ghana Oil Palm Development Association slowly became defunct. The new owner of GOPDC sought to work individually; TOPP and BOPP became vertically integrated into Unilever; and Norpalm was preoccupied with creating a commercially viable company. The three large estates (counting BOPP and TOPP as one) acted as islands, and competition for raw material supply increased among them with little cooperation in addressing collective industry issues and problems. Furthermore, the chairman of the association, who was the owner of Juaben Oil Mills, did not demonstrate much leadership in getting the existing medium and large mills to work together.[20] Many of the other medium mills were struggling and had little clout with the large estates or with the association chairman.

By 2010, there was almost no formal collective organizing or networking among the palm oil mills. The only case of collective action that staff at the mills could identify was their work together on Ghana's interpretation of the criteria and principles of the Roundtable on Sustainable Palm Oil, which would in the future constitute new global standards for palm oil production. This process was led by GOPDC, which did export some of its crude palm oil and thus had a vested interest in meeting the new global standards. Otherwise, there was limited sharing of knowledge among the estates. GOPDC management staff indicated that the best practices and guidelines produced by companies in the Malaysian palm oil sector to share knowledge were a dream for Ghanaian estates.

Challenges Facing Industrial Palm Oil Processing in the 2000s

The privatization process in the 1990s and early 2000s reinforced the dualistic structure of the palm oil industry, which had two subsectors with different end markets: industrial processing for sale to domestic manufacturing companies or export, and small-scale processors for sale at the local markets for consumption. The industrial use subsector consisted of four large-scale palm oil estates and roughly twelve medium-size processing mills. Compared to oil palm cultivation and processing for the home consumption end market, the industrial

[20] This point was raised several times in interviews with the medium-size mills and some of the large-scale estates.

subsector was characterized by more efficient technology, economies of scale, higher productivity on farms (in terms of yields of oil palm bunches) and in mills (in terms of quantity of oil extracted), and by its better quality of crude palm oil as well as further refined palm oil products.[21]

However, a study by the Food and Agricultural Organization of the United Nations conducted in 2006 indicated that at least four of the existing twelve medium-size mills were not viable companies; in other words, they were not making the requisite profit margins.[22] Of these medium-size mills, which were all private companies owned by Ghanaian nationals, only Juaben Oil Mills was doing well. Notably, the owner of Juaben Oil Mills was able to access concessional (below market rate) financing through donor projects, which he used to set up an outgrower scheme and upgrade the company's mill.[23] He later expanded the mill in size and capabilities, including a refinery and fractionation plant as well as a shea butter plant. Notably, the other medium-scale mills did not have their own oil palm plantations due to problems acquiring land, nor did they have outgrower schemes, which were too expensive to establish.[24] The dependence of these mills on acquiring all their raw material from independent smallholders cultivating oil palm trees was part of the reason for their poor performance. These mills registered a much lower extraction rate because they relied largely on buying from independent smallholders who grew an oil palm variety that had lower oil content, but also because they used less efficient technology than the large-scale estates.[25]

The home consumption subsector consisted of private smallholder oil palm cultivators, who largely sold their fresh fruit bunches to

21 Ecorys and CDC, "Oil Palm Value Chain, Final Report," 2010, submitted to the Ministry of Trade and Industry, Ghana, by Ecorys Nederland BV and CDC Consult Ltd.

22 Emma Nikki Owiredu, "Business Management Report: Diagnostic Surveys on the Prevalent Conditions and Capacity Building Needs of Associations and Companies," Report by Food and Agricultural Organization (FAO) consultant, January 2006.

23 On the Juaben paramount chief and his business Juaben Oil Mills Ltd, see Berry (2013).

24 Interviews with staff at Ayiem Mills and Obooma Farms, both medium-sized mills.

25 Ecorys and CDC, "Oil Palm Value Chain, Final Report, 2010, submitted to the Ministry of Trade and Industry, Ghana," by Ecorys Nederland BV and CDC Consult Ltd.

small-scale processing units or household (manual) processors. There was an estimated 400 of such small-scale processing units. Smallholder cultivators used a low-yielding oil palm variety; the farms and processors were characterized by lower productivity, and the processors produced a low-quality crude palm oil that was sold in villages or at small town markets. Nevertheless, the home consumption subsector consumed over half of the fresh fruit bunches (ffb) produced in Ghana. One study undertaken in 2010 calculated that small-scale and village processors utilized about 68 percent of the ffb in Ghana and accounted for 55 percent of the crude palm oil produced.[26] In contrast, the medium-size mills used about 12 percent of total ffb (but this is an overestimation because one of the mills stopped operating), and the large-scale estates used about 19–20 percent of total ffb. The remaining percentage was accounted for by household production.

The total area of oil palm trees cultivated in 2002 was approximately 175,000 hectares, which rose to 300,000 hectares in 2008, but the increased production of ffb was still not enough to meet the needs of the existing mills. None of the mills were operating at 100 percent capacity at the end of the 2000s due to the shortage of raw material.[27] Although the large-scale estates had the highest productivity in oil palm cultivation on their nucleus plantations compared to other cultivators, it was still lower than yields achieved on plantations in Malaysia. Malaysia oil palm trees yield 17.6 tons per hectare, whereas the large-scale estates in Ghana did not get more than 10 tons per hectare on their nucleus plantations. Furthermore, smallholder yields were as low as 2 tons per hectare, and all of the mills depended on smallholders for at least half of their ffb supply. Thus, the processing mills suffered from a *shortage of raw materials* and *low productivity among smallholder oil palm cultivators*.

These problems with expanding the supply of fresh fruit bunches and improving processing quality constrained the development of further downstream industries and exporting possibilities. The secondary processing of crude palm oil involves producing a refined, deodorized, bleached oil: a neutral oil of bland flavor and nearly white color. To attain refined oil of high quality, processing must be designed to minimize the development of free fatty acids and oil oxidation. For

[26] Ibid. [27] Ibid.

Ghana to develop secondary processing, the palm oil industry has to be highly organized in order to generate the most efficient processing (high rates of oil extraction) and the best quality oil (low fatty acid). This level of organization is hard to achieve, because the existing mills depend on scattered, independent smallholder cultivators to supply a significant portion of the fresh fruit bunches that they process. Fresh fruit bunches need to be collected and processed within 48 hours after harvesting in order to ensure low fatty acid content, and thus a neutral oil suited for refining. Furthermore, higher-yielding oil palm varieties are better suited for industrial milling due to their higher oil content, but smallholders neglected to adopt this variety because it was less desirable by local consumers of crude palm oil for cooking purposes (Huddleston 2006).

The individual estates could not overcome these problems on their own; it required collective action among industry actors as well as between industry actors and the government. Expanding the volume of crude palm oil produced in the industrial subsector depended on access to land, the organization of smallholders and better integrating their production with existing mills, and ensuring that smallholders cultivated a higher-yielding variety of oil palm. For the medium-size mills, issues also included access to finance for capital investments and working capital (as many had poor financial records with the banks); increasing efficiency in management; and training and retaining skilled workers.

The large-scale estates were constrained in their ability to increase production of crude palm oil due to lack of raw materials from smallholders and their inability to access more land with which they could expand their nucleus oil palm plantations. There was limited land in large contiguous quantities available near existing estates. Land was available for sale, but it was fragmented among many owners, whose actual ownership was often disputed due to the lack of formal titles. Leasing land was also difficult because it entailed a long process of negotiations with chiefs, indigene landowners, and people living on the land, and it involved compensation for the land as well as the people, structures and even trees (if cocoa trees, for example) on the land. Accessing land was more difficult for the foreign-owned palm oil estates due to sentiments in the traditional oil palm belt about past government expropriations and about foreign companies. Ghanaian mill owners could access land through the *abusa* system (see

Chapter 2), but they had insufficient working capital to finance cultivation of oil palm on their own plantations. Therefore, both foreign and Ghanaian owned mills came to depend on smallholders for increasing the supply of raw materials.

Smallholder cultivators were not well integrated into the industrial processing subsector. There were three categories of smallholders: (1) those who participated in outgrower schemes and were under contractual agreements to deliver ffb to a particular estate; (2) those who operated on land owned by the large estates as the result of resettlement schemes when the estates were created and who were independent producers that often sold their crop to traditional processors or processed small quantities of oil themselves; and (3) those who operated on land near large estates and medium-size mills and sold both to the modern mills and to the small village mills.

Only the first category of smallholders in outgrower schemes had a definite connection to the estates. Outgrower schemes served the dual purpose of expanding raw material and legitimizing the estates (which had expropriated land) by bringing benefits to the surrounding villages, such as schools and health clinics located on estate land and paid for by the company. These schemes also involved the provision of high-yielding seedlings to outgrowers, along with agronomic advice and the application of fertilizers and other inputs and services. The costs of these inputs were then added to the individual outgrower's account, and would be repaid after a certain period. However, the outgrower schemes were extremely costly, given the extension services, collection, and monitoring involved. In addition, despite monitoring, outgrower farmers could (and did) sell their fresh fruit bunches to small processors in the villages or to other estates. The outgrower schemes that existed had been created in the 1980s and 1990s through subsidies that came from donor projects. Estates not benefiting from such donor subsidies were not interested in establishing outgrower schemes because they were expensive to establish and run, and those costs would not necessarily be recouped if outgrowers sold their fruits to other buyers.

Finally, there was increasing competition for the fresh fruit bunches being sold by all three types of smallholders. This led to bidding wars on the price, not only between industrial estates during the peak season but also between mills and "market queens" who regulated the domestic market of crude palm oil for home consumption. It was common for agro-processing factories and market queens to compete over the supply of produce that had an existing high demand in domestic consumption markets.

Conclusion

By the turn of the twenty-first century, all of the large-scale palm oil estates wanted to expand their processing capacity, but the major constraint was the supply of raw materials. In order for estates to increase their access to raw materials, they needed to acquire more land for their own production; to improve yields on their existing plantations; and to increase oil palm cultivation and yields among smallholder farmers. Furthermore, an estimated 250,000 hectares of oil palm trees, representing 80 percent of fresh fruit bunches produced in Ghana, was produced by scattered, unorganized farmers who had no connection to an industrial palm oil mill, and the productivity of these farmers was very low compared to farmers linked to industrial mills.

This was the context in which the NPP government launched its President's Special Initiative in Oil Palm in 2003. The aim of the initiative was to assist the unorganized, small-scale farmers to adopt improved planting materials and production techniques in order to increase their output as well as to link them to modern processing mills. The PSI in Oil Palm had a modest impact on expanding oil palm cultivation and generally failed to better integrate smallholders into the industrial production chain. This was because the design and implementation of the PSI in Oil Palm had few linkages with the existing industrial mills. Instead, the group of NPP political elites pursuing the initiative opted for a state-led industrial policy that was designed along lines similar to the Farmapine pineapple exporting firm based on the farmer-owned model discussed in the previous chapter. In the PSI in Oil Palm, the state played the central role in creating new oil palm plantation cooperatives and wanted to link these cooperative plantations to new processing mills in which they would have shares along with core investors that would manage the mills. Implementation of the initiative was hampered by internal NPP politics, as the next chapter shows, but the design of the PSI in Oil Palm also generally failed to address the constraints on productivity and expansion facing the existing industry.

7 NPP Government and the Not So "Golden Age of Business"

President Kufuor and the New Patriotic Party (NPP) proclaimed that its tenure in government would be a Golden Age of Business, distinguishing itself from former President Rawlings and the NDC's hostilities towards private business. Despite this proclamation, the NPP government did not support domestic capitalists much more than the preceding NDC government did. In the context of competitive clientelism, NPP ruling elites generally prioritized distributive expenditures. When they pursued industrial policies, they were designed in such a way as to be implemented and controlled by the state, or they supported new private investments through initiatives that did not include and connect with existing firms in the industry. Because the industrial policies were not linked up to existing farmers and businessmen, whatever economic impacts they had usually disappeared when the financing stopped, as participants were not interested in continuing after the easy economic opportunities and rents ceased.

This chapter provides further evidence for this argument by focusing on the industrial policies that were intended to support the horticulture export and palm oil sectors: the President's Special Initiative in Oil Palm and the Millennium Challenge Account in commercial agriculture. The President's Special Initiatives (PSIs) and the Millennium Challenge Account (MCA) grant from the US government also constituted the largest initiatives related to developing productive sectors implemented during the Kufuor administrations.

President Kufuor launched the PSIs in August 2001, not long after assuming office, as his major program to create new pillars of growth by accelerating the development of selected products into leading export earners. The selected sectors mainly included agro-industries, but also garments and textiles in order to capture benefits from the African Growth and Opportunity Act created by the US in 2000. The PSIs were described as a public-private partnership, involving a government-directed effort to secure land, capital and other resources to facilitate the expansion of an existing industry or to pioneer a new one. The PSIs were clearly a form of industrial policy, one initiated and driven by the NPP government.

In 2004, the Millennium Challenge Corporation, the US agency administering the new Millennium Challenge Account aid program, offered Ghana the opportunity to propose a project that would improve economic growth and reduce long-term poverty. In late 2006, the NPP government signed the compact, which emphasized commercial agriculture and horticulture exports in particular and was worth US$547 million, the largest bilateral grant in Ghana's history. Implementation took place between 2007 and 2012, and President Kufuor heralded the MCA compact as one of his legacies.

The PSIs and the MCA provide windows into the everyday political maneuvering that occurred within the NPP over resource allocations, policymaking and implementation, but given their size and importance to President Kufuor, the political struggles were more visible and the stakes were higher. They are good cases with which to illustrate the causal linkages between the government's policy choices and expenditure patterns and ruling political elites' political survival strategies. These cases demonstrate the preference of NPP ruling elites for distributive expenditures and state-led industrial policies, and demonstrate the paradox of Ghanaian ruling elites trying to ambitiously implement state-led industrial policies in the context of competitive clientelism – it does not work.

This analysis is based on empirical material generated and collected through several periods of fieldwork. Sources on the PSIs include interviews with civil servants within the Ministry of Trade and Industry and the PSI Secretariat, combined with written documents including World Bank reports, FAO reports, consultancy reports, and reports from the Ministry of Trade and Industry and the Ministry of Food and Agriculture. In particular, documentation on the formulation and implementation of the PSI in Oil Palm was obtained from the first coordinator of the Oil Palm PSI, who provided files from the period when he was coordinator, including internal communication with key actors, annual reports, and designs and work plans.[1] For the

[1] This material was obtained by Elizabeth Asante and then shared with me as part of the Ghana country team research in the Elites, Production and Poverty research program (2008–2012) based at the Danish Institute for International Studies.

MCA case, sources include interviews with the MCA proposal drafting team and access to all written documents and drafts at various stages of the proposal process, as well as interviews with staff members at the Millennium Development Authority during the period between 2008 and 2009, and again in 2015 after the MCA was completed; interim implementation reports and the final completion report published by the Millennium Development Authority; field visits to sites with components related to the horticulture export industry and interviews with relevant industry actors.

The first part of the chapter describes the origin of the President's Special Initiatives and contextualizes them within the broader policy approach of the Ministry of Trade and Industry under the leadership of Alan Kyerematen. It then analyzes the economic challenges to implementing the Cassava Starch PSI, which involved the creation of a state-owned enterprise in cassava starch processing. This attempt to use state-owned enterprises to pioneer a new industry was no more successful than previous governments in the 1960s and 1970s. The chapter then turns to the Oil Palm PSI and explains the political drivers and economic challenges to implementing the Oil Palm PSI, which involved state-led attempts to improve smallholder cultivation of oil palm trees and catalyze private investment in new processing mills. The second part of the chapter explains the political drivers that shaped how the MCA compact was formulated with the focus on horticulture exports, and then how it was turned into a largely distributive initiative.

President Kufuor and the President's Special Initiatives

When the NPP formed a government in 2001, newly elected President Kufuor turned to Alan Kyerematen for ideas on how to support industrial development, particularly in rural areas. Kyerematen was the driving force behind most of the Kufuor administrations' industrial initiatives, even before he became Minister of Trade and Industry, including the District Industrialization Program and President's Special Initiatives. The ideas for these initiatives partly came from Kyerematen's experience working for Enterprise Africa, a project funded by the United Nations Development Programme, and he brought former members of the Enterprise Africa project into the Ministry of Trade and Industry as politically appointed civil servants to help run his initiatives. But they also had clear political drivers.

The District Industrialization Program and President's Special Initiatives had limited impacts on agro-processing and industrial development in the country. The explanation behind the limited economic outcomes is still very salient, not only for the broader argument that this book seeks to make but also because after the NPP won the December 2016 elections and formed a government, Kyerematen was appointed Minister of Trade and Industry and these initiatives were revived. Kyerematen's District Industrialization Programme in the 2000s are the inspiration behind the "one district one factory initiative" that appeared in the NPP's 2016 election manifesto and campaign. Only this time Alan Kyerematen seems to have the political backing of Nana Akufo-Addo and his faction, which has resulted in the Akufo-Addo administration signing an agreement with the Chinese government that is intended to finance the implementation of the "one district one factory" policy, including the construction of turnkey factories.[2] Only time will tell if the program will turn out differently.

In the 2000s, Kyerematen's District Industrialization Programme aimed to create "commercially viable, export oriented and domestic import competing business activities at the district level."[3] It attempted to harness the capital of the Ghanaian diaspora to invest in rural industrialization enterprises, but the investments were envisioned to occur through a Corporate Village Enterprise model. In this model, small and medium rural enterprises would be established with community ownership alongside individual private investors and institutional investors such as domestic banks and district assemblies. The implementation model involved community workshops to get support, the creation of district oversight committees, the development of business plans for selected district projects, identification of private

[2] "One District One Factory Implementation Plan Revealed," January 14, 2017, http://citifmonline.com (last accessed on August 3, 2017); "China Gives Ghana $2 Billion for 'One District One Factory' Project," June 23, 2017, http://3news.com (last accessed on August 3, 2017); "Government Releases 465 Million Ghana Cedis for One-District-One-Factory Project," April 11, 2017, http://dailyguideafrica.com (last accessed on August 3, 2017); "How NPP Will Implement 'One District, One Factory' Policy," January 23, 2017, www.graphic.com.gh (last accessed on August 3, 2017).

[3] "Brief on District Industrialization Programme," Ministry of Trade and Industry, May 2005. This paragraph also draws on interviews with former members of the District Industrialization Program team at the Ministry of Trade and Industry, Accra, September 17, 2008 and September 24, 2008.

investors, incorporation of companies and mobilization of finance. Consultants were hired to prepare business plans for one project for each district, and they produced eighty-six business plans. These business plans were poorly done, generic assessments of agro-processing potential in rural areas. Not surprisingly, the ministry had a hard time to attract individuals to invest or buy shares in these "projects," and concluded that the government would have to facilitate access to credit and infrastructural support, and to provide a grant to each district as start up capital for the "project."

Government resources on this scale were not available. The NPP government was implementing a "bail out" program with the IMF due to the 2000 economic crisis, and austerity measures were in place, which meant lower government expenditure. Therefore, Kyerematen's initiatves were scaled down. The District Industrialization Programme focused on reviving a few state-owned enterprises in collaboration with foreign and domestic private investment. The ministry refurbished the Northern Star Tomato Company in partnership with Trusty Foods Company Limited in Tema, which had a factory that imported bulk tomato paste and repackaged it for sale in Ghana. Northern Star was going to produce in bulk and sell to Trusty Foods for further processing. The factory opened in 2007, but closed down (again) after one season due to disputes with the farmers supplying tomatoes over the price, which was unresolved at the time of the December 2008 elections, which the NPP lost.[4] The Brong Ahafo tomato cannery in Wenchi faced similar problems, even though it was reopened through a public-private partnership with the private firm managing it. It was not able to source a sufficient volume of high-quality tomatoes at a competitive price and closed down after a pilot season, while the owner explored the option of sourcing raw material from its own dedicated farm.

Some of the PSIs came to incorporate ideas similar to the District Industrialization Program, especially around the Corporate Village Enterprise model. Kyerematen sought funding for the PSIs anywhere he could find it, and turned to the United Nations Development Programme (UNDP) Ghana office to provide initial financing for the PSI in Cassava Starch in the early 2000s. Initially, the PSIs were

[4] "Refurbished Ghanaian Tomato Factory Remains Idle," *Ghanaian Times*, posted November 19, 2008, at http://africanagriculture.blogspot.com (last accessed in 2008).

supposed to be implemented by the Federation of Associations of Ghanaian Exporters, but in close collaboration with the government through an interministerial team, which was needed to address problems such as the provision of water, roads and electricity. Implementation of the Cassava Starch and Garment PSIs began through collaboration between the head of the federation and the UNDP office. Alan Kyerematen became Minister of Trade and Industry in 2003, at which time he moved the PSI Secretariat to the Office of the President and appointed PSI coordinators who were politically connected. It is not clear whether he did this because he thought it would give him greater leverage in getting them implemented, but the move meant that the PSIs had become state-led and not private-sector-led. As a result, the federation withdrew from the initiative in 2004.

Despite President Kufuor's support for the PSIs, they lacked general support among NPP ruling elites. In fact, the group of NPP ruling elites supporting the PSIs was very small, including Kufuor, Kyerematen and a handful of others. The PSIs were not in the NPP's 2000 election manifesto, which in any case had very little to say about the productive sectors. They were only designed after the NPP formed the government, when President Kufuor was looking for a flagship project and asked Alan Kyerematen to lead a team to devise ideas on what the government could do to address rural poverty but with a business model. As a result, this small group backing the PSIs did not wield enough authority within the NPP party organization or over the NPP members of Parliament who formed the government, despite including President Kufuor. Furthermore, many NPP politicians saw the PSIs as a patronage resource with which Alan Kyerematen sought to build a personal political base ahead of his bid for the party's presidential nomination for the 2008 national elections.

When the PSI proposal went to Cabinet, Cabinet voted for it, but it was not made a priority over areas such as healthcare reform, school feeding program, roads, building schools, and water provision. The small group of NPP elites pushing the PSIs could not convince the rest of Cabinet of the importance of the PSIs over these distributive expenditures. In 2006 there was a drought and the Akosombo hydroelectric dam (the major source of electricity) dried up, leading to an energy crisis, which required putting money in energy production at the expense of other sectors. Furthermore, some Cabinet members such as

Yaw Osafo Marfo, minister of finance from 2001 to 2004, said that the government should not fund the PSIs, but rather the private sector should. It is worth noting that Osafo Marfo contested to be the party's 2008 presidential candidate and was an ardent member of the Akufo-Addo faction within the NPP. The politicization of the PSIs, combined with the limited involvement of domestic capitalists, resulted in weak implementation or their discontinuation after Kyerematen left the Ministry of Trade and Industry to stand in the presidential primaries. The inability to secure financing for the PSIs was another factor undermining their implementation. The PSI Secretariat had to piece together funding from a myriad of donor projects that were already in the works or which were being negotiated at the time when the PSI idea was launched.

The Cassava Starch PSI: Creating Another State-Owned Enterprise

The idea behind the Cassava Starch PSI was that cassava accounts for 22 percent of agricultural GDP, has the lowest entry barriers to production compared to other major crops in Ghana, and over 90 percent of farmers cultivate cassava.[5] Cassava can be processed into industrial starch, which has numerous uses in food, paper, pharmaceuticals, textiles and petrochemicals. The plan was to enhance production, add value to the crop by processing into starch, and supply export markets. It was in the Cassava Starch PSI that the corporate village enterprise model was first put into practice. The plan envisioned four factories in the first phase. Ayensu Starch Company, the first and only cassava starch factory to be established, was located in Awutu-Efutu-Senya district (in the Central Region), and it ran into significant problems.[6]

5 The President's Special Initiative on Job Creation and Poverty Reduction through Agribusiness. Project No. 2 The Integrated Action Programme for Cassava Starch Production and Export (Incorporating the Enterprise Africa COVE Model), A briefing document. Prepared by Enterprise Africa and UNDP Ghana, June 1, 2001.

6 This district was supposedly selected based on technical assessments of cassava producing districts done by contracted local technical assistance. However, Jens Thomsen from the Starch Institute in Denmark, which was working on the project, claims that this is not the best cassava producing area in the country, but

A turnkey factory was ordered in November 2001 from the International Starch Institute in Denmark, and a South African company was contracted to install it and supply the remaining components for the factory. Financing for the factory came from national banks. The PSI Secretariat secured US$6 million for the Ayensu Starch Company business plan from the Agricultural Development Bank, National Investment Bank and Ghana Commercial Bank, all of which was needed to pay for the factory, which according to UNDP documentation cost US$7 million. The two people appointed as the Cassava Starch PSI coordinator and the general manager of Ayensu Starch Company had previously worked at Unilever Ghana, so they had management experience.

The ownership structure is not clear from early UNDP documentation, but it seems that the company was envisioned to be some kind of donor-government financed factory with expert management. There is a strong precedent in Ghana of creating modern industries using this method, which started under Nkrumah's CPP government in the 1960s and continued with the way that Ghana Oil Palm Development Corporation was set up with World Bank financing in the 1970s and with the creation of Farmapine in the late 1990s.

To secure a supply of raw materials for the Ayensu Starch Company, the PSI Secretariat mobilized 2,500 farmers in the district to participate in the initiative. It gave the farmers seed and credit to clear new land for cassava production and to help them increase yields and produce cassava with the appropriate starch content. These farming activities were started on the back of collaboration with the Ministry of Food and Agriculture, which was implementing the Roots and Tubers Project, financed by the International Fund for Agricultural Development, in the Eastern Region. The PSI Secretariat recruited a technical adviser who had worked on this project at the district level to do the farmer mobilization. Nurseries had to be set up to supply cassava sticks appropriate for industrial production. Each farmer was given agricultural inputs and technical assistance, and requested to crop a minimum of 2 hectares, which was considered by the PSI Secretariat to be the minimum size required for profitability. Each participating farmer was to be allotted a number of shares in the

rather was selected because it was an opposition (NDC) stronghold area. Interviewed January 30, 2008.

Ayensu Starch Company, which would give the farmer the right and obligation to deliver an agreed quantity of cassava to the factory. The management would notify farmers of delivery dates and pay the minimum guaranteed price.

The company began production in June 2003. The original business plan was for the South African company that set up the factory to buy the starch produced at Ayensu, but that company did not honor its commitment. The company was itself producing cassava starch for the South African market but had to import from Asia to meet the high demand in South Africa, and thought it could get a better deal in Ghana. However, at that time, the international price of cassava starch fell *and* the cost of Ghana's starch was higher than anticipated. The latter was the result of the starch content of the cassava used in the Ayensu factory being lower than expected and thus the cost of production higher to produce a ton of starch. The factory managers secured a new arrangement, where the International Starch Institute in Denmark set up a trading company, the International Starch Trading Company, which would buy Ayensu starch and sell it to the European market under the existing preferential trade agreement.[7] The institute also arranged to provide training and technical assistance for the operation of the factory, which was funded by Danida through its Business-to-Business Program. In particular, it paid for a technical expert to work as the factory's operations manager for one and a half years. The training program was successful in that it was able to open up markets for the Ayensu factory by bringing its operations up to international standards and getting certificates by the end of 2004.[8]

The trading company had built up sales, but then the Aysenu factory began not delivering due to inadequate supply of raw materials. Several factors interacted to cause this problem. The company did not have enough working capital to pay farmers promptly for their crops and its

[7] Initially, the plan was to sell to Nestle in the Nigerian market, but Nigeria had a ban on the importation of cassava products. Then the trading company looked to Asian markets, but the prices offered were too low, so Ghana could not compete.

[8] Cassava Starch Production and Export in Ghana Cooperation Document, from the Danish Embassy. Interviews with Danish Embassy staff involved and with the technical expert from the International Starch Institute.

field workers who harvested cassava on the nucleus farm.[9] Then the farmers started asking for higher prices, and in mid-2003 threatened to stop supplying the factory. The price had been negotiated between the factory management and farmers' organization; it was lower than the farmers wanted but had been accepted on the condition that the government would help the farmers to increase productivity and pay them promptly.[10] However, it seems that buyers of cassava for the local market upped the market price in a bid to secure cassava for their trade, which led farmers to complain about the price offered by the company. Some farmers started selling to the local markets. What the farmers received from the PSI Secretariat in terms of production inputs added up to more than the price offered by buyers of cassava for the local market, but farmers did not see it that way; they only saw the difference in the cash price. In addition, because it was a government program, the farmers thought everything should be free. Finally, the selling of the cassava crop to the Ayensu factory became politicized in the run up to the December 2004 elections, with some farmers telling other farmers not to sell to the factory.

Thus, Ayensu's raw material supply problems started in 2003 but peaked around the December 2004 elections. Farmers stopped supplying the factory because they could get a higher price right away in the local market, and Ayensu could not afford to pay a higher price due to low international prices for its starch and the company's high production costs. Eventually, the company raised the price paid to the farmers and the pricing issue was resolved, but at the expense of removing the corporate village enterprise concept in which part of the price was to be kept as money for shares in the factory. By 2005, the company was operating at 20 percent capacity due to inadequate supply of cassava roots as well as low export prices in the European market.[11] The company's production costs were too high for it to compete in European markets with exports from Thailand.

9 This point was raised in interviews with the Technical Advisor for the Cassava Starch PSI, and is also stated by Tonah (2006) in his study of the Ayensu Starch Factory.

10 "Nobody Promised Ayensu Farmers 500,000 Cedis per Ton – Coordinator," GNA, July 25, 2003, www.ghanaweb.com (last accessed in 2008).

11 "Bleak Future for Ayensu Starch Factory," Jonathan Ababre, *Public Agenda*, February 21, 2005.

Ayensu's productions costs were high for several reasons. The cassava being supplied to the factory had a low starch content, which meant more cassava had to be used. The technical adviser for the Cassava Starch PSI argued that a good variety was used, but the starch content was lower than expected due to variations in soil type, as the variety was sensitive to soil types, and the lack of fertilizer use (which had not been encouraged). However, others interviewed argued that the farmers needed to use varieties specifically created for commercial cassava starch processing that have a higher starch content but that the Crop Research Institute in Ghana was not asked to collaborate with the PSI project to help in supplying appropriate seed varieties. The supply to the factory was poorly organized, with no transport organized by the company from farm gates to the factory, leaving farmers to organize it themselves. In addition, the company had not managed its nucleus farm successfully. The government interministerial team overseeing the PSIs was supposed to ensure the adequate provision of infrastructure (roads, electricity and water), but this was not done, and the quality of the water was not always good and the electricity was not stable. The standby generator was too small to run the whole factory. The cost of transporting the starch to the Tema port was also higher than necessary. Lastly, there were problems with the management of the factory. After the Danish technical adviser left Ayensu in the beginning of 2005, the quality of the product supplied to the trading company declined. Then there was the issue of not having enough working capital, which brought about a series of knock-on effects and problems. It seems the feasibility study underestimated the costs of production in Ghana, and that the corporate village enterprise model anticipated getting equity for the factory from the famers, but very little money came out of this effort. As of late 2008, the farmers association owned only 0.033 percent of the company.[12]

The Ayensu Starch Company managed to secure a new buyer in 2005: a long-term contract selling to Nestle's Yopougon factory in Côte d'Ivoire at a price much higher than the international price, which gave Ayensu a very good profit margin.[13] Then a final problem appeared. The company increased operations from 20 percent of its

12 Revival Operational Plan for Ayensu Starch Company for the Year 2008/2009, Ministry of Trade and Industry.

13 "Ayensu Starch in Big Deal," Daily Graphic, January 14, 2005, www.ghanaweb .com (last accessed in 2008).

capacity to 80 percent in order to meet the order of 8,000–9,000 tons per year, but the effluent pond had not been constructed to deal with that volume. It broke down, creating an environmental problem, and the factory was shut down. The Danish technical adviser who was involved in the installation of the factory with the South African company argued that the latter had cheated the Ghanaians by not providing a generator large enough to supply the whole factory and by not providing a waste water treatment facility that was sufficient. In mid-2006, the debts Ayensu had to the three Ghanaian banks were liquidated and turned into equity stakes in the company, bringing the banks on the Board of the company. A plan to revitalize the company was devised, but the company stalled, as government financing was not forthcoming.

Notably, the company stalled during a time of intense contestation within the NPP. It was in 2006 that the Kufuor faction lost control of the national party executive positions to the Akufo-Addo faction in internal elections, and then in 2007 the NPP presidential primary was held in which seventeen top NPP members competed for the nomination, including Alan Kyerematen who faced off against Nana Akufo-Addo and only barely lost. The PSIs were used against Kyerematen during intense campaigning for the presidential nomination, in which it was proclaimed that they were a failure. It was not until late 2008, after Nana Akufo-Addo had secured the presidential nomination and the December election was approaching, that the government provided additional equity and the Export Development Investment Fund provided an interest free loan to finance the revitalization plan. Ayensu was recommissioned in December 2008, just before the national elections.

The government and bank resources invested in Ayensu Starch Company were not completely lost, as the Mills and then Mahama-led NDC governments kept the company going, although always trying to find an investor to take over from the government. The factory kept operating but at very low capacity due to challenges in getting enough raw materials (ACET 2015). The main buyer for the company during this time period was Guinness Ghana, for the making of its new cassava beer, as part of the new policy of Guinness to increase its use of local materials. Even then, the company had problems meeting its contracts with Guinness Ghana, and the Ministry of Trade and Industry wanted to privatize it as a means to inject new capital and management into the company. But, given its raw material supply problems, it was hard to sell.

This situation seems to be a familiar one in Ghana: state-owned enterprises are created as pioneers, but then they face the same constraints on productivity that keep private investment out and that the state's investments do not seem able to overcome, and then try to sell it off when it becomes a financial liability. The PSI in Oil Palm was equally unsuccessful, even though it followed a different model. In the case of the palm oil sector, where there was an existing industry, the choice of NPP elites to adopt a farmer-ownership model rather than work with existing mills to develop more oil palm plantations can only be explained by the political imperatives driving these NPP elites.

The President's Special Initiative in Oil Palm: A Failed Industrial Policy

The PSI in Oil Palm was announced in October 2002 with the long-term vision of developing an oil palm industry that could deliver palm oil-based value added products for the domestic and regional markets. Domestic demand for palm oil was not being met by existing production, and so the country imported palm oil from Asia. The immediate objective was to expand oil palm cultivation among smallholders as a way to address the raw material supply issue described in the previous chapter. The target was to increase the supply of fresh fruit bunches (ffb) through the cultivation of 100,000 hectares, later expanding a further 200,000 hectares. This increased production of ffb would be accompanied by an expansion in processing, refining, marketing and downstream products. The plan stated that thirty new palm oil refining facilities were to be established over ten years.[14]

Initially, palm oil was selected as the focus of a President's Special Initiative because a group of NPP members had connections with the palm oil sector. A member of this group, Kwasi Poku, was selected to lead implementation of the Oil Palm PSI and became a political appointee in the PSI Secretariat under the Office of the President. Furthermore, there is evidence that lobbying from the Unilever-owned palm oil estates TOPP and BOPP also influenced the selection of palm oil for a PSI. Unilever is one of the largest companies in Ghana, and it paid for President Kufuor and a group of ruling elites to visit Malaysia's palm oil sector. But the mutual interests fell apart quite early in the process.

[14] Document accessed from the Oil Palm PSI Coordinator.

Two meetings were held with existing palm oil mills and a broader group of experts in 2004 to discuss the Oil Palm PSI. The outcome was a strategic framework report that provided a more comprehensive approach to supporting the oil palm industry. It highlighted the key constraints on the industry and addressed the issues of land, provision of infrastructure in the traditional palm belt, supporting the government's Oil Palm Research Institute to play a more strategic role in research and development, access to finance for capital investments, export markets, establishing a machinery manufacturing workshop to reduce costs of imported equipment, and so on.

Land availability was a key problem, as highlighted in the previous chapter. The report noted that there were some lands that could be considered immediately for use in the PSI initiative, but in general that the government needed to facilitate the acquisition of land given the complex nature of the land tenure system. The report did not support having only the corporate village enterprise model for expanding oil palm cultivation, but rather proposed a plurality of models such as expanding existing estates with outgrower schemes, establishing block cooperatives for small-scale farmers, and facilitating farmer-based organizations bound by legally enforceable laws.

Regarding the issue of access to finance, the report stated that it was absolutely imperative for the government to act as a venture capital fund provider. Industry actors and experts recommended that the government provide long-term equity funds to private firms in order to encourage firms to own the plantations, processing and refineries that the PSI initiative planned to develop, and advised the government to get concessional credit and pass it on to the participating companies. Notably, the report states,

> There are nagging fears about the Government of Ghana's willingness to share financial risks with the private sector. The program needs long-term equity funds and local investors are expecting that the government will borrow at concessionary rates and pass the funds on as equity. The private sector perceives this government to be averse to sharing financial risks. Therefore, it is likely that the private sector will adopt a "wait and see" attitude to the Initiative for the first few years if steps are not taken to remove the negative perception.[15]

[15] The President's Special Initiative on Oil Palm, April 27, 2004, p. 19.

The report also stated that the initiative needed to be driven by direct presidential oversight exercised through an Advisory Board and proposed a strong organizational structure to manage implementation of the initiative that included a National Oil Palm Board with members coming from the palm oil industry.

An advisory board was established to provide advice on decisions and supervise implementation, and the PSI Oil Palm coordinator invited industry actors to join the board. However, the board never really worked, its members had little influence, and the proposed framework had little impact. Instead, Kyerematen and the coordinator pushed their own strategy.

The PSI Secretariat decided that expropriating land was not an option given the political problems it had caused in the past and ongoing land litigations after the privatization of the large-scale palm oil estates. Thus, an approach like the FELDA scheme in Malaysia was not feasible in Ghana. Under the FELDA scheme, the Malaysian government created palm oil estates on large tracts of contiguous land, resettled landless farmers within the estate and required them to farm a small tract under supervision of state-led management. Instead, the PSI Secretariat asked landowners to contribute land within a certain radius that could be used for a group of farmers to cultivate oil palm, and ultimately both landowners and farmers would constitute a palm oil processing company together with a strategic investor who financed and managed the palm oil mill.

In short, the PSI in Oil Palm included three elements: (1) establishing nurseries; (2) developing smallholder-based plantations; and (3) establishing new mills. The Oil Palm Research Institute (a public agency) was charged with producing transplantable seedlings and selecting nursery operators. Nursery operators were to raise the seedlings that would be given to the farmers. Smallholder-based plantation units were to cover 5,000 hectares and be within a 20–30 kilometer radius around the nursery. These plantations would involve farmers interested in oil palm cultivation and willing to bring their land as equity for the incorporated plantation company. The benefit of the shareholder system was supposed to be the extra incentive for farmers to increase yields and keep supplying the mill (to solve the side-selling problem). Farmers were provided with credit and inputs, both of which were to be paid back when the farmers starting supplying the mill linked to the plantation. A mill was supposed to be set up with the help of a "strategic investor." The investor would establish the mill as part of his equity share contribution of 70–80 percent, with the plantation company's land and agriculture assets constituting the remaining equity in the company. The investor would sign an agreement that it would continue microfinance to the farmers, and farmers would sign an agreement to deliver to the mill. In the case of existing mills, they were asked to allow farmers to buy shares in the estate company with part of their produce. The PSI Secretariat was to lead the whole process and fund everything, but the money would be recouped when the government transferred its role to private actors.

Without broader political support, particularly within Cabinet, the PSI Oil Palm could not get the financial support it needed. The Ministry of Finance cut every PSI budget by three-fourths, and then there were problems with the budgeted money being released on time from the Ministry of Finance. Although these problems are widespread within the bureaucracy and not necessarily specific to the PSIs or the Ministry of Trade and Industry, they underscore the challenges of implementing industrial policies and the continuing level of dependence on donor projects. Donor support came in at the beginning, but it was limited and short-lived. And even then, some of this donor funding was meant for other projects, but the ruling elite leading the PSIs managed to get access to some of it.

The nursery program was started in June 2003. The Oil Palm Research Institute selected twelve nursery operators, which included Norpalm, the four medium-sized mills that were still operating, and seven new private companies led by individuals with experience in the palm oil sector. In 2006, the PSI Oil Palm coordinator selected an additional twenty-one nursery operators, almost all of which were led by individuals that had no experience in the sector and several were based in Accra. The PSI Secretariat gave the Oil Palm Research Institute money to raise pregerminated seed nuts and pass them on to the contracted nursery operators. The Ministry of Food and Agriculture provided financing for the Institute to modernize its operations through a funding scheme under the World Bank AgSSIP loan in the agricultural sector.[16] The PSI Secretariat also used AgSSIP funds to pay for the

[16] This included upgrading its laboratory and IT equipment, training in overseas research organizations for its research and technical staff, and intensifying its breeding program for higher-yielding varieties. Ghana had a large number of decaying agricultural research and development institutes, which were set up in

seedling production by the nursery operators. The secretariat secured further financing for developing the nurseries from the HIPC debt relief funds and from the Export Development Investment Fund. Nursery operators provided the land and raised the seedlings, while the secretariat paid for high-tech irrigation equipment, provided all the consumables to run the nurseries, and provided a commission to the nursery operators based on the percentage of total seedlings delivered.

It took one and a half years to set up the farmer associations that were to cultivate the new oil palm plantations. An outgrower support unit was set up at each nursery site to select and organize farmers. Each unit had an agronomist and a land surveyor, and it was charged with the task of providing extension services and for receiving the seedlings and other inputs for delivery to the farmer association. Private extension agents, NGOs and consultants constituted the outgrower support units, and they were paid using AgSSIP funds and trained by the Oil Palm Research Institute. The PSI secretariat used government funds to provide credit to the farmers, as donors would not fund that part.[17] The credit was to be repaid starting after five years, when the oil palm trees began producing, and to be repaid over a ten-year period as the fresh fruit bunches were sold to the mills. This system worked relatively well until late 2006, when financing for the outgrower support units ceased because the AgSSIP project ended, and the units disbanded. From that time forward, there were financing problems, with seedlings not being paid for and small farmers not being supported.

By the end of 2009, the nurseries had produced at least 2.84 million hybrid seedlings, which were planted on an estimated 30,000 hectares out of a total of 240,000 hectares mobilized for the PSI.[18] However, since the PSI Secretariat did not continue to support farmers through

the 1960s and 1970s, that received few resources from the government budget, with the exception of the Cocoa Research Institute.

17 The size of the oil palm plantation under the PSI was larger than the typical size cultivated by smallholders using their own and family's labor. The larger size required employing labor to work on the plantation and thus required working capital.

18 Data on the outcomes of the PSI Oil Palm was difficult to obtain due to the politically sensitive nature of the initiative. The information presented in this paragraph is based on three documents: Report on the President's Special Initiative on Oil Palm (2003–2009), Council for Scientific and Industrial Research, Oil Palm Research Institute, W.O. Danso, May 2010; Draft final report, April 2010, evaluation of Oil Palm PSI commissioned by the Ministry of Trade and Industry and paid for by EuropeAid under its Private Sector and

the whole five-year investment period (before trees begin yielding properly), many farmers did not (or could not) maintain their farms and they were taken over by the "bush," reducing the total area planted to about 25,000 hectares as well as reducing the potential yield of farms with poor maintenance. About 11,000 farmers were involved in the PSI, with about 77,000 workers involved in plantation preparation and maintenance, before government revenues dried up in 2006. Only twenty-two nurseries continued to operate in 2010, while four were inactive and three were abandoned, but even the active nurseries had serious problems with damaged or stolen equipment. A total of 2.3 billion cedis was spent on the Oil Palm PSI, mobilized in small amounts from various government sources as well as a loan from a domestic bank (excluding interest on the loan). The AgSSIP funds amounted to about US$1.5 million.

Contestation among NPP ruling elites and the lack of consensus within the Cabinet on the PSIs in general, which led to the financing problems, was not the only factor that negatively affected the implementation of the Oil Palm initiative. The PSI Secretariat was not able to shield itself from demands by members within the ruling coalition to benefit from the Oil Palm PSI. Members of Parliament pressured the PSI Secretariat to establish nurseries in their localities, which led the secretariat to select twenty-one new nursery operators. In most cases approvals were given at the secretariat without asking the Oil Palm Research Institute for feasibility studies on the location. As a result, some of the locations selected were not suitable. Furthermore, many of the additional nursery operators selected by the PSI Secretariat had connections to the ruling party. However, the contract of one nursery operator connected to the ruling party was terminated for nonperformance, so the PSI Secretariat had some ability to operate outside of factional demands. Nevertheless, the sudden increase in nurseries in 2006 could not be matched with corresponding funds, which undermined the viability of all of the nurseries.

Implementation of the PSI in Oil Palm was disconnected to a large extent from the existing palm oil estates and mills. The PSI Secretariat insisted on supporting the smallholders directly, instead of connecting the new nursery operators and PSI smallholders to existing mills.

Trade Enabling Programme; and a report on the PSIs undertaken by the Mills' government upon entering office in 2009.

On their part, the existing palm oil estates were not organized and did not present a unified front, as their industry association was not really operating. When it was clear that the PSI Secretariat was adopting the corporate village enterprise model, three out of the four large estates disengaged from the process. Norpalm and the medium-sized mills chose to participate as nursery operators in order to set up their own nursery, which they did not previously have, at a subsidized cost. None of the existing mills participated as strategic investors in the way envisioned in the design of the PSI.

By the time the Mills-led NDC government took power in 2009, the Oil Palm PSI had largely stalled. The oil palm strategy was full of easy rent opportunities with no incentives for learning, so when these rent opportunities vanished most of the investments collapsed. Nursery operators did not have to invest their own money in the nurseries, so when the PSI secretariat stopped paying them to produce seedlings, most of them did not expend their own money to keep it up, and when the government changed, they basically abandoned the nurseries. Likewise, the PSI Secretariat paid for the establishment and cultivation of the oil palm plantations, so when the money stopped flowing to finance the plantations, most farmers left. However, PSI farmers working plantations located near the existing mills, some of whom were also outgrowers for the estates, kept up their farms using their own resources. Lastly, the only "strategic investor" in a new mill as envisioned in the PSI design was a NPP regional party executive who had personal connections to the technical adviser on the Oil Palm PSI. He continued with the construction of his mill after the ruling party changed, but his management staff claimed that the Mills-led NDC government did not support the firm but rather was hostile towards it.[19]

Implementation of the Oil Palm PSI was largely disconnected from the existing estates and mills, which negatively affected the overall outcome of the industrial policy. When the PSI Secretariat could no longer finance its implementation and the initiative collapsed, it was not easy for the private firms to take over. In the cases where PSI plantations were located near existing mills, those mills tried to forge

[19] Interview with the Operations Manager at Sarpcoe Enterprise, July 7, 2011. Sarpcoe was a nursery started under the Oil Palm PSI, and its owner, the NPP regional party executive, decided to invest in a mill linked to the nursery and oil palm farmer units.

relations with the PSI smallholders and buy their fresh fruit bunches, and in some cases, farmers participating in the PSI were already cultivating oil palm and supplying ffb to those mills. In other cases, PSI plantations were not located near any existing mill, and no new mills were established under the PSI, so the PSI smallholders were abandoned with a supply of fresh fruit bunches that was too much for the village small-scale processors and no means to get the ffb to existing mills. For example, three nurseries were established in the upper part of the Volta region, along with 106 farmer-based organizations on 1,563 hectares of land. There was no existing mill in the Volta region, so when the PSI ended, these farmers had an oversupply of fresh fruit bunches and stopped keeping up the farms.

Nevertheless, the PSI initiative laid a foundation on which some private investors chose to build. To return to the same case in the Volta region, in 2012 a small group of British investors established the company Volta Red by buying a large-scale oil palm plantation (3,750 hectares) from an American company that set it up but then ran into issues with the landowners and local community and wanted to sell it.[20] A year later the investors established a small mill that was supplied by the company's plantation as well as an outgrower scheme that the company created out of the smallholders who had planted oil palm as part of the PSI. The company also bought a large PSI plantation (115 hectares) worked by an Accra resident, which the owner had neglected, and the company had to replant the oil palm trees. It was possible to establish a large-scale plantation in the upper part of the Volta region because competition over land was not as great as in the traditional oil palm belt stretching across the Western Region to the Eastern Region. Nevertheless, the company had to provide public goods and social services to the community in order to keep conflicts from emerging with landowners from whom the land was leased and local communities from which workers came. This is something that existing large-scale estates in the traditional oil palm belt also had to do. The outgrower scheme was likely to encounter fewer difficulties with side-selling because there were no other mills in the area to compete for their fresh fruit bunches. Volta Red began producing

20 See the company's website, www.voltared.com (last accessed January 17, 2017); "Land Grabbing in Africa: Kerakles Farms' Failed Venture in Brewaniase, Ghana," October 2014, Africa Faith and Justice Network, www.afjn.org (last accessed January 17, 2017).

crude palm oil for the domestic market and the West African region, as well as branded products for retail.

The Volta Red company was established using the standard estate model that was used in the past: a nucleus plantation with mill combined with an outgrower scheme. Notably, TOPP also instigated a new outgrower scheme in 2007 through a project where the Ministry of Agriculture and Agence Francaise de Developpment subsidized the cost. TOPP management designed the outgrower scheme in a way that incorporated its experiences with outgrower schemes at the estate that had failed in the past.[21] It is important to note that this donor-funded project was going on at the same time as the Oil Palm PSI, but there was no connection or coordination between the two initiatives. The Volta Red and TOPP outgrower scheme also shows that the nucleus-outgrower model for expanding the cultivation of oil palm could be made to work when designed to take into account sensitive community and land relations around the estate, and that this was the model preferred by private investors – a point made during the earlier discussions around how to support the palm oil industry and one ignored by the PSI Secretariat.

In sum, contestation among NPP elites resulted in an underfunded initiative, but that was only one reason for the failed industrial policy. The PSI in Oil Palm was poorly implemented by the PSI Secretariat with the limited finance it received due to the inability to keep distributive demands within the ruling coalition from undermining the economic objectives of the initiative. Furthermore, the PSI was not designed and implemented in collaboration with existing palm oil mills or prospective investors (foreign or domestic). The NPP ruling elites leading the PSIs and the PSI Secretariat staff were clearly not interested in working with the existing mills or in setting up a scheme that would be attractive to private investors. The medium-sized mills and the financially troubled Norpalm participated in its implementation at the margins in order to benefit their own companies by acquiring a nursery at a subsidized cost. The main aims of the NPP elites and their politically appointed technocrats implementing the Oil Palm PSI were to bring benefits directly to small farmers and to be seen doing it, so that they could take credit at election time. Thus, they were not interested in subsidizing the costs of setting up outgrower schemes for the existing

[21] Interview, TOPP Acting Director, Accra, July 13, 2011.

mills or for new investors as a way to incentivize new private investment in the industry. Some NPP party members benefited directly from participating in the Oil Palm PSI, but this collusion was an outcome of decentralized rent creation and management within the NPP and was not a driving factor behind its design and implementation. The political driver behind adopting the state-led corporate village enterprise model seems to have been for the NPP to win support (had the industrial policy been successful), and in particular for Kyerematen to expand his political support within the party at the local level.

MCA Compact in Commercializing Agriculture: A Giant Distributive Project

What the PSIs and the Millennium Challenge Account (MCA) compact share in common is the political imperative to distribute resources and economic opportunities to benefit a large number of smallholder farmers across different regions of the country. Whether this is through state-led initiatives or through donor-driven projects, the focus converges on smallholder farmers. This can be explained by the imperative of winning elections and the nonthreatening nature of accumulation among small farmers, should the projects be successful. Furthermore, ruling political elites and donor agency staff interests converge in this regard, as the MCA case and other examples such as Farmapine show. Donor agency staff typically want to support "poverty reduction" and argue that this is best achieved through direct support to a large number of small farmers. In the MCA case, the convergence of ruling elites and donor staff on supporting the "livelihoods" of small farmers resulted in the MCA compact becoming a farmer training scheme, but one that consumed a large amount of resources and had little impact on commercial agricultural production among small farmers.

Upon qualifying for the Millennium Challenge Account in 2004, President Kufuor charged the Minister of Finance to come up with a proposal. The first concept paper from the Ministry of Finance emphasized commercializing agriculture and agribusiness, but it was vaguely formulated and accompanied by several other priorities from various ministries. Horticulture was neither mentioned nor a thought at that time, but rather came in due to a chance opportunity. The Millennium Challenge Corporation (MCC) staff based in Ghana rejected the government's first concept note, and organized a meeting with business associations to discuss potential ideas. At that meeting, the head of the Federation of Associations of Ghanaian Exporters made the case for horticulture export. The Horticulture Export Industry Initiative had been drafted by that time (see Chapter 5), and his idea was to build on it and to include the northern part of Ghana, where there was some commercial horticulture production. The MCC staff were interested in his ideas, and he was brought into a new team constituted by the Ministry of Finance to revise the concept paper. The team included a representative from the Ministry of Finance, two Ghanaian consultants hired by the Ministry of Finance, the head of the federation, and a representative from the Ministry of Food and Agriculture since agriculture was the main focus of the initiative. The team adopted horticulture as the focus, and the MCC staff accepted the new concept note. The more difficult part was deciding exactly how to support the development of horticulture exports.

The process of writing the detailed project proposal for the MCC was a tug of war on multiple levels. On one level, there was a struggle between the horticulture export experts brought in to advise on writing the proposal, who pushed various ideas intended to develop Ghana's horticulture export industry, and the government's general consultants, who had no technical knowledge of the horticulture export industry but who had political backing and answered to the politicians. I refer to the latter as the power brokers. On a second level, there was a struggle between the power brokers and the MCC officials, who resided in Ghana and followed the proposal writing process closely. The power brokers were consultants who either had close connections to the Minister of Finance at that time, Yaw Osafo Marfo, or who were brought in because they had skills in writing project proposals that met the requirements of donors. The power brokers interacted directly with President Kufuor and the Cabinet as well as with the MCC officials. In the early part of the process, the horticulture experts had to constantly defend the focus on horticulture as the power brokers and politicians tried to bring in new ideas. For example, Osafo Marfo wanted the MCA project to focus on expanding cocoa production in the forest zone around the Afram Plains, which stretches across the Eastern and Ashanti regions.

Horticulture won out, but even then the horticulture experts had to convince the power brokers of their ideas, as the power brokers actually wrote the text and were constantly being pressured by the politicians and MCC officials. For example, the head of the federation advocated looking for new investment opportunities in "fresh cut" processed products. Blue Skies was the only company exporting "fresh cut" fruit products at that time, and he advocated creating a platform that would encourage more foreign investors like Blue Skies. Many on the team did not buy it, partly because of the implications of bringing in foreign investors, so they stayed with the idea of supporting whole fresh fruit exports. In this area, the head of the federation made suggestions on how the existing Ghanaian industry could benefit from good practices in other parts of the world. One of the suggestions was to create a Virtual Horticulture Faculty that would bring in practitioners from Costa Rica to share experiences and to entice Costa Rican companies to invest in Ghana with Ghanaian companies as junior partners for learning purposes. The idea was that the Ghanaian industry could be a second mover – copying and adapting new technology and research. This idea was too abstract for the Ghana team, and it had not been done before, so it would take a lot of time to create a technical proposal for it. Furthermore, it did not correspond with the needs expressed by the existing pineapple producer-exporters, who did not want to partner with foreign investors. In fact, there were several opportunities missed for foreign direct investments in pineapple export production in Ghana because the pineapple producer-exporters could not see the benefits and wanted to remain as individual exporters rather than working together or with a foreign partner. This was part of the second-order constraint on productivity, where domestic capitalists were still learning to learn (see Chapter 5). The horticulture experts tried to address this constraint, but were unsuccessful, as they could not convince the producer-exporters or the MCA proposal writing team.

In the end, the power brokers only accepted ideas on how to develop horticulture exports that they thought coincided with what the MCC officials would accept, especially when the pressure increased from President Kufuor to get the compact signed and implemented under his tenure. President Kufuor did not seem interested in what the project was about, only that it brought in money and as quickly as possible. The Ghana team submitted a proposal to the MCC officials in July 2005 that aimed to address the first-order constraints on productivity for existing horticulture export firms and to support small farmers through nucleus-outgrower schemes in the southern and northern horticulture belts. One of the inspirations for the proposal came from the Integrated Tamale Fruit Company located in Savelugu-Nanton district in the Northern Region, a company established with domestic and foreign investors to grow organic mango for export using a nucleus farm and a large outgrower scheme, which the MCC staff and MCA team visited. The proposal included the provision of credit, transport infrastructure and postharvest infrastructure to create a national cold chain from exporter farms to the port and airport, as well as agribusiness services and investment incentives in three targeted districts: one in the southern horticulture zone, Savelugu-Nanton in the northern horticulture zone, and one in the Afram Plains area. The inclusion of Afram Plains was defended on the grounds of opening this area up to commercial farming through the provision of infrastructure and incentives, as it had the potential to become the "bread basket" of Ghana. But the Afram Plains was included largely for political reasons, as NPP political elites involved in the MCA process sought to channel resources into their constituencies.

Between July 2005 when a first proposal was presented and August 2006 when the MCA compact was signed, the focus on the horticulture export industry was significantly diluted as the objectives broadened to include the commercialization of agriculture generally. The broadening of the objectives occurred because the power brokers wrote the final proposal and because the MCC staff increased the amount of money on offer. As a result, the power brokers also increased the number of targeted districts from three to twenty-three, as shown in Figure 7.1, increased the amount of transport infrastructure, and added public goods and services such as the provision of schools, water, and sanitation in the twenty-three targeted districts. With the increased amount of money on offer, the ruling elites and power brokers sought to distribute it widely rather than use it solely on developing the horticulture export industry.

Another major change was made to the proposal before the final compact was signed: the "enhanced business services component" intended to finance the cost of setting up nucleus-outgrowers schemes was replaced with a farmer-based organization model and a farmer training scheme. The original MCA proposal included a nucleus-outgrower model as the way to link smallholders to export markets, and it was the model used by the Blue Skies fruit processing company in the south and the Integrated Tamale Fruit Company in the north. These firms were supporting the production of a large number of outgrowers

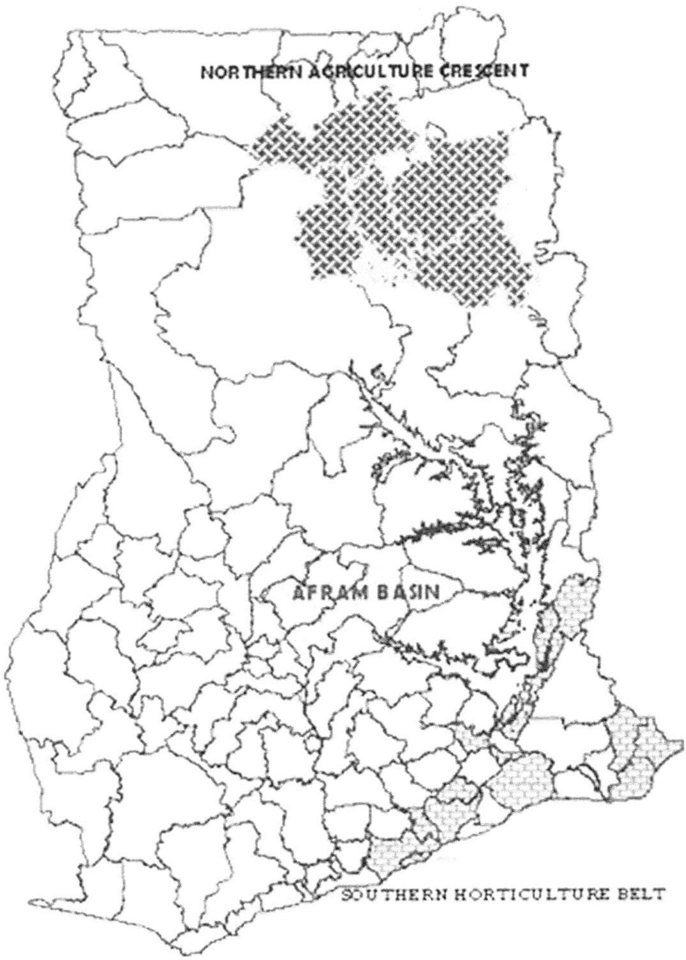

Figure 7.1 MCA Intervention Zones and Districts
Source: Millennium Development Authority, Accra

and buying their produce based on a contractual relationship. They provided not only a link to export markets for smallholder farmers, but also information and assistance. The horticulture experts on the MCA proposal writing team argued that the provision of information and assistance by firms to outgrowers should be seen as a "development" expenditure with positive externalities for the industry and country as a whole, and thus the state should finance this development cost, which would also reduce the overall production costs of firms. The idea of the "enhanced business services" was to allow skilled small farmers to become outgrowers through a demand-driven voucher scheme. The MCC officials were not convinced and kept asking the Ghana team to define the idea better, but they also preferred a farmer-based organization model, which was being used by the World Bank in its agriculture sector program in Ghana at that time. Furthermore, the MCC officials thought the nucleus-outgrower model would only benefit the nucleus commercial farmers and instead wanted to make outgrower farmers self-sustaining by organizing them and creating opportunities to link them directly to markets – which sounds very similar to the Farmapine model. The MCC officials won out, and the final compact focused on creating farmer-based organizations that would be provided with training.

The MCC officials won out because the horticulture experts on the MCA team did not have political backing. President Kufuor was in a hurry to start implementing the MCA compact so it could be his legacy. He appointed the Minister for Public Sector Reform, Paa Kwesi Nduom, to lead the Ghana team in the Washington negotiations. Nduom had not been part of the proposal writing process but was seen as someone who could negotiate with Americans and conclude the deal. However, he also had presidential ambitions and wanted to use his role in getting the MCA compact signed to foster his presidential credentials.[22] As a result, he made many concessions to what the MCC officials in Washington wanted, against what the Ghana team had been holding out for; advocated things that the Ghana team did not want but would be better politically (more social services); and pushed for creating an entirely new implementing agency. For example, a major aspect during the negotiations was the agricultural financial credit component. The Ghana MCA team wanted to provide credit to farmers and all along the value chain to help them improve quantity and quality

[22] The Minister was not from the ruling NPP but from the Convention People's Party (CPP). President Kufuor invited him to join the first Kufuor-led NPP government as a means of thanking the CPP for its support in the presidential runoff election, which helped Kufuor to win the presidential runoff in the 2000 elections and the NPP parliamentarians to form a majority. He was also part of the second Kufuor-led NPP government, and he ran for president in the 2008 elections on the ticket of the CPP.

of production. There was a big debate about the interest rate at which the credit should be provided. The MCC officials said that it had to be the going market rate, but the Ghana team argued that market rates in Ghana were too high to allow farmers to borrow and repay. The MCC officials won out, but the interest rate became a major issue during implementation and the access to finance component was largely a failure, as discussed below.

The Millennium Development Authority was set up to implement the MCA and formalized through an Act of Parliament in March 2006, before the MCA compact was actually signed. The Ghana team had not clearly articulated implementation arrangements but envisioned a low-profile, single-purpose unit. The MCC officials insisted on a special unit for implementation, but the idea of a broader multi-purpose agency seems to have come from the minister leading the negotiating team, Paa Kwesi Nduom. The Millennium Development Authority was intended to have a life after the MCA compact in the management of other development programs of the government or donors. It took the entire year of 2007 to negotiate the structure of the authority and salaries for staff, as it was all being paid by the MCC.

The final MCA compact contained three discrete components: agriculture, transportation and rural services (see Appendix A). The compact maintained the thrust of the original proposal, but with a diluted focus on the horticulture export industry. Only a few people who were involved in formulating the proposal and negotiating the compact were involved with implementing it. The Millennium Development Authority was a gigantic bureaucracy, and its organizational structure led to the further dilution of the focus on horticulture exports. Each of the three components was given a project management team with equal authority. The upshot was to create several disparate projects in agriculture, land administration, financial services and transportation, rather than an agricultural program in which these components were coordinated and focused on the horticulture export industry. Furthermore, most of the actual implementation was contracted out to private companies, something pushed for by the MCC. This was especially the case in the agriculture component, which involved three layers of consultancies in charge of training the farmer-based organizations: one company managing the national level, a company/NGO in charge of each regional zone, and then several training service providers in each region. Administrative offices for the authority were constructed in each of the regional zones.

The story of the MCA compact formulation indicates that there were strong overlaps between the interests of the NPP ruling elites and power brokers involved in the MCA process on the one hand and the MCC officials on the other hand. Both groups wanted a project that would benefit as many farmers as possible, and both wanted large visible activities for which they could take credit. For example, the Millennium Development Authority spent money on huge billboards in each beneficiary district to advertise its activities. The NPP government, as well as the MCC, wanted to be seen as the one providing the goods and services. Additionally, both groups preferred to support smallholder farmers as opposed to the existing commercial horticulture farmers, who were seen as rich commercial farmers. They could not see that the fortunes of the smallholder farmers in horticulture were linked to those of the commercial farmers, and thus they thought that supporting the commercial farmers would have no direct poverty reduction impacts.

During implementation of the MCA compact, the focus on building a competitive horticulture export industry was almost completely lost. Most importantly, the agricultural project became a farmer-training project. Everything became about training farmer-based organizations, and the needs of existing horticulture smallholder farmers, such as the outgrowers of the pineapple producer-exporters who were supposed to be supported to grow MD2 pineapples, were neglected. This happened because the implementation of the agricultural project was driven by bureaucratic imperatives of the Millennium Development Authority to achieve the target of training 60,000 farmers in 1,200 farmer-based organizations set sometime during the compact negotiation, or shortly afterwards. Everything else seems to have been tailored to achieve this goal. Farmer organizations were created by geographical location, so pineapple outgrowers were combined with food crop farmers. During the first phase of training, the farmer organizations wrote collective business plans that were submitted to banks and formed the basis of accessing credit, which the MCC gave to the banks. Some of the regional implementing agencies acknowledged the problem with combining crops, but said there was little flexibility within the system. In addition, an experimental monitoring and evaluation component was inserted into the implementation strategy by the MCC in order to rigorously test the impact of training on farmers. This experimental evaluation system required that farmer-based organizations pull lots for when they would go through training. This was not exactly amenable to achieving a competitive horticulture export industry. Lastly, the training provided was not very useful for pineapple outgrowers and was just a necessary means to access the credit. Thus, the agricultural project was not implemented in a way that helped to link small farmers to horticulture export chains.

In the northern horticulture belt, the MCA compact was supposed to help the Integrated Tamale Fruit Company to expand mango production among small farmers, but the company did not want to be involved with the agricultural project because the interest rate on credit was too high to make it useful for its outgrowers. Furthermore, mango was dropped as a crop that smallholders in the farmer-based organizations could grow because its gestation period would have been longer than the lifespan of the compact, which meant that farmers would not show results and that credit would have to have a longer moratorium. Thus, the intention to support mango production for export in the northern part of the country was abandoned completely. Implementation of the MCA compact in the targeted districts in the Northern Region only provided new roads in the villages where mango outgrowers were located and extended electricity to the area.

The Sea-Freight Pineapple Exporters of Ghana negotiated with Millennium Development Authority staff and MCC staff on the access to credit and postharvest equipment for pineapple producer-exporters. However, the association was not successful in getting the moratorium on repaying the loans extended and in the end, taking the MCA loan for equipment made the producer-exporters worse off when they could not repay it in the time period stipulated by the MCC (see Chapter 5).

The intention to create packhouses in the southern horticulture belt also turned out badly. The MCA project provided three state-of-the-art packhouses that were supposed to be run as a public-private partnership with 70 percent owned by the private investor (commercial farmer) and 30 percent by farmer-based organizations in the area. The commercial farmer was supposed to provide technical assistance to these farmer-based organizations, buy their produce and export it. In 2015, none of the three packhouses were in operation. The two packhouses built in pineapple growing areas and intended to be linked to specific pineapple producer-exporters were not being used because the two pineapple producer-exporter firms that were supposed to run them were struggling to export MD2 pineapples, and because there were no small farmers in the areas producing MD2 pineapples! The third packhouse was built in the Somanya mango-growing area of the southern horticulture belt. This packhouse had the potential to work, but the packhouse was initially given to a private company to manage that was not a commercial farmer, and that company quit when the packhouse encountered technical problems with the equipment installed. The owner of a large-scale mango farm in the area took it over, but it was still not operating when I visited in May 2015.

The problem was that the packhouses were not set up on a viable commercial model and not embedded in developments in the horticulture export industry, and they suffered from problems with the training scheme discussed above. Furthermore, construction of the packhouses was delayed by two years due to a "condition precedent" in the MCA compact that required the passage of the Plants and Fertilizer Act by the Ghanaian Parliament.[23] Lastly, the packhouses were crucial for securing a market for farmers producing pineapples and mangos, and a guaranteed market would have made it easier to repay loans. This is significant, as the credit component of the MCA compact turned out to be a disaster due to the poor repayment of loans by the first lot of beneficiary farmers, and as a result, further disbursements of credit to farmers was discontinued.[24]

In sum, the MCA compact achieved very little in terms of supporting the horticulture export industry, and arguably very little in terms of supporting commercial agriculture more generally. A large amount of resources were disbursed widely, but there was remarkably little to show for it in terms of improved agricultural production or horticulture exports. Evaluations of the farmer-training scheme undertaken for the Millennium Development Authority show limited impacts in terms of increasing yields, and noted that the gains did not seem

23 Compact Completion Report, Millennium Challenge Account Ghana Program, July 15, 2013, p. xxiv.

24 Ibid, pp. xvi and 23. The agricultural credit program had an overall recovery rate of 64 percent as of January 2012, but the residual portfolio was at a very high risk of default. The MCC held the Millennium Development Authority and the Bank of Ghana responsible for the shortcomings in the management of the program, and demanded a refund of the outstanding loans, which were originally supposed to be a grant that would be used as a revolving fund (p. 83).

sustainable.[25] The financial services project was not very successful, nor was the land registration project.[26] Perhaps the main achievements were in road infrastructure.

Conclusion

The MCA compact illustrates the first defining feature of Ghanaian political economy, where ruling elites pursue distributive expenditures as a political survival strategy due to short time horizons produced by their vulnerability in government. In this case, NPP ruling elites involved with formulating the MCA compact sought to use the grant to distribute public goods to communities across a large number of constituencies and to provide some benefits to as many smallholder farmers as possible. The original idea driving the MCA compact was to help overcome constraints on productivity in the horticulture export sector, but the Federation of Associations of Ghanaian Exporters had pushed this idea. Because the NPP politicians involved with the MCA did not have a real interest in supporting horticulture exports or the pineapple producer-exporters in particular, they failed to support this idea, especially during project negotiations with the Millennium Challenge Corporation staff in Washington, DC, on the final project design. As a result, the final project included social services, effectively adding general distributive expenditures to what was supposed to be a targeted industrial policy, and the conversion of specific activities to develop the horticulture export industry into generally distributive expenditures for smallholder farmers in the form of a training program. During implementation, the focus on horticulture was weakened even further, and in the end, the MCA compact had a limited impact on the horticulture export industry and even some unintended negative effects.

The Oil Palm PSI illustrates the second defining feature of Ghanaian political economy, where ruling elites seek to support productive sectors through industrial policies in which the state plays a central role in implementation, often as manager or owner of the productive

[25] "An Impact Evaluation of the MIDA FBP Training: Final Report," submitted to the Millennium Development Authority, by Institute of Statistical, Social and Economic Research, University of Ghana, February 2012.

[26] These points are made in the Compact Completion Report, Millennium Challenge Account Ghana Program, July 15, 2013.

investment, and in which domestic capitalists are neglected or marginalized. The political imperatives driving the design of the Oil Palm PSI were that it *directly* benefit farmers, be feasible within the land tenure restrictions in southern Ghana, and *be carried out by the state* so that the NPP could take credit for it at election time. President Kufuor, Alan Kyerematen and the small group of NPP elites driving the Oil Palm PSI wanted the initiative to do something that was "additional" to the existing palm oil industry and did not work with the existing palm oil estates to address the challenges in the sector.

However, the political rivals of Alan Kyerematen perceived that he was trying to use the PSIs to build a personal political support base in rural areas and did not want to see him succeed with the PSIs, which would have given him an edge in political contests. The story of the PSIs reveals the extreme factionalism within the NPP between the Kufuor/Kyerematen and the Akufo-Addo factions discussed in Chapter 3, and illustrates how this factionalism as well as other distributive demands associated with competitive clientelism negatively affected the formulation and implementation of the PSIs.

Thus, we can see that the NPP political elites leading the MCA compact and PSIs perceived distributive expenditures and state-led industrial policies as important political survival strategies. The chapter also demonstrates the paradox of state-led industrial policies in Ghana: while NPP elites were drawn to the state-led and -controlled implementation design on the PSIs for political reasons, implementation of such policies encounters problems as aspects of competitive clientelism undermine the state's ability to play the dominant role set out for it. In the case of the Oil Palm PSI, factional struggles within the party over who would benefit from the outcomes and contestation over the allocation of resources in the budget led to its underfunding, while at the same time distributional demands from members within the ruling coalition increased the scale of the initiative. Lower-level members of the ruling coalition sought to benefit from the implementation of the Oil Palm PSI, but were not serious about the investments in oil palm nurseries and plantations; thus, when the easy rent opportunities ended, they largely abandoned the investments.

Underfunding and the lack of political oversight in the implementation of Cassava Starch PSI resulted in an inefficient state-owned enterprise in cassava starch processing, which encountered the same type of constraints on productivity that all start-ups in Ghana do but which the state management was not able to address. In particular, securing a sufficient supply of raw materials from smallholder farmers remained a problem for Ayensu Starch Factory, just as it has for all agro-processing factories in Ghana, and the problem was more intense for the state-owned company as issues of price and factory-farmer relations became entangled with electoral politics.

It is the rather small, and often unsustainable, impacts of such initiatives that explain why Ghana's economy remains untransformed. Money is spent, but very little is achieved in terms of expanding production, increasing productivity and diversifying exports. Resources are consumed without increasing the ability to produce more resources in the future.

8 *NDC II Government and Managing the New Oil Wealth*

The incumbent NPP lost the December 2008 elections by a very small margin, and the NDC returned to government in January 2009. J.A. Mills beat Akufo-Addo in a presidential runoff election by a mere 40,586 votes, and the NDC had an equally slim majority in Parliament. With the discovery of oil in 2007, this election decided which party would manage the new oil revenues, and hence it was a closely fought election. President Mills died while in office in July 2012, and Vice President John Mahama took over the presidency and became the NDC's presidential candidate in the December 2012 elections. Mahama won the elections, and the incumbent NDC retained a majority in Parliament. In this chapter, I refer to the Mills and Mahama administrations as the NDC II government, in order to make a clear distinction between the NDC administrations in the 1990s.

The NDC II government presided over the beginning of oil production in December 2010. There were high expectations among the population of what the new oil wealth would mean, despite the fact that the country's oil production was modest. As a result of the oil revenue management system established in the Petroleum Revenue Management Act passed by Parliament in 2011, more oil revenues were spent than were saved in the two sovereign wealth funds. Furthermore, of the revenues spent, a majority went to the oil and gas sector through direct transfers to the state-owned Ghana National Petroleum Corporation (GNPC). After making transfers to GNPC, the remaining oil revenues were distributed across priority spending areas selected by the Minister of Finance. According to the Act, expenditures in these priority areas should maximize the rate of economic development. Under the NDC II government, paying off loans contracted to develop oil and gas infrastructure constituted one of these priority areas, further increasing the oil revenues flowing back to the sector. The remaining oil revenues available annually to spend on the three other priority areas were relatively small.

This chapter argues that competitive clientelism shaped the development of the oil and gas sector, as well as how oil revenues were allocated and actually spent. Competitive clientelism played out in terms of political strategies on how to use the discretionary oil revenues, and in terms of NDC factional fighting over how to develop the gas industry. Both aspects resulted in the suboptimal use of oil revenues.

The development of the oil and gas sector under the NDC II government involved a more ambitious role for GNPC than it had under the NPP government, which supervised the discovery of oil and awarded the initial exploration contracts. The group of NDC elites leading GNPC wanted it to become a significant player in upstream oil development, and they influenced the petroleum law so that GNPC would receive sufficient capitalization in order to realize this objective. Another faction of NDC elites felt that GNPC was becoming too powerful and wanted the development of the gas industry to be under the jurisdiction of a separate state-owned company, which they could control. Initially the latter group won this factional struggle, and as a result, Ghana National Gas Company was created and Chinese financing was used to build the gas-processing infrastructure. However, this solution turned out to be extremely expensive and untenable because Ghana National Gas Company was not a credible buyer in the eyes of the multinational oil companies. In the end, GNPC had to assume responsibility for Ghana Gas. The high cost and inefficiency of this process can only be understood through the lens of elite factional struggle within the ruling party. In making this argument, the chapter draws on the few existing accounts of decisionmaking in the oil and gas sector.

Competitive clientelism also shaped the spending patterns regarding the use of discretionary oil revenues going into the annual budget. Despite the good intentions of the Petroleum Revenue Management Act that oil revenues be used to catalyze economic development, actual expenditures took a different path. The government spread oil revenues across a large number of ministries, departments and agencies, some of which were not even in the priority areas specified by the Ministry of Finance, as required by the petroleum law. Even within the priority areas, such as infrastructure, revenues were spread thinly across a large number of projects, undermining the effectiveness of public expenditures. Thus, much of the spending of discretionary oil revenues had a distinctly distributional and consumptive character, in that wealth was spread around and largely "consumed" without contributing directly to reproducing wealth.

The exception was in some of the spending related to the agriculture priority area, in which the NDC II government tried to increase agriculture production and agro-processing. However, in this area, we see the predilection for state-led industrial policies again. The government's initiatives included state-managed block farms, state-owned enterprises used to stabilize prices in food crops, state-run programs to support import-substituting production in poultry, and the creation of state-owned factories in sugar and fish processing. Many of these state-led industrial policies followed the same approach and structure of previous governments, including those of the preceding NPP government. They also clearly neglected to engage with domestic firms and to incentivize or build on private investments, and preferred state control of implementation and separate, isolated investments that the government could claim was increasing incomes and creating jobs. The economic impact of these expenditures was modest, at best.

The evidence on oil revenue allocations presented in this chapter comes from compiling data in annual reports of the Ministry of Finance, which it is required by law to make publicly available. However, these annual reports on petroleum revenues initially only stated the allocation of revenues to the priority areas and not how the government further allocated and spent the funds within each priority area. The latter only began with the 2015 Annual Report on Petroleum Revenues. For the earlier years, the analysis of spending within the priority areas is based on general budget statements in order to identify the projects funded with oil revenues, combined with reports by research institutes, consultancy firms and donor agencies in order to determine how these projects were implemented and their impacts.

The chapter begins by providing an overview of the oil and gas sector as it developed between 2007 and 2015, focusing on the companies involved and the magnitude of the resources discovered. It provides the necessary background for understanding the factional struggles within the NDC II government over the sector's development. The chapter then describes the oil revenue management structure, showing how and why GNPC received a significant proportion of oil revenues. The final part of the chapter describes how the oil revenues that did not go into the oil and gas sector were spent, illustrating how the two features – distributive, consumption-driven expenditures and state-led industrial policies – characterized the NDC II government's allocation and spending of the discretionary oil revenues.

Overview of the Oil and Gas Sector

Kosmos Energy made the first discovery of viable oil deposits in 2007 in its block within the Tano Basin, followed by Tullow Oil in its adjacent block, constituting the Jubilee Field, which is illustrated in Figure 8.1. Oil production in the Jubilee Field began in October 2010, with the field producing around 100,000 barrels per day (bbl/d) in 2014. Since Jubilee, twenty-three new discoveries have been made (as of 2015). In addition to the Jubilee Field, two other major oil fields were being developed: the TEN Field comprising Tweneboa, Enyenra, and Ntomme, and the Sankofa Field comprising Sankofa, Sankofa East, and Gye Nyame. Tullow Oil led the development of the TEN Field, which started producing oil in August 2016 and gas production was expected to follow a year or two later. There was a dispute over the TEN Field, with the neighboring Côte d'Ivoire government claiming it was in their country's waters. The International Tribunal for the Law of the Sea ruled in 2015 that the Ghanaian government could continue developing the TEN Field, but disallowed any further drilling in the disputed area with Côte d'Ivoire until the tribunal gives its decision on the maritime boundary dispute, which was expected in September 2017. The development plan of the Sankofa Field produced by the international oil company ENI was approved in 2015 and started producing oil in July 2017, with gas production expected by mid-2018.[1]

1 On the TEN Field, see www.tullowoil.com/operations/west-africa/ghana/ten-field (last accessed August 21, 2017). Regarding the Sankofa Field, Eni owns a 47.2 percent share in the block, with Vitol Upstream Ghana Limited having a 37.8 percent share and GNPC a 15 percent share. See www.offshoreenergytoday.com/eni-moves-step-ahead-with-6b-sankofa-development/ (last accessed on December 8, 2015), and https://www.reuters.com/article/us-ghana-oil-idUSKBN19R1R9 (last accessed on August 17, 2017).

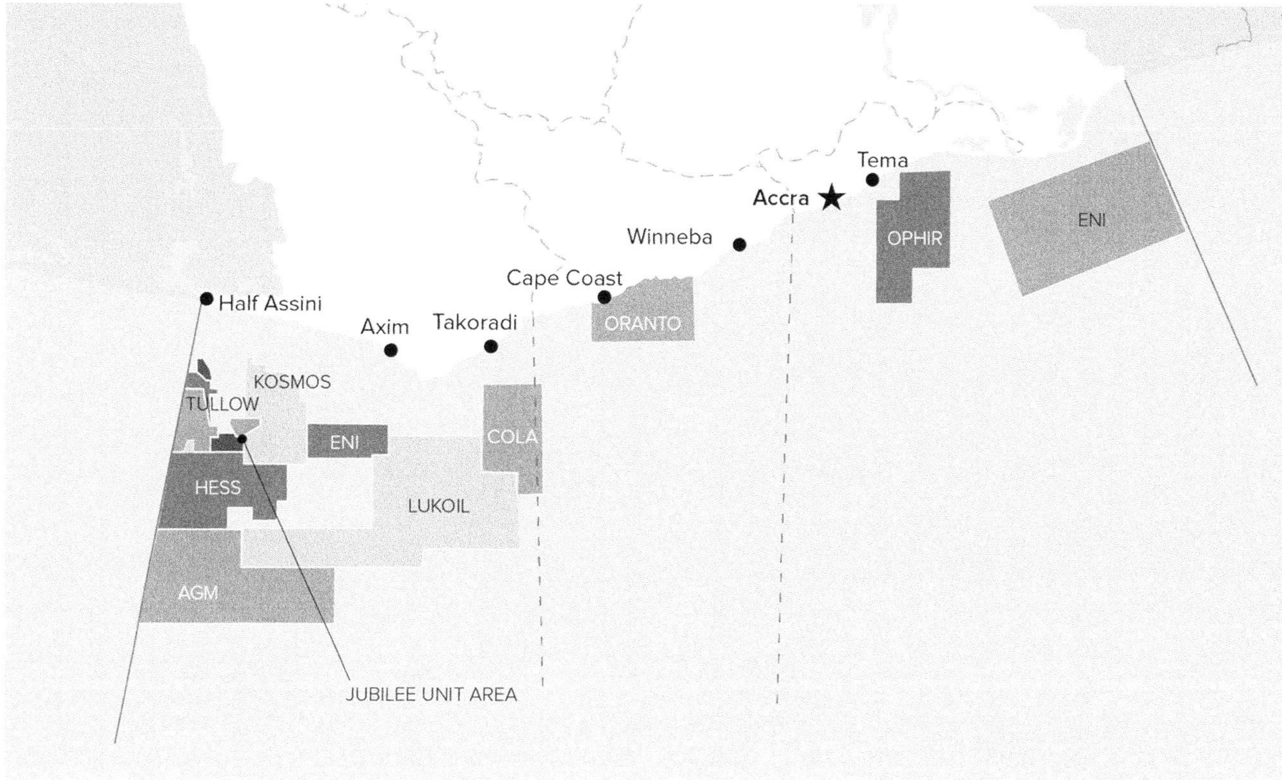

Figure 8.1 Ghana's Offshore Licensed Oil Areas
Courtesy of Oxford Analytica 2015.

The other oil discoveries were at various stages of appraisal in the mid-2010s. Mahogany Deep, Teak and other minor discoveries in the West Cape Three Points license were unlikely to support a standalone development, but could be developed as Jubilee satellites in the future. According to a World Bank report, none of the other pre-2012 discoveries were likely to mature into development projects (World Bank 2013: 45), but the international oil companies Ophir and ENI were positive about the potential of the Accra-Keta Basin. The Tano Basin exploration agreements are summarized in Table 8.1, and the status of commercial development in Table 8.2. The NDC II government signed further exploration petroleum agreements after 2008, which are summarized in Table 8.3. By law, GNPC is a party to all upstream petroleum agreements.

The World Bank developed projections for oil production up to the year 2036, the year that the Jubilee production license expires. These projections suggest that oil production will peak in 2019–2020 at around 230,000 bbl/d (World Bank 2013: 46). Total production over the period 2010–2036 will be 1.1 billion barrels. The long-term

Table 8.1 *Tano Basin Exploration Blocks and Discoveries*

Block designation	Lead operator	Contract ratified	Exploration period ended	Discoveries
Deepwater Tano	Tullow	July 2006	February 2013	Jubilee, Tweneboa, Enyenra, Ntomme, Wawa
West Cape Three Points	Kosmos	May 2014	May 2011	Jubilee, Teak, Mahogany Deep, Akasa, Bada, Odum
Offshore Cape Three Points	Eni	March 2006	March 2013	Sankofa, Gye Nyame, Sankofa East
Deepwater Tano/ Cape Three Points	Hess	July 2006	July 2013	Paradise, Pecan, Beech, Hickory North, Almond, Cob, Pecan North
Cape Three Points Deepwater	Vanco/ Lukoil	August 2002	June 2013	Dzata

Source: World Bank (2013: 43), based on GNPC website and company press releases.

Table 8.2 *Oil Field Appraisal Activity*

Field area	Status
Jubilee	Field development plan approved July 2009. In production since December 2010.
Tweneboa, Enyenra, & Ntomme (TEN)	Development plan approved in 2013.
Sankofa, Sankofa East, Gye Nyame (Sankofa)	Development plan approved in 2015.
Teak	Uncertain. Possible future Jubilee satellite.
Mahogany Deep	Uncertain. Possible future Jubilee satellite.
Odum	Uncertain. Thin pay zone.
Dzata	No data released. Presumed unsuccessful.

Source: World Bank (2013: 44), based on staff calculations and company press releases. Updated by the author.

Table 8.3 *Other Exploration Petroleum Contracts, 2008–2014*

Block name	Contractor parties	Effective agreement date
Offshore Saltpond	GNPC; Oranto; Stone Energy	July 3, 2008
Offshore Accra	GNPC; Ophir, Tap Oil; Azonto Petroleum; Vitol; Afex	March 24, 2010
Offshore Keta	GNPC; ENI, Mitsui, Afren;	February 19, 2010
East Cape Three Points	GNPC; Cola Natural Resources, Medea	December 4, 2013
South Deepwater Tano	GNPC; AGM, GNPC ExplorCo	December 4, 2013
Expanded Shallow water Tano	GNPC; Camac Energy; Base Energy; GNPC ExplorCo	March 27, 2014
Central Tano	GNPC; Amni Development Ghana Ltd	March 27, 2014

Source: Created by the author with data from the GNPC website.

upside potential, assuming future development of Pecan, Mahogany, Teak, Akasa and Bada, is estimated at around 300,000 bbl/d within the 2020–2024 timeframe. Projections for local gas estimate that gas production will peak in 2020–2022 at about 345 million cubic feet per day, while estimated total gas sales over the period 2010–2036 will be 1.9 trillion cubic feet.

These World Bank projections show government oil and gas revenue increasing steadily from US$542 million in 2012 to US$1 billion by 2016 and then surging in 2017 to hit a peak of almost US$4 billion in 2019–2022 as a result of the TEN and Sankofa Fields coming online and the exhaustion of cost recovery at the Jubilee Field (World Bank 2013: 47).[2]

Government oil revenues come from four main sources: royalties, surface rentals, income and capital gains taxes, and carried and participating interest of the national oil company GNPC. Under Ghana's petroleum laws, the state is entitled to a 10 percent interest in each contract area, through GNPC, and has the option to buy additional interest for which it is responsible for full operating costs during the development and production phases. The former is referred to as the "carried" interest and the later as "participating" interest. GNPC has taken additional participating interest in all contracted areas, which was about 4 percent in the early agreements under the NPP government but rose to around 13 percent in agreements signed between 2008 and 2014 (Hickey et al. 2015: 24). Thus, the government earns what is referred to as "carried and participating interest" from each developed oil field. Sam Hickey and colleagues (2015) argue that the NPP government offered generous terms that reduced the government's revenue from oil, which the NDC II government changed in petroleum agreements signed after 2008. The NDC II government also doubled the royalty rates, from 4–5 percent between 2002 and 2006 to 10 percent for agreements signed between 2008 and 2014.[3] Additional state participation also increased after 2006.

For the Jubilee Field, the state's carried and participating interest is 13.64 percent, the royalty is 5 percent of gross production, and corporate income tax is 35 percent.[4] However, the existing Petroleum

[2] These projections are based on an oil price of US$100 per barrel and gas prices of US$1.25 per million British thermal units (MMBtu) for Jubilee, US$6 per MMBtu for TEN, and US$8 per MMBtu for the Sankofa Fields.

[3] Notably, these Petroleum Agreements were signed with weaker consortiums than previous concessions.

[4] 2015 Annual Report on the Petroleum Funds, submitted to Parliament by Seth Terkper, Minister for Finance, as part of the presentation of the 2016 budget statement and economic policy, Republic of Ghana, p. 14.

Income Tax Law from the 1980s allowed companies to amortize exploration expenditure against income tax over the first five years of commercial operations, resulting in low corporate tax revenues in the first years (ACEP 2013). Furthermore, the rules allowed oil companies to deduct large levels of debt interest payments from their corporate income tax. Probably as a result, the NDC II government developed a new Petroleum Bill that increases the fiscal terms for new oil contracts. To date, the majority of government oil revenue comes from royalties and the carried and participating interest through GNPC.[5]

The primary responsibility of GNPC is to manage the country's commercial interests in upstream petroleum operations. A significant part of that role includes marketing the country's royalty oil and managing the state's carried and participating interests in petroleum developments. GNPC separately markets its crude oil production. There was only one oil refinery in Ghana: the state-owned Tema Oil Refinery. It previously imported crude oil from Nigeria for processing, but it became plagued by debts resulting from successive governments' subsidy of fuel prices without making payments to the Refinery, leaving it without the revenues to invest in upgrading technology over the years – similar to what happened with the public utility companies. By the 2000s, its operations were inadequate, and the government imported most of its finished petroleum products, and continued to do so in the 2010s. In mid-2016, there was an attempt at debt restructuring to make the Refinery profitable again. The sustainability of this endeavor was not yet clear.

Competitive Clientelism and State-Owned Companies in the Oil and Gas Sector

The NDC II government's official vision for the oil and gas sector included two main elements. The first was creating linkages with the rest of the economy through employing and training skilled labor, local content requirements, and building the capacity of local firms to supply international oil companies. The second was building the capacity of state-owned companies to participate in operating, processing and

[5] Based on a reading of the Annual Reports on the Petroleum Funds from 2012, 2013, 2014 and 2015. Available on the website of the Ministry of Finance, www.mofep.gov.gh (last accessed on December 8, 2015).

distributing oil and gas. In practice, the NDC II government put more emphasis on the second element, rather than helping build the capacities of local private firms to supply oil companies. However, GNPC became caught up in political battles, first between the NDC and NPP, and then among different groups of political elites within the NDC. These political battles, especially the ones among NDC elite factions, had significant effects on the development of the oil and gas sector. In particular, they resulted in the creation of a state-owned company to run the gas sector that was not capable of doing so and in a gas infrastructure project that cost the government more than it should have due to delays and corruption.

The Ghana National Petroleum Corporation was set up by the PNDC government in order to pioneer oil exploration and development, and it was mandated to be both industry regulator and commercial entity.[6] Tsatsu Tsikata, a key member of the PNDC ruling elite, was put in charge of GNPC and established the initial legal framework of the sector. After 1992, and under the NDC government, Tsikata remained head of GNPC and continued to undertake oil exploration in collaboration with a few international oil companies, although unsuccessfully (Mohan and Asante 2015: 8). However, during this period, significant technical capacity was built within the GNPC by investing in the training of GNPC staff (Hickey et al. 2015: 17).

Given the strong linkages between the GNPC and P/NDC political elites, when the NPP came to government in the 2000s, it pursued a different strategy for political and economic reasons. The NPP government restructured the corporation, significantly downsizing it, and prosecuted and sentenced Tsikata to prison for "causing financial loss to the state" (Hickey et al. 2015: 23). The NPP government also changed the incentive structure for attracting foreign direct investment by offering more generous terms and shifted negotiations away from the GNPC and into the hands of NPP political appointees. Notably, this is how the Kosmos-EO Group deal was possible, which was the

[6] The PNDC Law 64 of 1983 mandates that the corporation undertake the exploration, development, production and disposal of petroleum, and allows it to enter joint ventures and production-sharing agreements on behalf of the government. PNDC Law 84 establishes the legal framework governing the contractual relationship between the State, GNPC and the prospective investor in upstream petroleum operations.

first exploration petroleum agreement that the NPP government signed. Kosmos Energy, a small Texan oil exploration company backed by US equity finance, entered Ghana. The exploration agreement was brokered by EO Group, an inexperienced Ghanaian oil company that had close links to President Kufuor, which in return acquired a 3.5 percent equity stake in Jubilee (see Chapter 3). The agreement with Kosmos was more generous than those signed afterwards with other oil companies exploring the same offshore territory, allegedly costing the government US$3.8 billion in tax revenues compared to the terms offered to Tullow Oil in the adjacent Deepwater Tano block (Phillips et al. 2015).

The Jubilee Field development plan was approved in 2009, and Kosmos Energy, which had entered Ghana as an oil exploration company, sought to sell its stake in the Jubliee Field and exit at the onset of commercial production. Kosmos wanted to sell its stake to ExxonMobil, but GNPC was opposed to the deal because it wanted to buy the stake. Upon the NDC's return to government in 2009, a key member of the NDC dating back to the PNDC days, Ato Ahwoi, was made board chairman of GNPC, and Tsatsu Tsikata acted as an advisor to President Mills (Hickey et al. 2015: 18). Under NDC leadership, GNPC declared that its ambitions were greater than that of regulator and facilitating investment.[7] GNPC did not have the right of first refusal, but it made a counteroffer in a joint bid with the Chinese National Offshore Oil Company, which saw this bid as a way to enter Ghana's oil industry. After a year of wrangling with the NDC II government, Kosmos decided to hold on to its stake and develop its commercial interests as a partner in the Jubilee Field, and the EO Group sold its stake to Tullow Oil in a deal worth US$305 million (Phillips et al. 2015).

At the same time that GNPC's struggle for Kosmos' stake in the Jubilee Field was going on, another struggle was unfolding around how to develop the new gas industry, but this time it was between elite groups within the NDC.[8] The struggle pitted NDC elites connected

7 Notably, even though the Ministry for Energy was formally the regulator of the oil sector under the NPP government, GNPC held all the expertise and thus became the de facto regulator. I thank Jon Phillips for pointing this out.

8 This paragraph and the next paragraphs are based on empirical research carried out by Jon Phillips and available in his PhD thesis (Phillips 2017). I thank him for sharing it with me.

with GNPC, such as Tsatsu Tsikata and Ato Ahwoi, against a group of NDC elites outside of the energy sector, in particular a "kitchen cabinet" of economic advisors to President Mills. GNPC was judged to have moved slowly in initiating the gas infrastructure project, and a task force was created to determine alternative institutional arrangements. The task force included representatives from both sides. In the end, it concluded that GNPC should concentrate on becoming an upstream operator and that a separate state company should be created. Kwesi Botchwey, backed by President Mills, forced through a decision within the task force to sideline GNPC in the gas industry by creating the National Ghana Gas Company. Their decision was driven by the perception that GNPC would be too powerful if it was given the mandate to develop the gas industry as well, and that a separate company to manage the gas infrastructure would also provide significant opportunities for patronage and could be used to reward NDC elites that had been instrumental in Mills' victory in the 2008 elections.

While members of the task force were struggling over the institutional arrangements for the gas industry, they were also divided on the financing arrangements. GNPC political leaders and the energy minister preferred a joint venture involving technology transfer from the National Gas Company of Trinidad and Tobago and had initiated negotiations to raise its own finance for the project. Sidelining GNPC, Botchwey and his allies sought to contract the international oil companies ENI and Lukoil to build and operate the gas infrastructure needed to process oil-associated and non-oil-associated gas and transmit it for electricity generation in the country. However, the energy minister preferred that the gas infrastructure be owned by the state, in order to capture more value from gas. The Ministry of Finance was also in discussions with the World Bank on financing the gas infrastructure and providing technical assistance. In the end, President Mills decided to go for Chinese financing, through which SINOPEC (China's third largest oil and gas company) would build and then transfer the gas processing plant to the National Ghana Gas Company for operating. Jon Phillips (2017) argues that the promise of quick dispersal, especially procurement procedures, was critical to this decision.

The National Ghana Gas Company was created in April 2011, with Botchwey as Chairman of the Board and George Sipa-Yankee as Chief Executive Officer. Later that year, the government signed the agreement with the China Development Bank to finance the Western Corridor Gas Infrastructure Project, as part of the larger US$3 billion Master Facility Agreement, after the IMF approved the raising of Ghana's debt ceiling. The terms of financing with the China Development Bank were not that favorable. The project included a loan of US$850 million (at nonconcessional rates) from the Chinese Development Bank and 15 percent counterpart funding from the government, bringing the expected cost to US$1 billion. The government committed future oil to repay the loan through a direct resource swap, which would give UNIPEC, the oil-trading business of SINOPEC, a monopoly on marketing its oil for fifteen years.

President Mills put a lot of political emphasis on the Master Facility Agreement, but details of the subsidiary agreement subsequently cast doubt on his assumptions that the Chinese loan offered a cheaper, quicker and less stringent alternative to the World Bank. The deal did not make the supply of oil to UNIPEC contingent on loan disbursement for the gas project and thus there was little incentive for disbursement, especially when the government paid a 1 percent fee on the nondispersed parts of the loan. The biggest plus about the arrangement was that SINOPEC agreed to start construction in 2012 by prefinancing the work. However, delays in the disbursement of the loan by the China Development Bank caused delays in the construction. The Atuabo gas processing plant was finally completed in mid-2014 and began commercial operations in mid-2015, sending gas to the Volta River Authority to fuel the Abaodze Thermal Plant.

It was not just delays on disbursement that caused the gas plant to take longer to build than anticipated. The slow pace and high cost were due to poor management by Ghana Gas and what many insiders saw as quite blatant corruption associated with the procurement process. Details of Ghana Gas' procurement practices and transfer mispricing by SINOPEC were leaked by GNPC to the public through nongovernmental organizations scrutinizing the oil and gas sector.

The significant delays in completing the gas project associated with mismanagement had substantial costs for the government, in addition to the inflated price of the project itself, as the government had to keep importing crude oil for electricity generation at the Abaodze thermal plant, and oil production had to be slowed down due to the limited amount of gas that could be reinjected.[9] The (compromise) outcome of creating Ghana Gas must be seen as a product of Ghana's particular form of competitive clientelism, in which NDC elite factions were vying for political influence and economic opportunities in a context of a range of international finance options. Relatedly, the NDC placed a premium on developing the oil and gas sector as quickly as possible, in order to benefit within its time in office. Notably, Jubilee was the fastest oil field development in the world.[10]

However, the arrangement with Ghana Gas was untenable. GNPC had to take over Ghana Gas to provide security for ENI and Vitol, the multinational oil companies selling gas from the Jubilee, TEN and Sankofa fields. This was a requirement in order for the Sankofa gas development project to go through. Unlike oil, the gas was to be sold to the domestic market, where margins are much smaller and the multinational companies would be dependent on one government buying agency. As a result, the multinational oil companies faced higher risks than in oil production; they stood to lose money if the government buying agency defaulted on its buying contract. ENI and Vitol did not see Ghana Gas as a credible buying agency because it did not own any significant assets: GNPC technically owned the gas, the state-owned Bulk Oil Storage and Transport Company had been granted the transmission license, and GNPC invested in building the pipelines (World Bank 2013: 38–39). GNPC also owned significant assets and had a revenue stream from the sale of Jubilee oil. Even then, ENI and Vitol required guarantees from the World Bank to reduce the risk of government default.[11]

The NDC elites were focused on fighting over the management of the state-owned oil and gas companies. They were not very concerned with promoting local private firms' participation in the sector, despite formulating the Petroleum Local Content and Local Participation Regulations, which Parliament passed in 2013. This local content law officially aimed to promote linkages between the country's oil and gas

9 In the first half of 2015, the fuel import bill rose dramatically, by about US$27 million per month, because gas supplies from Nigeria through the West African Gas Pipeline slowed and domestic gas was not yet available (World Bank 2015: 1).

10 I thank Jon Phillips for pointing this out.

11 On the guarantees and the Sankofa gas development project, see World Bank (2015).

sector and the rest of the economy through including Ghanaian nationals in the management of oil and gas resources, sourcing local goods and services and engaging local contractors and consultants.[12] The government's main initiative to operationalize the local content law was the Enterprise Development Centre, which was not very ambitious and was not even funded by the government. It was funded by a consortium of the multinational oil companies operating in Ghana that provided US$5 million over a five-year period.[13] The main aim of the center was to help Ghanaian businesses to improve their competitiveness (and thereby be better positioned to win business opportunities in the sector) through training in business and financial management, procurement policies and regulations, quality awareness and excellence, and health safety and environment.

Research on the Enterprise Development Centre concluded that its impact would be limited (Ablo 2015; Ablo and Overå 2015). Of the firms that qualified in 2014, only twenty-five businesses completed the training program out of the first batch of forty. Many of these firms were supplying services to mining companies, or were formed by Ghanaian entrepreneurs who had worked in the oil industry in other countries and returned to Ghana after oil was discovered in 2007. For these firms, the training program was largely a platform for them to expand their operations and to make contacts and networks with Ghanaians working for the multinational oil companies and their subcontractors. According to Austin Dziwornu Ablo (2015), the center did not have any significant effects on local firms' ability to meet the administrative and financial requirements of winning contracts.

[12] Under the legislation, all multinational oil companies operating in Ghana must have at least 5 percent indigenous Ghanaian equity stake in their organizations in order to qualify for new exploration licenses; subcontract only to vendors and organizations with a 10 percent indigenous Ghanaian equity stake; utilize local goods in their operations, as long as their costs are not more than 10 percent above those of foreign suppliers and after ten years, procure 90 percent of all goods and services from indigenous companies regardless of costs; and employ Ghanaians in 70–80 percent of all managerial and technical posts, and 100 percent of all middle- and junior-level jobs by 2023.

[13] The participating companies included Tullow Ghana, Anadarko, Kosmos Energy, Petro SA, and GNPC. USAID was also funding a project aimed to increase the participation of Ghanaian small businesses in the oil and gas sector, but whether and how it collaborated with the Enterprise Development Center was not clear (Ablo 2015: 323).

In sum, state-owned companies were the focus of the NDC II government in developing the oil and gas sector, and they became embroiled in elite factional struggle to control the revenues flowing from the sector. This struggle cost the government a lot of money and resulted in the suboptimal development of the sector. GNPC did emerge as a very capable state-owned enterprise, but its confidence in its capabilities also led the NDC elites to pursue an ambitious strategy for the GNPC.

Ambitions of the Ghana National Petroleum Corporation

A large portion of the oil revenue that does not go into the sovereign wealth funds goes back into the oil and gas sector, largely through GNPC. This situation results from the design of the oil revenue management structure as set out in the Petroleum Revenue Management Act, which GNPC officials had a significant say in designing because they held most of the knowledge in the country regarding the oil sector. This section describes the oil revenue management structure before turning to the ambitions of GNPC in the upstream oil sector, which required massive capitalization.

The Petroleum Revenue Management Act is very clear on how to use oil revenues, but it is also rather complex. The Act requires petroleum revenue from all sources to be deposited in a Petroleum Holding Fund.[14] First, revenue from GNPC's stakes in the oil fields is used to meet GNPC's equity financing costs in respect of its share of development and production costs. The net proceeds from GNPC's carried and participating interest are then split between GNPC and the government. The Act sets the maximum share of net revenue from participating interests that GNPC can receive at 55 percent. The split is supposed to be reviewed every three years, and GNPC submits its annual budget to Parliament for approval.

The remaining oil revenue from the net carried and participating interest, combined with the other sources of oil revenue (royalties, corporate taxes, surface rentals), constitute the actual oil receipts, which is divided between money available to be spent in the annual budget and money that will go into two Ghana Petroleum Funds: the Heritage Fund and the Stabilization Fund. The Heritage Fund's aim is

14 The Petroleum Holding Fund was opened at the Federal Reserve Bank of the United States on April 11, 2011.

to save surplus oil revenue for use after Ghana's oil runs out. The Stabilization Fund, as the name indicates, is intended to stabilize public expenditure given the volatility in oil revenues as international oil prices fluctuate. These two funds are sovereign wealth funds, managed by the Bank of Ghana in line with the investment strategy designed in collaboration with the Minister of Finance and under advice from an Investment Advisory Committee.

For the purposes of budget planning, the Ministry of Finance makes the allocation of funds for current spending and saving in advance using a Benchmark Revenue calculation. The ministry calculates the Benchmark Revenue on the basis of averages of historical and expected values of both oil price and production.[15] The allocation of petroleum revenue to the current year budget, the Annual Budget Funding Amount, is limited to 70 percent of the Benchmark Revenue. The remaining 30 percent is saved in the Heritage and Stabilization Funds. When actual revenue exceeds the Benchmark Revenue, the excess is directed to the Stabilization Fund. Withdrawals from the Stabilization Fund to cushion the Annual Budget Funding Amount are permitted only when actual revenue falls short of the Benchmark Revenue. Table 8.4 provides an overview of the total petroleum receipts for the years 2011 to 2015, and shows how oil revenues were distributed between the transfers to GNPC, transfers to the budget, and transfers to the two sovereign wealth funds.

The ambitions of GNPC, and the capital requirements required to fulfill those ambitions, resulted in a significant amount of oil revenues flowing to it. In the first three years of oil production, revenue from the net carried and participating interest (after deducting equity financing costs of GNPC) was split between GNPC and the government on a 40/60 basis. After the first three-year review, GNPC's portion was reduced to 30 percent in 2014. Nevertheless, this amounted to a large portion of oil revenues going back to GNPC, with the explicit objective of building GNPC to be a world-class commercially independent oil company.

Due to its equity share in each field development, GNPC has future investment requirements estimated at over US$600 million between 2013 and 2023 (World Bank 2013: 54). In most cases, the petroleum agreements allow GNPC to finance its capital requirements with the oil

[15] The Petroleum Revenue Management Act was amended in 2015 to allow for some flexibility in the determination of the Benchmark Revenue, at the time of laying the budget or during the midyear review of the budget, in the context of significant changes in the oil price.

Table 8.4 *Total Oil Revenue and Allocation, 2011–2015 (in US$)*

	2011	2012	2013	2014	2015* (up to September)
Total petroleum receipts	444,124,724	541,620,000	846,770,000	978,890,000	341,500,000
Transfer to GNPC	207,960,000	230,949,926	222,421,416	180,712,503	98,300,000
Net Government Oil Receipts	236,160,241	310,673,815	624,345,768	797,305,285	244,068,246
o/w Annual Budget Funding Amount	166,955,067	286,554,461	273,197,567	409,072,777	227,465,322
o/w Infrastructure Investment Fund	–	–	–	–	39,806,431
o/w Transfer to Petroleum Funds	69,205,354	24,119,354	351,048,145	388,232,507	16,602,925
o/w Heritage Fund (30%)	14,400,002	7,235,806	105,314,444	116,469,752	4,980,877
o/w Stabilization Fund (70%)	54,805,353	16,883,548	245,733,702	271,762,755	11,622,047
(o/w Sinking and Contingency Funds)	–	–	–	305,684,687**	95,020,291

Source: Created by the author with data from the Annual Reports on the Petroleum Funds from 2012, 2013, 2014 and 2015, including the Reconciliation reports for 2013 and 2014. The 2015 data only goes up to September 2015, because the Annual Reports only cover the first nine months of the year, as they are submitted alongside the next year's budget. Fourth quarter data is then presented in a Reconciliation report produced in the following year.

Notes:

* Even though three months of receipts are not indicated for 2015, the significantly lower amount than the previous year is due to the rapid decline in crude oil prices, and to lower corporate tax income.

** Of this amount, US$17.43 million was used to set up the Contingency Fund, and US$288.25 million was transferred to a Debt Service Account. In the latter, US$179.81 million was used to retire domestic marketable debt, and the remaining US$108.44 was used to set up the Sinking Fund account. However, the Bank of Ghana "swept" this amount at the end of 2014. The public financial management reforms are being pursued to ring-fence oil revenues from such "sweeping."

company partners in exchange for a reduced share of future petroleum production. Capital costs plus its operating costs (corresponding to its carried and additional participating interests in each field) will average roughly US$180 million per year over the same ten-year period. The World Bank calculated that the revenue allocated to GNPC through its 30–40 percent share of the carried and participating interests would provide GNPC with an average of US$150 million per year above its capital and operating costs, which would grow to over US$400 million per year when new fields come into production.

This additional cash allocation is clearly intended to capitalize GNPC in order to achieve its ambitious vision of becoming a commercially independent operator with investments in new exploration and production ventures.[16] Under the NDC II government, GNPC's strategy to achieve this goal included entering joint venture/operator arrangements with foreign operators to achieve rapid transfer of operating capabilities.[17] To this end, GNPC established a joint venture with Technip, an exploration and production engineering company, to help build its capabilities in engineering services and project management onshore and offshore. It also established a subsidiary, GNPC Exploration and Production Company (Explorco), focused on the exploration and production of hydrocarbons that could partner with foreign firms in jointly operating selected blocks. In 2013, the government signed an agreement in the South Deepwater Tano block with GNPC Explorco and AGM Petroleum Ghana as joint operators, in addition to GNPC's stake on behalf of the government (see Table 8.3).[18] Another agreement was signed in 2014 in which Explorco was also a joint operator.

The objective to make GNPC a world-class oil company reduced the oil revenues flowing into the Petroleum Holding Fund and thus potential revenues for the annual budget. For example, the 2015 annual

[16] Notably, GNPC took a US$700 million commercial (but low interest) loan in 2014, just prior to the steepest oil price decline, which was a bone of contention in the IMF bailout negotiations around that time. I thank Jon Phillips for pointing this out.

[17] 2013 Annual Report on the Petroleum Funds, submitted to Parliament by Seth Terkper, Minister for Finance, Republic of Ghana, p. 7; 2014 Annual Report on the Petroleum Funds, submitted to Parliament by Seth Terkper, Minister for Finance, Republic of Ghana, pp. 8–9.

[18] AGM is a consortium of Norway's AGR Energy (49.5 percent), Israeli-owned Minexco (48 percent) and local player MED Songhai Developers (2.5 percent).

report on petroleum revenues (from January to September) shows that carried and participating interest constituted 69.62 percent of total petroleum receipts, while Jubilee Field royalties accounted for 26.86 percent, and corporate income tax and surface rentals for the small remaining part. However, investing in building GNPC as a world-class oil company will have limited effects on catalysing broader economic transformation in the country, relative to alternative investments that could be made with the money.

Priority Areas for Spending Oil Revenues

After the transfers to GNPC and to the two sovereign wealth funds, the remainder of the oil revenues goes into the Annual Budget Funding Amount. The Minister of Finance is required to prioritize not more than four areas for spending the Annual Budget Funding Amount, which have to be approved by Parliament, and the areas are revisited every three years. Under the NDC II government, the four priority areas included expenditure and amortization of loans for oil and gas; road and other infrastructure; agricultural modernization; and capacity building (including oil and gas). Table 8.5 summarizes the expenditures of oil revenue by priority area from 2011 to 2015, based on data extracted and compiled from the government's annual reports on the petroleum funds. The table indicates that more oil revenue was spent on the oil and gas sector, which received the second-largest amount of revenue after infrastructure.

The revenue allocated to "expenditure and amortization of loans for oil and gas" went to pay for the government's matching fund requirements for the Western Corridor Oil and Gas Infrastructure Project, as well as its principal and interest payments for the first tranche of the Chinese Development Bank Master Facility. According to the Minister of Finance, as of September 2015, the total disbursement from the Chinese loan was US$857.63 million, with the government contributing US$128.64 million from oil revenues.[19] The Master Facility Agreement governing the Chinese loan included twelve projects divided into two tranches of US$1.5 billion to be disbursed over a six-

[19] 2015 Annual Report on Petroleum Funds.

Table 8.5 *Budget Expenditure of Oil Revenues by Priority Areas, 2011–2015 (Ghanaian Cedis)*

Priority Area	2011	2012	2013	2014*	2015 (Jan–Sept)	Total
Expenditure & amortization of loans for oil and gas	20,000,000	100,000,000	137,920,847	163,084,572	390,517,533	811,522,952
Road and other infrastructure	227,641,768	232,403,269	372,074,147	215,691,357	451,586,162	1,499,396,703
Agriculture modernization	13,147,652	72,471,824	13,604,329	170,624,180	27,043,457	296,891,442
Capacity building (including oil and gas)	750,000	111,959,738	20,183,359	–	135,948,665	268,841,762
Total	*261,539,420*	*516,834,831*	*543,782,682*	*549,400,109*	*1,005,095,819*	

Source: Created by the author with data from the Annual Reports on the Petroleum Funds from 2012, 2013, 2014 and 2015, including the Reconciliation reports for 2013 and 2014.

Note:

* In 2014, 1,215,460 million cedis were allocated to the ABFA. However, at year's end, only 549.40 million cedis were spent, leaving a balance of 666.06 million cedis (equivalent to US$222.93 million). According to the 2015 Annual Report on Petroleum Funds, this balance on the ABFA account was "swept" by the Bank of Ghana, which means that oil revenue was being used in ways not intended, as a result of the macroeconomic crisis.

year period and to be repaid within twenty years.[20] The first tranche included the Western Corridor Gas Infrastructure project and two small projects, but only the former was implemented and included the gas infrastructure and development of an ICT platform for surveillance of the oil and gas field. In 2013, the Chinese Development Bank's delay in disbursing payments to SINOPEC, which was implementing the project, cost the government US$54 million in "commitment fees." The loan agreement included a clause stating that the government must pay a commitment fee of 1 percent annually on the undrawn and uncancelled balance of the loan. The payment of the commitment fee became a source of public debate in Ghana, used by the opposition NPP to discredit the NDC II government.

In mid-2014, the Mahama administration renegotiated the terms of the loan, cancelling the second half of the loan (tranche two) and thus effectively cancelling the commitment fee. The cancellation also stemmed from disagreements between the government and the Chinese Development Bank over the pricing of oil in the resource swap. Even the remaining money in the first tranche of the loan was not released, which was earmarked for the rehabilitation of Tema Oil Refinery, Takoradi port and "oil enclave" roads.

Allocation of the remaining revenue in the Annual Budget Funding Amount was not in accordance with the priority areas of infrastructure, agriculture and capacity building of local firms to participate in the oil and gas sector. An analysis by the African Center for Energy Policy of the 2011, 2012 and 2013 budget statements shows that the allocation of oil revenues across ministries, department and agencies did not strictly follow the three priority areas, as ministries completely unrelated to these priority areas received oil revenues (ACEP 2014). When revenue was allocated for activities falling within the three priority areas, it was spread widely over many projects. This was particularly true for the infrastructure area. Moving from budget statements to the field, African Center for Energy Policy staff tracked expenditures on the road projects partly funded from oil revenues and found that they were at different stages of completion, with few actually completed, which in turn led to costly extensions and thus cost overruns.

[20] Information about the Chinese Development Bank loan and Master Facility Agreement are based on documents accessed from the Ministry of Finance.

This experience is not particular to projects being funded by earmarked oil revenues, but rather represents a general trend of public financial management in Ghana. Ruling political elites not only pursue distributive expenditures, but also distribute them widely due to political imperatives generated by competitive clientelism. All politicians want to bring distributive expenditures to their electoral constituencies in general, and their core supporters in particular, in order to increase their chances of reelection. This leads them to push for spending on projects in their constituency, and ministers to push for allocations to their sectors. Building roads is seen as a particularly useful form of distributive expenditure for gaining political support. In the 2014 budget, the Minister of Finance recognized the problems of spreading the oil money across too many projects and stated that Annual Budget Funding Amount expenditure would be more focused in the future. However, according to the 2015 Annual Report on Petroleum Revenues, money continued to be spread widely.

The priority area in capacity building was used to meet these political pressures as well. There are years for which the NDC II government did not account for expenditures under this priority area, especially during the 2012 election year, which received and spent an unusually large amount in this priority area, as shown in Table 8.5. In 2015, when the government did account for expenditures under this priority area, it indicated that funds were spent on "improving the capacity of teachers across the country" by supplying teaching and learning materials, financing the feeding and capitation grant for schools, and paying the subsidy for 2015 secondary school examinations, as well as providing scholarships for advanced learning, including in oil and gas training. These are clearly distributive, consumption-driven expenditures.

Oil revenue allocations in the priority area of agricultural modernization were used to support economic development directly. The NDC II government's objective was to increase agricultural productivity, especially among smallholders, through utilization of agricultural machinery, investments in small irrigation facilities, promoting the formation of cooperatives, and investments to irrigate large tracts of land in the Northern Savannah and Accra Plains.[21] In particular, the

[21] The vision of the NDC II government was contained in the Agenda for Shared Growth and Development, which the Mills administration produced and submitted to parliament as the government's Coordinated Programme of Economic and Social Development Policies, which it is required to do by the

NDC elites wanted to increase domestic production of major imported agricultural products (rice, sugar, wheat, tomato, poultry, frozen fish, and vegetable cooking oil) in order to reduce the import bill, and thus reduce the trade deficit, at the same time as increasing the incomes of Ghanaian producers. This strategy has been pursued many times by Ghanaian government since the 1960s, as shown throughout this book, and like previous governments, the NDC ruling elites primarily chose to achieve these objectives through state-led industrial policies.

Oil-Financed Industrial Policies in Agriculture and Agro-processing

The NDC II government's key initiatives in agriculture included mechanization centers, fertilizer subsidies, block farms, and instituting a national buffer stock. The Mills administration not only continued with the Agricultural Mechanization Services Centers project started by its NPP predecessor, but also rapidly expanded it and linked it to block farms. Block farms grouped small farmers on contiguous land where the government provided them with subsidized mechanization services, fertilizers, credit for improved seed and pesticides, extension services, and guaranteed minimum prices. The block farm model was dependent on the government to provide everything, a model that rarely worked in the Ghanaian political economy, as demonstrated with the fate of the Oil Palm PSI in the previous chapter. While the NDC II government was better able to cover the financial costs through oil revenues, implementation was still plagued by political problems.

An evaluation carried out by the International Food Policy Research Institute office in Ghana shows that the block farms had a significant impact on increasing small farmers' access to mechanization services, and that the fertilizer subsidy program contributed to an increase in the application of fertilizers, but the costs of the programs were high due to the amount of government subsidy and the low recovery rates on loans in the block farm and mechanization centers schemes (Benin et al. 2013). Historically in Ghana, state-led loan schemes have not worked because farmers see them as political largesse, and are not wrong in

constitution. The Mahama administration adopted this Agenda, but more sharply defined its priority programs in the NDC's 2012 election manifesto.

thinking so given the way that politicians use them in political campaigning. The nonrepayment of loans in the past caused the failure of such state-led agricultural projects and brought them closer to distributive expenditures. In this case, oil revenues were used to keep the project going, but it absorbed a large amount of resources.

Complementing the block farms, the Ministry of Food and Agriculture created the National Buffer Stock Company to provide an alternative market for farmers producing cereals and one that offered guaranteed minimum prices. The model was that the company purchased maize and rice from smallholders during harvest time (when supply outstrips demand, causing prices to fall) at a guaranteed minimum price, distributed it around the country and to other government organizations, and saved the excess as an emergency stock. The company began purchasing rice from farmers in northern Ghana in 2010, and its purchases accounted for nearly 5 percent of local rice production between 2010 and 2015.[22] Initially the company did the purchases itself, but then moved to using private licensed buying companies. The company then contracted several small-scale processors to parboil the paddy, which was then milled at two state-owned rice mills in northern Ghana. The operational stocks of the company were used to supply government agencies and programs such as the school feeding program and the prison service. One evaluation of this policy notes that it was extremely expensive and wasteful in regards to *rice* purchases[23], while the evaluation by the International Food Policy Research Institute states it was financially viable in relation to *maize* purchases but that this viability could change when the market price falls below the floor price (Benin et al. 2013).

In theory the model was a good one, which used government demand and state-owned enterprises to stabilize agricultural prices in food crops. But this model is very expensive and, as before, problems often arise in the implementation, in which state-owned agro-processing companies are not run well. Notably, the Ghana Grains Council (a private initiative of leaders in the grains business with the aim of achieving greater commercialization and quality) was developing a warehouse receipt system where privately-owned warehouses

[22] Summary of Rice Market System Analysis Report, DFID Market Development in Northern Ghana Programme, submitted to DFID Ghana, by DAI in association with Nathan Associates London Ltd, August 11, 2015, p. 24.

[23] Ibid.

provide an important intermediary node in the marketing and distribution of food crops by reducing the high transportation, transaction and information costs of smallholder farmers (Benin et al. 2013: 93). While not the same as a buffer stock system, it shared the same objective of stabilizing agricultural prices. The NDC II government did not work with the Ghana Grains Council to expand this initiative, but rather pursued its own initiative implemented through state-owned enterprises.

Despite these agricultural initiatives, five years later, the agricultural sector's performance was still poor according to the government budget statement in late 2015.[24] The agricultural sector as a whole was expected to grow less than 1 percent in 2015, with the crops sub-sector recording negative growth and being the reason for the generally poor performance of the sub-sector. While the aggregate numbers were not impressive, local production of rice expanded, but whether this was because of government initiatives in the rice sector is not clear.

The NDC II government specifically targeted rice because it was the second most important food staple, especially in urban areas, and two-thirds of domestic consumption of rice was imported. Targeting rice was a way to boost local agricultural production and farmers' incomes while also reducing the import bill. The Mills administration increased import duties as an incentive for local investment in rice production and a disincentive for importing. It restored the 15 percent rice tariff in 2010, as part of a general restoration of levies on grains and poultry that had been removed by the NPP government during the 2008 global food crisis, and then added a 5 percent increment. In addition to the 20 percent import duty on rice, a myriad of other levies brought the effective tax on rice to 37 percent in 2015. However, raising the tariff on rice had a limited effect because urban consumers preferred imported rice over local rice due to its characteristics and were willing to pay the higher price.[25]

[24] The Budget Statement and Economic Policy of the Government of Ghana for the 2016 financial year, presented to Parliament on 13 November 2015, by Seth Terkper, Minister for Finance, pp. 14–15.

[25] Urban areas accounted for 76 percent of the demand in rice, much of which was met by imported rice. Domestically produced rice is sold mainly in rural markets, with only 20 percent of local rice being consumed in urban markets. Urban rice consumers prefer imported rice because it is fragrant, long-grained, white rice (better cleaned, destoned and polished compared to local rice). Only rural consumers in the north remained loyal to local, parboiled, nonaromatic

One study showed that Ghanaian farmers could compete with imported rice on price, but not on quality.[26] Thus, the challenge was for small farmers and processors to produce better quality rice that met urban consumer tastes.[27] Furthermore, the major rice importers could be convinced to purchase local aromatic rice from processors and act as distributors for the domestic market, if sufficient quantities of local rice of high quality existed. A few importers dominated rice distribution and marketing in the country, with Finatrade and OLAM together capturing 60 percent of the domestic market. These two importing firms already had begun to purchase and distribute local aromatic rice produced by private rice mills that emerged in the early 2010s.[28]

As with previous policies, when the NDC II government sought to increase local rice production, it largely did so through state-led approaches. The main government effort to increase rice production was through the Aveyime Rice project in the Volta region. The Aveyime Rice Project was started under the Rawlings-led NDC government in the 1990s as a joint venture between the government and a US company called Quality Grain, on a large tract of land that the state had acquired in the 1970s. The project ended in the Quality Grain scandal, and the project collapsed in 2003.[29] However, in the year of the 2008 elections,

rice. Summary of Rice Market System Analysis Report, DFID Market Development in Northern Ghana Programme, submitted to DFID Ghana, by DAI in association with Nathan Associates London Ltd, August 11, 2015, pp. 6–7.

26 Bill and Melinda Gates Foundation Report, Developing the Rice Industry in Africa: Ghana Assessment, July 2012.

27 The International Rice Research Institute developed an aromatic rice that could compete against imports and released it in Ghana in 2009, but small farmers had to be convinced that they would be compensated for the cost of investing in seeds and other modern inputs by higher returns, and farmers needed finance to pay for the inputs and labor. Achieving the rice quality that would meet urban consumers' preferences required not only the right seed type but also appropriate harvesting, postharvesting and processing techniques at rice mills.

28 Bill and Melinda Gates Foundation Report, Developing the Rice Industry in Africa: Ghana Assessment, July 2012.

29 The scandal involved fraud by the Chief Executive Officer of Quality Grains, a US company, in relation to the Aveyime Rice Project, in which the government was to enter a joint venture company with Quality Grains to produce and mill rice. The joint venture with a US firm was necessary in order to access external finance from the US Export-Import Bank. The US company was dubious, but no proper background check and monitoring was carried out by the NDC government, resulting in a liability of over US$22 million for the government (see *Africa Confidential* 2003 Vol. 44, No. 10, p. 1). The NPP government

the NPP government decided to revive the Aveyime Rice Project. It sold the state's existing assets to a US company in return for shares in the new company called Prairie Volta Limited, and it guaranteed access to loans provided by state-owned banks to rehabilitate equipment neglected on the farm and to get production started. The NDC II government continued to see the Aveyime Rice Project as a strategic way to meet domestic demand for polished rice and rehabilitated the irrigation facility at Aveyime to serve small-scale farmers in the area who sold their rice to Prairie Volta Limited.[30] While Prairie Volta was the first large-scale rice farm and mill in the Volta Region and marketed rice under its own brand, its operations suffered difficulties with its minority government ownership.[31]

The most promising development in producing high-quality rice in Ghana to compete with imports was not driven by the NDC II government, but rather by several private rice mills established in the Northern and Volta Regions, which initiated smallholder and outgrower schemes to supply their mills in addition to their nucleus farms.[32] These new investors aimed to capture the lucrative local market away from imported rice, and some were teaming up with the dominant rice-importing firms in order to use their distribution channels. In the Northern Region, the main investor was Avnash, an Indian conglomerate that already had diversified investments in Ghana and Nigeria. In the Volta Region, the main investors were GADCO and Brazil Agro Investment.[33] Avnash and GADCO had extensive plans for working with smallholder farmers to produce high-quality rice and to improve their processing techniques.

prosecuted and convicted the former Minister of Finance (1995–2000), the former Minister of Agriculture, and a former Ministry of Finance official for "wilfully causing financial loss to the state" as a result of this scandal.

30 "Government committed to seeing Aveyime rice project flourish – Ahwoi," Ghana News Agency, April 6, 2009, accessed at www.modernghana.com/news/210002/1/government-committed-to-seeing-aveyime-rice-projec.html (last accessed on December 15, 2015).

31 These difficulties are documented in Bill and Melinda Gates Foundation Report, Developing the rice industry in Africa: Ghana assessment, July 2012.

32 Ibid.

33 GADCO was established by two businessmen previously in the global consulting and advisory services businesses. They used private equity raised from global venture capital firms and investment banks to establish their rice milling business in the Volta Region. See http://gadcompany.com/foundation.php (last accessed December 15, 2015).

The predilection of the NDC II government for state-led industrial policies occurred in the other import substituting sectors as well, such as poultry and sugar. Similar to rice, the Mills administration restored the 20 percent tariff on imported poultry products, with the effective rate around 37 percent when factoring in taxes and levies. Over the course of the 2000s and early 2010s, imports of chicken had quadrupled due to growing urban demand. Imported chicken as a percentage of the total supply of chicken in Ghana increased from 38 percent in 2001 to 68 percent in 2010 (FAO 2014). Imported poultry products tended to be 30–40 percent cheaper than domestically produced chicken.[34] The high cost of domestic poultry products was due to importing fertilized eggs or day-old chicks, inefficient production methods, and high energy costs, among others. The Mills administration sought to increase the access of broiler farms to cheaper local corn as feed (rather than expensive imports) through the fertilizer subsidy for maize farmers and the National Buffer Stock Company to provide bulk storage facilities for maize. However, this approach did not have a significant impact on the local poultry sector, and poultry imports continued to grow (Kumi 2015: 33).

In response, the Mahama administration launched the Broiler Revitalization Project in mid-2014, which placed poultry import quotas on importing firms, such that importers had to buy 40 percent of their produce from local sources in order to access licenses to import poultry. In order to make this policy feasible, the project aimed to increase local poultry production through direct support and created a 20 million cedis Poultry Stimulus Fund. The existing poultry firms were in dire need of access to investment and working capital in order to replace old equipment in hatcheries and revive parent stocks, and to employ and train workers, as most had stopped producing broiler chickens a decade ago.[35] However, the design of the project was such that it did not just provide cheaper inputs and access to credit, but

[34] Analysis Poultry Sector Ghana, Netherlands Enterprise Agency, October 16, 2014.

[35] In 2014, there were less than twenty large-scale private poultry firms, most of which produced mainly eggs, with limited production of broilers (chickens raised specifically for meat production, rather than laying eggs). Some of these firms operated their own feed mills, hatcheries and parent stock. The vast majority of poultry producers were medium and small-scale businesses, with the small-scale ones mainly producing broiler birds and the medium-scale businesses mainly producing eggs. Ibid.

rather had the state directly intervening to manage the supply chain. The Ministry of Food and Agriculture, which was implementing the project, selected the participating firms and coordinated inputs to firms along the supply chain by supplying fertilized eggs to hatcheries for the production of day-old chicks and by making their buffer stock of maize available for feed, as well as contracting firms to provide feed and contracting firms to provide chicks and birds for customers arranged by the project (Kumi 2015: 36–37). The role of the Ministry in the Broiler Revitalization Project was similar to that played by the PSI Secretariat in the PSI in Oil Palm (see Chapter 7).

While supermarkets had not yet complied with the import quota on poultry in 2015 due to insufficient local supply, local poultry traders were doing so, but complained that customers were not interested in buying the local chicken due to poor packaging and quality.[36] Similarly to the challenges in the rice sector, the problem was not just one of reducing the cost of production and thus prices of poultry, but also improving quality and developing marketing, branding and distribution of local products. In the poultry case, the direct intervention by the state in coordinating firms' production processes, instead of supporting firms to act on their own, was likely to result in lower not higher quality.

State-controlled industrial policy approaches by the Mahama administration were also found in the sugar sector. The administration sought to revive the Komenda sugar factory in the Central Region, which was established in the 1960s by the CPP government. The government used a US$35 million line of credit from the Exim Bank of India to finance a new sugar factory, and provided counterpart funding of US$1.26 million. At the time, critics argued that the plans to revive Komenda were unrealistic because the factory was undercapitalized and the catchment area around the factory was not large enough to grow sufficient sugar cane to feed the factory.[37] The factory was inaugurated by President Mahama in May 2016, but did not have sufficient

[36] "Poor Packaging of Local Birds Affecting Poultry Business," McAnthony Dagyenga, News Ghana, February 18, 2015, http://newsghana.com.gh/poor-packaging-of-local-birds-affecting-poultry-business (last accessed on December 15, 2015).

[37] "$36m Can't Revive Komenda Sugar Factory – IMANI," General News of Friday, August 22, 2014, Ghanaweb news, www.ghanaweb.com/GhanaHomePage/NewsArchive/36m-can-t-revive-Komenda-sugar-factory-IMANI-322455 (last accessed on November 24, 2015).

raw material and stopped working.[38] This experience is strikingly similar to the story of the Ayensu Starch Factory set up under the NPP government (see Chapter 7). It is also a repeat of the CPP government's strategy that set up the original Komenda sugar factory in 1967, which was financed and supplied by Czechoslovakia, but later collapsed as it was poorly planned and managed.

Conclusion: Return to Macroeconomic Crisis

A large proportion of the oil wealth was invested in the oil and gas sector with the objectives of making GNPC a strong state-owned oil company and building the infrastructure and processing plant required to use natural gas as a source of energy. Gas was expected to lower the cost of electricity generation by replacing expensive imported fuels used by the power sector with domestically produced and reasonably priced natural gas. The use of gas was also expected to reduce the need for fuel subsidies for the power sector and reduce overall oil imports. The gains were going to be significant. But the project to build the gas infrastructure was delayed by several years and cost much more than expected due to elite fragmentation and contestation within the NDC.

Outside the oil and gas sector, oil revenues were spent on infrastructure, but were spent very inefficiently, characterized by what IMF and World Bank reports refer to as "poor public financial management." What this really means is that Ghanaian governments have problems with prioritizing the allocation of budget revenue, in actually disbursing money as budgeted, and in keeping within budget ceilings. This in turn is driven by political pressures generated by competitive clientelism to distribute resources widely among the general population in order to win elections and remain in government. MPs and ministers fight over the allocation and spending of resources in their sectors and

38 "Komenda Sugar Factory Stops Working," Myjoyonline, www.myjoyonline.com/news/2016/June-24th/komenda-sugar-factory-shuts-down.php (last accessed January 17, 2017); "Komenda Sugar Factory to Resume Operations in November," Citifmonline, http://citifmonline.com/2016/10/07/komenda-sugar-factory-to-resume-operations-in-november (last accessed January 17, 2017); "Economic Plan for Komenda Sugar Factory Lacked 'Common Sense'," myjoyonline www.myjoyonline.com/news/2017/January-18th/economic-plan-for-komenda-sugar-factory-lacked-common-sense.php (last accessed January 17, 2017).

electoral constituencies so that at election time, they can point to their individual accomplishments. Spreading resources widely leads to spreading them thinly: starting too many projects with not enough resources to complete them, causing delays in disbursements, leading to delays in completions, and thus to costly extensions. Furthermore, resources were not always disbursed according to budget allocations, as occurred with the oil revenues when it was given to ministries not associated with the priority areas.

The NDC II government also used oil revenues to implement its key initiatives in agriculture and agro-processing, but most, if not all, of these initiatives followed a state-led approach. Notably, its block farms initiative and the creation of state-owned factories with foreign loans bear a strong resemblance to the state farms and factories set up under the CPP government in the 1960s. Notably, the Kufuor-led NPP government pursued similar initiatives, which highlights the broader tendency for politicians to be drawn to state-led industrial policies. The NDC II government did not seek to support local private firms in addressing production and productivity constraints in existing agro-industries, and when it did in the case of poultry, it sought to control the whole process. Nor did the NDC II government seek to incentivize domestic or foreign direct investments in new economic activities, such as sugar, but rather to set up factories itself.

The initiation of oil exports increased government revenues available for budgetary expenditure, but this did not stem the cyclical macroeconomic crises that occurred under the Fourth Republic. New oil wealth in the context of competitive clientelism led to spending what was available and more, as usual, leading to trade and fiscal deficits. This spending was characterized by distributive, consumption-driven expenditures and state-led investments in productive sectors, neither of which stimulated production and productivity gains to a significant extent. Despite growing private investments in agriculture and agro-processing, the economy remained too shallow, narrow and thin. As a result, when the international prices of gold and cocoa dropped at the same time, this external shock precipitated a significant macroeconomic crisis starting in 2012.

The fiscal deficit was not only due to overspending and the poor investments and management of public spending discussed above, but also to the growing public sector wage bill. As discussed in Chapter 4, the wage bill constituted a high proportion of government expenditure and had been a persistent source of budget overruns, but it was even higher than normal due to the implementation of the new Single Spine Pay policy in 2010.[39] This policy aimed to harmonize remuneration in the public service and to enhance the pay of public workers in a manner that was equitable and would improve productivity in the public sector. This pay reform had been a long time in the making and was not a spontaneous and reckless policy as many international financial commentators claimed. The introduction of the new pay structure led to an increase in almost all civil servants' salaries for several years in a row, while delays in moving staff to the single spine system also resulted in large salary arrears, leading to higher than budgeted costs. Furthermore, the growing energy shortage, with demand for electricity outstripping supply, led to short-term and more expensive measures such as buying oil to fuel the thermal plant, and then costly energy subsidies. Government overspending more than offset higher revenue from oil and led to a double-digit fiscal deficit in 2012 (Okudzeto et al. 2015: 6).

To fund the fiscal deficit, the NDC II government resorted to issuing short-term domestic bonds with high interest rates, which increased the cost of financing the domestic debt and the proportion of government revenue spent on servicing interest payments. At the same time, the current account deteriorated significantly, despite significant foreign direct investments, loans and portfolio inflows attracted by the high interest rates on domestic bonds. The growing trade deficit was the product of falling international prices of gold and cocoa beans since 2011 and thus lower than expected export receipts, combined with higher imports associated with the country's large foreign direct investments in the oil and gas sector. As a result of the fiscal and trade deficits, the government's net public debt increased, the currency depreciated, the Bank of Ghana's international reserves dwindled, and economic growth slowed as a result of weaker non-oil GDP growth.

The Mahama administration attempted to rectify the twin deficits after the 2012 elections by imposing taxes on certain imports and on profits in certain sectors, eliminating fuel subsidies, sharply raising electricity and water tariffs, and compressing other spending – the

39 This paragraph and the following ones draw on IMF and World Bank documents (IMF 2014, 2015; World Bank 2014). Information on the Single Spine Pay policy comes from Seniwoliba (2014).

classic austerity measures of Ghanaian governments. However, the government's efforts were thwarted by several external and domestic factors. Continued disruptions in the power supply and high interest rates on credit (due to the government's borrowing needs) led to slower growth. The value of exports fell faster than imports due to continued declines in international prices for gold and cocoa beans, especially gold. Growing oil production made up for most of the losses from lower gold and cocoa exports, but the imports of goods and services outpaced exports, causing the trade deficit to grow. As a result, the cedi depreciated almost 15 percent in 2013. Inflation surged due to the removal of subsidies and the pass-through effects of currency depreciation in an economy that depended heavily on imported goods, as well as to deficit financing by the government through the Bank of Ghana.

Then the cedi experienced a shockingly steep depreciation between January and August 2014 caused by net outflows from the capital account – in other words, capital flight. The government had become more reliant on private foreign capital through domestic debt instruments, which made the country vulnerable to capital flight. The depreciation of the cedi in 2013 caused foreign investors currency translation losses that exceeded their interest rate gains.[40] When this happened, they exited their investments, which further accelerated the currency's depreciation.[41] Another source of capital flight was speculative trading in foreign exchange.

The Mahama-led NDC government produced its own austerity plan in the first half of 2014, but when it declared in July 2014 that it would not seek support from the IMF, the cedi took a steep fall indicating foreign investors' lack of confidence in the government's ability to implement economic austerity without IMF backing. Returning to where this book began with Kwesi Botchwey's words, the Ghanaian economy was clearly in a crisis and had to seek an IMF bailout, both for balance of payments support and to signal confidence in its currency.

40 "Ghana Looks to Reverse Capital Flight," July 24, 2014, www.ghanaweb.com/GhanaHomePage/NewsArchive/artikel.php?ID=318350 (last accessed on September 7, 2015).

41 "During the first half of 2014, non-residents repatriated US$1.1 billion of income generated in Ghana, almost doubling the US$0.6 billion repatriated during the first half of 2013" (World Bank 2014: 3).

Conclusion: Can Industrial Policy Work in Ghana?

This book has shown that Ghana experienced limited progress in transforming its economy away from the colonial trading economy inherited at independence. While the structural adjustment reforms implemented in the 1980s stopped the economic decline and led to renewed growth, they served to rehabilitate the colonial trading economy structure, rather than transform it. Subsequent economic policies in the 1990s and 2000s did not result in substantial advances in export diversification, increasing agricultural productivity, industrial upgrading or deepening, or increasing the technological capabilities of locally owned firms and farms. In short, new productive sectors were not developed that generated exports or substitutes for imports and created forward and backward linkages on a scale that significantly broadened and deepened the "fragile" economic structure. Furthermore, governments continued to overspend, largely due to distributive expenditures, and finance fiscal deficits through domestic and external debt. As a result, the country found itself back in a macroeconomic crisis after the 2012 elections, and the Mahama-led NDC government had to ask for an IMF bailout in 2014.

While Ghana experienced sustained economic growth since the structural adjustment period, what matters for economic transformation are the specific drivers of growth. Between 1985 and 2000, growth was driven by initial gains from liberalization policy changes, increased imports funded by World Bank and IMF lending, the rehabilitation of the traditional gold and cocoa export sectors, investments in infrastructure, and increased government spending supported by foreign aid. Increased growth rates in the second half of the 2000s were driven by increased production of gold and cocoa exports on the back of increasing international prices for these commodities after a decade of stagnant world prices, as well as growth in services. The growth spike after 2010 was due to the start of oil production and exports, but the sharp decline in global commodity prices between 2012 and 2014 led to a similarly sharp drop in growth.

From the 2000s, economic growth was increasingly consumption driven and led by services. By 2014, the service sector contributed 50 percent of GDP, followed by the industry sector (which in Ghana's statistical accounts includes mining, manufacturing and construction) at 28.5 percent of GDP, and the agricultural sector at around 21 percent. More than one-third of the service sector involves public and government-related services such as administration, health and education. The share of industry remained almost constant, but within the industry sector, the share of manufacturing declined. Within agriculture, there were significant differences between growth rates in cocoa and in staple crop production. Most of the increased agricultural production was due to expansion in the land area cultivated rather than improved productivity, and the main driver was cocoa cultivation. Yields were stagnant, with the Ministry of Food and Agriculture noting that yields for most crops were 20 to 60 percent below their achievable level with available technologies, including fertilizers and improved seeds.

In other words, extensive constraints on agricultural and industrial transformation remained. The NDC and NPP governments in the 1990s, 2000s and the first half of the 2010s had a poor record with pursuing and successfully implementing industrial policies aimed at overcoming these constraints. The sector case studies in horticulture export and palm oil processing presented in this book illustrated in detail the range of first- and second-order constraints on productivity that domestic firms and farms faced.

First order constraints on productivity concern factors external to firms that lead to high production costs, but which are costly or impossible for individual firms or farms to address on their own. They include a lack of infrastructure or the poor state of infrastructure, the lack of reliable access to electricity, and the lack of finance at modest interest rates and moratorium periods conducive to risky investments in commercial farming, agro-processing and manufacturing. Other constraints included the limited supply of skilled labor such as engineers and electricians and the absence of skilled labor with technical and practice experience in new industries, which required firms to cover the cost of training labor. The absence of public institutions in research and development that worked with firms, except in the cocoa sector, meant that firms had to bear the costs of research and development individually, if they undertook it at all. Agribusiness and agro-processing firms faced additional challenges regarding access to land and organizing a sufficient supply of raw materials as well as enforcing property rights in land, which led to higher costs of production and in the case of the agribusiness firms in the southern horticulture belt, insecurity about the future of their farms.

Second order constraints concern factors internal to firms, in particular their technological capabilities, which are knowledge-based assets regarding the technical, managerial and organizational skills necessary to make firms function efficiently. They involve tacit knowledge that can only be acquired through learning by doing, and require conscious investments in building such capabilities in order to reach international levels of efficiency and to maintain them, as international competition, global standards and buyers' requirements constantly change. Investing in building capabilities is costly and risky, and thus entrepreneurs, especially first generation capitalists, undertake the minimum required and do not invest in continuous learning and moving into new economic activities.

The high production costs due to first-order constraints, combined with the hard-to-acquire technological capabilities required to create profitable businesses, deter private investment because these investments involve a period of loss making and risk due the uncertainty that firms will eventually become profitable. Industrial policy is necessary to encourage private investments by solving first-order constraints and underwriting the risk and financing losses incurred while firms are becoming competitive in domestic and international markets. The next question, then, is why Ghanaian governments did not perform better in terms of implementing industrial policies. The elaborated political settlements theoretical framework presented in Chapter 1 argued that rather than state insulation from business interests, collusion between ruling political elites and capitalist firms is necessary if governments are to pursue and successfully implement industrial policies. But not just any kind of collusion will work.

The Politics of Industrial Policy Implementation in Ghana

The key factor that makes industrial policies work is whether they address the concerns of investors about their ability to profit in the future from investment decisions. Investors do not pursue new economic activities if the risk of not succeeding (becoming competitive) is too high. Government support can reduce uncertainty, but investors want predictability of government actions, including that the promised political support will be provided. This predictability has been referred to as a credible commitment that government will do what it says. This kind of predictability and credible commitment can occur even when the overall business environment is poor. What is required are close relations between ruling elites and relevant investors, and for close relations to emerge, ruling elites and investors must have mutual interests.

Ruling elites in all countries need investment in order to maintain or increase the rate of economic activity, to enlarge the tax base, to increase national wealth and the geo-political or military power of the state, and to keep a sufficient part of the population satisfied so that the incumbent government will win the next election and/or face less public dissent (Moore and Schmitz 2008). The higher the proportion of the population depending on formal employment generated by private investment, the greater is the dependence of ruling elites on capitalists for political survival. The capacity of investors to withhold this investment is conventionally termed the structural power of capitalists. However, in developing countries such as Ghana, the structural power of capitalists is weak and a small proportion of the population depends on formal employment generated by private investment. In Ghana, not only does a small percentage of the population depend on capitalists for employment, but also the public sector employs slightly more people than the formal private sector.

Thus, whether ruling elites have an interest in supporting domestic capitalists depends on whether they need those capitalists for their primary objective of political survival. Mutual interests in Ghana have been rare. Domestic capitalists with capabilities in productive sectors have been small in number, and they have not been important players in the major pillars of the economy. Even foreign firms have not been able to create strong mutual interests with ruling political elites, as shown in the case of the Oil Palm PSI. This is because the high level of elite fragmentation within the NDC and NPP political parties makes it difficult for such mutual interests to really drive policy implementation unless a large enough group of ruling elites can be brought on board. When there is intense jockeying for the top political positions among ruling elites, this situation is difficult to achieve. Weak domestic capitalists and a lack of mutual interests have meant that ruling elites did not typically pursue industrial policies in collusion with a group of domestic capitalists.

In other countries where ruling elites were not dependent on (a group of) domestic capitalists for their political survival or for financing the state, they have relied on foreign direct investment and state-owned enterprises. The political incentive to take this route was to avoid promoting the development of an independent local capitalist class that might threaten their own rule.[1] While state-led industrial policies in which the state plays a central role as manager or owner of the productive investment, through state-owned or party-owned enterprises for example, are a strategy that worked in some countries, they worked because of the particular political context, or distribution of power, in those countries. State-led industrial policies have not worked in Ghana due to competitive clientelism.

Competitive clientelism occurs in Ghana because ruling elites face a high vulnerability in government due to powerful political factions outside the ruling coalition that are capable of winning elections (or in earlier periods, capable of mounting a coup), combined with a high level of fragmentation within the ruling coalition and a high degree of fragmentation among ruling elites. High vulnerability led to short time horizons of ruling elites, while dependence on an array of local groups and alliances meant a large number of distributional demands being placed on ruling elites in return for that support. Ruling elites distributed state resources and economic opportunities linked to the state as patronage to keep the ruling political coalition together and as a strategy to win elections. However, the high degree of elite fragmentation within political coalitions meant that no one group of ruling elites could centralize control over the distribution of resources and opportunities.

This dispersion of power within the ruling coalition made it difficult for ruling elites pushing industrial policies to secure the financing required for large state interventions, and made it difficult for bureaucrats designing and implementing the policies to resist distributional demands from within the ruling coalition that could distort the

[1] For example, this political strategy was evident among ruling elites in Vietnam (Moore and Schmitz 2008).

economic objectives and implementation of such industrial policies. In other words, it was difficult for pockets of efficiency to emerge, much less pockets of efficiency that could successfully implement state-led industrial policies. Nonetheless, there are some cases of pockets of efficiency within the state bureaucracy in Ghana since the 1980s.

These cases where a pocket of efficiency has emerged include the state-run Cocoa Marketing Board, especially the Cocoa Marketing Company; the Ministry of Health in implementing industrial policies for the pharmaceutical industry; and the state-owned Ghana National Petroleum Company and its role in the oil industry discussed in the previous chapter. In concluding, the chapter considers the conditions under which the pockets of efficiency emerged in the cocoa export and pharmaceutical industries and the lessons that can be learned from these cases when thinking about what kind of industrial policies could work in Ghana.

Exceptional Cases of Pockets of Efficiency in Ghana

The Cocoa Marketing Board from the 1980s onward became a pocket of efficiency within the state bureaucracy, which is ironic given that many observers singled out the marketing board as the cause of economic decline in the postindependence period. The types of industrial policies implemented by the Cocoa Board include its large role in the internal marketing of cocoa, quality control, setting the producer price, and monopoly on export marketing – functions that it has performed well since the reforms in the 1980s and that have resulted in Ghanaian cocoa beans receiving a premium on the international market.

Several factors explain the creation and maintenance of the pocket of efficiency within the Cocoa Marketing Board.[2] First, the technical expertise built up over time among local staff in the Cocoa Board was not lost during the years of economic decline or during the structural adjustment reforms. Compared to other parts of the state bureaucracy, the quality control and export management functions of the cocoa marketing system always functioned relatively well (Hubbard 2003; Williams 2009). The Cocoa Marketing Company had an institutional

[2] This analysis is a summary of the more detailed discussion in Whitfield et al. (2015: 236–243).

history of recruiting staff based on merit and providing extensive training to its employees, and its officials interacted primarily with international buyers and maintained a great deal of autonomy from the rest of the state bureaucracy.

Second, PNDC elites supported measures to make the operations of the Cocoa Board as a whole more efficient and decrease its operating costs, in order to increase the producer price paid to farmers. The political driver was the economic importance of the cocoa sector in the 1980s in terms of GDP, exports, and government revenue, rather than mutual interests. Third, the PNDC government and then the NDC government gradually reduced its reliance on revenue generated by taxing the cocoa export sector, and the value-added tax introduced in the late 1990s became the new source of generating government revenue. Furthermore, foreign aid inflows from the 1980s onward provided a new source of financing for distributional expenditures, reducing the need to tax the cocoa sector for this purpose as in the past. The NDC and NPP governments had political imperatives to keep the producer price of cocoa high as an electoral strategy, given the large proportion of the population dependent on incomes from the cocoa sector. Lastly, the Cocoa Marketing Company became financially self-sufficient during the 1990s, raising international finance with which to buy the cocoa crop and finance its operations. However, there are clear limits to this pocket of efficiency, in terms of increasing the productivity of cocoa farmers, as discussed in Chapter 4.

Another case of a pocket of efficiency in the state bureaucracy can be found in the department of the Ministry of Health responsible for pharmaceutical services and the pharmaceutical division of the state-owned Ghana Industrial Holding Corporation before it was privatized in the late 1990s. The Ministry of Health implemented a series of industrial policies with the explicit aim of developing a local pharmaceutical manufacturing industry. It is necessary to summarize what these industrial policies entailed, before trying to explain how this pocket of efficiency emerged.[3]

The industrial policies included the creation of a protected market through a ban on importing specified basic medicines, a 15 percent marginal preference to local drug manufacturing firms in public

[3] The empirical details of the pharmaceutical industry and industrial policies targeting it are drawn from the research conducted by Wong (2017).

procurement processes involving government money (donors did not follow this policy), and an exemption from value added tax on ingredients for manufacturing essential drugs.[4] Furthermore, the Ministry of Health pushed local manufacturing firms to upgrade their facilities and manufacturing practices in order to comply with international standards, so that more medicines could be procured locally.[5] These measures led to private domestic and foreign investment in the sector in the 1990s and early 2000s, resulting in 30 percent of drugs purchased by the Ministry of Health being procured locally by 2016.

Why were bureaucrats in the Ministry of Health able to transcend the usual politics of industrial policy in Ghana, despite the pharmaceutical industry being small and not a major pillar of the economy? The import ban had been in place since the early 1970s, with an expansion over time of the list of banned imported medicines. Pharmaceutical products that could be produced locally were banned, probably due to severe balance of payments constraints at the time, although the ingredients still had to be imported. But the ban was only possible because local production already existed by the State Pharmaceutical Corporation, which was established in 1967 and subsumed as a division of the Ghana Industrial Holding Corporation (GIHOC) in 1968. GIHOC Pharmaceuticals was the best performing division of the state-owned holding company and relatively profitable due to the financial and technical support provided by the United Nations Industrial Development Organization (UNIDO) in the 1970s, but also due to the specific economic relationship between GIHOC Pharmaceuticals and the Ministry of Health. GIHOC Pharmaceuticals was protected from international competition through the ban on some imported drugs, was able to access foreign exchange and import licenses to import key ingredients (even during the economic downturn of the 1970s) due to its special "social welfare" status, and had a secured market and constant demand through public procurement at the Ministry of Health. Thus, mutual interests, even

4 The marginal preference is effectively a 15 percent tariff on the prices of foreign firms in public procurement tenders where foreign and local firms are bidding to provide the same drugs.

5 Donor funds could only be used to procure medicines from manufacturing firms that complied with international standards, as specified by the World Health Organization.

mutual dependence, developed between GIHOC Pharmaceuticals and the Ministry of Health, as the former was the main domestic supplier and the latter was the main domestic buyer, and increasing the capacity of GIHOC Pharmaceuticals was in the interest of the Ministry, which wanted to source cheaper medicines locally. UNIDO programs provided the technical expertise to help GIHOC Pharmaceuticals to increase its capabilities.

The Ministry of Health managed to maintain the import ban, and later extend the list of medicines banned, despite trade liberalization in the 1980s and 1990s, based on the argument that having a local pharmaceutical manufacturing industry increased social welfare (Wong 2017). The ban encouraged new firms to invest in pharmaceutical manufacturing in the 1990s. Many of them had been importers and distributors of medicines, but as the cedi depreciated in the 1990s, they looked into local manufacturing with imported ingredients. The list of medicines that were banned from import gave them an incentive, and these investors used capital from their trading businesses to enter manufacturing. Several joint ventures also emerged. But new entrants into the industry declined in the mid-2000s, as the Ministry of Health started to require that firms meet the basic international standards set by the World Health Organization in order to get a license to manufacture medicines. To help the existing firms upgrade their factories and practices to comply with international standards, several international organizations provided technical and financial support. When GIHOC Pharmaceuticals was privatized in 1998, retrenched staff found jobs in the new local drug manufacturing companies, which benefited both sides, as the new local firms were able to access skilled labor and tacit knowledge. As the main buyer, the Ministry of Health encouraged and in some cases demanded that the firms develop new drugs. Having the government as the main buyer created a constant and secure market demand for these firms. Lastly, but equally important, the manufacturing process involved mostly imported materials and was not dependent on domestically produced raw materials.

Several key features of this case explain why the Ministry of Health was able to implement industrial policies rather successfully. Mutual interests developed between the Ministry of Health and GIHOC Pharmaceuticals, which was later extended to include the new local firms as well. The interest on the side of the Ministry was a genuine belief that having a local pharmaceutical manufacturing industry was vital for public health. These industrial policies supporting the pharmaceutical industry garnered support from NDC and NPP elites because supporting the pharmaceutical sector industry was legitimized as supporting the health sector, and expanding and upgrading local pharmaceutical manufacturing had a direct impact on a large percentage of the population through greater access to medicines and cheaper medicines. This does not mean that competitive clientelism had no effects. Wong (2017) indicates that implementation of direct support to pharmaceutical manufacturers by the Mahama-led NDC government in 2015 went to some firms and not others, and anecdotal evidence indicates that the owners of these firms were said to be politically aligned with the NDC.

There are several aspects that the cocoa and pharmaceutical cases share in common. Economically, the industrial policies involved only partial liberalization of the sectors. While the partial liberalization served different purposes in the two industries, the point is that gradual liberalization was a key feature of the industrial policy. This required that ruling political elites and civil servants counter arguments of the World Bank and IMF staff for full liberalization. Notably, international agencies and corporations operating in the sectors also supported these counter arguments. These sectors garnered the interest of ruling political elites even under the Fourth Republic because the industries had a significant impact on a large proportion of the population and achievements in these industries could be used as campaign tools during election time, and thus made good sense as part of the general political survival strategies. The bureaucratic agencies involved had significant technical expertise accumulated over time. The mutual interests that drove the industrial policy were between the government agency and state-owned enterprises, at least initially, and not between political elites and domestic capitalists. Most notably, these industrial policies did not require major resources and depend on budgeted revenues actually materializing. The Cocoa Marketing Board became financially self-sufficient through raising finance on international capital markets. The industrial policies in the pharmaceutical industry did not involve significant government expenditures but rather changes to institutions, such as an import ban. The Ministry of Health incentivized firms to increase their capabilities, but international donors such as UNIDO provided the financial and technical resources with which to do so.

Industrialization and Industrial Policies: Which Way Forward?

In concluding, let us consider what kind of industrial policies could work in Ghana in light of these exceptional cases and the cases of failed industrial policies discussed in earlier chapters of the book. In doing so, it is important to consider the different paths of industrialization and the different kinds of industrial policy required to facilitate them. Paths to industrialization typically have been discussed in terms of import substitution industrialization *or* export-oriented industrialization, but this is a false dichotomy. Import-substitution and export-oriented industrializations were and remain inherently linked.

Historically, Asian countries used both industrialization strategies simultaneously. Japan, South Korea and Taiwan used import protection extensively for some final consumer goods as part of import substitution industrialization strategies, but also had liberal policies toward the import of intermediate goods for assembly and manufacture in export processing zones.[6] While Asian countries are most known for export-oriented industrialization and leveraging participation in global production networks to transform their economies, most value added occurred in production for the domestic market. In a background paper for UNCTAD's 2016 Trade and Development Report, Cornelia Staritz (2016) notes that in eleven Asian countries, domestic market-targeted value added was between 50 to 80 percent, with production for global and regional value chains claiming the remainder. Christina Wolf (2017) also emphasizes that key to South Korea, Taiwan and China's successful transformation was a process of domestic-market formation, including growth in domestic demand for both final consumer products and intermediate products across sectors.

Export-oriented industrialization was also important, because it increased the foreign exchange earnings of developing countries in light of the continuously declining and volatile international prices for agricultural and natural resource commodity exports. Foreign exchange was needed to pay for the imported capital and intermediate goods necessary for import substitution. Export-oriented industrialization was also useful for overcoming limited domestic demand due to generally low incomes in developing countries. Engaging in production

[6] On this point, see the work of Alice Amsden, Robert Wade and Peter Evans, as well as the UNECA's Economic Report on Africa 2016, Greening Africa's Industrialization.

for export also required obtaining state-of-the art technology and learning how to produce efficiently (raise productivity to be able to compete with international prices) and meet international quality standards. In other words, engaging in exports required technology transfer in ways that producing for the domestic market did not.

However, the nature of export-oriented industrialization changed significantly as international trade became less and less about producing final consumer products in one country and shipping them to another country for sale, and more about global production networks. Since the 1970s, corporations in the United States, European countries and Japan began setting up production facilities in East Asia, Mexico and other locations, in order to reduce production costs and export finished goods back to their home markets. After 1989, transnational corporations also set up operations in China, India and Brazil. As these countries also developed locally owned firms with manufacturing capabilities, Western transnational companies increasingly outsourced to them, and began focusing on marketing, branding and retailing rather than production. The result was to break up the production process and disperse it across multiple countries, leading to what are called global production networks, or global value chains. Regional global value chains also emerged, for example in Asia, where countries' economies and firms are integrally linked in the production of capital, intermediate and final consumer goods, especially in electronics.[7] By 2009, world exports of intermediate goods exceeded the combined export values of final and capital goods for the first time (Staritz 2016). Thus, creating nontraditional export sectors in manufacturing and even agro-processing now means entering global value chains.

In many ways, this global dispersion of production makes it easier for African countries to export, as they do not have to create entire industries that are internationally competitive but rather master one step or task in the global value chain. The first step is typically the labor-intensive assembly of inputs manufactured in other countries. This makes it easier for African countries in that the technologically advanced and capital-intensive economic activities take place elsewhere. Participating in global value chains still provides the same

[7] The literature on global value chains is vast. A good entry piece is the relatively recent article by Gary Gereffi (2014).

opportunities as in the past, in terms of technology transfer and productivity increases through learning international best practices and state-of-the art technology as well as achieving economies of scale (lower production costs from producing a large volume of goods, which would not be possible if only producing for the domestic market, where demand is lower due to lower incomes) and economies of scope (lower production costs from producing a variety of complementary products).

However, exporting through global value chains has disadvantages compared to the previous export-oriented industrialization process in which entire industries, such as textile and apparel or automobiles, were created in one country. Labor-intensive assembly manufacturing for export initially has limited linkages to the rest of the domestic economy and net foreign exchange earnings are low. High competition in this segment of global value chains has reduced unit values, leading to falling international prices. Nevertheless, developing country firms still have to meet increasingly stringent requirements with regard to quality, fast delivery, and compliance with safety, social and environmental standards (which raise the start-up costs of investment). This means that even with large supplies of low cost unskilled labor, African countries have not easily entered the low value segments of manufacturing global value chains such as apparel and footwear. Profit margins are low, so firms have to reach high productivity levels in order to be viable in labor-intensive assembly manufacturing.

Labor-intensive assembly also provides limited linkages to the domestic economy and limited opportunities for creating skilled labor and building the capabilities of domestic firms. Buyers prefer supplier firms to source inputs from their global supplier networks, so that they can ensure consistency in products produced in multiple countries. Buyers can approve the use of locally produced inputs once they reach international standards of quality and consistency, but that can take some time. Moving into higher value added activities within global value chains is not always easy, and can be actively discouraged by global buyers and retailers. Furthermore, as all developing country firms attempt to upgrade – move into higher value activities – at the same time, the increasing competition and asymmetric power relations with buyers force unit prices down and result in less value added actually being achieved.

Therefore, developing greater linkages within the domestic economy and producing products with greater value added and requiring greater skills and capabilities among domestic firms is more likely to occur with production for the domestic market, at least initially. This is why import-substitution industrialization is equally important for economic transformation. The growth of domestic manufacturing industries in consumer products initially with largely imported inputs can provide sufficient demand to make it possible for industries to emerge that produce intermediate inputs locally. Thus, import-substitution industrialization creates more backward and forward linkages in the manufacturing process, as well as "side" linkages through the creation and growth of the transport, communications, marketing, distribution and other services linked to domestic manufacturing and retail.

The type of industrial policies needed to promote exports through entering global value chains are very different from those required to facilitate import substitution industrialization. Furthermore, in Ghana, the specific types of industrial policies used to promote import substitution need to distinguish between manufacturing production for the domestic market with imported inputs, and manufacturing production for the domestic market with locally produced agricultural inputs. Increasing agricultural productivity is necessary to solve the raw material supply problem and make agro-processing industries viable. Rather than combining initiatives to promote agriculture and agro-processing as in the past, they should be considered separately, as discussed below.

Export-oriented industrialization has become GVC-oriented industrialization, and it requires thinking about industrial policies to promote this kind of industrialization (Gereffi and Sturgeon 2013). Retailers and branded manufacturers in wealthy countries specialize in international sourcing from supplier firms, and depend on what are called first-tier suppliers that manage and coordinate production and sourcing networks. These first-tier suppliers are also transnational producers as they invest in production facilities around the world to produce manufactured goods as well as source them from independent suppliers. While retailers and branded manufacturers can source directly from developing country suppliers, new suppliers are more likely to enter global value chains as second-tier suppliers selling to these transnational producers/first-tier suppliers. It is these global first-tier suppliers that are responsible for most of the foreign direct investment in manufacturing in developing countries. But retailers and branded manufacturers (who often just own brands and no longer actually manufacture) "drive" the global value chains because they specify the exact characteristics of what their suppliers must produce and how they should produce it.

Thus, industrial policies promoting GVC-industrialization must help locally owned firms build manufacturing capabilities, such as meeting rigorous international standards regarding efficiency, quality and delivery deadlines, as well as non-manufacturing capabilities, such as establishing connections and interacting with buyers. This is difficult for African governments to do, as bureaucratic agencies initially have little knowledge about international standards and marketing relationships. Therefore, the method of entering global value chains used by almost all, if not all, developing countries has been to attract foreign direct investment from transnational producers already participating in these global value chains, and then build linkages with these foreign suppliers. The linkages can be through interactions between locally owned firms and foreign firms, including subcontracting arrangements, or through local employees in foreign firms that later leave and set up their own companies after having gained knowledge and experience from the foreign firm. After the simple skills are mastered, industrial policy can aim at creating more linkages between the domestic economy and assembly for export, through developing input supplier firms.

In sum, entering global value chains at the assembly stage requires industrial policy aimed at attracting strategic foreign direct investment. This is what the Ethiopian government has done in order to increase apparel exports, albeit after several attempts at other kinds of industrial policies to promote apparel exports with minimal results (Staritz and Whitfield 2017). The Ethiopian government, like the Ghanaian government with the Garment PSI, initially sought to promote locally owned firms in apparel exporting through financial incentives and infrastructural support, but this was not sufficient for them to succeed. Then the Ethiopian government courted retailers and branded manufacturers, which in turn encouraged their preferred first-tier suppliers to set up factories in Ethiopia. The government also engaged in direct discussions with first-tier suppliers.

Foreign direct investment is crucial for facilitating GVC-industrialization, but in Ghana, governments have not been interested in promoting foreign direct investment. There are historical reasons for this. Colonial rule led to a domestic economy that was dominated by foreign firms and investors, and political independence was equated with economic independence. In the absence of domestic capitalists with capabilities in large-scale production, Ghanaian governments turned to state investment or joint ventures between the state and foreign capital, but always with a dominant role for the state. Government attempts to privatize state-owned enterprises usually met with resistance from leftist intellectuals against foreign participation, but also from domestic entrepreneurs. Since the 1980s, that has changed somewhat, as the privatization drive in the 1990s and 2000s led to domestic entrepreneurs taking over some state-owned enterprises and an increase in foreign direct investments. Nevertheless, NDC and NPP governments have not promoted industrial policies that seek to encourage foreign direct investment and use it to build local manufacturing expertise. For example, during deliberations on how to use the money in the MCA compact, horticulture experts suggested encouraging foreign direct investment and using it as a means to help local exporters improve their capabilities, but this idea was rejected. Ghanaian governments will have to change their view of foreign direct investment if they want to develop nontraditional export sectors and enter global value chains. This type of industrial policy could be politically feasible if sold to politicians on the grounds of creating jobs, and it is more likely to succeed in that the implementing role of the state is minor and it does not involve substantial outlays from the government budget.

Industrial policy for domestic market production generally requires a different approach than industrial policies to promote GVC-industrialization. It typically targets goods where there is already a high domestic demand that is being met with imports, but, as mentioned earlier, we should distinguish between production with locally sourced raw materials, and production with mostly imported raw materials.

In Ghana, industrialization is typically thought of in terms of processing raw materials in the country, either agricultural products or minerals. For example, the District Industrialization Program and the President's Special Initiatives under the Kufuor administrations embodied this idea of industrialization through processing local agricultural crops. The NDC II government also pursued this idea in its focus on promoting agro-processing in sugar, fish and rice, and Akufo-Addo's NPP government continued to pursue the idea of the District Industrialization Program under the colloquial name "one district, one factory."

However, much of the existing industrial production in Ghana does not use raw material produced in the country, but rather relies on imported inputs, as evident from the enterprise mapping done by Sutton and Kpentey (2012). Furthermore, the exceptional success case of the pharmaceutical industry and the failed cases of industrial policy in cassava starch and palm oil indicate that strategies of import-substitution in Ghana need to abandon the idea of value-added processing of locally produced raw materials, at least initially. Just because the raw material is traditionally produced in Ghana does not make it a good candidate for import-substitution, in fact, probably the opposite. This is because the production of traditional crops is embedded in particular social relations and structured by existing marketing arrangements, which means that industrial production competes for the supply of raw material and it is hard to get farmers to adopt industrial varieties of the crop.

In promoting agro-processing, it would be better to select processed goods that involve producing nontraditional crops, and thus do not have a parallel market, or where the raw material is imported initially. Productivity in agricultural crop production needs to be increased before trying to create agro-processing industries using locally sourced raw materials. Factories could function first with imported materials, and later source domestically. This strategy involves working to increase the productivity of agricultural production and specific agro-processing firms separately.

In order for smallholder farmers to invest in productivity, they must have access to credit but also a secure market and good prices, which in turn requires an efficient distribution system and wholesale outlets. The spread of supermarkets in Ghana provides an incentive, as they can offer higher prices to farmers whose produce meets their quality standards, but this requires investments in a distribution system and cold chain infrastructure. The challenge for industrial policy in this area is to find a private investor model that works. Access to fertilizer and irrigation is important for increasing agricultural productivity among smallholder farmers, but they might succeed better through outgrower schemes in which commercial farmers provide such inputs with some kind of indirect support from the government. The government could encourage commercial farms and firms to come together and act collectively through industry associations to solve first- and second-order constraints, and the government could partially finance the solutions along with firms. The main risk is that the government would have to monitor the industry associations to ensure that the firms use the money as envisaged and are investing in learning. But even part of this role of monitoring could be given to the industry association, using a mechanism of peer monitoring where infringements of one firm affect them all.[8]

Existing industries in Ghana producing goods for the domestic market, such as cement, plastics and chemicals, are small and dominated by a few large firms. They import most of their raw materials, and they are not large enough to create the demand necessary to stimulate local production of raw materials or to catalyze the development of upstream industries. Such industries must grow if they are to facilitate industrialization through backward and forward linkages in the economy. Industrial policy to support such industries entails the standard tools used by other developed countries, including now wealthy countries when they were industrializing. They include import tariffs to temporarily shield local producers from international competition while they are increasing productivity and learning to produce higher-quality products, use of local content regulations in public procurement to increase demand, access to low-cost, long-term financing to reduce start-up investment costs and provide working capital, and subsidizing the cost of accessing technical and tacit knowledge through foreign experts and learning by doing.

The Ghanaian economy continued to teeter on the edge of macroeconomic instability and a looming debt crisis in 2017.[9] Fiscal targets

[8] This kind of business-led industrial policy has worked in many countries. See the country chapters in Maxfield and Schneider (1997) as well as Schneider's work on Latin American countries (Schneider 2004).

[9] IMF Press Release, "Ghana: Staff Concluding Statement of the 2017 Article IV Consultation Mission and Discussions for the Fourth Review under the Extended Credit Facility," April 13, 2017, www.imf.org/en/News/Articles/2017/04/13/ms041317-ghana-staff-concluding-statement-of-the-2017-article-iv-consultation-discussions-for-ecf (last accessed on August 28, 2017); 2017 Post-Budget Analysis, ISSER Policy Brief, Vol. 5, March 2017, Institute of Statistical, Social and Economic Research (ISSER), University of Ghana.

under the IMF lending agreement were missed in 2016 as a result of overspending in the lead up to the December 2016 elections, which the NDC lost. The budget deficit was 8.7 percent of GDP, more than 3 percent of GDP above the target. The NDC II government financed the spike in the budget deficit largely through domestic debt. According to government accounts, "nonbanks" hold a large amount of domestic debt, which is an indicator of the importance of foreign investors in the domestic bond market, since these nonbank investors are largely international funds. This situation further undermined debt sustainability, with possible pressures on the exchange rate if financing conditions deteriorate. By December 2016, the country's debt stock reached a level of about 73 percent of GDP, which was in excess of the debt sustainability threshold of 70 percent. Total debt represented 266 percent of exports, 363 percent of budget revenue, and 475 percent of tax revenue. The rising public debt stock resulted in high debt-service costs, with interest payments consuming nearly 42 percent of tax revenue. Of the total public debt, 68.9 percent was external debt. Continuing currency depreciation could lead to a rapid increase in the value of the external debt, putting its sustainability further in doubt.

This book has argued that Ghana's recurrent macroeconomic and debt problems arise not only from the "fragile" structure of the colonial trading economy, but also from the combination of competitive clientelism with weak domestic capitalists that shape the political survival strategies of ruling elites across both political parties in Ghana. The high degree of vulnerability in government and the high degree of intraelite contestation within the political parties produce short time horizons among political leaders. As a result, ruling political elites prioritize distributive expenditures that can be used to reward patron-client networks and provide public and quasi-public goods and services to a large number of voters. The political pressures to distribute resources widely even affected the content and implementation of industrial policies. Both NDC and NPP governments used state-led investments in agriculture, agro-processing and manufacturing as a way to try to do two things at once: promote economic transformation and win more votes. The success record with this approach has not been very encouraging. Because the formal private sector in Ghana is small, domestic capitalists have had only limited political influence on the content and implementation of industrial policies. As a result, industrial policies in Ghana have rarely involved supporting existing domestic firms to expand production and increase productivity, or incentivizing them to move into new economic activities or upgrade in existing ones.

The kinds of industrial policies suggested in this chapter will be politically less attractive to politicians than distributive spending and state-led industrial policies, but they are cheaper and likely to have a much bigger impact in terms of facilitating economic transformation. Such industrial policies will have to be "sold" to political elites as a good political strategy for winning elections. Assessments of the likely impacts of a particular industrial policy on job creation and increased incomes would help to convince politicians, as well as targeting investments to locations in the "swing" regions of the electoral landscape. To be well implemented, they will have to find support within the state bureaucracy and some kind of mutual interests that can drive implementation and lobby for the policy when it hits resistance or challenges. Getting the politics of industrial policy right is indeed much harder than "rolling back the state" or "getting the prices right."

Appendix A: MCA Compact

The five-year (2007–2012), approximately US$547 million Millennium Challenge Compact was aimed at reducing poverty by raising farmer incomes through private sector-led, agribusiness development. The project focused on increasing the production and productivity of high-value cash and food staple crops in twenty-three districts across the Northern Region, Afram Basin region and the southern horticultural belt, and at enhancing the competitiveness of Ghana's export base in horticultural and other traditional crops. The program consisted of three projects:

Agriculture Project:

- *Farmer and Enterprise Training in Commercial Agriculture*: Accelerate the development of commercial skills and capacity among farmer-based organizations (FBOs) and their business partners, including entities adding value to agricultural crops such as processors and marketers.
- *Irrigation Development*: Establish a limited number of retention ponds and weirs requested by the FBOs and FBO partnerships for whom access to water is critical to the success of their businesses.
- *Land Tenure Facilitation*: Improve tenure security for existing land users and facilitate access to land for higher-value agricultural crops in the Intervention Zones.
- *Improvement of Post Harvest Handling and Value Chain Services*: Facilitate strategic investments by FBOs and FBO partnerships in postharvest infrastructure improvements and build the capacity of the public sector to introduce and monitor compliance with international plant protection standards.

- *Improvement of Credit Services for On-Farm and Value Chain Investments*: Augment the supply of, and access to, credit provided by financial institutions operating in the Intervention Zones, providing seasonal credit to FBOs through commercial and rural banks, as well as through nontraditional channels such as input suppliers, and medium-term credit through banks to finance capital goods such as irrigation and postharvest processing and storage facilities.
- *Rehabilitation of Feeder Roads*: Rehabilitate up to 950 kilometers of feeder roads in eight districts in the intervention zones to reduce transportation costs and time, to increase access to major domestic and international markets, and to facilitate transportation linkages from rural areas to social service networks (including, for instance, hospitals, clinics and schools).

Transportation Project:

- *Upgrades to Sections of N1 Highway*: Reduce the bottleneck in accessing the International Airport and the Port of Tema and support an expansion of Ghana's export-directed horticulture base beyond current production, by upgrading of 14 kilometers of the National Highway (N1 Highway) between Tema and Accra.
- *Improvements of Trunk Roads*: Facilitate the growth of agriculture and access to social services by rehabilitating or constructing up to 230 kilometers of trunk roads in the Afram Basin region.
- *Improvements of Lake Volta Ferry Services*: Facilitate the growth of agriculture in the Afram Basin region by improving the ferry service of Volta Lake Transport Company that connects Adawso on the southern shore to Ekye Amanfrom on the northern shore.

Rural Services Project:

- *Strengthening of Public Sector Procurement Capacity*: Support the development of procurement professionals and reinforce the capabilities of the Government of Ghana to procure goods and services, reinforcing execution of the overall program and, in particular, the community services.
- *Support for Community Services*: Complement the Agriculture Project by funding construction and rehabilitation of educational

facilities, construction and rehabilitation of water and sanitation facilities and electrification of rural areas, and by providing capacity building support to local government institutions.

- *Strengthening of Rural Financial Services*: Automate and interconnect 121 rural banks that are private, community-owned banks, and provide other improvements in the national payments systems that will draw a large number of people currently not served or underserved into the financial system.

Appendix B: Interviews

Horticulture Exports Sector

John Lawrence Farms (no longer exists): John Opoku-Acquah, owner, 04/29/09, 03/08/10

Farmex (no longer exists): Rami Jebeile, Exports logistics manager, and Jonas Quaye, General Manager, now work at Air Ghana, 05/06/09

Combined Farms (no longer exists): Mr. Safo, 07/31/09

Milani: Koumbou Some, Managing Director, 08/03/09; Jerome Buchwalder, Production Manager, 05/12/15.

Georgefields: George Donkor, owner, 04/30/09; Coulibaly Moussa, Operations Manager, 08/05/09.

Bomarts: Daniel Asherow, General Manager, 05/01/09; Antony Botchway, CEO, 05/02/09, 08/04/09, 01/10/10, 03/09/10, 07/04/11, 05/09/15; T. Lewis Pels, Bomarts worker who was also a small farmer outgrower, 08/04/09; Kweku Seko, Bomarts small farmer outgrower, 08/04/09.

Prudent Exports: Edward Antwi-Twum, owner, 08/05/09, 05/13/15; Samuel Mintah, General Manager and outgrower, 05/01/05, 08/05/09

Koranco Farms: Mr. Koranteng, owner, 05/04/05

Pioneer Quality Farms: Victor Peasah, owner, and Dominic Donkor, Farm Manager, 05/05/09

Chartered Impex: Solomon Benjamin, owner, 05/05/09, 03/09/10, 05/13/15.

Greenspan Farms: Kwabena Afari, owner, 08/06/09, 03/07/10, 07/04/11, 05/10/15

Golden Exotics: George Kporye, Corporate Affairs and Human Resources Manager, 03/06/10, 05/15/15, 05/17/15; Jean-Michel Blanc, Pineapple Production Manager, 03/09/10

JEI River: Kwesi Korboes, General Manager, 04/29/09; Eric Afeadongor, Chief Accountant, 05/04/09; Samuel Yeboah, Farm Manager, 05/12/15

Gold Coast Fruits: Samuel Borlu, majority shareholder, 05/15/15; George Dzibolosu, Farm Manager, 05/11/15.

2K Farms (papaya and other tropical fruit): Emmanuel and Love Carr, owners, 04/30/09, 08/03/09, 05/13/15.

Sea-freight Pineapple Exporters of Ghana: Stephen Mintah, General Manager 05/28/09 (telephone), 07/31/09, 05/15/15; Kwaku Amoafo-Yeboah, operations manager, 05/07/09, 05/08/15

Farmapine: Chris Foli, Managing Director (since 2004), 07/29/09, 08/13/09; Gabriel Anani Deku, Managing Director, Kokobin Farm (brought into Farmapine, no longer producing), 07/29/09;

Oboadaka Pineapple Cooperative, Philip Osafo Amoah, Vice chairman (interviewed at a cooperative meeting), 08/07/09

PeelCo (fresh cut fruit export): Frank Oberschlip, General Manager, 08/05/09

Integrated Tamale Fruit Company (mango, the only commercial farm in northern Ghana at that time): Juliana Bostic, Manager, 07/20/09

HPW Fresh and Dry Ltd: Maik Blaser, General Manager, 05/11/15.

Vegpro Ghana Limited: Jagdish Patel, General Manager, 05/14/15.

Davis Korboe, Member of Yilo Krobo Mango Farmers Association, Owner of Weblink Farms (mango), CEO of Farm Management Service Limited (mango), 08/06/09, 01/09/10; Weblink Farm Manager, Frank Wilson, 05/14/15.

Palm Oil Sector

Ghana Oil Palm Development Corporation (GOPDC): Anke Massart, Director of Agriculture, 03/02/10; Michael Kemeh-Mensah, Outgrower Manager, 03/02/10.

Norpalm: Eric Anang, General Manager, 03/04/10.

Benso Oil Palm Plantations Limited (BOPP): Samuel Ayaala, Estate Manager, 03/04/10.

Twifo Oil Palm Plantations Limited (TOPP): Emmanuel Ahiable, Acting Director, telephone interview, 07/13/11.

Ayiem Mills: Mr. Biney, Mill Manager, and Mr. Yamson, Manager of Palm Kernel Oil mill, 03/03/10.

Obooma Farm Products Ltd (medium-sized mill): Daniel Anane, Senior Manager of Operations, and son of the owner, 03/02/10.

Ameen Sangari (manufacturing firm): Wessel Ameen Sangari, Chairman, and Absallam Alamedene, Managing Director, 03/03/15.

PZ Cussons: Emmanuel Awotwi, Head of Supply Chain and Distribution, 03/05/10.

Millennium Challenge Account (MCA)

P.K. Mensah, MAP Consult, consultant on MCA proposal team, 09/24/08, 11/05/08, 03/08/10

Ben Nyamadi, Deputy Director, Irrigation Development Authority, Ministry of Food and Agriculture, member of MCA proposal team, 11/05/08

Robert Osei, Research Fellow at Institute for Statistical, Social and Economic Research, member of extended MCA proposal team, 11/06/08

Joseph Chognuru, Ministry of Finance, member of MCA proposal team, 08/12/09

Matthew Armah, Chief Operating Officer, Millenium Development Authority (MiDA), 11/10/08

Michael Asomani-Adem, Commercialization of Agric Projects Manager, MiDA, 11/14/08, 05/08/09, 05/10/15

Isaac Karikari, Land Administration Project Manager, MiDA, 11/10/08

Yaw Brantuo, Agricultural Financial Services and Bank Capacity Building Project Manager MiDA, 05/08/09

David Owusu, Southern zonal MiDA office, Bawjiase, zonal agriculture manager, 05/04/09

Northern zonal MIDA office, Tamale: Alabira Ibrahim,, zonal monitoring and evaluation manager, 06/20/09; Rashid Yakubu, Pentax, implementing agent for MIDA Financial services project; Rashid Abdallah, Borimanga Rural Bank, project officer/deputy manager. 06/21/09

DAI, Central Managing Consultant, agricultural project for MiDA: John Engle. Project Manager, and John Nene-Osom Azu, Training Manager, 08/12/09

IFDC, MCA regional implementing consultant for northern zone: Kofi Debrah, 07/29/09

ACDI/VOCA, MCA regional implementing consultant for southern zone: Dr. Sakyi-Dawson employee, 07/31/09; Kwesi Korboe, employee (and former General Manager of JEI River Farms), 11/14/08, 04/29/09, 05/04/09, 06/27/09, 08/13/09, several informal interviews in 2010, 2011 and 2015, and email correspondence

Augustine Adongo, Integrated Business Consulting, formerly Executive officer of the Federation of Associations of Ghana Exporters and member of MCA proposal team, 11/05/08 and 04/28/09, 01/06/10, and many email communications.

President's Special Initiatives (PSIs)

Kwamena Bartels, NPP Member of Parliament for the Ablekuma North constituency, Minister in charge of Private Sector Development and President's Special Initiatives (2005–2006), 07/05/11.

Alan Kyerematen, Minister for Trade and Industry (2003–2007), 04/10/07.

Francis Kusi, political appointee to Ministry of Trade and Industry, Coordinator for the PSIs, 04/03/07, 09/22/08, 07/14/11.

Patrick Nimo, political appointee to Ministry of Trade and Industry, Coordinator for the Private Sector Development Strategy, 04/05/07, 09/25/08.

A.K. Boateng, Sarpcoe Enterprises (PSI nursery operator that invested in a mill), Operations Manager, 07/07/11.

W.O. Danso and Felix Swanzy, Oil Palm Research Institute, Commercialization and Information Division, 07/07/11.

Dr. Wonkyi-Appiah, Oil Palm PSI Technical Adviser, PSI Secretariat, 09/23/08, 11/14/08.

Papa Bartels, Cassava Starch PSI Technical Adviser, PSI Secretariat, 09/22/08.

Jens Thomsen, International Starch Institute, Aarhus, Denmark, (telephone) 01/30/08.

Sam Mensah, consultant, author of report on PSIs commissioned by the Ministry of Private Sector Development, 09/24/08.

Ernest Agyepong, former employee of Enterprise Africa (UNDP program), political appointee, assistant to Patrick Nimo, Ministry of Trade and Industry, 11/14/08.

Robert Baffour Tandor, Ministry of Trade and Industry, SME/Technical division, 03/11/10.

Patricia Boateng, Ministry of Trade and Industry, SME and Technology Division, formerly part of the District Industrialization Program team, 09/17/08.

Clement Nminibapiel, formerly part of the District Industrialization Program team at the Ministry of Trade and Industry, seconded from the National Board of Small Scale Industries (1979–2002) to work at the Ministry of Trade and Industry (2002–2004), then worked for World Bank Community-Based Rural Development project, 09/24/08.

Government Officials and Bureaucrats

Lena Otto, Policy Planning and Analysis Unit, Ministry of Food and Agriculture, 07/28/09.

Mawuli Agboka, Horticulture Development Unit, Ministry of Food and Agriculture, coordinator of Horticulture Export Industry Initiative and coordinator of the Export Marketing & Quality Awareness project, 11/11/08, 04/27/09, 03/13/10

Eric Bentsil Quaye, Horticulture Development Unit, worked on HEII and EMQAP, 04/27/09, 03/12/10

Eleanor Swatson, Horticulture Development Unit, Ministry of Food and Agriculture, 03/10/10

Emelie Monney, Head of the Horticulture Development Unit, Ministry of Food and Agriculture, 03/11/10

Harry Bleppony, Horticulture Development Unit, Ministry of Food and Agriculture, 03/12/10

Mallam Seidu, formerly Ministry of Food and Agriculture (retired), Coordinator of AgSSIP implementation, now a commercial horticulture farmer in the northern region, 07/24/09

Peter Obeng, Ghana Export Promotion Council, 25/05/09 (telephone), 07/24/09

Kofi Djin, former Minister of Trade and Industry under PNDC government, 07/27/09, 07/30/09, 08/01/09

Agyabeng Antwi-Agyei, Export Development and Investment Fund, CEO, 07/29/09.

Ibrahim Adam, Regional Deputy Minister of Agriculture for the northern region (1984–1985), PNDC Deputy Secretary of the Ministry of Food and Agriculture in charge of crops (1985–1992), Acting Secretary (1992–1993), NDC Minister for Agriculture (1993–1996), Member of Parliament (1997–2000). Interviewed in relation to oil palm initiatives under PNDC and NDC governments, 07/06/11.

Benson Poku-Kyei, former Executive Secretary for the Divestiture Implementation Committee (2001–2003), 07/08/11.

Mallam Sediu, worked in the Ministry of Food and Agriculture (retired), was Coordinator of AgSSIP implementation, 07/24/09.

Donor Agencies and International Consultants

Patience Mensah, formerly at World Bank Ghana office (retired), worked on the Agricultural Diversification project, 05/06/09

Gayatri Acharya, formerly at World Bank Ghana office (changed position), HEII implementation, 07/15/09 (telephone)

Patrick Labaste, World Bank headquarters, involved with horticulture research, 04/10/09 (telephone).

Robert Epworth, World Bank, was involved with AgSSIP, email communication.

Lauren Ruth, USAID TIPCEE project: Deputy chief of party, employed by Chemonics; Pearl Ackah, public relations officer, employee of Care International, 05/06/09; Emmanuel Muange, fresh pineapple commodity leader, 06/02/09 (telephone).

Nana Frimpong, DfID Ghana, Adviser for Private Sector Development, 09/22/08.

Erik Rasmussen, former Danida Ghana office, interviewed in Copenhagen, 01/29/09.

Andrew Sergeant, Accord Associates, 04/17/09 (telephone).

Grahame Dixie, formerly at Accord Associates, now at the World Bank, 03/23/09 (telephone).

Peter Jaeger, Accord Associates, 03/24/09 (telephone), 01/10/10 in Accra, February 2010 by telephone, and many email communications.

Stuart Honeysett, Palm Oil Mills Consultants, 11/23/11.

Bibliography

Abdulai, Abdul-Gafaru. 2012. State Elites and the Politics of Regional Inequality in Ghana, PhD thesis, University of Manchester.

Abdulai, Abdul-Gafaru, and Sam Hickey. 2016. "The Politics of Development under Competitive Clientelism: Insights from Ghana's Education Sector," *African Affairs* 115(458): 44–72.

Ablo, Austin Dziwornu. 2015. "Local Content and Participation in Ghana's Oil and Gas Industry: Can Enterprise Development Make a Difference?," *The Extractive Industries and Society* 2: 320–327.

Ablo, Austin Dziwornu, and Ragnhild Overå. 2015. "Networks, Trust and Capital Mobilisation: Challenges of Embedded Local Entrepreneurial Strategies in Ghana's Oil and Gas Industry," *Journal of Modern African Studies* 53(3): 391–413.

(ACEP) African Center for Energy Policy. 2013. How a Good Law May Not Stop Oil Money from Going Down the Drain: The Two Sides of Ghana. Report by ACEP Staff. Sponsored by Oxfam.

(ACEP) African Center for Energy Policy. 2014. Tracking Budget Expenditure of Extractive Resource Revenues in the 2014 Budget and Policy Statement of the Government of Ghana. Report by ACEP staff. Sponsored by Oxfam.

(ACET) African Center for Economic Transformation. 2015. Promoting Sustainable Rural Development and Transformation in Africa. Ghana Country Report. ACET, Accra.

Agbodeka, Francis. 1992. *An Economic History of Ghana: From the Earliest Times*. Accra: Ghana Universities Press.

Agyeman-Duah, Ivor. 2006. *Between Faith and History: A Biography of J. A. Kufuor*. Banbury: Ayebia Clark Publishing.

Akyeampong, Emmanuel. 1996. "What's in a Drink? Class Struggle, Popular Culture and the Politics of Akpeteshie (Local Gin) in Ghana, 1930-67," *Journal of African History* 37(2): 215–36.

Alence, Rod. 2001. "Colonial Government, Social Conflict and State Involvement in Africa's Open Economies: The Origins of the Ghana Cocoa Marketing Board, 1939–46," *Journal of African History* 42: 397–416.

Allen, Chris. 1995. "Understanding African Politics," *Review of African Political Economy* 65: 301–320.

Allman, Jean Marie. 1990. "The Youngmen and the Porcupine: Class, Nationalism and Asante's Struggle for Self-Determination, 1954–57," *Journal of African History* 31(2): 263–279.

Amanor, Kojo S. 2008. "The Changing Face of Customary Land Tenure," In *Contesting Land and Custom in Ghana: State, Chief and the Citizen*, (eds.) J. Ubink and Kojo S. Amanor. Amsterdam: Leiden University Press, pp. 51–81.

Amanor, Kojo S. 2010. "Family Values, Land Sales and Agricultural Commodification in South-Eastern Ghana," *Africa* 80(1): 104–125.

Amoako, K.Y. 2011. "Transforming Africa – Start Now, We Can't Wait," *African Business* 45: 24–27.

Amsden, Alice. 2001. *The Rise of the Rest*. Oxford: Oxford University Press.

Anyemedu, K. 1991. "Export Diversification under the Economic Recovery Programme." In *Ghana: Political Economy of Reform*, (ed.) Donald Rothchild. Boulder: Lynne Reinner, pp. 209–220.

Appiah, Kweku, Lionel Demery and S. George Laryea-Adjei. 2000. "Poverty in a Changing Environment." In *Economic Reforms in Ghana: The Miracle and the Mirage*, (eds.) Ernest Aryeetey, Jane Harrigan and Machiko Nissanke. Oxford: James Currey, pp. 304–320.

Appiah-Kubi, Kojo. 2001. "State-Owned Enterprises and Privatization in Ghana," *Journal of Modern African Studies* 39(2): 197–229.

Apter, David. 1972. *Ghana in Transition*. Princeton: Princeton University Press.

Armstrong, Robert. 1996. *Ghana Country Assistance Review: A Study of Development Effectiveness*. Washington, DC: The World Bank.

Arthur, Peter. 2002. "Ghana: Industrial development in the Post-Structural Adjustment Program Period," *Canadian Journal of Development Studies* 23(4): 717–742.

Arthur, Peter. 2006. "The State, Private Sector Development, and Ghana's 'Golden Age of Business,'" *African Studies Review* 49(1): 31–50.

Ayee, Joseph, Tina Søreide, G.P. Shukla and Tuan Minh Lee. 2011. "Political Economy of the Mining Sector in Ghana," Policy Research Working Paper. Washington, DC: The World Bank.

Aryeetey, Ernest, and Jane Harrigan. 2000. "Macroeconomic and Sectoral Policies in Ghana 1970–1997." In *Economic Reforms in Ghana: The Miracle and the Mirage*, (eds.) Ernest Aryeetey, Jane Harrigan and Machiko Nissanke. Oxford: James Currey, pp. 5–31.

Aryeetey, Ernest, and Ravi Kanbur (eds.). 2008. *The Economy of Ghana: Analytical Perspectives on Stability, Growth and Poverty*. Oxford: James Currey/Boydell & Brewer.

Aryeetey, Ernest, and Ravi Kanbur (eds.). 2017. *The Economy of Ghana Sixty Years after Independence*. Oxford: Oxford University Press.

Aryeetey, Ernest, and Nkechi Owoo. 2015. "Ghana's Experiments with Business-Government Co-Ordination," WIDER Working Paper 2015/099. World Institute for Development Economics Research, Helsinki, Finland.

Aryeetey, Ernest, and Andrew McKay. 2007. "Ghana: The Challenge of Translating Sustained Growth into Poverty Reduction." In *Delivering on the Promise of Pro-Poor Growth: Insights and Lessons from Country Experiences*, (eds.) Timothy Besley and Leslie Cord. New York: Palgrave Macmillan, pp. 147–168.

Aryeetey, Ernest, and Finn Tarp. 2000. "Structural Adjustment and After: Which Way Forward?" In *Economic Reforms in Ghana: The Miracle and the Mirage*, (eds.) Ernest Aryeetey, Jane Harrigan and Machiko Nissanke. Oxford: James Currey, pp. 344–365.

Aryeetey, Ernest, Jane Harrigan and Machiko Nissanke (eds.). 2000. *Economic Reforms in Ghana: The Miracle and the Mirage*. Oxford: James Currey.

Aryeetey, Ernest, Joseph Ayee, Kwame Ninsin and Dzodzi Tsikata. 2007. "The Politics of Land Tenure Reform in Ghana: From the Crown Lands Bills to the Land Administration Project," ISSER Technical Publication No. 71, Institute of Statistical, Social and Economic Research, University of Ghana, Legon.

Asante, Elizabeth. 2012. "The Case of Ghana's President's Special Initiative on Oil Palm." DIIS Working Paper 2012: 11, Danish Institute for International Studies, Copenhagen.

Austin, Dennis. 1961. "The Working Committee of the United Gold Coast Convention," *Journal of African History* 2(2): 273–297.

Austin, Dennis. 1964. *Politics in Ghana, 1946–1960*. London: Oxford University Press.

Austin, Dennis. 1985. "The Ghana Armed Forces and Ghanaian Society," *Third World Quarterly* 7(1): 90–101.

Austin, Gareth. 1987. "The Emergence of Capitalist Relations in South Asante Cocoa-Farming, 1916–1933," *Journal of African History* 28: 259–279.

Austin, Gareth. 1996. "National Poverty and the "Vampire State" in Ghana: A Review Article," *Journal of International Development* 8(4): 553–573.

Austin, Gareth. 2003. "African Rural Capitalism, Cocoa Farming, and Economic Growth in Colonial Ghana." In *Ghana in Africa and the World: Essays in honor of Adu Boahen*, (ed.) Toyin Falola. Trenton, NJ: Africa World Press, pp. 437–453.

Austin, Gareth. 2005. *Labour, Land and Capital in Ghana: From Slavery to Free Labour in Asante, 1807–1956*. Rochester, NY: University of Rochester Press.

Barrientos, Stefanie, Kwadwo Asenso-Okyere, Samuel Asuming-Brempong, Daniel Sarpong, Nana Anyidoho, Raphael Kaplinsky, and Jennifer Leavy. 2008. Mapping Sustainable Production in Ghanaian Cocoa. Report to Cadbury. Institute of Development Studies and the University of Ghana.

Barthel, Fabian, Matthias Busse, and Robert Osei. 2008. The Characteristics and Determinants of FDI in Ghana. HWWI Research Paper 2–15. Hamburg Institute of International Economics.

Bauer, Peter. 1954. *West African Trade: A Study of Competition, Oligopoly and Monopoly in a Changing Economy.* Cambridge: Cambridge University Press.

Beckman, Bjorn. 1976. *Organizing the Farmers: Cocoa Politics and National Development in Ghana.* Uppsala: Scandinavian Institute of African Studies.

Behuria, Pritish. 2016. "Centralising Rents and Dispersing Power while Pursuing Development: Exploring the strategic uses of military firms in Rwanda." *Review of African Political Economy* 43 (150): 630–647.

Benin, Samuel, Michael Johnson, Emmanuel Abokyi, Gerald Ahorbo, Kipo Jimah, Gamel Nasser, Victor Owusu, Joe Taabazuing, and Albert Tenga. 2013. "Revisiting Agricultural Input and Farm Support Subsidies in Africa: the case of Ghana's mechanization, fertilizer, block farms and marketing programs," IFPRI Discussion Paper 01300, Development Strategy and Governance Division, International Food Policy Research Institute, Washington, DC.

Berry, Sara. 1993. *No Condition Is Permanent: The Social Dynamics of Change in Sub-Saharan Africa.* Madison: University of Wisconsin Press.

Berry, Sara. 2001. *Chiefs Know Their Boundaries: Essays on Property, Power and the Past in Asante, 1896–1996.* Oxford: James Currey.

Berry, Sara. 2009. "Property, Authority and Citizenship: Land Claims, Politics and the Dynamics of Social Division in West Africa," *Development and Change* 40(1): 23–45.

Berry, Sara. 2013. "Questions of Ownership: Proprietorship and Control in a Changing Rural Terrain—A Case Study from Ghana," *Africa* 83(1): 36–56.

Boahan, A. Adu. 1975. *Ghana: Evolution and Change in the Nineteenth and Twentieth Centuries.* London: Longman.

Boamah, Festus. 2014. "How and Why Chiefs Formalise Land Use in Recent Times: The Politics of Land Dispossession through Biofuels Investments in Ghana," *Review of African Political Economy* 41(141): 406–423.

Bob-Milliar, George. 2011. ""We Are Holding the Umbrella Very Tight!": Explaining the Popularity of the NDC in the Upper West Region of Ghana," *Africa* 81(3): 455–473.

Bob-Milliar, George. 2012a. Political Party Activism in Ghana: Factors Influencing the Decision of the Politically Active to Join a Political Party. *Democratization* 19 (4): 668–689.

Bob-Milliar, George. 2012b. "Party Factions and Power Blocs in Ghana: A Case Study of Power Politics in the National Democratic Congress," *Journal of Modern African Studies* 50(4): 573–601.

Bob-Milliar, George and G.K. Bob-Milliar. 2010. "The Economy and Intra-Party Competition: Presidential Primaries in the New Patriotic Party of Ghana," *African Review of Economics and Finance* 1(2): 51–71.

Boone, Catherine. 1992. *Merchant Power and the Roots of State Power in Senegal, 1930–1985*. New York: Cambridge University Press.

Boone, Catherine. 2003. *Political Topographies of the African State: Territorial Authority and Institutional Choice*. Cambridge: Cambridge University Press.

Boone, Catherine. 2013. *Property and Political Order in Africa*. Cambridge: Cambridge University Press.

Boone, Catherine and Dennis K. Duku. 2012. "Ethnic Land Rights in Western Ghana: Landlord-Stranger Relations in the Democratic Era," *Development and Change* 43(3): 671–693.

Booth, David and Frederick Golooba-Mutebi. 2012. Developmental Patrimonialism? The Case of Rwanda. *African Affairs*. 111: 379–403.

Booth, David, Richard Crook, Emmanuel Gyimah-Boadi, Tony Killick and Robin Luckham. 2004. "Drivers of Change in Ghana: Overview Report," Report for DFID Ghana for the country situation assessment based on a Drivers of Change analysis.

Brautigam, Deborah. 2009. Coalitions, Capitalists and Credibility: Overcoming the crisis of confidence at independence in Mauritius. Research Paper 4, Developmental Leadership Program. Accessed at www.dlprog.org.

Breisinger, Clemens, Xinshen Diao, Sashi Kolavalli, and James Thurlow. 2008. The Role of Cocoa in Ghana's Future Development, IFPRI GSSP Background Paper 11. International Food Policy Research Institute, Accra Office.

Busia, K.A. 1956. The Present Situation and Aspirations of Elites in the Gold Coast. *International Social Science Bulletin* 8(3): 424–31.

Chang, Ha-Joon. 2009. "Rethinking Public Policy in Agriculture: Lessons from History, Distant and Recent," *Journal of Peasant Studies* 36(3): 477–515.

Chazan, Naomi. 1983. *An Anatomy of Ghana Politics: Managing Political Recession, 1969–1982*. Boulder, CO: Westview Press.

Cheeseman, Nic, Gabrielle Lynch and Justin Willis. 2017. "Ghana: The Ebbing Power of Incumbency," *Journal of Democracy* 28(2): 92–104.

Cheng, Tun-jen. 1990. "Political Regimes and Development Strategies: South Korea and Taiwan." In *Manufacturing Miracles: Paths of Industrialization in Latin America and East Asia*, (eds.) Donald Wyman and Gary Gereffi. Princeton: Princeton University Press, pp. 139–178.

Crook, Richard. 1986. "Decolonization, the Colonial State, and Chieftaincy in the Gold Coast," *African Affairs* 85(338): 75–105.

Crook, Richard. 1989. "Patrimonialism, Administrative Effectiveness and Economic Development in Cote d'Ivoire," *African Affairs* 88(351): 205–228.

Crook, Richard. 1990. "State, Society and Political Institutions in Cote d'Ivoire and Ghana." In *Rethinking Third World Politics*, (ed.) James Manor. Harlow: Longman, pp. 213–241.

Crook, Richard with Simplice Affou, Daniel Hammond, Adja Vanga, and Mark Owusu-Yeboah. 2007. "The Law, Legal Institutions and the Protection of Land Rights in Ghana and Cote d'Ivoire: Developing a more effective and equitable system," IDS Research Report 58, Institute of Development Studies at the University of Sussex, Brighton.

Daddieh, Cyril. 1994. "Contract Farming and Palm Oil Production in Cote d'Ivoire and Ghana." In *Living Under Contract: Contract farming and agrarian transformation in Sub-Saharan Africa*, (eds.) Peter Little and Michael Watts. Madison: University of Wisconsin Press, pp. 188–215.

Daddieh, Cyril and Bob-Milliar, George. 2012. "In Search of "Honorable" Membership: Parliamentary Primaries and Candidate Selection in Ghana," *Journal of Asian and African Studies* 47 (2), pp. 204–220.

Diao, Xinshen, Frances Cossar, Nazaire Houssou, and Shashidhara Kolavalli. 2014. "Mechanization in Ghana: Emerging Demand and the Search for Alternative Supply Models," *Food Policy* 48: 168–181.

Dinh, Hinh, Vincent Palmade, Vandana Chandra, and Frances Cossar. 2013. *Light Manufacturing in Africa: Targeted Policies to Enhance Private Investment and Create Jobs*. Washington, DC: World Bank.

Doner, Richard. 2009. *The Politics of Uneven Development: Thailand's Economic Growth in Comparative Perspective*. Cambridge: Cambridge University Press.

Doner, Richard and Ansil Ramsay. 1998. "Competitive Clientelism and Economic Governance: The case of Thailand." In *Business and the State in Developing Countries*, (eds.) Sylvia Maxfield and Ben Ross Schneider. Ithaca: Cornell University Press, pp. 237–276.

Dowse, Robert. 1975. "Military and Police Rule." In *Politicians and Soldiers in Ghana*, (eds.) Robin Luckham and Dennis Austin. London: Cass, pp. 16–36.

Dumett, Raymond. 1983. "African Merchants of the Gold Coast, 1860–1905: Dynamics of Indigenous Entrepreneurship," *Comparative Studies in Society and History* 25: 661–693.

ECA. 2011. "Governing Development in Africa: The Role of the State in Economic Transformation," Economic Report on Africa. Addis Ababa: United Nations Economic Commission for Africa.

Esseks, John. 1971. "Government and Indigenous Private Enterprise in Ghana," *Journal of Modern African Studies* 9(1): 11–29.

Esseks, John. 1975. "Economic Policies." In *Politicians and Soldiers in Ghana*, (eds.) Robin Luckham and Dennis Austin. London: Cass, pp. 37–55.

Faber, Mike. 1990. "The Volta River Project: For Whom the Smelter Tolled." In *Towards Economic Recovery in Sub-Saharan Africa: Essays in Honour of Robert Gardiner*, (eds.) James Pickett and Hans Singer. London: Routledge, pp. 65–91.

(FAO) Food and Agriculture Organization of the United Nations. 2014. "Poultry Sector Ghana." FAO Animal Production and Health Livestock Country Reviews. Rome: FAO.

Farole, Thomas. 2011. *Special Economic Zones in Africa: Comparing Performance and Learning from Global Experiences*. The World Bank, Washington, DC.

First, Ruth. 1970. *The Barrel of a Gun: Political Power in Africa and the coup d'etat*. London: Allen Lane.

Fischer, Andrew. 2009. "Putting Aid in Its Place: Insights from Early Structuralists on Aid and Balance of Payments and Lessons for Contemporary Aid Debates," *Journal of International Development* 21 (6): 856–867.

Fold, Niels. 2002. "Lead Firms and Competition in "Bi-Polar" Commodity Chains: Grinders and Branders in the Global Cocoa-Chocolate Industry," *Journal of Agrarian Change*, 2(2): 228–247.

Fold, Niels. 2003. Re-Entering the Global Circuit? Upgrading and Differentiation in Ghana's Palm Oil Industry. Paper for the Annual Meeting of the Association of American Geographers, March 4–8, New Orleans.

Fold, Niels and Katherine Gough. 2008. "From Smallholders to Transnationals: The Impact of Changing Consumer Preferences in the EU on Ghana's Pineapple Sector," *Geoforum* 39: 1687–1697.

Fold, Niels and Lindsay Whitfield. 2012. "Developing a Palm Oil Sector: The Experiences of Malaysia and Ghana Compared", DIIS Working Paper 2012:08, Danish Institute for International Studies, Copenhagen, Denmark.

Foster, Mick, Adrienne Brown and Felix Naschold. 2000. "What's Different about Agricultural Swaps?," paper presented at DFID Natural Resources Advisers conference, July 10–14, 2000. Accessed at www.odi.org/resources/docs/2231.pdf (last accessed 24 August 2017).

Frimpong-Ansah, Jonathan. 1991. *The Vampire State in Africa: The Political Economy of Decline In Ghana*. London: James Currey.

Geddes, Babara. 1994. *Politician's Dilemma: Building State Capacity in Latin America*. Berkeley: University of California Press.

Genoud, Roger. 1969. *Nationalism and Economic Development in Ghana*. London: Frederick A. Praeger.

Gereffi, Gary. 2014. "Global Value Chains in a Post-Washington Consensus World," *Review of International Political Economy* 21(1): 9–37.

Gereffi, Gary and Timothy Sturgeon. 2013. "Global Value Chain-Oriented Industrial Policy: The Role of Emerging Economies," In *Global Value Chains in a Changing World*, (eds.) Deborah Elms and Patrick Low. World Trade Organization, in cooperation with the Fung Global Institute and the Temasek Centre for Trade and Negotiations, pp. 329–360.

Goldstein, Markus and Christopher Udry. 2008. "The Profits of Power: Land Rights and Agricultural Investment in Ghana," *Journal of Political Economy* 116(6): 981–1022.

Gray, Hazel and Lindsay Whitfield. 2014. Reframing African Political Economy: Clientelism, rents and accumulation as drivers of capitalist transformation. LSE International Development Working Paper Series No. 14–159, London School of Economics and Political Science, London.

Gray, Hazel and Mushtaq Khan. 2010. "Good Governance and Growth in Africa: What Can We Learn from Tanzania?" In *The Political Economy of Africa*, (ed.) Vishnu Padayachee. London: Routledge, pp. 339–356.

Gyasi, Edwin. 1992. "Emergence of a New Oil Palm Belt in Ghana," *Tijdschrift voor Econ. En Soc.* Geografie 38(1): 39–49.

Gyasi, Edwin. 1994. "The Adaptability of African Communal Land Tenure to Economic Opportunity: The Example of Land Acquisition for Oil Palm Farming in Ghana," *Africa* 64(3): 391–405.

Gyasi, Edwin. 1996. "The Environmental Impact and Sustainability of Plantations in Sub-Saharan Africa: Ghana's Experience with Oil-Palm Plantations." In *Sustaining the Future: Economic, social and environmental change in Sub-Saharan Africa*, (eds.) E. Gyasi and J. Uitto. Tokyo: United Nations University Press, available at http://archive.unu.edu/unupress/unupbooks/80918e/80918E10.htm (last accessed February 13, 2018).

Gyimah-Boadi, Emmanuel. 2009. *A "Liberal" Developmental State in Ghana: An Emerging Paradigm for Democracy and Economic Growth?*

Paper presented at the conference 'From Asymmetry to Symmetry? The West, Non-West and the Idea of Development as Conceptual Flow," University of Heidelberg, Germany, July 13–16, 2009.

Gyimah-Boadi, Emmanuel and Richard Jeffries. 2000. "The Political Economy of Reform." In *Economic Reforms in Ghana: The Miracle and the Mirage*, (eds.) Ernest Aryeetey, Jane Harrigan and Machiko Nissanke. Oxford: James Currey, pp. 32–50.

Gyimah-Boadi, Emmanuel and Kwasi Prempeh. 2012. "Oil, Politics and Ghana's Democracy," *Journal of Democracy* 23(3): 94–108.

Haggard, Stephen. 1994. "Business, Politics and Policy in Northeast and Southeast Asia." In *Business and Government in Industrializing Asia*, (ed.) Andrew MacIntyre. Ithaca: Cornell University Press, pp. 268–301.

Handley, Antionette. 2008. *Business and the State in Africa: Economic Policymaking in the Neo-Liberal Era*. Cambridge: Cambridge University Press.

Hansen, Emmanuel. 1991. *Ghana under Rawlings: Early Years*. Oxford: Malthouse.

Harrigan, Jane and F. Younger. 2000. "Aid, Debt and Growth." In *Economic Reforms in Ghana: The Miracle and the Mirage*, (eds.) Ernest Aryeetey, Jane Harrigan, and Machiko Nissanke. Oxford: James Currey, pp. 185–208.

Hart, Elizabeth and Emmanuel Gyimah-Boadi. 2000. *Business Associations in Ghana's Economic and Political Transition*. Critical Perspectives No. 3. Ghana: Center for Democracy and Development.

Herbst, Jeffrey. 1993. *The Politics of Reform in Ghana, 1982–1991*. Berkeley: University of California.

Hickey, Sam, Abdul-Gafaru Abdulai, Angelo Izama and Giles Mohan. 2015. The Politics of Governing Oil Effectively: A Comparative Study of Two New Oil-Rich States in Africa. ESID Working Paper No. 54. Effective States and Inclusive Development Research Centre, University of Manchester.

Hill, Polly. 1963. *The Migrant Cocoa-Farmers of Southern Ghana: A Study in Rural Capitalism*. Cambridge: Cambridge University Press.

Hilson, Gavin. 2009. "Small-Scale Mining, Poverty and Development in Sub-Saharan Africa," *Resources Policy*, 34(1–2): 1–86.

Hilson, Gavin and Chris Garforth. 2013. " "Everyone Now is Concentrating on the Mining": Drivers and Implications of Rural Economic Transition in the Eastern Region of Ghana," *The Journal of Development Studies* 49 (3): 348–364.

Hirvi, Marja and Lindsay Whitfield. 2015. "Public Service Provision in Clientelist Political Settlements: Lessons from Ghana's Urban Water Sector," *Development Policy Review* 33(2), 2015: 135–158.

Hopkins, A. G. 1966. “Economic Aspects of Political Movements in Nigeria and in the Gold Coast, 1918–39,” *Journal of African History* 7: 133–152.

Howard, Rhoda. 1976. “Differential Class Participation in an African Protest Movement: The Ghana Boycott of 1937–38,” *Canadian Journal of African Studies* 10(3): 469–480.

Hubbard, Michael. 2003. “Reforming the Role of Government in Agricultural Markets.” In *Developing Agricultural Trade: New Roles of Government in Poor Countries*, (ed.) Michael Hubbard. Basingstoke: Palgrave Macmillan, pp. 120–142.

Huddleston, Paul. 2006. Contract Farming in Oil Palm: The Case of Ghana and the Philippines. PhD thesis, University of Western Australia, Faculty of Natural and Agricultural Sciences.

Huddleston, Paul and Matthew Tonts. 2007. “Agricultural Development, Contract Farming and Ghana’s Oil Palm Industry,” *Geography* 92(3): 266–278.

Hutchful, Eboe. 1979. “A Tale of Two Regimes: Imperialism, the Military and Class in Ghana,” *Review of African Political Economy* 14: 36–55.

Hutchful, Eboe. 1989. “From ‘Revolution’ to Monetarism: The Economics and Politics of the Adjustment Programme in Ghana.” In *Structural Adjustment in Africa*, (eds.) Bonnie Campbell and John Loxley. Basingstoke: Macmillan, pp. 92–133.

Hutchful, Eboe. 2002. *Ghana’s Adjustment Experience: The Paradox of Reform*. Oxford: James Currey.

Ichino, Nahomi and Noah Nathan. 2012. “Primaries on Demand? Intra-Party Politics and Nominations in Ghana,” *British Journal of Political Science* 42(4): 769–791.

(IMF) International Monetary Fund. 1998. *The Price Incentive to Smuggle and the Cocoa Supply in Ghana, 1950–1996*. IMF Working Paper 98/88. Washington, DC: IMF.

(IMF) International Monetary Fund. 2014. *Ghana: Staff Report for the 2014 Article IV Consultation*. Washington, DC: IMF.

(IMF) International Monetary Fund. 2015. *Ghana: First Review under the Extended Credit Facility Arrangement*. IMF Country Report No. 15/245. Washington, DC: IMF.

ISSER. 2012. *State of the Ghanaian Economy Report 2011*. Institute for Statistical, Social and Economic Research, University of Ghana, Accra.

Jacobeit, Cord. 1991. “Reviving Cocoa: Policies and Perspectives on Structural Adjustment in Ghana’s Key Agricultural Sector.” In *Ghana: The Political Economy of Recovery*, (ed.) Donald Rothchild. Boulder: Lynne Rienner, pp. 221–232.

Jeffries, Richard. 1978. *Class, Power and Ideology in Ghana: The Railwaymen of Sekondi*. Cambridge: Cambridge University Press.

Jeffries, Richard. 1980. "The *Ghanaian* Elections of 1979," *African Affairs* 79(316): 397–414.

Jeffries, Richard. 1982. "Rawlings and the Political Economy of Underdevelopment in Ghana," *African Affairs* 81(324): 307–317.

Jeffries, Richard. 1989. "Ghana: The Political Economy of Personal Rule." In *Contemporary West African States*, (eds.) Donald Cruise O'Brien, John Dunn and Richard Rathbone. Cambridge: Cambridge University Press, pp. 75–98.

Jeffries, Richard. 1998. "The Ghanaian Elections of 1996: Towards the Consolidation of Democracy?," *African Affairs* 97: 189–208.

Jeffries, Richard and Claire Thomas. 1993. "The Ghanaian Elections of 1992," *African Affairs* 92: 331–366.

Jerven, Morten. 2013. "For Richer, for Poorer: GDP Revisions and Africa's Statistical Tragedy," *African Affairs*, 112(446): 138–147.

Jerven, Morten and Duncan, Magnus. 2012. "Revising GDP Estimates in Sub-Saharan Africa: Lessons from Ghana," *African Statistical Journal* 15: 13–24.

Kang, David. 2002. *Crony Capitalism: Corruption and Development in South Korea and the Philippines* Cambridge: Cambridge University Press.

Kay, G.B. 1972. *The Political Economy of Colonialism in Ghana: A Collection of Documents and Statistics, 1900–1960*. Cambridge: Cambridge University Press.

Kelsall, Tim. 2011. "Rethinking the Relationship between Neopatrimonialism and Economic Development in Africa," *IDS Bulletin* 42 (2): 76–87.

Kelsall, Tim with David Booth, Diana Cammack, Brian Cooksey, Mesfin Gebremichael, and Fred Golooba-Mutebi. 2013. *Business, Politics and the State in Africa: Challenging the Orthodoxies on Growth and Transformation*. London: Zed Books.

Kennedy, Arthur. 2009. *Chasing the Elephant into the Bush: The Politics of Complacency*. Bloomington, IN: AuthorHouse.

Khan, Mushtaq. 2000a. Rents, Efficiency and Growth. In *Rents, Rent-Seeking and Economic Development: Theory and Evidence in Asia*, (eds.) M. Khan and K.S Jomo. Cambridge, UK: Cambridge University Press, pp. 21–69.

Khan, Mushtaq. 2000b. Rent-Seeking as Process. In *Rents, Rent-Seeking and Economic Development: Theory and Evidence in Asia*, (eds.) M. Khan and K.S Jomo. Cambridge, UK: Cambridge University Press, pp. 70–143.

Khan, Mushtaq. 2005a. "Markets, States and Democracy: Patron-Client Networks and the Case for Democracy in Developing Countries," *Democratization* 12(5): 704–724.

Khan, Mushtaq. 2005b. "The Capitalist Transformation." In *The Origins of Development Economics: How Schools of Economic Thought Have*

Addressed Development, (eds.) K.S. Jomo and Erik Reinert, London: Zed Press, pp. 69–80.

Khan, Mushtaq. 2009. Learning, Technology Acquisition and Governance Challenges in Developing Countries' Research Paper Series on Governance for Growth. School of Oriental and African Studies, University of London: London. Available at http://mercury.soas.ac.uk.

Khan, Mushtaq. 2010. Political Settlements and the Governance of Growth-Enhancing Institutions. Research Paper Series on Governance for Growth. School of Oriental and African Studies, University of London: London. Accessed at http://mercury.soas.ac.uk/users/mk17

Khan, Mushtaq. 2012a. "Governance and Growth: History, Ideology and Methods of Proof." In *Good Growth and Governance in Africa: Rethinking Development Strategies*, (eds.) Akbar Noman, Kwesi Botchwey, Howard Stein and Joseph Stiglitz. Oxford: Oxford University Press, pp. 51–79.

Khan, Mushtaq. 2012b. "Governance and Growth Challenges for Africa." In *Good Growth and Governance in Africa: Rethinking Development Strategies*, (eds.) Akbar Noman, Kwesi Botchwey, Howard Stein and Joseph Stiglitz. Oxford: Oxford University Press, pp. 114–139.

Killick, Tony. 1966a. "The Possibilities of Economic Control." In *A Study of Contemporary Ghana, Volume One The Economy of Ghana*, (eds.) Walter Birmingham, I. Neustadt, and E.N. Omadboe. London: George Allen and Unwin, pp. 411–438.

Killick, Tony. 1966b. "Economics of Cocoa." In *A Study of Contemporary Ghana, Volume One The Economy of Ghana*, (eds.) Walter Birmingham, I. Neustadt, and E.N. Omadboe. London: George Allen and Unwin, pp. 365–390.

Killick, Tony. 1978. *Development Economics in Action: A Study of Economic Policies in Ghana*. London: Heinemann.

Killick, Tony. 2000. "Fragile Still? The Structure of Ghana's Economy 1960–94." In *Economic Reforms in Ghana: The Miracle and the Mirage*, (eds.) Ernest Aryeety, Jane Harrigan and Machiko Nissanke, Oxford: James Currey, pp. 51–67.

Killick, Tony. 2008. "What Drives Change in Ghana?" In *The Economy of Ghana: Analytical Perspectives on Stability, Growth and Poverty*, (eds.) Ernest Aryeetey and Ravi Kanbur. Oxford: James Currey, pp. 20–35.

Killick, Tony. 2010. *Development Economics in Action: A Study of Economic Policies in Ghana*, Second Edition. London: Routledge.

Kilson, Martin. 1970. "Emergent Elites of Black Africa." In *Colonialism in Africa 1870–1960*, (eds.) P. Duignan and L.H. Gann. Cambridge: Cambridge University Press, pp. 351–398.

Kimble, David. 1963. *A Political History of Ghana: The Rise of Gold Coast Nationalism, 1850–1928*. Oxford: Clarendon Press.

Kleist, Nauja. 2011. "Modern Chiefs: Tradition, Development and Return among Traditional Authorities in Ghana," *African Affairs* 110(441): 629–647.

Kolavalli, Sashi and Marcella Vigneri. 2011. "Cocoa in Ghana: Shaping the Success of an Economy." In *Yes Africa Can: Success Stories from a Dynamic Continent*, (eds.) Punam Chuhan-Pole and M. Angwafo. Washington, DC: World Bank, pp. 201–217.

Kolavalli, Shashi, Elizabeth Robinson, Xinshen Diao, Vida Alpureto, Renato Folledo, Mira Slavova, Guyslain Ngeleza, and Felix Asante. 2012. "Economic Transformation in Ghana: Where Will the Path Lead?," *Journal of African Development* 14(2): 41–78.

Konings, Piet. 1986. *The State and Rural Class Formation in Ghana: A Comparative Analysis*. London: KPI Limited.

Krassowski, Andrzej. 1974. *Development and the Debt Trap: Economic Planning and External Borrowing in Ghana*. London: Croom Helm Ltd and the Overseas Development Institute.

Kraus, Jon. 1980. "The Political Economy of Ghana," *Africa Report* 25(2): 9–16.

Kraus, Jon. 1982. "Rawlings' Second Coming," *African Report* 27(3): 59–66.

Kraus, Jon. 1991. "The Political Economy of Stabilization and Structural Adjustment in Ghana." In *Ghana: The Political Economy of Recovery*, (ed.) Donald Rothchild. Boulder: Lynne Rienner, pp. 119–155.

Kraus, Jon. 2002. "Capital, Power and Business Associations in the African Political Economy: A Tale of Two Countries, Ghana and Nigeria," *Journal of Modern African Studies* 40(3): 395–436.

Kumi, Yasmin. 2015. We Are a Chicken Family: The History of a Ghanaian Family Business and Its Changing Relationships with State and Markets. MSc Dissertation in African Studies, African Studies Centre, University of Oxford.

Ladouceur, Paul. 1979. *Chiefs and Politicians: The Politics of Regionalism in Northern Ghana*. London: Longman.

Lall, Sanjaya. 1996. *Learning from the Asian Tigers: Studies in Technology and Industrial Policy*. Basingstoke: Macmillan Press.

Lall, Sanjaya and Francis Stewart. 1996. "Trade and Industrial Policy." In *Agenda for Africa's Economic Renewal*, (eds.) Benno Ndulu and Nicolas van de Walle. New Brunswick and Oxford: Transaction Publishers.

Lall, Sanjaya, Giorgio Barba-Navaretti, Simon Teitel and Ganeshan Wignaraja. 1994. *Technology and Enterprise Development: Ghana under Structural Adjustment*. New York: St. Martin's Press.

Laven, Anna. 2010. The Risk of Inclusions: Shifts in Governance Processes and Upgrading Opportunities for Small-Scale Cocoa Farmers in Ghana. Published doctoral dissertation. Amsterdam: Royal Tropical Institute (KIT) Publishers.

Leftwich, Adrian. 2005. "Democracy and Development: Is There Institutional Incompatibility?" *Democratization*. 12(5): 686–703.

Leite, Sergio Pereira, Anthony Pellechio, Luisa Zanforlin, Girma Begashaw, Stefania Fabrizio, and Joachim Harnack. 2000. "Ghana: Economic Development in a Democratic Environment," IMF Occassional Paper 199, Washington, DC: International Monetary Fund.

Lentz, Carola. 2002. "'The Time When Politics Came': Ghana's Decolonization from the Perspective of a Rural Periphery," *Journal of Contemporary African Studies* 20(2): 245–274.

Lindberg, Staffan. 2010. "What Accountability Pressures Do MPs in Africa Face and How Do They Respond? Evidence from Ghana," *Journal of Modern African Studies* 48(1): 117–142.

Lindberg, Staffan. 2013. "Have the Cake and Eat It: The Rational Voter in Africa," *Party Politics* 19(6) pp. 945–961.

Lindberg, Staffan and Minion Morrison. 2005. "Exploring Voter Alignments in Africa: Core and Swing Voters in Ghana," *Journal of Modern African Studies* 43(4): 565–586.

Lindberg, Staffan and Minion Morrison. 2008. "Are African Voters Really Ethnic or Clientelistic? Survey Evidence from Ghana," *Political Science Quarterly* 123(1): 95–122.

Lindberg, Staffan with Yongmei Zhou. 2009. "Co-optation despite Democratization in Ghana." In *Legislative Power in Emerging African Democracies*, (ed.) Joel Barkan. Boulder: Lynne Rienner, pp. 147–176.

Ludvigsen, Rasmus. 2012. *Global Value Chains and Cocoa Processing in Ghana*. Master thesis, Aalborg University, Denmark.

Marshall, Judith. 1976. "The State of Ambivalence: Right and Left Options in Ghana," *Review of African Political Economy* 5: 49–62.

Martin, Matthew. 1991. "Negotiating Adjustment and External Finance: Ghana and the International Community, 1982–1989." In *Ghana: The Political Economy of Recovery*, (ed.) Donald Rothchild. London: Lynne Rienner, pp. 235–263.

Maxfield, Sylvia and Ben Ross Schneider (eds.). 1997. *Business and the State in Developing Countries*. Ithaca, NY: Cornell University Press.

Mkandawire, Thandika. 2015. "Neopatrimonialism and the Political Economy of Economic Performance in Africa: Critical Reflections," *World Politics* 67(3): 563–612.

Migdal, Joel. 1988. *Strong Societies and Weak States: State-Society Relations and State Capabilities in the Third World*. Princeton: Princeton University Press.

Mikell, Gwendolyn. 1989. "Peasant Politicisation and Economic Recuperation in Ghana: Local and National Dilemmas," *Journal of Modern African Studies* 27(3): 455–478.

Mohan, Giles and Kojo Asante. 2015. Transnational Capital and the Political Settlement of Ghana's Oil Economy. ESID Working Paper No. 49. Effective States and Inclusive Development Research Centre, University of Manchester.

Moore, Mick and Hubert Schmitz. 2008. Idealism, Realism and the Investment Climate in Developing Countries. IDS Working Paper 307. Institute of Development Studies, University of Sussex.

Mulangu, Francis, Mario Miranda and Maiga. 2015. Is More Chocolate Bad for Poverty? An Evaluation of Cocoa Pricing for Ghana's Industrialization and Poverty Reduction. AGRODEP Working Paper 0014. African Growth and Development Policy Modeling Consortium, facilitated by the International Food Policy Research Institute.

Nin-Pratt, Alejandro and Linden McBride. 2014. "Agricultural Intensification in Ghana: Evaluating the Optimist's Case for a Green Revolution," *Food Policy* 48: 153–167.

Ninsin, Kwame. 1996. "Ghana beyond Crisis and Adjustment," *Africa Development* 21 (2&3): 25–42.

Noman, Akbar, Kwesi Botchwey, Howard Stein, and Joseph Stiglitz (Eds.). 2012. *Good Growth and Governance in Africa: Rethinking Development Strategies*. Oxford: Oxford University Press.

Nti, Kofi. 2011. Ghana Economic Transformation Case Study. Paper prepared for the African Center for Economic Transformation, Accra, Ghana. Unpublished report.

Nugent, Paul. 1995. *Big Men, Small Boys, and Politics in Ghana: Power, Ideology and the Burden of History, 1982–94*. London: Pinter.

Nugent, Paul. 1999. "Living in the Past: Urban, Rural and Ethnic Themes in the 1992 and 1996 Elections in Ghana," *Journal of Modern African Studies* 37(2): 287–319.

Nyanteng, V.K. and A.W. Seini. 2000. "Agricultural Policy and the Impact on Growth and Productivity, 1970–95." In *Economic Reforms in Ghana: The Miracle and the Mirage*, (eds.) Ernest Aryeetey, Jane Harrigan and Mashiko Nissanke. Oxford: James Currey, pp. 267–283.

Oelbaum, Jay. 2002. "Populist Reform Coalitions in Sub-Saharan Africa: Ghana's Triple Alliance," *Canadian Journal of African Studies* 36(2): 281–328.

Okudzeto, Eline, Wilberforce A. Mariki, Radhika Lal, and Sylvia S. Senu. 2015. "Ghana: African Economic Outlook." African Development Bank, Organization for Economic Co-operation and Development, United Nations Development Programme.

Onoma, Ato. 2010. *The Politics of Property Rights Institutions in Africa.* Cambridge: Cambridge University Press.

Opoku, Darko. 2010. *The Politics of Government-Business Relations in Ghana, 1982–2008.* New York: Palgrave Macmillan.

Oquaye, Mike. 1980. *Politics in Ghana, 1972–1979.* Accra: Tornado.

Oqubay, Arkebe. 2015. *Made in Africa: Industrial Policy in Ethiopia.* Oxford: Oxford University Press.

Osei, Phillip. 2000. "Political Liberalization and the Implementation of the Value Added Tax in Ghana," *Journal of Modern African Studies* 38(2): 255–278.

Osei, Anja. 2015. "Elites and Democracy in Ghana: A Social Network Approach," *African Affairs* 114(457): 529–554.

Osei, D.K. 2008. "Ambassador D.K. Osei." In *An Economic History of Ghana: Reflections on a Half-Century of Challenges and Progress*, (ed.) Ivor Agyeman-Duah. Banbury: Abyeia Clarke, pp. 124–125.

Ouma, Stefan. 2012. "Agro-Business and the Precarious Making of Fresh-Cut Markets," *Journal of Development Studies* 48 (3): 322–334.

Ouma, Stefan. 2015. *Assembling Export Markets: The Making and Unmaking of Global Food Connections in West Africa.* West Sussex: Wiley Blackwell.

Owusu, Maxwell. 1970. *Uses and Abuses of Political Power: A Case Study of Continuity and Change in the Politics of Ghana.* Chicago: Chicago University Press.

Owusu, Maxwell. 1979. "Politics without Parties: Reflections on the Union Government Proposals in Ghana," *African Studies Review* 22(1): 89–108.

Peasah, J.A. 1975. "Politics in Abuakwa." In *Politicians and Soldiers in Ghana, 1966–1972*, (ed.) Dennis Austin and Robin Luckham. London: Cass, pp. 214–231.

Phillips, Jon. 2017. Contested Spaces of Offshore Oil and Gas in Ghana: Territory, Materiality and Politics in Ghana. PhD thesis, Geography Department, King's College London, London.

Phillips, Jon, Elena Hailwood, and Andrew Brooks. 2016. "Sovereignty, the 'Resource Course' and the Limits of Good Governance: A Political Economy of Oil in Ghana," *Review of African Political Economy* 43 (147): 26–42.

Pinkney, Robert. 1972. *Ghana under Military Rule, 1966–1969.* London: Methuen.

Price, Robert. 1984. "Neo-Colonialism and Ghana's Economic Decline: A Critical Assessment," *Canadian Journal of African Studies* 18(1): 163–193.

Quarcoo, Rosemary, Modesta Gavor and Doreen Tetteh-Coffie. 2013. "Challenges Facing Garment Producing Industries under AGOA in Ghana," *International Journal of Clothing Science* 2(1): 9–14.

Rankin, Neil, Måns Soderbom, and Francis Teal. 2002. *The Ghanaian Manufacturing Enterprise Survey 2000*. Centre for the Study of African Economies, University of Oxford, UK.

Rathbone, Richard. 1968. "Education and Politics in Ghana," *Africana Collecta* [offprint]. Gütersloh: Bertelsmann-Universitätsverlag.

Rathbone, Richard. 1973. "Businessmen in Politics: Party Struggles in Ghana, 1949–57," *Journal of Development Studies* 9(3): 391–401.

Rathbone, Richard. 2000. *Nkrumah and the Chiefs: The Politics of Chieftaincy in Ghana 1951–60*. Oxford: James Currey.

Ray, Donald. 1986. *Ghana: Politics, Economics and Society*. London: Pinter.

Reinert, Erik. 2007. *How Rich Countries Got Rich ... and Why Poor Countries Stay Poor*. London: Constable and Robinson.

Rimmer, Douglas. 1992. *Staying Poor: Ghana's Political Economy, 1950–1990*. Oxford: Pergamon.

Robinson, Elizabeth and Shashi Kolavalli. 2010. The Case of Tomato in Ghana: Processing. Ghana Strategy Support Program Working Paper No. 21, International Food Policy Research Institute, Accra.

Rodrik, Dani. 2007 *One Economics, Many Recipes: Globalization, Institutions and Economic Growth*. Princeton: Princeton University Press.

Ruf, François. 1995. "From Forest Rent to Tree-capital: Basic 'Laws' of Cocoa Supply." In *Cocoa Cycles: The Economics of Cocoa Supply*, (eds.) Ruf François and P.S. Siswoputranto. Cambridge: Woodhead Publishing, pp. 1–53.

Sandbrook, Richard. 1985. *The Politics of Africa's Economic Stagnation*. Cambridge: Cambridge University Press.

Sandbrook, Richard. 2000. *Closing the Circle: Democratization and development in Africa*. London: Zed Books.

Sandbrook, Richard and Jay Oelbaum. 1997. "Reforming Dysfunctional Institutions through Democratisation? Reflections on Ghana," *Journal of Modern African Studies* 35(4): 603–646.

Schneider, Ben Ross. 2004. *Business Politics and the State in Twentieth-Century Latin America*. Cambridge: Cambridge University Press.

Schwartz, Herman. 2010. *States versus Markets: The Emergence of a Global Economy*. Basingstoke: Palgrave Macmillan. Third Edition.

Seniwoliba, Joseph A. 2014. "The Single Spine Pay Policy: Can Ignorance Derail the Benefits It Has on the Ghanaian Public Service Worker?," *European Scientific Journal* 10(8): 437–460.

Shepherd, Andrew. 1981. "Agrarian Change in Northern Ghana: Public Investment, Capitalist Farming and Famine." In *Rural Development in Tropical Africa*, (eds.) Judith Heyer, Pepe Roberts and Gavin Williams. London: Macmillan, pp. 168–192.

Shepherd, Andrew and Onumah, G. 2003. "Changing Role of Government in Agricultural Trade in Ghana." In *Developing Agricultural Trade: New Roles of Government in Poor Countries*, (ed.) Michael Hubbard. Basingstoke: Palgrave Macmillan, pp. 65–76.

Simensen, Jarle. 1974. "Rural Mass Action in the Context of Anti-Colonial Protest: The Asafo Movement of Akim Abuakwa, Ghana," *Canadian Journal of African Studies* 8(1): 25–41.

Simensen, Jarle. 1975. "The Asafo of Kwahu, Ghana: A Mass Movement for Local Reform under Colonial Rule," *International Journal of African Historical Studies* 8(3): 383–406.

Stanliland, Martin. 1975. *The Lions of Dagbon: Political Change in Northern Ghana*. Cambridge: Cambridge University Press.

Staritz, Cornelia. 2016. "Global Value Chains, Industrialization and Industrial Policy in Developing Countries," Background paper for UNCTAD's 2016 Trade and Development Report. Unpublished.

Staritz, Cornelia and Lindsay Whitfield. 2017. "Made in Ethiopia: The Emergence and Evolution of the Ethiopian Apparel Export Sector," CAE Working Paper 2017:3, Center of African Economies, Roskilde University, Denmark.

Stiglitz, Joseph, Justin Yifu Lin, and Ebrahim Patel, (eds.). 2013. *The Industrial Policy Revolution II: Africa in the Twenty-First Century*. New York: Palgrave Macmillan.

Stockwell, S.E. 2000. *The Business of Decolonization: British Business Strategies in the Gold Coast*. Oxford: Oxford University Press.

Sutton, John and Bennet Kpentey. 2012. *An Enterprise Map of Ghana*. London: International Growth Centre, in association with the London Publishing Partnership.

Sutton-Jones, Stuart. 1979. "Ghana: Yesterday's Men versus the Day before Yesterday's Men?," *Africa* 91: 10–15.

Takane, Tsutomu. 2002. *The Cocoa Farmers of Southern Ghana: Incentives, Institutions and Change in Rural West Africa*. IDE Occasional Papers Series No. 37, Institute of Developing Economies, Japan External Trade Organization.

Tangri, Roger. 1992. "The Politics of Government-Business Relations in Ghana," *Journal of Modern African Studies* 30(1): 97–111.

Tangri, Roger. 1999. *The Politics of Patronage in Africa: Parastatals, Privatization and Private Enterprise*. Oxford: James Currey.

Targetti, Ferdinando and A. P. Thirwall (eds.). 1989. *The Essential Kaldor*. New York: Holmes and Meier.

Taylor, Ayowa Afrifa. 2006. *Sam Jonah and the Making of Ashanti*. Accra: Sub-Saharan Africa publishers.

Taylor, Scott. 2007. *Business and the State in Southern Africa: The politics of economic reform*. Boulder: Lynne Rienner.

Teal, Francis. 2013. "An Agricultural Revolution in Ghana?" Paper presented at the CSAE Conference Economic Development in Africa, University of Oxford, 17–19 March.

Tignor, Robert. 2006. *W. Arthur Lewis and the Birth of Development Economics*. Princeton: Princeton University Press.

Tonah, Steve. 2006. "The Presidential Special Initiative on Cassava: A Bane or Blessing to Ghana's Smallholder Farmers," *Ghana Journal of Development Studies*, 3(1): 66–84.

Tsikata, Dela, Ama Pokuaa Fenny, and Ernest Aryeetey. 2008. China-Africa Relations: A Case Study of Ghana. A Draft Scoping Study Prepared for the African Economic Research Consortium.

Twerefou, D., E. Aryeetey and O. Bafour. 2007. "Impact of Mining Sector Reforms on Ouput, Employment and Incomes in Ghana, 1980-2002," Technical Publication No. 75, Institute of Statistical, Social and Economic Research, University of Ghana.

Vagneron, Isabelle, Guy Faure & Denis Loeillet. 2009. "Is There a Pilot in the Chain? Identifying the Key Drivers of Change in the Fresh Pineapple Sector," *Food Policy* 34: 437–446.

Voisard, Jean-Michel and Peter Jaeger. 2003. "Ghana Horticulture Sector Development Study, including Agriculture Sub-Sector Investment Program Restructuring." Report prepared for ESSD, Department of the World Bank by Accord Associates, UK.

Vrolijk, Kasper J. 2016. On Technology: Second-Order Constraints in Underdeveloped Economies, with Special Reference to Ethiopia. PhD dissertation in International Development, Department of Economics, SOAS, University of London.

Weghorst, Keith and Staffan Lindberg. 2013. "What Drives the Swing Voter in Africa?," *American Journal of Political Science* 57(3): 717–734.

Whitfield, Lindsay. 2006. "The Politics of Urban Water Reform in Ghana," *Review of African Political Economy* 33(109): 425–448.

Whitfield, Lindsay. 2009. "'Change for a Better Ghana': Party Competition, Institutionalization and Alternation in Ghana's 2008 Elections," *African Affairs* 108: 621–641.

Whitfield, Lindsay. 2017. "New Paths to Capitalist Agricultural Production in Africa: Experiences of Ghanaian Pineapple Producer-Exporters," *Journal of Agrarian Change*, 17(3): 535–556.

Whitfield, Lindsay and Emily Jones. 2009. "Ghana." In *The Politics of Aid: African Strategies for Dealing with Donors*, (ed.) Lindsay Whitfield. Oxford: Oxford University Press, pp. 185–216.

Whitfield, Lindsay, Ole Therkildsen, Lars Buur, and Anne Mette Kjær. 2015. *The Politics of African Industrial Policy: A Comparative Perspective*. Cambridge: Cambridge University Press.

Wight, Martin. 1947. *The Gold Coast Legislative Council*. London: Faber and Faber.

Willems, Sabine. 2006. The Ivorian Pineapple: Social Action within the International Pineapple Commodity Network. PhD thesis in Rural Development Sociology, Wageningen University, the Netherlands.

Williams, Tracy. 2009. An African Success Story: Ghana's Cocoa Marketing System, IDS Working Paper 318, January 2009, Institute of Development Studies, University of Sussex.

Williamson, John, (ed.). 1993. *The Political Economy of Policy Reform*. Washington, DC: Institute for International Economics.

Wolf, Christina. 2017. "Industrialization in Times of China: Domestic-Market Formation in Angola," *African Affairs* 116(463): 435–461.

Wong, Hilary. 2017. "For the Sake of Health: The Development of the Ghanaian Pharmaceutical Sector," master's thesis, Oxford Department of International Development, University of Oxford.

Wood, Ellen Meiksins. 2002. *The Origin of Capitalism: A longer view*. London: Verso.

World Bank. 2013. Energizing Economic Growth in Ghana: Making the Power and Petroleum Sectors Rise to the Challenge. Energy Group, Africa Region, Report no. 79656. Washington, DC: World Bank.

World Bank. 2014. Ghana Economic Update. Report No. 91809. Africa Region. Washington, DC. World Bank.

World Bank. 2015. Project Appraisal Document on Proposed IBRD Enclave Guarantees in the Amount of Up to $200 Million and a Proposed IDA Guarantee in the Amount of $500 Million for the Republic of Ghana in Support of the Sankofa Gas Project. Energy and Extractives Global Practice, Africa Region. Report No. 96554-GH. Washington, DC: World Bank.

Index